TOWARD A LIVING ARCHITECTURE?

TOWARD A LIVING ARCHITECTURE?

COMPLEXISM AND BIOLOGY IN GENERATIVE DESIGN

CHRISTINA COGDELL

MINNESOTA

University of Minnesota Press
Minneapolis | London

The University of Minnesota Press gratefully acknowledges financial support for the publication of this book from the Office of Research and College of Letters and Science, University of California, Davis.

This title is freely available in an open access edition thanks to the TOME initiative and the generous support of the University of California, Davis. Learn more at openmonographs .org.

Background image: Soap bubble morphology by Dr. Jeremy Burgess / Science Photo Library (Figure 1.6).

Published by the University of Minnesota Press
111 Third Avenue South, Suite 290
Minneapolis, MN 55401–2520
http://www.upress.umn.edu

Printed in the United States of America on acid-free paper

The University of Minnesota is an equal-opportunity educator and employer.

25 24 23 22 21 20 19 18   10 9 8 7 6 5 4 3 2 1

Library of Congress Cataloging-in-Publication Data
Names: Cogdell, Christina, author.
Title: Toward a living architecture? : complexism and biology in generative design / Christina Cogdell.
Description: Minneapolis : University of Minnesota Press, 2018. | Includes bibliographical references and index. |
Identifiers: LCCN 2018008959 (print)| ISBN 978-1-5179-0537-8 (hc) | ISBN 978-1-5179-0538-5 (pb)
Subjects: LCSH: Architecture and biology.
Classification: LCC NA2543.B56 C64 2018 (print) |DDC 720/.47–dc23
LC record available at https://lccn.loc.gov/2018008959

CONTENTS

INTRODUCTION

Evolutionary Architecture—Genetic Algorithm—Generator—Evolutionary Computation—Complexity Architecture—Architectural Genetics—Embryological House—Generative Components—Generative Design—Breeding Architecture—Genetic Architectures—Architectural DNA—Morphogenetic Design—Morpho-Ecologies—Architecture of Emergence—Self-Organizing Architecture—Autopoiesis of Architecture—Parametric Design—Protocell Architecture—Generative Architecture

The above list, drawn from architectural history of the past fifty years, offers a composite overview of the field referred to most commonly as "generative architecture." The latter phrase has gained sway owing to its general reference to the use of digital computational tools to generate architectural form. Although digital tools have been integral to and inseparable from the founding and development of generative architecture, other modes of using digital technologies in architecture exist beyond those associated with generativity. Generative architecture is thus a subset, albeit a prominent one, of what architectural historian Mario Carpo terms, in the title of the collection he edited, *The Digital Turn in Architecture, 1992–2012.*[1] What binds the above disparate architectural approaches into an identifiable genre, therefore, is most often a certain computational approach. Yet frequently, the final products share a common aesthetic, one that entails an interconnected proliferation of component-based forms that morph through different curvatures, resulting in a stylized organic appearance.[2] Two well-recognized multimillion-dollar built structures created using generative techniques are the Beijing National Stadium ("The Bird's Nest," $423 million USD) and the Beijing National Aquatics Center ("The Water Cube," $140 million USD), both from the 2008 Olympics (Figure I.1).

The use of computational tools and algorithmic structures to generate solutions to complex problems and to create forms is not unique to the discipline of architecture. While arising out of cybernetics and then computer science, generative techniques are used as well by scientists, engineers, linguists, musicians, and artists. For comparison, art historian Philip Galanter defines "generative art" as "'any art practice where the artist uses a system, such as a set of natural language rules, a computer program, a machine, or other procedural invention, which is set into motion with some degree of autonomy contributing to or resulting in a completed work of art.' The key element in generative art is the use of an external system to which the artist cedes partial or total subsequent control."[3] Architects using generative software—such as Generative Components or genetic algorithm–based plug-ins like the Galápagos feature

in Grasshopper with Rhino—also cede partial control to their computers. After establishing the basic parameters, fitness criteria, and approach to a particular problem, they sit back and wait for the computer to generate a population of solutions, from which the architect then selects and refines chosen designs. Often, computers generate solutions that an architect would not have imagined, so generative design is frequently viewed as human–computer collaboration.

FIGURE I.1. Beijing National Aquatics Center, Beijing, China. Building designed by PTW Architects with CSCEC, 2008. Photograph by Daniel Case (CC BY-SA 3.0). Beijing National Stadium. Building designed by Herzog & de Meuron, 2008. Photograph by David Dong (CC by 2.0). By mimicking the geometry of soap bubbles and the structure of a bird's nest, while using ETFE plastic and tons of steel, these buildings reference ideas of "self-organizing" pattern formation in nature while relying heavily on advanced technologies of computation and engineering.

But as the opening list clearly demonstrates, much of the terminology associated with generative architecture sounds very biological. While this is partially due to the "gen-" root in all variations of "generative" and "genetic," the commonalities between computation and biology in fact run deep. After all, in computer science this overlap is the conceptual origin for the pursuit of artificial life, as well as the root of techniques of evolutionary computation and genetic algorithms, which generate solutions based on the principles of neo-Darwinian biological evolution. Yet, as architect Karl Chu points out, "The meaning of both terms, genetics and gene, are sufficiently abstract and general enough to be used as concepts that have logical implications for architecture without being anchored too explicitly to biology. Implicit within the concept of genetics is the idea of replication of heritable units based on some rule inherent within the genetic code," he writes. "Embedded within the mechanism for replication is a generative function: the self-referential logic of recursion. Recursion is a function or rule that repeatedly calls itself or its preceding stage by applying the same rule successively, thereby generating a self-referential propagation of a sequence or a series of transformations. It is this logic encoded within an internal principle, which constitutes the autonomy of the generative that lies at the heart of computation."[4]

Chu's explanation of the generative leans heavily toward the computational realm while abstractly relying on principles of biology. Other architects affiliated with generative architecture, however, are promoting "genetic architectures," which in this case refer not just to techniques of evolutionary computation but also to the literal use of genetic engineering to grow living buildings. Alberto Estévez, director of the Genetic Architectures graduate program at the Escuela Arquitectura (ESARQ) of the International University of Catalunya in Barcelona, describes his goal as "the fusion of cybernetic–digital resources with genetics, to continuously join the zeros and ones from the architectural drawing with those from the robotized manipulation of DNA, in order to organize the necessary genetic information that governs a habitable living being's natural growth, according to the designs previously prepared on the computer."[5] While such a vision's practical realization is debatable, it reveals a fundamental conflation and coordination of the technologies used in both architecture and synthetic biology. Estévez boldly states, "The architect of the future will no longer direct masons but genetic engineers."[6] Others, like Marcos Cruz at the Bartlett School of Architecture, University College London, look to integrating the techniques of tissue engineering. They point to living works like *Victimless Leather* (2007) by artists Oron Catts and Ionat Zurr as prototypes for architecture of the future (Plate 1). As these examples show, the lines between computation, architecture, and biology begin to blur, for all three disciplines address potentially overlapping aspects of generativity.

One final thread interwoven into the above list of terms associated with generative architecture is the language of complexity theory, including self-organization, emergence, and autopoiesis. While complexity may seem like an outlier to the nexus of computation, biology, and architecture, in fact it is integral to current understandings of the generation of pattern and structure in inorganic, organic, and cultural dynamical systems. Furthermore, the historical development of complexity theory overlaps significantly with that of cybernetics and generative architecture, arising in the late 1950s and early 1960s. Complexity theory offers a means to understand and simulate the organization of matter from disorder or chaos into order, using the mathematics of nonlinear nonequilibrium dynamic systems. Such systems include the weather, traffic, the economy, the growth of the internet, social behavior patterns such as flocking and swarming, and life itself, for organisms are open systems that continually exchange energy and materials with their environment to fend off equilibrium, which is death. Architects are adapting the process of self-organization of natural systems as a means for pattern and form generation in architecture. This framework helps theorize the proliferating interconnected component aesthetic of generative architecture that has resulted from the limited bed size of 3-D printers, although recently, the scale and types of materials used for 3-D printing are increasing. For example, Michael Hansmeyer's and Benjamin Dillenburger's *Digital Grotesque II* (2017) for the Centre Pompidou was printed using additive manufacturing in synthetic sandstone at a scale of over fifty cubic meters.[7] Although it was printed in sections (maximum eight cubic meters per print), they scaled the sections to pallets for transportation and the carrying capacity of four humans. The increasing capacity of 3-D printers makes the modular design of large numbers of components less obligatory moving forward, a prospect that will likely shift the general aesthetics of generative architecture. Yet when this limitation held, generative architects explained the component-based approach by turning to the definition of self-organization, which posits that multiple components interacting with one another locally according to rules, without reference to a central control, produce emergent patterns at the next higher level of their organization. Architect Michael Weinstock, in his article "Morphogenesis and the Mathematics of Emergence" (2004), urges architects to integrate these mathematical processes into architectural and urban systems design, so that architecture more quickly becomes "intelligent" with responsive emergent forms and behaviors that demonstrate higher levels of complexity.[8]

Given these major themes in generative architecture, this book critically examines and unravels this complicated nexus of architecture, computation, biology, and complexity. In doing so, it offers a conceptual scaffold for parsing various goals of those working under the rubric of generative design, which is often confusing because of the overlapping terminology across these disciplines. As the title *Toward a Living Architecture?* implies, its overall narrative moves from the computational toward the biological and from current practice toward visionary futures. It addresses architects' dreams of generating buildings from living cells or "protocells," demystifying the scientific advances necessary to shift these dreams from the realm of science fiction to reality, finding that for many reasons their visions are unlikely to be realized. To what ends, then, is this rhetorical biologization of architecture working, besides serving as a gloss of "sustainability" over high-tech avant-garde architecture-as-usual? Sustainability, in its most basic definition, implies maintaining ecological balance and functionality for generations to come. The book ultimately positions generative architecture as one of many arenas today where "complexism" as our current scientific ideology has become a player affecting the broader debates over design, production, and consumption and the economic and environmental effects of this cycle.

How complexism is functioning now as an ideological foundation for generative architecture serves in some ways as contemporary, scientifically updated parallel to the argument that my earlier work made about how eugenics functioned ideologically in relation to streamline design. In *Eugenic Design: Streamlining America in the 1930s* (2004), eugenics functioned as the reigning scientific ideology at work across many cultural domains.[9] It influenced and in turn was promoted by the material and rhetorical strategies used by designers to justify their architectural and design style as appropriately modern. Today, complexism offers generative architecture a naturalizing scientific framework that, reciprocally, is then reified by generative approaches across disciplines, not just in architecture, utilizing its concepts of self-organization, emergence, contingency, and the ever-onward march of increasing hierarchy and complexity. Yet, while *Eugenic Design* was primarily historical, this current project on complexism and generative architecture is more contemporary criticism than history, more science studies than history of science. Only one very short section of this book addresses interwoven historical threads at the origins of cybernetics, systems theory, and generative architecture that placed them early on in conversation with each other (see the Appendix). *Let me be clear that my intent has never been to write a history of generative architecture.* The majority of this book focuses on predominant themes that arise from the *intersections* of contemporary science, computation, and generative architecture in the last fifteen to twenty years, with special emphasis on the scientific portion owing to three of the book's major themes. These critically examine (1) the roles of complexism in discourses of generative architecture, (2) some generative architects' claims to be promoting environmental "sustainability" in their work, and (3) others' claims to be moving architecture toward newly designed and engineered *living* materializations.

Appropriately then, my current methodology integrates a new approach to design studies and criticism, one that uses common practices and insights from science and technology studies (STS) alongside my earlier interdisciplinary approach merging archival research and wide reading across disciplines combined with visual and rhetorical analysis. In particular, STS methods utilizing participant observation as an "ethnographic" approach at multiple sites for studying and working alongside both scientists and architects came naturally for this project. I put "ethnographic" in quotes here because doing design ethnography is not my primary intent, but just one of the general modes of research I used for this project. This stemmed directly from the type of funding I received to pursue the bulk of the research. Two Mellon

Foundation fellowships—a Penn Humanities Forum Postdoctoral Fellowship at the University of Pennsylvania (2008–9) and a New Directions Fellowship (2011–13)—supported twenty-five months of interdisciplinary postdoctoral study with release from teaching, in the fields of generative architecture, physics (self-organization and complexity), philosophy of science (emergence), epigenetics, and evolutionary biology.

In many cases, I was privileged to study with the very scientists and architects whose work I wanted to better understand. For example, at Penn I participated in Jenny Sabin's and Peter Lloyd Jones's LabStudio seminar "Nonlinear Biological Systems and Design," where I was a student alongside the others, being introduced for the first time to generative software and scripting, theories of epigenetics, and lab protocols. While I did not join one of the groups for the studio projects, in every other way I studied under Sabin and Jones, even if at the same time I critically observed and questioned the underlying assumptions at play in the course. At the same time, conversations outside the classroom over the nine months clarified the course material and LabStudio's broader research aims; these served as a second major source of information about their collaborative work. A few years later in 2011, I became a graduate student and participant observer for one term in the Emergent Technologies and Design program at the Architectural Association in London, including the preliminary Boot Camp, Michael Weinstock's Emergence seminar, and George Jeronimidis's Biomimicry studio. Upon returning to UC Davis in January 2012, I participated in physicist and mathematician James Crutchfield's two-quarter graduate seminar "Natural Computation and Self-Organization: The Physics of Information Processing in Complex Systems," as well as in philosopher of science James Griesemer's seminar on "Philosophy of Emergence." I co-led a faculty and graduate student discussion group on "Self-Organization and Evolutionary Biology" with members from physics, evolution and ecology, entomology, philosophy, cultural studies, and anthropology. Finally, I spent time in independent study the following year with Eva Jablonka, University of Tel Aviv, studying epigenetics, and with Evelyn Fox Keller, Massachusetts Institute of Technology, studying self-organization. In all these situations, while I was occupying the role of a student, I was also still professor, historian, and critic, so the positions I occupied in relation to those with whom I studied were multifaceted—studying under but also studying across.

This educational mode of research does not quite fit the standard rubric for STS scholars, who are often trained in the social sciences and versed in the scientific theories and practices prior to being on-site at one or more laboratories. But this experiential, observational approach poses a new method for design studies scholars and critics, affording the chance to learn not only about the intersections of design with contemporary science, but also about the material and rhetorical practices of design within the classroom and the studio. Few precedents for design ethnographies exist, although versions influenced primarily by anthropology are becoming increasingly common. Recent examples include the anthology *Design Anthropology: Theory and Practice* (2013) and

Swedish Design: An Ethnography by Keith Murphy (2015), as well as the project Experimental Collaborations: Ethnography beyond Participant Observation, headed by Adolfo Estalella, Andrea Gaspar, and Tomás Sánchez Criado.[10] Even fewer design ethnographies are influenced by STS rather than anthropology, one of which is Albena Yaneva's recent book *Made by the Office for Metropolitan Architecture: An Ethnography of Design* (2009).[11]

STS approaches matter for understanding aspects of generative architecture not only because practitioners claim the terminology of the "laboratory" for the studio but also because of their heavy reliance on different scientific theories and practices. STS approaches matter as well for design studies that engage with issues of design in relation to science, the environment, and "sustainability." These methods and the knowledge they have produced offer means to better understand the science and weigh the environmental impact of different modes of design production. Like most academic disciplines, STS has transformed significantly since its inception in the 1970s from "first generation" STS to "second-" and now "third-generation" approaches. A short review of these is useful for helping those in design studies consider a variety of STS approaches and some of their implications.

First-generation STS scholars, under the influence of Bruno Latour and Steven Woolgar's pathbreaking *Laboratory Life,* stressed ethnographic observation within a single laboratory to reveal, as their subtitle stated, *The Construction of Scientific Facts* (1979).[12] While this approach carried the powerful punch of destabilizing the authority of scientific fact-hood as objective knowledge of reality, its focus within a single laboratory ignored the larger influences of social forces outside the laboratory as having influence on scientific knowledge-making. Furthermore, the entrée of social constructivism into the realm of science, as distinct from the arts and humanities, brought with it certain challenging implications. For example, if scientific knowledge is a social construction, then why should the educated public believe scientists over creationists on such topics as evolution and global warming? Second-generation STS scholars of the 1990s and 2000s (including George Marcus, Jan Golinski, Annemarie Mol, Stefan Helmreich, and Christine Hine, among others), under the influence of comparative anthropology, began to practice multisite ethnographies focused on more than one scientific laboratory, in part to engage social forces outside of and in between laboratories as active participants in the making of scientific knowledge. This approach forced researchers to pay closer attention to their own relations to their subjects, which differed from site to site. This self-consciousness resulted in the idea of not *studying up* or *studying down* but rather *studying across.* Self-conscious research under this model, which examined simultaneously different "worlds" and spaces and the social forces at play within and between, often did so to a particular end, engaging an activist cause addressing particular concerns. This brought STS scholarship into closer engagement with problems affecting different groups, a major one of which is environmental devastation.

I have already alluded to the influence of this approach in my own research in terms of my multiple roles as student, observer, peer, professor, historian, and critic at different academic institutional sites. The idea of studying across applies to more than just one's positional relations as an observer, however. It can also be a self-conscious mode of analysis that treats theory as transversal, as socially constructed concepts that cut across different lines of thought and different worlds while producing measurable material effects. In this study, I approach complexity theory by studying across in this latter sense. I recognize complexity as a scientific theory of natural processes of organization, but I also analyze it as an ideology of complexism that is infusing many fields, including generative architecture. It thereby influences disciplinary practices that produce real material and environmental effects.

One example of this mode of studying across from STS scholarship that is particularly useful as a parallel approach to my own study is Helmreich's essay from 2011, "Nature/Culture/Seawater." He explores seawater theoretically and materially: as the spatial divider of "nature" and "culture" historically under colonialism as that which falls in between during travel; as the flux and flow between concepts and materializations of nature and culture, some of which are leading to rising sea levels; and as the site of major oil spills, understood both through scientific data and computer simulations. He uses what he calls working "athwart theory," a conceptual approach of studying across, thinking of "theory neither as set above the empirical nor as simply deriving from it but, rather, as crossing the empirical transversely."[13] With regard to seawater, he writes, "I am interested in how simultaneously to employ water as a theory machine, when useful, and to treat both water and theories as things in the world," drawing attention to their materializations. "I think of this approach as operating *athwart theory*: tacking back and forth between seeing theories as explanatory tools and taking them as phenomena to be examined. Such an account does not separate meaning and materiality, since such sequestering only reinstalls a pre-analytic nature/culture."[14] He considers "theory (and, for that matter, seawater)" to be both "at once an abstraction as well as a thing in the world; theories constantly cut across and complicate our descriptive paths as we navigate forward in the 'real' world."[15] He thus accepts and interprets seawater as both a "theory machine" and as known materially through the tools and methods of science.

Like seawater, complex systems are positioned both at and beyond the nature/culture binary. Human "cultural" systems like urban traffic, the Occupy movement, or generative architecture are interpreted as complex systems just as often as are physical and biological "natural" systems, such as the weather or an ant colony. Yet all of these are "natural" material systems that produce transformative, measurable environmental effects. At the same time, complexity functions as a "theory machine" driving scientific research questions and experiments as well as ideologically shaping how academics in many fields interpret the systems they study or create. My study of generative architecture and complexity theory therefore works "athwart theory," tacking back and forth between complexity as an explanatory tool and ideology *and* as a material phenomenon to be explained, one that has environmental effects as real as we can be sure of as an oil spill in seawater.

How do we know about the material effects of oil spills, seawater, or complex systems, if scientific knowledge is a social construction? Third-generation STS scholars—including Helmreich, Harry Collins, and Paul Edwards, among others—are carrying forward second-generation activist concerns while facing directly the difficulties posed by first-generation scientific social constructivism. They pragmatically differentiate scientific theory-making from political and environmental policy-making. While scientific theories are necessarily socially constructed, scientific infrastructure also has a material basis that tends to reify past accepted knowledge. Yet, they argue, the knowledge that mainstream scientists provide is the "best knowledge" we have about the material world.[16] Pointing out the social construction of science was not intended to be "anti-science," Collins states, but rather was meant to serve as a caution to scientists to not promise more than they could deliver.[17] So when it comes to policy-making, political and environmental leaders should rely, Collins and Edwards argue, on mainstream scientific knowledge generated by the largest group of respected scientists or "experts," rather than on knowledge promulgated by fringe theories.[18]

Edwards's book *A Vast Machine: Computer Models, Climate Data, and the Politics of Global Warming* (2010) specifically tackles the profound difficulties of acquiring knowledge about climate change and global warming. One process he explores is how historical climate data, which originally was only national and not global and was based on earlier scientific technological infrastructures, must be revisited again and again upon the advent of new knowledge-making tools and theories in order to incorporate its information into current climate modeling. Yet, this process of revisiting data and method again and again, in combination with looking at scientific evidence of climate change from multidisciplinary perspectives including those the earth and environmental sciences, along with the stringent thoroughness and integrity of the Intergovernmental Panel on Climate Change, leads to a growing certainty of the probabilistic likelihood that our knowledge of climate change is the "best" it can be. Edwards concludes his book, "We have few good reasons to doubt these facts and many reasons to trust their validity. The climate's past and its future shimmer [probabilistically] before us, but neither one is a mirage. This is the best knowledge we are going to get. We had better get busy putting it to work."[19]

In our current era of climate change and global warming, design studies scholars can benefit from the methods and knowledge produced by STS as they observe and critique efforts in design and architecture aiming for "sustainability." STS methods can help design studies move beyond decades of exploring design predominantly as social construction, to add to this understanding insight into how theory inspires creative practice while also moving transversely across domains, producing real material effects. Design production, hand in hand with consumption, utilizes vast amounts of the earth's materials and energy, effecting not only climate change but also direct environmental devastation. Architecture does, too; a common statistic is that buildings in the United States consume approximately 48 percent of the energy the nation produces and release about 45 percent of the nation's carbon dioxide emissions.[20] It is thus from the vantages of second- and third-generation STS insights and scholarship that important contributions for design studies arise. Potentially useful methods, some of which are already beginning, include participant observation and ethnographic study of studios and classrooms; moving beyond the nature/culture binary; multisite analysis; careful consideration of one's relationship to different sites; studying across rather than up and down; working "athwart theory" to consider theories—scientific or otherwise—as explanatory tools and also as shapers of material effects; directing studies with an activist's eye for change; and integrating into policy *and* design ideation and production the "best" scientific knowledge we have.

These approaches lay a methodological foundation for this particular study in a number of ways, as explained above and as demonstrated throughout the book. One criteria by which I evaluate generative architects' claims of sustainability is by considering life cycle analysis and embedded energy, a strategy that environmental architecture and design educators and analysts use but which apparently has largely gone by the wayside as something that somehow did not catch hold. I am unwilling to let it go, for it offers arguably the best tool for considering the environmental and (socio)material effects of design and architecture, which depend on the life cycle of the materials included in all forms of design ideation and production. With regard to a specific life cycle analysis of generative architecture, the closest this study comes is a brief synopsis of the life cycle of transistors, silicon chips, and computers at the end of chapter 2 as well as brief mention of the greenhouse gas output and embedded energy in some materials used in well-known buildings. I use this tool because, like Edwards, I accept that climate change science is some of the best and most important knowledge we have, and I believe that most, maybe even all, forms of architecture should integrate this knowledge into architectural curricula, as well as all phases of design ideation and production. Yet I am not an absolutist, and I accept that architecture has critical significance beyond its environmental impacts.

I therefore will clarify that I do not consider environmental pragmatism to be the end-all and be-all of architecture and design or design studies, exclusive of its aesthetic and cultural representations and creative expressions. Architecture functions holistically: materially, environmentally, culturally, socially, aesthetically, economically, politically, et cetera. It can be celebrated and critiqued for functioning well but doing so only partially. It is when some architects directly claim that their work promotes "sustainability" that they specifically invite themselves into the arena of life cycle analysis. A number of historical vernacular examples demonstrate that it is possible to use relatively low amounts of energy in design production with relatively low hazardous environmental outputs while also aptly expressing culture and aesthetics. The true challenge here lies not in architecture alone, per se, but in its practitioners' and educators' acceptance of the capitalist modes in which architecture functions in the global economy: promoting continual economic growth through continual harvesting and processing of new materials, largely disregarding reuse and historical preservation, choosing highly processed rather than minimally processed, high-embedded-energy rather than low-embedded-energy materials, and continuing to relish the aura of and economically reward avant-garde "starchitects" rather than those making more holistically considered decisions. I therefore choose to evaluate generative architecture in relation to the sciences that its practitioners reference—complexity theory in general, including self-organization, emergence, and natural computation, complex biological systems, genetic and tissue engineering, and synthetic biology; as well as in relation to the sciences that some of them ignore, namely, epigenetics, climate change, and global warming. This valuation is based on my acceptance of what I think is the best knowledge we have.

In addition to posing an approach to design studies informed by STS methodology and insights, this book also offers the first significant critical interrogation of the major scientific themes at play in generative architecture. These include, in addition to complexity, self-organization, and emergence: natural and material computation; morphogenesis, evolutionary development, epigenetics, and evolutionary computation; biosynthesis in biological systems design; tissue and genetic engineering; and synthetic biology in its two forms, as "bottom-up" protocell research and as "top-down" bioengineering. The book therefore functions in part as a primer on contemporary biological sciences for those interested in architecture who may know less about biology. I historically contextualize contemporary theories by placing them in relation to predecessor theories of the twentieth century: Lamarckian and neo-Darwinian evolution, eugenics and early genetics, the modern synthesis, and Richard Dawkins's selfish-gene theory. This foundation provides a knowledge base for readers—and for prospective students of generative architecture—to better assess the claims of generative architects with regard to scientific approaches and their visions of the near future. It also clarifies the confusing discourses of generative architecture caused by overlapping terminologies from the disciplines of complexity theory, biology, computer science, and architecture. Words like "gene," "DNA," and "biocomputation," which mean one thing in the discipline where they first arise, do not necessarily translate into other disciplines carrying the same meaning. For example, the words "gene" and "DNA" in the writings of architects almost never refer to the molecular substances in cells. Yet such language has wooed more than one aspiring graduate student into an architectural movement that was far less biological and more computational than he or she had expected. This book therefore demystifies the terminology of generative architecture by identifying, as best as possible, when architects use terminology to refer to computational versus biological processes.

Besides these contributions, two other major reasons motivate this study. The first is to ascertain what practitioners mean when they claim some version of "sustainability" as an effect of their biologically inspired approaches. Does simply referencing some aspect of biology—like coining the word "morphoecologies" to describe organic-looking, high-performance, high-tech, big-data but generally small structures—suffice to deem a process and its resulting structures "sustainable"?[21] Achim Menges, who coined the word "morphoecologies" in 2004, and his collaborator Michael Hensel both decry the shallowness and small-mindedness of most "sustainable" or "green" architecture. They aim instead for a "more developed paradigm" integrating form and function and connecting the structure to its environment. To generally evaluate how successful they are in comparison to, say, approaches in vernacular architecture utilizing traditional layers, screens, and semipermeable shading structures, the simple concept of "life cycle analysis" offers a guide for critique. Life cycle analysis is useful to designers and people who care about doing less harm to the environment. It helps them choose materials and production processes that require less energy input, produce less toxic outputs, and can more quickly and readily decompose and return to full ecological use at the end of life. It is difficult to deny that the actual energetic and material formations of architecture, biology, and computation can be very different and can produce very different environmental effects. This is another reason why clarifying the terminology matters. Most digital technologies and works of generative architecture—for that matter, most works of contemporary architecture—do not fare very well.

Consider another example of "sustainable" generative architecture. Looking to the future, architect Rachel Armstrong aspires to create "genuinely sustainable homes and cities" using what she calls "protocells," which are actually pre-protocells since the first protocell has not yet been created.[22] These pre-protocells are tiny sphere-like droplets with semipermeable lipid membranes that coagulate in a beaker at the boundary between olive oil and water, with the addition of a few other chemicals. Architect Philip Beesley, at the University of Waterloo, crafts exquisite digitally designed and manufactured container systems as installations for their display (Plates 2 and 14). Pre-protocells have been created by origin of life and artificial life researchers trying to re-create how cells may have first formed in the earth's early marine environment. Some pre-protocells can precipitate tiny calcium carbonate particles by taking carbon dioxide out of the air, so Armstrong imagines "protocell" cities made with calcium carbonate built from "the bottom up" serving as carbon sequestration zones.[23] Given the scale differential and other feasibility issues between pre-protocell secretions in a beaker and an actual city, her claims sound fantastic, yet her 2009 TED talk "Architecture That Repairs Itself?" as of this writing, has been viewed more than a million times.

Only Michael Weinstock and Alberto Estévez openly scoff at the concept of "sustainability." Estévez sports the familiar architect-as-god / genetic engineer mentality, writing, "The new architect creates nature itself. Therefore, there is no point in being environmentally friendly since we are about to recreate the environment anew."[24] Weinstock more interestingly bases his rejection of sustainability on his deep belief in complex systems theory, which posits processes where abrupt phase changes reorganize systems far from equilibrium into ever more complex systems. Weinstock thinks "sustainable" architecture is just a "Band-Aid" on a complex system on the verge of phase change, as current environmental and economic conditions are tending toward global collapse (he might say reordering).[25] Accordingly, students in the Fall 2011 EmTech program had to beg the tutors to teach Ecotec, the then-current software used to analyze sun angle at different latitudes throughout the year in order to design for energy efficiency. Possibly owing to Weinstock's direction, the tutors did not think graduate architectural students needed to learn it. At the Architectural Association and other architectural schools around the world, graduate programs teaching "green" or "sustainable design" have been historically separate from those teaching generative design. A simple perusal of every issue of *AD (Architectural Design)* on these topics from the 1960s to the present reveals this split as well until only recently. Students entering programs teaching generative architecture should know where their professors and program generally stand on the issue of architectural design in relation to environmental concerns, as should clients hiring the professors' architectural firms for design work.

The second major reason motivating this project besides a critical analysis of sustainability discourse is the importance of historically contextualizing generative architecture in relation to its precedent, eugenic design of the interwar period. I do so to caution against the eugenic thought that is embedded into today's genetic algorithms and some aspects of genetic engineering. The similarity of the language of generative architecture to that of the 1930s designers that I critiqued in *Eugenic Design: Streamlining America in the 1930s* is remarkable. Simply seeing the words "architecture," "design," "genetic," and "morphogenetic" together on the covers of early major publications in the field—such as *Genetic Architectures* (2003) and the *AD* issue "Emergence: Morphogenetic Design Strategies" (2004)—stunned me. Inside this *AD* issue, the Foreign Office Architects (FOA) diagram of their firm's work in the form of a "phylogenetic tree" (Plate 3) reads as a new version of Raymond Loewy's evolution charts of the 1930s (Figure I.2).[26] The name of FOA's 2003 exhibition at the Institute for Contemporary Art in London, *Foreign Office Architects: Breeding Architecture,* simply reinforces this. The language of evolution, phylogenesis, species, breeding, genotype, phenotype, DNA, and fitness optimization pervades generative architecture, much as it did eugenic design. Despite so much being familiar, however, new words are in the mix—computation, algorithm, emergence, self-organization, complexity. These point to significant differences between contemporary science and architecture and that of the 1930s, although Martin Bressani and Robert Jan van Pelt's essay "Crystals, Cells, and Networks: Unconfining Territories," written for *The Gen(H)ome Project* at the MAK Center (2006), argues that lebensraum German design under the Third Reich proceeded hand in hand with the state's eugenic program in the annexed territories based on natural design principles, both organic and inorganic.[27]

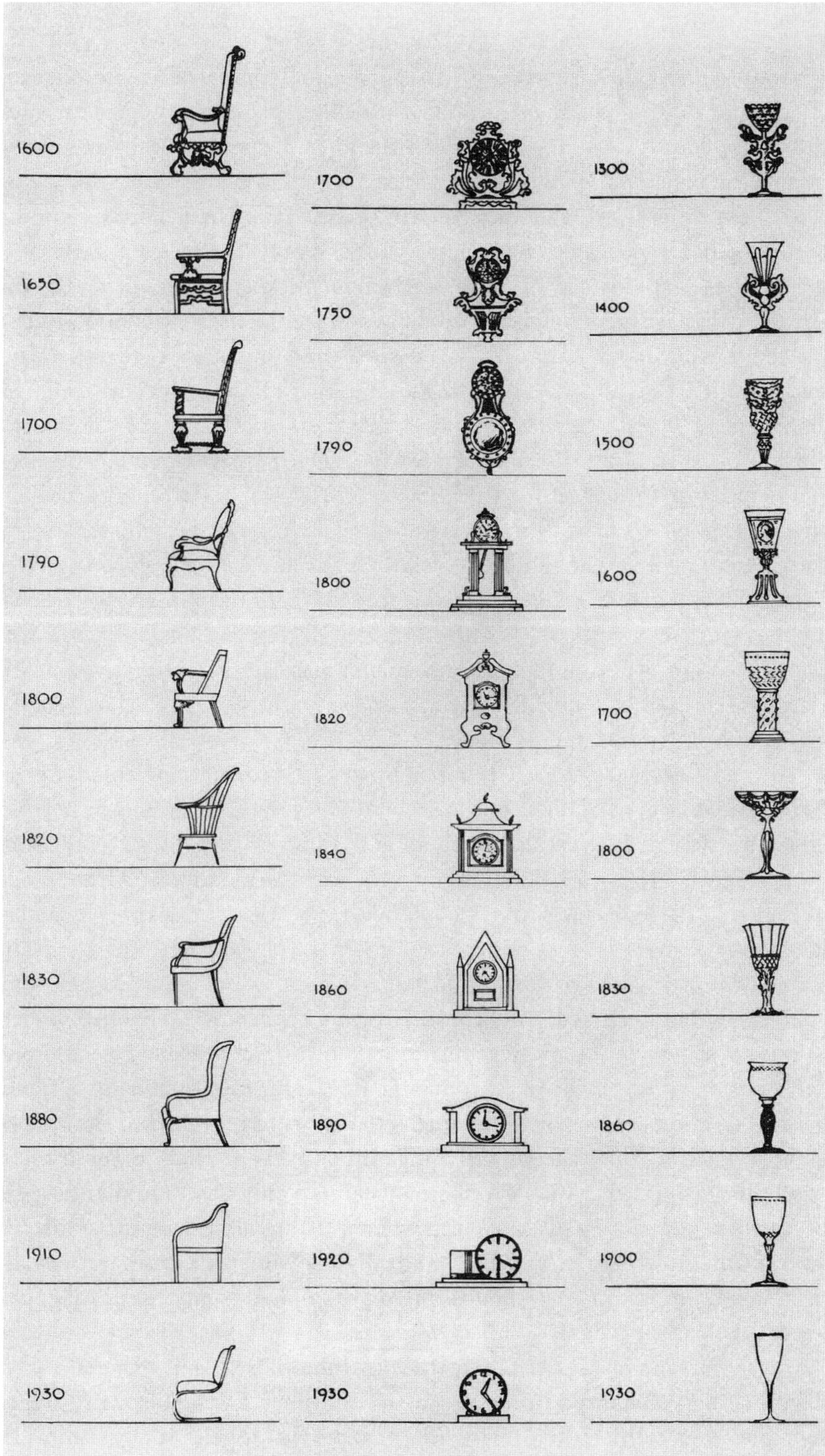

FIGURE I.2. Evolution charts, by Raymond Loewy, 1934. Provided by Loewy Design LLC, http://www.raymondloewy.com. By depicting historical changes in product design in the form of linear evolution charts, industrial designer Raymond Loewy suggests that clean modernist design was produced by natural progression of biological evolution rather than by designers working in particular contexts.

I therefore highlight when today's discourses and approaches resemble those of eugenics to bring a critical awareness to its re-occurrence in generative architecture, for it is also re-occurring in the form of contemporary eugenic sociopolitical policies and medical practices.

Although the word "eugenics" became taboo after the Holocaust and has been largely forgotten by the general public, its ideals and even some of its practices persist. Instead of "race betterment" and "positive eugenics" that tried to increase the number and quality of "fit" citizens, people now speak of "designer babies" and "enhanced" or "disease-free" humans. As regards "negative eugenics" that aimed to decrease the number of "defective" or "unfit" humans, the U.S. state sterilization laws that inspired Germany's Law for the Prevention of Hereditarily Diseased Offspring (1933) remained on the books and in practice until as late as the 1980s. In 2013, North Carolina became the only state to pass a law offering reparations to living victims who were sterilized involuntarily, although of the nearly eight hundred people who applied only about a quarter have been approved.[28] As North Carolinians were debating the law, CNN investigated California's sterilizations, asking why California was not also considering reparations when it was the state that involuntarily sterilized the highest number of citizens, nearly a third of the national total of around seventy thousand people.[29]

Yet just one year after CNN ran its piece, California news media broke a story investigated by Justice Now about the forced sterilization between 2006 and 2010 of 148 female prisoners in the state.[30] In 2014, governor Jerry Brown signed into law SB 1135 banning prisoner sterilizations.[31] Other modes of limiting the reproduction of people with qualities not desired by a state (or its politicians) have been proposed recently as well. In 2008, Louisiana state senator John LaBruzzo proposed that poor women be paid $1,000 to voluntarily be sterilized. The *Times-Picayune* reported, "LaBruzzo said he worries that people receiving government aid such as food stamps and publicly subsidized housing are reproducing at a faster rate than more affluent, better-educated people who presumably pay more tax revenue to the government."[32] And in 2008, the United Kingdom passed the Human Fertilisation and Embryology Act, which forbids medical personnel from implanting embryos with "hereditary disease" into women using in vitro fertilization. The law classifies deafness as a "defect" and "disease" and forbids a parent selecting a "deaf" embryo, ascertained through pre-implantation genetic diagnosis, even if the parent is deaf.[33]

These current instances of eugenics in the political and medical realms might feel very distanced from the practices of generative architecture and design. But when architectural forms are generated using genetic algorithms, the logic of design and production is almost identical to that of eugenics. Consider this description offered by Keith Besserud and Joshua Ingram, of BlackBox Studio at Skidmore, Owings & Merrill, in their paper "Architectural Genomics" presented at the 2008 ACADIA conference Silicon + Skin: Biological Processes and Computation:

1. Define the fitness function(s) . . . what performative metric(s) is(are) being optimized?
2. Define a genome logic (the number of characters in the genome string and the relationship between the individual characters and the expression of the design geometry)
3. Randomly generate an initial population of genomes
4. Test the fitness of the designs that are generated from each genome
5. Identify the top performers; these will become the selection pool for the next generation
6. From the selection pool build the population of the next generation, using methods of cloning, cross-breeding, mutation, and migration
7. Test all the new genomes in the new population
8. If the performance appears to be converging to an optimal condition then stop; otherwise repeat starting from step #5[34]

From defining "fitness" and embedding it in a "genome," to evaluating individuals in populations against the fitness criteria to "identify the top performers" as the "selection pool," to breeding only the top performers with each other thereby eliminating all "unfit" designs from future populations, to aiming overall for the "optimal condition," this logic is virtually identical to eugenics of the interwar period. LaBruzzo, too, expressed the same aim that during the Great Depression had exerted a powerful appeal: more of the "fit" and less of the "unfit" to supposedly save state funds. The differences between Besserud and Ingram's description and the ideals of eugenics in the 1930s are in the medium and location of design and production, in silico rather than in vivo; in the kinds of traits or parameters being optimized, architectural ones rather than human or cultural ones; and the extent to which eugenic opinions, sociopolitical policies, and medical practices are enacted publicly in our time.[35] Genetic algorithms should therefore be referred to as "eugenic algorithms" (EuAs) in order not to evade consciously recognizing this increasingly internalized and common mode of thought—for example, the ways that listeners of Pandora streaming service, which is driven by the "Music Genome Project," optimize their playlists with votes up or down.[36]

Chapter Overview

As previously stated, the book's overall narrative moves from the computational toward the biological and from current practices to visionary futures. The first half focuses more on ideals of complexism in generative architecture and the second half addresses more of the biological aspects, from actual scientific experimentation to architects' dreams of generating buildings from living cells and pre-protocells. The book explains the scientific reasons why these dreams from the realm of science fiction are unlikely to become reality based on today's knowledge.

At one end of this spectrum, some generative architects might not ever think about using biological materials for building; they use biology only as an analogy or inspiration for computational techniques. They do not work in scientific laboratories, and may even be offended that I include those who want to grow living buildings under the label "generative architecture." At the opposite end of the spectrum—those who dream of mixing up pre-protocell concoctions and pouring them on the earth to have buildings slowly materialize—are those whose practice need not involve computers at all; theirs is more akin to cooking and chemistry, some of which they do mix up in laboratories. This is not to say computers and generative processes are not involved in the envisioning process. As the image of Philip Beesley's *Hylozoic Ground* shows (Plates 2 and 14), everything surrounding the beaker is digitally designed and manufactured, albeit hand-assembled, for every one of Beesley's installations, and I think it is unquestionably characterized as generative architecture. And then there are those in the middle, whose work transitions between the purely computational and biological: Jenny Sabin and Peter Lloyd Jones, as well as others involved with LabStudio, David Benjamin and Fernan Federici, and Oron Catts and Ionat Zurr. These truly interdisciplinary teams work both in scientific laboratories and in the practices of architecture, design, and art, and perhaps owing to their serious exploration of these two domains, their work is the most astute as well as the most scientifically informed and up-to-date. As will become clear, Estévez rhetorically positions himself in this middle arena, yet in fact, his publications do not address the results of laboratory experimentation and reveal little current knowledge about the science he promotes.

My goal in including all these concepts, practices, and visions in the same book—one titled *Toward a Living Architecture?*—is to explore, by comparison, the meanings of their shared rhetoric as well as the interrelations and disjunctions of their practices and the larger questions raised by doing so. I expect that the crucial differences in media that these practitioners use, or envision using, for architecture and the contexts that inform their function will help distinguish different practices and disciplines that are being theoretically conflated or merged under contemporary materialist philosophical concepts. I hope this facilitates a deeper and more critical discussion about the ways that humans and their architecture affect the environment. I do not think that merely talking about and claiming "sustainability" as has thus far been manifested through generative architecture is anywhere near substantial enough. Shifting from steel, concrete, and glass in the shape of organic forms, to turning buildings into living organisms or living organisms into buildings, is not a good answer either for many reasons. My hope is that this book brings some clarity to a murky terrain to allow for more informed discussions and well-considered practices.

Chapter 1 opens with an exploration of the most fundamental concepts of complexism, those of self-organization and emergence, particularly with regard to how they interest certain architects. By definition, emergence is closely tied to self-organization. These terms are therefore explored in this chapter based primarily on Weinstock's overall argument in *The Architecture of Emergence: The Evolution of Form in Nature and Civilisation* (2010). The chapter begins with the Boot Camp project that EmTech students, including myself, were assigned in 2011 to introduce ideas of self-organization and emergence in architecture. The brief called for creating a design using multiple components that connect locally following rules to "emerge" into a "global" structure. This fundamental design approach contributes a particular aesthetic to "emergent architecture" that extends far beyond EmTech. The chapter then analyzes Weinstock's writings on emergent architecture in relation to his dismissal of "sustainability," in order to contrast his approach with emergent architecture as proposed by Menges and Hensel under the term "morpho-ecologies." Because Weinstock, Menges, and Hensel publish together often, many in the field see them as part of a single school of thought, but in fact their views differ significantly. This chapter therefore parses some of their major differences, including Menges and Karola Dierichs's research into aggregate architecture in relation to the ideas of self-organization and self-assembly, and Menges and Hensel's support for heterogeneity in contrast to Patrik Schumacher's call for a monolithic parametric homogeneity.

Chapter 2 compares generative architects' ideas of "material computation" with a number of very similar-sounding concepts—natural computation, biocomputation, biomolecular computation, protoputing, and programming matter. It does so to clarify the potential confusion surrounding these terms in relation to one another and to point out where they overlap. "Material Computation" is the title of a special issue of *AD* in 2012 edited by Menges, who currently directs the Institute for Computational Design at the University of Stuttgart. He is an expert in wood, particularly in terms of current scanning and digital technologies that offer detailed and precise information about wood and its material performance under many different conditions. Many of the pieces he and his students create are wooden designs that intentionally feature its dynamic, performance-based, "emergent" properties. I therefore interpret his use of "material computation" in multidirectional comparison: first, with a few of the self-assembling and aggregate structures he includes in the journal issue, those of Dierichs and also Skylar Tibbits, of the Massachusetts Institute of Technology; and second, with the term "biocomputing" used by architect David Benjamin, founder of the firm The Living and an instructor at Columbia University's Graduate School of Architecture, Planning, and Preservation. Benjamin and his collaborator, synthetic biologist Fernan Federici, recently published a chapter called "Bio Logic," where they put forward the term "biocomputing" in contrast to "biomimicry." I explain what their version of biocomputing means, since there also is a scientific process called biomolecular computing that is developing at the intersection of computer science, engineering, and molecular biology.[37] This field is "known variously as biocomputing, molecular computation, and DNA computation," molecular bioengineer Pengcheng Fu writes, so therefore it is important to understand the different meanings given to these very similar-sounding, even identical, terms.

Additionally, Menges's phrase "material computation" sounds very much like a related concept in complex systems theory, what physicist James Crutchfield and others refer to as "natural computation." Menges likely chose the term he did since so much of his, Hensel's, and Weinstock's ideas are shaped by complexity theory. I took Crutchfield's graduate physics course Natural Computation and Self-Organization at UC Davis in 2012, and in this chapter, I use my research into the self-organization of a particular biological system, as measured through Crutchfield's technique of "computational mechanics," as an example to highlight the differences between "material computation" and "natural computation" and to point out the different ways that "computing" and computers are used in these different disciplinary contexts. Studying the same topic—tendril coiling—from different disciplinary perspectives (biomimetic architecture, mathematics, biology, physics, computation) offered deep insights into the differences of terminology and tools of analysis used across different fields. I end the chapter by discussing the actual life cycle materiality of computers as a fitting contrast to "material computation": the increasingly rarer earth substances from which they are made, the high embodied energy in transistors and chips that are integral to every digital technology today, and the toxic effects of their production on workers and the environment.

The third chapter covers the history of ideas of morphogenesis and evolutionary computation as related to each other and to generative architecture. The branch of computer science referred to as evolutionary computation draws its analogies from biological theories of morphogenesis and evolution, and its techniques are the source for the "generative" computational portion of generative architecture and design. As a whole, however, evolutionary computation contributes far more to studies of artificial life and general complex problem-solving in many different fields than it does to biology. On the one hand, architectural students and those interested in generative techniques should understand how and where evolutionary computation fails to mimic biological processes, in order not to presume that by using generative techniques they are somehow creating biologically relevant design. On the other hand, for those interested in biology, developments in knowledge of processes of biological morphogenesis (aka biological development from embryo to adult) and their relationship to evolution have made the last couple of decades the most exciting in over a century of pursuing answers to some of biology's biggest questions. Although embryology and evolutionary studies began side by side in the late nineteenth century, during most of the twentieth century during the development of genetics they functioned as separate fields. The recent theory known as evo-devo (evolutionary developmental biology) has brought them together again, and just as it is prompting new research in biology, it is posing a new approach in evolutionary computation known as "computational development." Additionally, new knowledge of epigenetics is transforming understanding of how organisms interact with their environment to regulate gene action appropriately and responsively, sparking new conversations about the ongoing relevance of Lamarckism and encouraging the development of epigenetic algorithms. While I learned about evo-devo at both Penn and EmTech, only at Penn was epigenetics discussed. Later, independent study with geneticist and philosopher of science Eva Jablonka convinced me of the importance of this new field of scientific knowledge that is virtually ignored by generative architects.

While some generative architects are creating genetic algorithms integrating principles from evo-devo, to my knowledge none besides John Frazer has recently tried epigenetic algorithms as a tool for architectural morphogenesis. Because buildings, like organisms, interact with their environments in multiple ways, perhaps these approaches could push architects to think of morphogenesis not just as something that happens during the design phase in silico but also during the life of the building, including not just the "ecology" of humans but ecology writ large. After all, other theories of morphogenesis—beginning with D'Arcy Thompson's pathbreaking foray *On Growth and Form* (1917) and Alan Turing's prescient essay "The Chemical Basis of Morphogenesis" (1952)—are influencing generative architects.[38] Mid- to late twentieth-century neo-Darwinian theories of genetics offered the theories on which genetic algorithms were structured, and now generative architects are adapting evo-devo, as explained in Sean Carroll's *Endless Forms Most Beautiful* (2005), for computational design strategy. It is crucial to realize, however, that these approaches in architecture mostly contribute to "the evolution of things," as noted in a 2015 article in *Nature*, through digital design and manufacture.[39] But the developments in biological theories are relevant to those architects serious about biological sciences or envisioning growing living buildings, as the second half of the book discusses.

This leads directly to the fourth chapter, "Context Matters: LabStudio and Biosynthesis," the first to focus more on biological experimentation than computation. Jenny Sabin and Peter Lloyd Jones have been two of the most prominent figures in generative architecture to understand and integrate the most recent "postgenomic" knowledge of epigenetics and systems biology into their work and teaching.[40] Jones's first lectures in their co-taught 2008 seminar, Nonlinear Biology and Design at Penn, introduced epigenetics and the ways it is transforming knowledge of gene regulation and systems biology. He shared ideas from Eva Jablonka and Marion Lamb's important book *Evolution in Four Dimensions: Genetic, Epigenetic, Behavioral, and Symbolic Variation in the History of Life* (2005), as well as the work of his postdoctoral mentor, Mina Bissell. Bissell's groundbreaking work on cancer morphogenesis focuses on epigenetic triggers and controls of the disease, particularly with regard to the extracellular matrix that surrounds cells in tissues. The experiments that Sabin and Jones prepared for interdisciplinary teams of graduate students in their seminar focused on cell behaviors in different matrix conditions, in order to develop tools to see and identify healthy and unhealthy behaviors appearing through cell patterning in surface design, grouping, and motility. This is the only chapter in the book that focuses on the work of just one collaborative entity, since for many years they were the only team working in generative architecture that included a molecular biologist / biomedical researcher; the only team that taught the most current scientific theories pertaining to biological systems, although their close collaboration ended in 2011 when Sabin relocated to the Department of Architecture at Cornell University; and the only group that paired graduate students in architecture with those in molecular biology, making teams do research in both a scientific laboratory and a computational studio. The chapter evaluates some of the contributions of LabStudio's efforts both for biomedical research and for architecture, as manifest in Sabin's recent accomplishments.

Generative architects who want to grow living buildings using either tissue or genetic engineering most certainly need to understand postgenomic theory, for it seriously complicates their endeavors. Chapter 5 examines the goals of those architects envisioning or claiming to want to work with genetics and living cells or flesh as their media for architecture. These prominently include Alberto Estévez (ESARQ, Barcelona), Marcos Cruz (Bartlett School of Architecture, UCL), Matthias Hollwich (Penn Design and Hollwich Kushner), and, for a short while, SPAN Architects (Matias del Campo and Sandra Manninger), who collaborated with mechanical engineer Wei Sun of Drexel University's Lab for Computer-Aided Tissue Engineering. Their visions are examined in relation to the technologies they propose to use—usually tissue or genetic engineering. The chapter opens with a discussion of Catts and Zurr's *Victimless Leather,* shown at the Museum of Modern Art in the exhibition *Design and the Elastic Mind* in 2008. Both before and after this exhibition, architects upheld Catts and Zurr's work as the prototype of a future living architecture. For example, Cruz with Steve Pike published "Neoplasmatic Architecture" in *AD* (2008). They invited Catts and Zurr to contribute an article, and then later invited Catts to come to the Bartlett to guest lecture on how to apply tissue technologies to architecture. Overall, though, architects completely miss Catts and Zurr's critical views of these technologies. The chapter summarizes the limitations of living buildings in general, as well as limitations of scale in tissue engineering and the new field of 3-D "bio-printing," less often referred to as "organ printing." It introduces the difference between methods of tissue and genetic engineering, as distinct from synthetic biology. With regard to genetic engineering, I critique the video *Econic Design: A New Paradigm for Architecture* by Matthias Hollwich, Marc Kushner, and their students in 2008, as well as the descriptions of genetic architecture put forward by Estévez.

The last chapter addresses generative architecture and design in relation to the two branches of synthetic biology, research aiming to create protocells "bottom-up" as distinct from "top-down" engineering of synthetic life forms and products referred to here as "engineering synbio." "Protocell" architecture, as Armstrong calls it, returns us full circle to the initial ideas of self-organization and self-assembly, as it proposes to allow molecules in different solutions to form cell-like entities that secrete calcium carbonate to make buildings and cities. The most prominent promoters of "protocell" architecture are Rachel Armstrong, Neil Spiller, and Nic Clear, all with the Advanced

FIGURE I.3. *Hy-Fi,* by David Benjamin / The Living with Ecovative, 2014. Winner of MoMA PS-1 Young Architects Program, 2014. The bricks in this structure are created out of mushroom mycelium and corn stalks.

Virtual and Technological Architecture Research Group at the University of Greenwich, with their visions materialized through the work of artist Christian Kerrigan and architect Philip Beesley. Interestingly, Kerrigan's renderings for Armstrong's *Future Venice* project contradict some of her primary assertions. This raises questions about their collaboration and how the piece was intended to be received. Kerrigan's renderings suggest that theirs may be a work of "critical design" of the sort promoted by Anthony Dunne and Fiona Raby at the Design Interactions Department, Royal College of Art, but no one thus far has interpreted Armstrong's work in this way. Rather, she is usually given credit for being a medical doctor—implying she must understand biology—and is revered by many young architectural students for a "sustainable" vision that is not architecturally or scientifically credible.[41] For his part in "protocell" architecture, Beesley's digitally designed and manufactured sculptures create stunningly beautiful and thoughtful interactive environmental installations that happen to house "protocell" flasks. His work raises more interesting questions about "hard" artificial life than about protocells, which are characterized as a future form of "wet artificial life."[42]

The book concludes by considering new work in biodesign and in design using engineering synbio, which I refer to as "synbiodesign," first explaining the major differences between genetic engineering and engineering synbio. David Benjamin, who collaborated with synthetic biologist Fernan Federici in 2011, also worked with the new company Ecovative to grow mushroom

FIGURE I.4. *Walnut Legged Yamanaka McQueen,* by Phil Ross, 2012. Fungus and wood. Created at the Workshop Residence in San Francisco with the help of Michael Sgambellone, Caitlin Moorleghen, and Peter Doolittle. Courtesy of Phil Ross.

mycelium bricks for his installation *Hy-Fi,* which won the 2014 MoMA Young Architects Program at PS-1 (Figure I.3). Ecovative built on the preceding work of San Francisco artist and designer Phil Ross (Figure I.4). Ross is developing his company Mycoworks through the biotechnology-focused IndieBio start-up program in the Bay Area. For the last three years, he has been working at the lab of Stanford bioengineer Drew Endy, one of the founders of the field of synthetic biology. Ross knows that it is very difficult to genetically engineer fungi; they resist genetic manipulation, reverting to their age-old form and function. This has prompted him and his collaborators to work on engineering the media in which the mycelium grows, to shape the resulting composite into a new, low-energy, low-cost material that can serve ubiquitously for design.[43] The chapter explains both the appeal and the critiques of engineering synbio, which has a significant distance to go to live up to its most basic claims. If it does, along with genetic engineering it comes closest of all the methods discussed in this book to opening new modes of practicing eugenics. It is thus on a discordant tone that the book ends, weighing the former difficulties against the stark contrast that exists between Benjamin's *Hy-Fi* and Ross's relatively low-tech mycelium-based designs in comparison to the high-tech methods of generative architects of the computational variety—say, Menges, Hensel, or Schumacher.

CHAPTER 1

SELF-ORGANIZING AND EMERGENT ARCHITECTURE

In Fall 2011, the curriculum at the Emergent Technologies and Design Program (EmTech) at the Architectural Association (AA) opened with a three-week-long Boot Camp, which offered a crash course in EmTech's most basic version of the theory and practice of "emergent architecture." The specifications were given: Using only sheet material or fabric, design a component-based system that aggregates "through local, regional, and global hierarchies." Components should be formed using a "simple geometry"; their mode of connectivity to other components should be designed into them using "system-specific assembly logic." Teams of students had to design and manufacture these components using digital tools—Grasshopper or other "computational associative modeling" software and laser cutters for the sheet material—alternating between physical form-finding and digital experimentation. The "global array" should "demonstrate a clear hierarchical component logic, resulting in a final form with global curvature" that functioned as a "complex spatial configuration." It could be anchored in only three places to the floor, walls, or ceiling of the EmTech studio and should be self-supporting. It would be evaluated based on its "performative and structural qualities," as well as on the "emergent spatial and aesthetic" "ambient effects" of the "intervention."[1]

To my team, which included Spaniard Mara Moral-Correa and Italian Vincenzo Reale, the limitation of flat sheet materials suggested bending and folding to achieve three-dimensional form. This was not the only possible approach, though, as other groups used flat components connected into larger systems employing the principle of tensegrity structures. Whereas three-dimensional form could be achieved from bending a single cut shape, we designed smaller flat parts to bend and fit together to form a three-dimensional base component (Figure 1.1). This organization contributed toward the goal of having a hierarchy of forms, starting with "local" (interpreted as single parts in relation to one another) and moving to "regional" (a component in relation to other components) and then "global" (the final installation, featuring *lots* of components in relation to one another). Since the aggregate had to be self-supporting and would be evaluated based on its structural performance

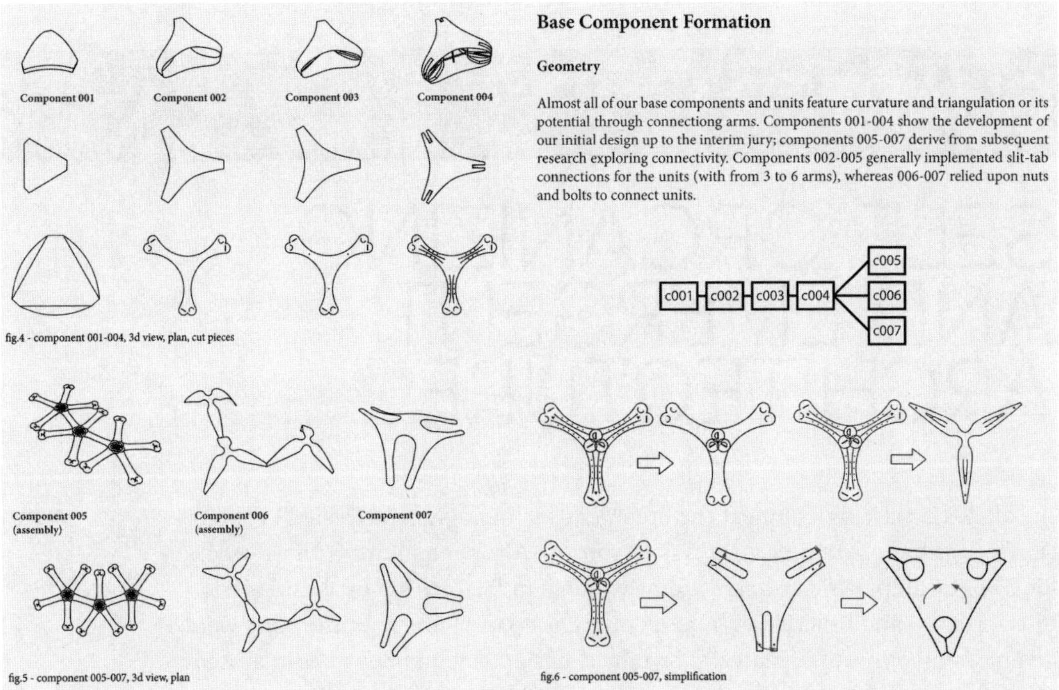

FIGURE 1.1. Component design, by Vincenzo Reale, Mara Moral Correa, and Christina Cogdell. Boot Camp project for Emergent Technologies and Design Program, Architectural Association, Fall 2011. Using EmTech terminology, our base components (001–004) evolved into a family of related forms, from which we experimented with three different morphologies and their connectivity (005–007).

and aesthetics, teams tried different materials and forms. Paper was easiest to experiment with but was weak; thin polypropylene sheets were thicker, stronger, flexible in any direction, and translucent (Figure 1.2). We finally selected 1.5-millimeter birch plywood, which owing to its cellular structure can only bend in certain directions; this was made much easier to work with by soaking it in water. Depending on the orientation of the triangular form with rounded corner cutouts in relation to the grain of the wood, and depending also on how large the rounded corner cutouts were, we achieved a wide range of curvatures. The most difficult challenge was the "assembly logic." The bone-shaped parts with moon-sliver slits in the ends did slot together to form round lantern-like shapes, but the other types of components we experimented with needed either string, tiny nuts and bolts, or both to become an aggregate assembly (Figures 1.3 and 1.4).

Our first critique midway through the studio was dismal. Our rather floppy "pile of plastic" made up of repeating "dog-bone" ball components (system 004 in Figure 1.1), connected to one another with nuts and bolts and string pulled taut, apparently had few redeeming, much less emergent, properties. I personally was not discouraged, though, since my primary goal was trying to understand what counts as an "emergent property" in the first place.[2] Hopefully not to my teammates' chagrin, I politely asked fundamental questions such

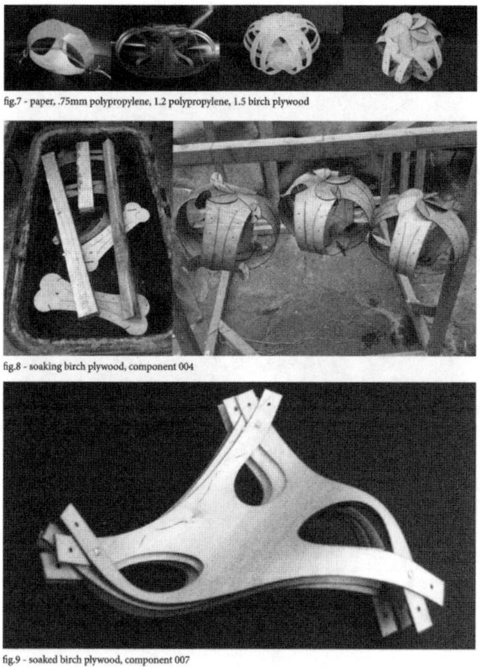

FIGURE 1.2. Component material experimentation, by Vincenzo Reale, Mara Moral Correa, and Christina Cogdell. Boot Camp project for Emergent Technologies and Design Program, Architectural Association, Fall 2011. Our experiments moved from paper to different thicknesses of polypropylene sheet material to thin birch plywood, soaked in water to enhance ease of curvature. Connections were made through slits with tab inserts or with the addition of string and/or nuts and bolts.

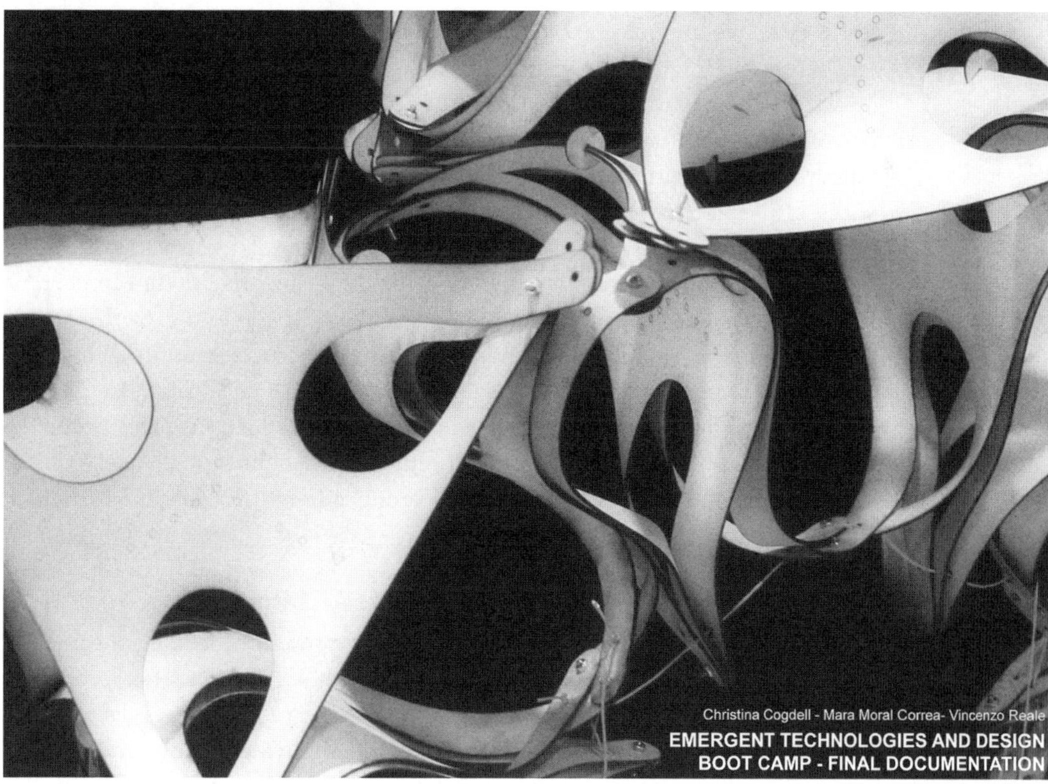

FIGURE 1.3. Assembly logic, by Vincenzo Reale, Mara Moral Correa, and Christina Cogdell. Boot Camp project for Emergent Technologies and Design Program, Architectural Association, Fall 2011. Two different base components work together to provide differentiation across the aggregated system.

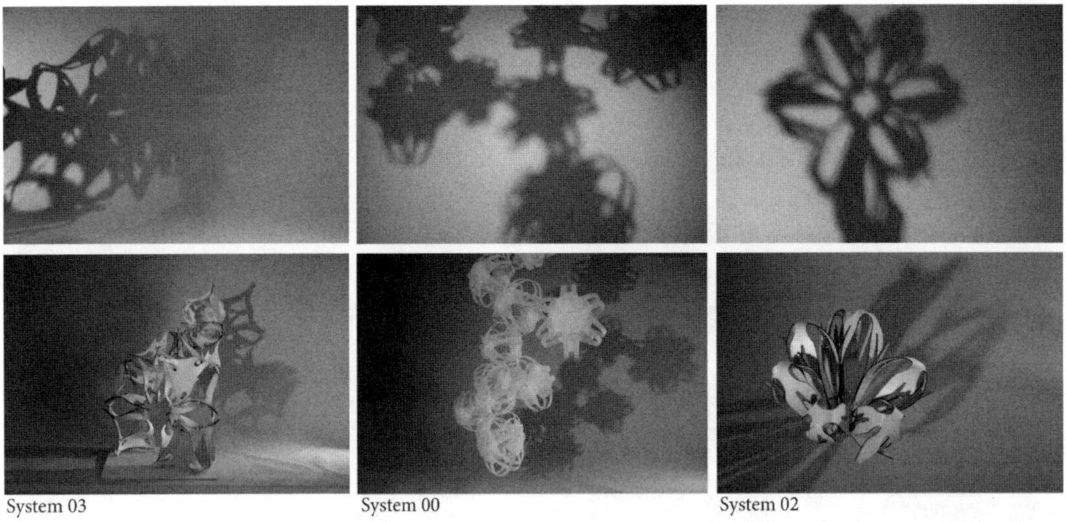

FIGURE 1.4. Emergent aesthetics, by Vincenzo Reale, Mara Moral Correa, and Christina Cogdell. Boot Camp project for Emergent Technologies and Design Program, Architectural Association, Fall 2011. Each of our component-aggregate systems, owing to their repetitive geometries in connection, produced organic-looking two-dimensional shadow patterns and three-dimensional morphologies.

as "Why do we have to start with components?" and "What distinguishes the local from the regional from the global?" It seemed grandiose that "global" referred to something that would fit inside one corner of the room where we worked, although our class did consist of students from twenty-three countries. Our final critique went better, for we eliminated the structurally unsuccessful plastic, worked with different curvatures of wood based on its material performance capacities, and used our triangular components in different ways through different modes of connection. This made a few important differences, including not only a more stable foundation and growth pattern for the "global array" but also the production of "differentiation" across the system. This means that parts are used differently to add variety or distinction, or parts are slightly changed, or a new part is added into the system in order to allow for differentiation to occur. As the light studies and shadow patterns show, our various systems all produced organic-looking aesthetics.

Introduction to Complexism in Generative Architecture

EmTech is and has been the primary academic program focusing specifically on emergence in architectural design. Although faculty at other programs around the world have undoubtedly used generative techniques and expressed interest in complexity or biological systems, no equivalent program has been in existence as long as EmTech, since 2001. Furthermore, the publications by its three main founders—Michael Weinstock, Michael Hensel, and Achim Menges—constitute the theoretical core for the application of principles of self-organization and emergence into architecture. This chapter, therefore, explores their writings to elucidate how they envision transforming architecture through these concepts. Although in the early to mid-2000s they published together, after this period Hensel and Menges diverged from Weinstock in their focus and in their joint publication efforts. Weinstock discounts sustainability and has moved toward the macroscale, applying emergence to the study of urban "metabolism" and urban systems. Hensel and Menges, however, have developed the concept of "morpho-ecology" that applies the rhetoric of sustainability, specifically interpreted, to performance optimization at the scale of a pavilion or building. They use associative computer modeling (parametric tools) to integrate data from the microscale of material structure with other design factors in order to design environmentally responsive structures that offer "heterogeneous" interior spaces, sometimes with different temperature gradients owing to gradated permeable membrane facades. Taken together, Weinstock's, Hensel's, and Menges's modes of applying self-organization and emergence to architecture span different scales and tend toward different ends. This chapter explores which ideas and thinkers from scientific complexity theory they rely on to frame their divergent approaches, and how they propose to integrate these ideas into design.

First, though, scientific definitions of the three most basic terms—complex systems, self-organization, and emergence—raise some interesting issues, for these terms are closely interrelated. Computer scientist Melanie Mitchell, in *Complexity: A Guided Tour,* defines a nonlinear complex adaptive system as one "in which large networks of components with no central control and simple rules of operation give rise to complex, collective behavior, sophisticated information processing, and adaptation via learning or evolution." More succinctly, she states that it is "a system that exhibits non-trivial emergent and self-organizing behaviors."[3] Biologist and physician Scott Camazine and others, in *Self-Organization in Biological Systems* (2001), define self-organization as "a process in which pattern at the global level of a system emerges solely from numerous interactions among the lower-level components of the system. Moreover, the rules specifying interactions among the system's components are executed using only local information, without reference to the global pattern."[4] Self-organization is closely related to the concept of emergence, which is generally understood to mean that "the whole is more than the sum of its parts," a phrase credited to Aristotle but repeated so many times it has become common knowledge.[5] According to Camazine and colleagues, "Emergent properties are features of a system that arise unexpectedly from interactions among the system's components. An emergent property cannot be understood simply by examining in isolation the properties of a system's components, but requires a consideration of the interactions among the system's components."[6] The title of 2001 *New York Times* best seller *Emergence: The Connected Lives of Ants, Brains, Cities, and Software,* by Steven Johnson, offers a few of the most popular examples of complex systems; add to the list in his title honeybee colonies, the internet, and urban transport systems and the catalog is virtually complete.

A few things about these definitions deserve special attention, beyond the fact that they are interrelated and by definition almost circularly self-constituting. The word "self" in self-constituting is used figuratively, since humans are the ones making these definitions and seeing the "components," "levels," and "systems" in the first place. This clarification pertains as well to the "self" in self-organization, discussed below. First, all three require parts or components, and quite a lot of them; just a couple is not enough. The generic terminology allows these things to be living or nonliving so long as they are multiple-to-many. Second, these units make up the "lower level" of a system, so by definition it is thereby presumed or called into being that multiple levels or some sort of hierarchy, layering, or nestedness exists in the system. This is important because emergence or an emergent property arises at the next level up from that of the components, and its occurrence depends upon there being many components that interact with one another according to the same rules. Third, no "central control" tells the components "top-down" what to do; the components use only "local information, without reference to the global pattern" as their inputs. This is referred to as "bottom-up." This means a component or group of components cannot see itself or themselves as if looking down from on high, cannot see the patterns the group is making, and then use the information from that seeing to shape its own or the group's actions. (In social and cultural manifestations of complex systems, human beings are frequently considered to be "components.") Fourth, there are "rules" that the components know and obey. The passive voice is used intentionally here since it is never even noted, much less explained, why there are rules or from whence the rules had come.[7] Rules simply exist and precede or are called into being by the components, which somehow all know and follow them.

The above points are troubling for three reasons. The first has to do with agency and the location or identity of the "self" in self-organization. It is unclear whether a component is considered to be a self, or whether the self is being organized or emerging from the organization. In other words, are lots of selves actively undertaking or passively undergoing the process of self-organization? Evelyn Fox Keller believes the self emerges from the organization at the next higher level, but still, she quotes cybernetician W. Ross Ashby stating, "Since no system can correctly be said to be self-organizing, and since use of the phrase 'self-organizing' tends to perpetuate a fundamentally confused and inconsistent way of looking at the subject, the phrase is probably better allowed to die out."[8] If components merely follow rules of interaction, and humans are the components of cultural or social systems, then humans are denied agency, intelligence, perspective, and free will; in other nonhuman systems, parts or all of this are true as well. Perhaps, instead of the components then, it is the system that is self-organizing. But the system is pre-assumed and pre-existent in the above definitions. When I asked scientists, "What is a system?" they replied, "Whatever you say it is." When I asked, "Where are a system's boundaries?" they responded, "Wherever you draw them, but usually there is some clearly defined yet semipermeable border." These are very flexible and convenient answers.

The second reason pertains to the idea of system hierarchy, which is defined into the idea of a complex system though the existence of levels. History shows that humans are very adept at conceiving of things as hierarchical, as well as at projecting beliefs like social hierarchy onto the behavior of "natural" things. Hierarchies imply power especially if the complex system is a human-related one (economic, social, cultural), even though scientists might interpret hierarchy simply as organization or structure or architecture, not power. The existence of rules also implies or creates power, and the origin of the rules is unclear. They cannot just emerge, since the rules cause emergence to happen.[9] Finally, the third reason the definitions and their interrelatedness (circular self-constitution) are troubling derives from their cohesiveness, which strongly resembles the cohesion of a highly successful intellectual, ideological, or religious system. If something cannot be explained by one part of the framework, it can be explained by another part or by redrawing the system's boundaries.

The flexibility inherent in these terms permits their application in many different disciplines, not just generative art and architecture.[10] While I use "complexity" to refer to the scientific theory and its scientific applications, I use "complexism" to call attention to its ideological instantiations that are widespread across the arts, humanities, and social sciences. Complexism is used to theorize political protests like the Occupy movement and revolutions like the Arab Spring to explain nonlinear dynamics of criminology or to posit "cryptohierarchies and self-organization in the open-source movement."[11] It offers new modes of writing history, new ways of theorizing pedagogy, new ways of understanding borderline personality disorder or anti-sociality.[12] Economists in the field of evolutionary economics have promoted the idea of *The Self-Organizing Economy* in support of deregulated global trade (the title of a book by Princeton professor Paul Krugman, who received the 2008 Nobel Prize for Economics).[13] Mainstream financial institution HSBC picked up on this, using emergence and self-organization to advertise their services in international airports in 2015 (Figure 1.5).[14] They use the typical examples of the honeybee, urban transportation design, and neural networks as their chosen metaphors. Complexism has even been used to bolster the assertion that "Fairness Is an Emergent Self-Organized Property of the Free Market for Labor"—an article title from the journal *Entropy* in 2010—an assertion with which many would disagree, including not only Occupy protestors but also sociologist Saskia Sassen.[15] Her recent book *Expulsions: Brutality and Complexity in the Global Economy* (2014) argues that the growth and complexity of the deregulated global economy has produced not fairness but brutal expulsions of individuals, small businesses, and wasted lands. Another way of saying this is that the boundaries delineating those entities *inside* from those *outside* the complex system of the global economy have shrunk, while the economic growth of the last thirty years has been channeled to those fewer entities that

FIGURE 1.5. HSBC advertising campaign, 2015. This campaign is built on principles in evolutionary economics that promote ideas of self-organization (e.g., the honeybee symbol) and emergence in complex systems that collapse the dichotomy of nature and culture.

remain inside the system's boundaries. As these examples begin to show, both promoters and critics of economic neoliberalism are able to use complexism to argue their case. Scientific ideologies are most powerful when their terminologies are sufficiently vague but still logically interconnected so as to be able to be used by people or groups with opposing perspectives to justify their views. Eugenics functioned this way in the 1930s, and complexism does so today.

The general allure of complexism for generative architects is thus multilayered, arising from its cachet and authority as a scientific theory with broad explanatory power, its ambiguity of agency, and its flexibility of application. Additionally, self-organization offers a useful framework for designers because it posits where and how order—pattern and form—arises in nature, be it organic or inorganic. With regard to living systems, self-organization is often interpreted with reference to homeostasis, which occurs within the bodies of individual organisms and collective groups such as termites in a mound. Homeostasis refers to the capacity to self-regulate to an internal norm in order to sustain comfort and life, both of which occur within narrow parameter ranges. Such is the function of a thermostat or "governor" in machines that senses changes externally or internally and offers positive or negative feedback to restore and maintain balance. In living organisms, common examples of homeostasis are the maintenance of body temperature, fluid or gas concentrations, and bone density, as well as the construction (self-assembly) of structures (hives, mounds, nests) by organisms that help regulate their immediate environment. Architects, therefore, find homeostasis to be an attractive model for architecture since buildings moderate environmental conditions (temperature, humidity, etc.) for human existence, often relying on large amounts of energy and material to do so. Menges and Hensel focus on minimizing the latter, although within a very narrow frame of consideration.

Yet, self-organization is by no means the *only* explanation of pattern formation in nature and culture, and for a long time now, humans have designed machines to function homeostatically, including for the regulation of building environments. Think about the use of sensors plus feedback to a central control or thermostat to regulate how a building maintains its temperature or lighting levels. This shows that both homeostasis and patterns frequently occur through the use of centralized processes such as "top-down" intention and design, as well as through sensor systems that are designed to be distributed and communicate with one another. Examples of other pattern-making processes are the human use of recipes in cooking, patterns for sewing, and blueprints for building; some nonhuman organisms use these processes, too. Alternately, cells function as "preformatted" templates for future cells, such that when a cell divides asexually, it creates a new copy of itself. This notion of copying, or repeating, of structures also inheres to the idea of a pattern, and is similar to sexual reproduction, which also includes mechanisms for slight differentiation from generation to generation. These reproduction processes do not exactly fit the definition of self-organization, however, which requires many nearly identical components, not just one, operating according to rules using only local information without a central control. Rather, reproduction performs the role of component multiplication. So, given that other modes of pattern-making exist in nature, why do generative architects focus almost exclusively on self-organization and emergence as their theoretical platform and justification for this particular mode of parametric design?

This chapter explores complexism as an ideological influence on the foundational architectural theories of complexity, self-organization, and emergence, and on the fundamental practices of generative architecture as taught at EmTech. It focuses on the published writings of its three main founders as interpreted through experiential insights gained during my time as a student there during the Fall 2011 semester. First, Weinstock's theories of emergent architecture are explained in conjunction with his opinion that sustainability need not be a significant concern for architecture. These are then contrasted with Menges and Hensel's advocacy for sustainability using complexity theory as developed in their concepts of morpho-ecology and heterogeneity in architecture. The final section reflects on historical and contemporary sociopolitical and economic developments that contribute to generative architects' current interests in self-organization and emergence as an architectural paradigm for today. These broader developments are explicated in part by Patrik Schumacher in his insistence on the superiority of homogeneity and his own streamlined version of parametricism as the only suitable architectural expression of the neoliberal era. Because of the contrast this offers to Hensel's and Menges's approaches, the chapter thus demonstrates the ideological power of complexism as used by generative architects to argue for different ends—for and against sustainability, for and against homogeneity—thereby cautioning its supporters against blithe acceptance.

Michael Weinstock's Architecture of Emergence

Weinstock, continuing director of EmTech since its beginning, certainly conceives of emergence as related to self-organization, even though the latter word was not used in the 2011 Boot Camp brief or in the name of the graduate program. His first major explication of emergent architecture in print from 2004 opens, "Emergence is a concept that appears in the literature of many disciplines, and is strongly correlated to evolutionary biology, artificial intelligence, complexity theory, cybernetics, and general systems theory." He cites the simplest definition: "Emergence is said to be the properties of a system that cannot be deduced from its components, something more than the sum of its parts." He then sets the task for architects to "delineate a working concept of emergence," "to outline the mathematics and processes that can make it useful to us as designers" by searching "for the principles and dynamics of organization and interaction." He describes these as "the mathematical laws that natural systems obey." But first, he asks, "What is it that emerges, what does it emerge from, and how is emergence produced?"[16] Images accompanying his article depict a satellite photograph of the patterns made by clouds in a turbulent weather system and photos of spiraling fractal helices of shells and the florets of broccoflower. These suggest that emergence occurs in nonliving systems and living organisms, both plants and animals. To these, he adds the dynamics of group behavior: "flocks of birds" and "schools of fish" that "produce what appears to be an overall coherent form or array, without any leader or central directing intelligence." He includes "bees and termites" that "produce complex built artefacts . . . without central planning or instructions."[17] Thus, in answer to his first questions, it is order or pattern in form and behavior that emerges "from the processes of complex systems."[18]

Weinstock's mention that no leader or central instructions are involved points directly to the idea of self-organization as a founding principle of both emergence and complex systems. Two years later he made this explicit: "The evolution and development of biological self-organisation of systems proceeds from small, simple components that are assembled together to form larger structures that have emergent properties and behaviour, which, in turn, self-assemble into more complex structures."[19] This time, his images included an electron micrograph scan of spongy bone tissue and a close-up of the structure of soap bubbles (Figure 1.6), upon whose geometry the "Watercube" National Swimming Centre in Beijing was then being built for the 2008 Olympics (Figure I.1).[20] His explanation of self-organization is very similar to how he defines complexity theory, which "focuses on the effects produced by the collective behaviour of many simple units that interact with each other, such

FIGURE 1.6. Soap bubble morphology, by Dr. Jeremy Burgess / Science Photo Library. Image previously published in Michael Weinstock, "Self-Organisation and Material Constructions," in "Techniques and Technologies in Morphogenetic Design," special issue of *AD,* ed. Michael Hensel, Achim Menges, and Michael Weinstock, 76, no. 2 (March–April 2006): 36. This morphology is used as the basis for the Beijing National Aquatics Center (Figure I.1).

as atoms, molecules or cells. The complex is heterogeneous with many varied parts that have multiple connections between them, and the different parts behave differently, although they are not independent." As we learned through the Boot Camp final critique, "complexity increases when the variety (distinction) and dependency (connection) of parts increases. The process of increasing variety is called differentiation, and the process of increasing the number or the strength of connections is called integration." Weinstock believes that "evolution produces differentiation and integration in many 'scales' that interact with each other, from the formation and structure of an individual organism to species and ecosystems."[21]

In retrospect, other parts of the initial Boot Camp assignment, besides the obvious requirement to create a hierarchy of connected components, explored fundamental concepts and processes associated with complex biological systems. By starting with flat sheet material, groups mimicked one way that three-dimensional tissues are created in some biological forms, as sheets of cells fold over on themselves to create cavities or layers. In Weinstock's 2004 article titled "Morphogenesis and the Mathematics of Emergence" he cites cybernetician Alan Turing's paper "The Chemical Basis of Morphogenesis" (1952). Turing proposes that some two-dimensional surface patterns in nature develop through a chemical process called "reaction diffusion," where gradients of chemicals in surface tissues of plants and animals trigger thresholds that produce patterns of branching or stripes and spots. "Turing's model operates on a single plane, or a flat sheet of cells," Weinstock writes. He continues, "Some current research in the computational modeling of morphogenesis extends the process that Turing outlined on flat sheets to processes in curved sheets. . . . Folding and buckling of flat sheets of cells are the basis of morphogenesis in asexual reproduction."[22]

Similarly, by designing components digitally, students were forced to think with the logic of software, describing form mathematically using software tools, or for those who were advanced programmers, by writing custom algorithms. This aligns the practice with a mode familiar to complexity theorists: "Mathematical models have been derived from natural phenomena, massively parallel arrays of individual 'agents' or 'cell units' that have very simple processes in each unit, with simple interactions between them. Complex patterns and effects emerge from distributed dynamical models."[23] To Weinstock, the use of digital technologies is mandatory, and not just because that is how contemporary architecture is mostly designed today. The rationale is higher, and one with a lengthy history in architecture: to base architecture on the principles of evolution. "Strategies for design are not truly evolutionary," he writes, "unless they include iterations of physical (phenotypic) modeling, incorporating the self-organising material effects of form finding and the industrial logic of production available in CNC and laser-cutting modeling machines."[24] Every studio at EmTech stressed this iterative cycle between physical form-finding and advanced digital modeling. Without having been a student or observer there, I would not have understood from just reading published articles how at its most basic level, EmTech weaves together these layers of meaning and process. Considering Weinstock's publications from the perspective of lived experience and personal observation opened up new modes of understanding the theoretical writings of generative architecture, thereby posing a new mode of research for design studies.

In his early elaborations of the theory of emergence for his architectural audience, Weinstock cites the work of twentieth-century scientists and thinkers whose contributions he considers influential. Because architects create three-dimensional forms, he explores theories that pertain to the emergence of form ("morphogenesis") and behavior in nature. He begins with the early twentieth-century Scottish biologist D'Arcy Thompson, whose book *On Growth and Form* (1917) established an original theory of evolution and organismal development using mathematical relationships between the physical forms of related and divergent species. Weinstock associates Thompson's ideas with those of mathematician and philosopher Alfred North Whitehead, whose writings emphasize the primary importance of process and interaction in nature more than just substance alone. Weinstock then turns to Norbert Wiener's cybernetic theory to establish that the only major systemic difference in how animals and machines—of the sort regulated by a governor guided by feedback from communication inputs—maintain themselves over time is in their "degree of complexity."[25]

This common pattern of behavior between animals and machines, Weinstock asserts, was further developed by the work of chemical physicist Ilya Prigogine, who argued that "all biological and many natural nonliving systems are maintained by the flow of energy through the system."[26] Prigogine is well known for his recognition and description of open systems, those whose sources of energy, in addition to material or informational inputs or both, are external to the system yet interact with and help maintain it. Open systems exhibit nonequilibrium thermodynamics, and the foregoing characteristics are integral to the formation of complex dynamic systems. Prigogine's publications of the 1970s and 1980s thus greatly furthered the interdisciplinary study of complex systems. Weinstock describes the general pattern of nonequilibrium systems: "The pattern of energy flow is subject to many small variations, which," as in cybernetics, "are adjusted by 'feedback' from the environment to maintain equilibrium," he writes.[27] "But occasionally there is such an amplification that the system must reorganise or collapse. A new order emerges from the chaos of the system at the point of collapse." More on this below, but many patterns in nature occur when a system is "far from equilibrium" or "on the edge of chaos," not in its closer-to-equilibrium states.[28] Weinstock continues describing what complexity theorists typically claim happens when a system reorganizes at this influx: "The reorganisation creates a more complex structure, with a higher flow of energy through it, and is in turn more susceptible to fluctuations and subsequent collapse or reorganisation. The tendency of 'self-organised' systems to ever-increasing complexity," he states, "and of each reorganisation to be produced at the moment of the collapse in the equilibrium of systems extends beyond the energy relations of an organism and its environment. Evolutionary development in general emerges from dynamic systems."[29]

Weinstock relies on two other basic principles that are widely accepted in complexity theory. The first was proposed by Francis Heylighen in the late 1980s and pertains to the idea of "assemblies." This sounds very similar to what Gilles Deleuze and Félix Guattari referred to in *A Thousand Plateaus* (1980) as "assemblages," a term also taken from dynamical systems theory but which they extend in different philosophical directions. For Heylighen, some component interactions (think of organisms in groups, or species in ecologies) evolve together as "assemblies" that "survive to go on to form naturally selected wholes, while others collapse to undergo further evolution. This process repeats at higher levels," producing the effect that "an emergent whole at one level" becomes "a component of a system emerging at a higher level."[30] The other fundamental concept of complexity theory that undergirds Weinstock's interpretation of his theory of emergent architecture is that "system theory argues that the concepts and principles of organisation in natural systems are independent of the domain of any one particular system. . . . What is common . . . is the study of organisation, its structure and function. Complexity theory formalizes the mathematical structure of the process of systems from which complexity emerges."[31] The concept of "independence" of domain presumes that any and all complex systems, regardless of which disciplinary area might study them, exhibit common processes and characteristics to the extent that their disciplinary domain becomes insignificant. Hence, Steven Johnson considers ants, brains, cities, and software in the same book, in order to point out common systemic processes of emergence across these different domains. Weinstock follows suit, discussing architecture, biology, computation, and other domains as systemically equivalent to the extent that at times it is unclear which domain he is discussing. This lack of specificity enhances the already existing confusion elicited by terminology across these domains, such as use of the words "gene," "genetic," and "evolution" that read as both biological and computational.

Weinstock develops these tenets much more fully in his book *The Architecture of Emergence: The Evolution of Form in Nature and Civilisation* (2010). His narrative is historicist, reinterpreting basic scientific knowledge about the formation and function of the earth's major natural systems through the lens of emergence. He writes, "Emergence requires the recognition of all the forms of the world not as singular and fixed bodies, but as complex energy and material systems that have a lifespan, exist as part of the environment of other active systems, and as one iteration of an endless series that proceeds by evolutionary development."[32] He begins with weather and the atmosphere, then moves to geology and landscape, then living organisms and their metabolisms. Humans are of course living organisms, and Weinstock makes it explicitly clear in his first chapter and throughout the book that he considers humans and their cultural forms (i.e., "civilization," meaning mostly cities) to be part of, not separate from, nature. "Humans are the work of nature, and all the works of man, their material practices, constructions and artefacts, evolve and develop over time as part of nature."[33] At the same time, he rejects the idea that an untouched nature exists: "There is no singular 'natural landscape' to be found, no ideal state of nature that can be reconstructed or modeled. The difficulty of hypothesising a landscape with little or no human influence is evident."[34]

Together, these two claims effectively dissolve the conceptual dichotomy between nature and culture, though he does acknowledge differences between biological and cultural processes. He effectively constitutes human actions as "natural" and, at the same time, positions the materiality and processes of the earth as having been seriously transformed by humans. He acknowledges that this has not always been to the benefit and often has been to the detriment of other living forms.[35] Yet, because he sees all the systemic processes discussed throughout the book as interconnected and "self-organizing" toward an inevitable, ever-greater complexity, the ethical consequences of human actions are mitigated, evaded, or dismissed since human actions simply become one more part of the current system leading toward the next near collapse and "higher" reorganization.

This attitude is likely a significant factor in Weinstock's discounting of current human efforts to use architecture and other cultural arenas to enhance "sustainability." The idea of sustainability is both a part of and at odds with his framework of the advance of complexity. On the one hand, homeostasis is a means whereby organisms *sustain* themselves within a variable environment, and this is seen as one example of "self-organization." Weinstock views this as a metabolic process and considers architecture to be an extension of the human metabolism. On the other hand, though, according to open systems and complexity theory, all systems are in flux, maintaining balance for a while but then reorganizing into a new form of complexity, one usually considered "higher" or "greater" than the previous one.[36] He writes, "The tendency of living systems and of cultural systems to ever increasing complexity, and of each reorganization to be produced subsequent to the collapse, suggests that the evolutionary development of all forms is regulated by the dynamics of energy flow." Because he thinks that "an increase in complexity is always coupled to an increase in the flow of energy through the system," it follows that to try to "save" energy or reduce the flow of energy through cities or the global economy would suggest a "rever[sion] to a simpler organisation."[37] Such an action would be tantamount to what modernists' decried as "degeneration."

In fact, this is the argument Weinstock develops toward the end of his book. He summarizes human history in relation to growth in population, technologies, and urbanism, as tied to the increase in the burning of fossil fuels, the only source besides nuclear power that is dense enough in energy to have powered the exponential increase in the flows of energy and information since the Industrial Revolution. This growth has proceeded hand in hand with deforestation, species extinctions, soil exhaustion, increasing desertification, changes in weather and the evaporative cycle, and a huge increase of atmospheric pollution owing to soot, carbon dioxide, and greenhouse gases.[38] These human-caused changes, however, while being cited, are cast as value-neutral in Weinstock's text. "There are many indicators that suggest that the system is close to the threshold of stability. Systems that have evolved close to their maximum capacity are poised at the critical threshold of stability," he writes, "and are consequently very sensitive to social, climatic and ecological changes. A local failure may trigger a cascade of failures that amplify each other right across the world and so trigger the collapse of the whole system."[39]

Weinstock goes so far as to predict the number of generations it will take to develop major new sources of energy and for population to decline. "Voluntary commitment to limiting the expansion of the population may begin to slow the rate of expansion within one generation," he writes, "but will have to be reinforced by strong societal commitment with some coercion if the world population is to be stabilized within two generations."[40] Notice his prediction that humans will have to be coerced to not reproduce, although no mention is made as to whether "fitness" determinations will be part of this process. In general, Weinstock seems closed to the idea and fact of the ongoing prevalence of eugenics.[41] He predicts that "world dissemination of free information . . . will then begin to have a significant impact on all energy and material transformations, and the transition to a truly 'distributed intelligence' world system will be accelerated." This is but one example of the "higher complexity" that will emerge. "All forms change over time," he states.[42] "It is clear that the world is within the horizon of a systemic change, and that transitions through multiple critical thresholds will cascade through all the systems of nature and civilization." He closes his book with this biblical-sounding prediction: "New forms will emerge down through all the generations to come, and they will develop with new connections between them as they proliferate across the surfaces of the earth."[43]

As his subsequent issue of *AD*, titled "System City" (2013), makes clear, these proliferating new forms that Weinstock imagines will emerge are not humans or even buildings but cities, considered as if they are organisms or "superorganisms."[44] Some of his verbiage suggests that he views humans as significantly subsidiary to cities. He describes humans as a "fluctuating discharge" that comes out of subway stations, and says that a city will be conscious of "its citizens."[45] In other words, he considers cities to be assemblies, per Heylighen's description, that will become the self-organizing components of the next higher order of complexity after collapse and reorganization. The buildings in these cities will be "smart"—both within their own walls through sophisticated sensor systems that feed back to homeostatic controls, as well as through linkage to their neighboring structures. "Linking the response of infrastructure systems to groups of environmentally intelligent buildings will allow higher-level behaviour to emerge," he wrote in 2004. By 2013, he was classifying the taxonomy of types of "intelligent cities" based on their scale of "cognitive complexity": "These cognitive categories are, in ascending order of complexity: situated, reactive/responsive, adaptive/attentional and self-aware. . . . The 'self-aware' city does not yet exist."[46]

For a city to be intelligent, what is first required is sentience, "a primary attribute of intelligence," which he defines as "the ability to sense the world external to the organism; no organism can respond to its environment or become better adapted to it over time without sentience."[47] Based on studies in the field of artificial intelligence on collective intelligence, such as is exhibited by insect societies that build "dynamically responsive" nests to regulate their proximal environment, he argues that "intelligence is not just the property of a singular brain, but is situated and socially constructed and emerges from the interaction of large numbers of relatively simpler individuals within fluctuating dynamical contexts. This suggests that collective intelligence is the appropriate model of intelligence for the integration of the systems of intelligent cities."[48] As the termite mound functions homeostatically to maintain a constant comfortable environment for the termite colony, owing to the self-organizing collective behavior of millions of termites, so, too, are cities imagined to function as homeostatic organisms with collective intelligence and infrastructure, made up from the interactions of populations of smart buildings that happen to be inhabited by humans.[49]

Thus, he proposes that "situated cities" at the most basic taxonomic level of urban intelligence and complexity have evolved over time to be very well suited ecologically to their climate and place. Situated cities can become "reactive and responsive," with "sentience, the ability to sense critical changes in the flows of the external environment and within itself, and to respond by modifying or changing some aspects of the behaviour of its own systems appropriately."[50] If a city has attained this level, it can then evolve to become "adaptive and attentional," meaning it "has the capacity to selectively change some aspects of both the behaviour and configuration of any of its infrastructural systems. It requires the capacity for selective attention to moderate changes that are beneficial at a local scale but potentially conflict with global system parameters."[51] Note that this description of adaptive and attentional cities has moved beyond the definition of self-organization, whereby components are not seemingly able to observe themselves as if from above to make decisions about and control subsequent behavior, but rather only exist on the local level following local rules without any "top-down" control. Finally, once these mechanisms are in place, a city can become "self-aware . . . 'conscious' of its citizens and the interrelation between all of its infrastructural systems, and able to synchronize its city systems with climatic and ecological effects at the regional scale." A self-aware city can "learn from experiences . . . run simulations to predict the effectiveness and long-term consequences of system modifications and reconfigurations . . . and is capable of planning its further expansions or contractions according to the fluctuations of its global and regional contexts."[52]

As becomes clear from Weinstock's writings, his most sacrosanct belief is that *everything* emerges from self-organizing dynamical system processes, including evolution, and the direction that emergence takes teleologically is toward ever greater complexity.[53] Higher levels of complexity supposedly have higher energy and informational flows; note that material flows are almost never mentioned, perhaps because matter is inconveniently finite. In other words, higher informational flows imply higher orders of intelligence, such as he predicts for the evolution of urban "organisms" (cities). The architecture of emergence that he seeks and is training students to design prioritizes digital information technologies—the use of associative modeling, the embedding of microprocessors, sensors, and digital feedback and control systems—throughout urban environments. Given his dismissal of current efforts toward future-oriented "sustainability," along with his characterization of humans as creatures of lower-level complexity compared to smart buildings and intelligent self-aware cities that plan their own futures, it seems that Weinstock is investing his time and energy into preparing for what he imagines to be the future.[54] If cities are to be the next organisms (components) in the march toward higher complexity, Weinstock is laying the theoretical groundwork for designing and installing their communication and control systems, on the questionable assumptions that materials will not run out and city infrastructures and buildings along with their many microprocessors will not collapse when the climate, economy, and energy infrastructures do.

Michael Hensel and Achim Menges's Morpho-Ecologies

From the early 2000s, along with Weinstock, Hensel and Menges offered formative contributions to the development of EmTech at the AA. Hensel codirected the program with Weinstock until 2009, and Menges taught as a Studio Master. All three also collaborated in a design practice, the Emergence and Design Group. Their component-based approach to creating emergent architecture, based on principles of self-organization and complex systems, is something they shared in the 2000s, although recent projects have broadened beyond this design method. They have followed different trajectories in their careers, each developing a unique focus for his research. Whereas Weinstock has remained at the AA and been the most heavily committed to developing emergence as a theory for architecture (actually as a theory of everything), Hensel and Menges have architectural practices, doing design work in addition to teaching at other European institutions. Hensel became a founding member of the architectural firm OCEAN in 1994, which has morphed since 2008 into two Norwegian nonprofits focusing on the human and built environments, the OCEAN Design Research Association and the Sustainable Environment Association (SEA), now fused into OCEAN/SEA.[55] These have focused more on research and publications than on built projects, with the SEA's promotion of "sustainability" following in line with Hensel and Menges's concept of morpho-ecologies, as explained below. Since 2011, he has directed the Research Center for Architecture and Tectonics at the Oslo School of Architecture and Design. He also taught some in the Scarcity and Creativity Studio there, a design-and-build studio focusing on lower-tech, lower-embedded-energy materials and construction approaches for local communities with few resources. The built practices of this studio, now directed by Christian Hermansen Cordua, tend more toward time-tested methods of vernacular architecture, although no doubt they are designed using advanced technologies. Although Menges taught at the AA until 2009, with ongoing visiting professorships and lectures since then, he also held positions at HfG Offenbach University for Art and Design, the Harvard Graduate School of Design, and founded the Institute for Computational Design at the University of Stuttgart in 2008, which he still directs. He also has his own architectural practice in Frankfurt, Germany.

Although generally Hensel has focused his research on sustainability and

Menges on understanding the material properties of wood and other materials through digital technologies and experimentation, they have coedited and copublished a number of articles and books owing to their common concept of morpho-ecologies. As early as 2004, Menges used this phrase in relation to "complex environments" (complex here references complex systems). The "morpho" part comes from morphogenesis, and "ecology" he defines as "all the relationships between human groups and their physical and social environments," by which he and Hensel consistently just mean buildings.[56] The term expresses their interest in creating parametric tools that can associate (link with feedback) many factors into the generation of a design: at the outset, these included ecology, topology, and structure, but soon this list came to include additional characteristics.[57] In the introductory essay to their book *Morpho-Ecologies* (2007), he and Hensel write, "The underlying logic of parametric design can be instrumentalised here as an alternative design method, one in which the geometric rigour of parametric modeling can be deployed first to integrate manufacturing constraints, assembly logics and material characteristics in the definition of simple components, and then to proliferate the components into larger systems and assemblies."[58] Using these associative tools, "if we change a variable of the basic outward proliferation, we may see an accompanying change in the number of components populating the surface. Indeed, as we introduce changes, we can identify results ranging from the 'local' manipulation of individual components to the 'regional' manipulation of component collectives to the 'global' manipulation of the component system."[59]

In general, Hensel and Menges aim for these tools to aid them in generating "heterogeneous space," in contrast to what they describe as the "homogeneous space" of modern architecture. In modernist homogeneous space, the interior of a building is regulated for uniformity—the building is closed off from the surrounding environment, generally with rectangular rooms, lighting, and air-conditioned temperature. With heterogeneous space, they aim to design structures that modulate the barrier between inside and outside, perhaps through the use of screens or layered walls with fractal, branching, or cell-shaped perforations that absorb heat and cast shadows for cooling. Inside, heterogeneous space is not uniform, but flows between different kinds of spaces—some cooler possibly, some warmer, but all flexible enough for multiple formal uses and types of human interactions. One example they offer of morpho-ecological design is a project Hensel designed with OCEAN and Scheffler + Partner, their unbuilt competition entry for the New Czech National Library (2006) (Figure 1.7). The design features "gradient spatial conditioning" as well as "intensive differentiation of material and energetic interventions that are evolved from their specific behavioural tendencies in a given environment and with regards to their mutual feedback relationship, passive modulation strategies that are sustainable, and speculation on the resultant relationship between spatial and social arrangements and habitational pattern and potentials."[60] The concept of morpho-ecologies thus describes

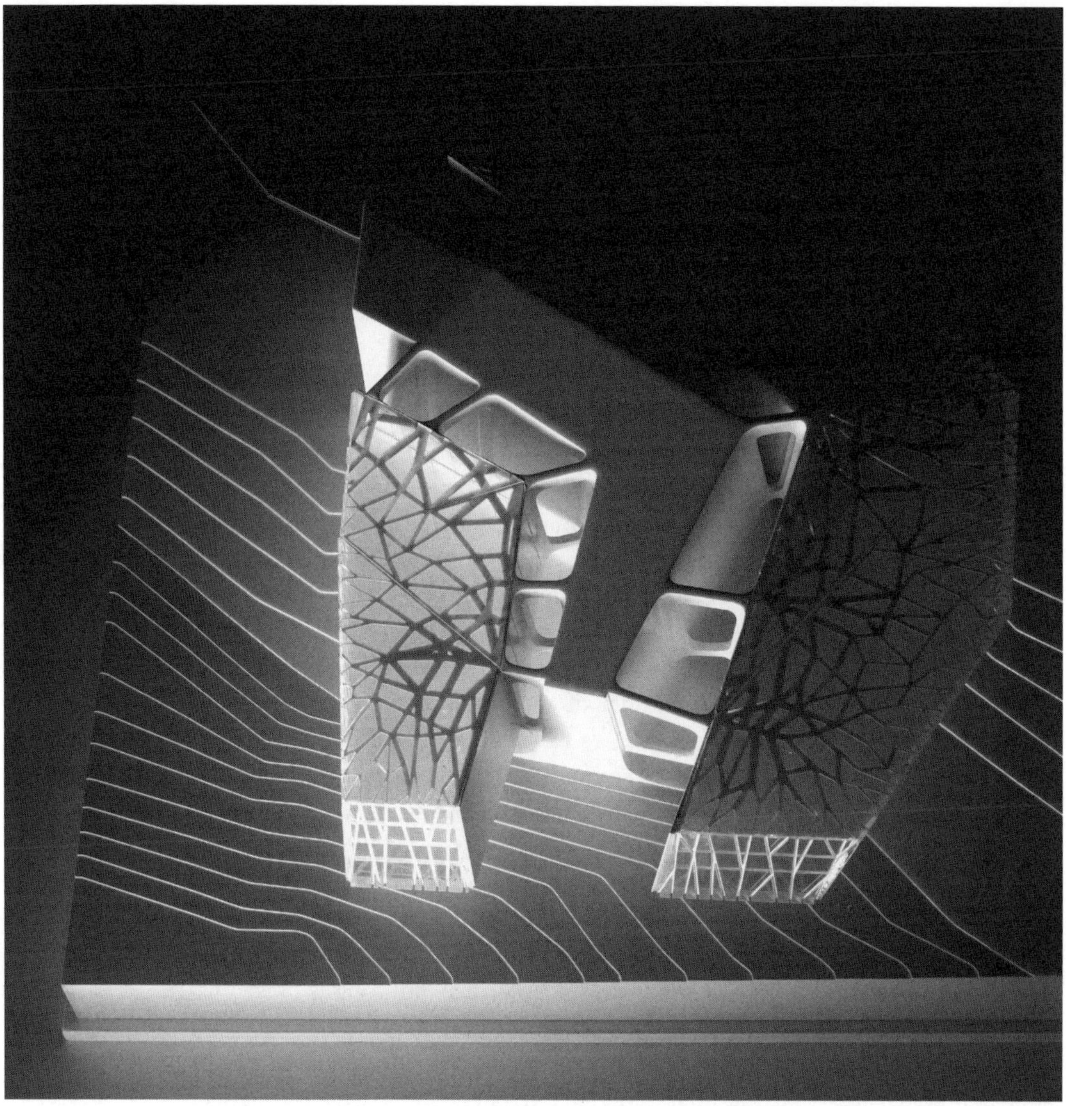

FIGURE 1.7. Competition model for New Czech National Library by OCEAN and Scheffler + Partner, 2006. From the opaque, enclosed central trunk of the library's collections and circulation center, the design branches outward in gradated permeability of light into the reading rooms, making for a "heterogeneous" "morpho-ecology." The reading room structural support system resembles both a tree canopy and the structure of lung trachea.

their multi-objective optimization parametric approach that integrates material and structural performance with environmental conditions—light, temperature, gravity, wind, humidity—flexible spatial program, and assembly and manufacturing logic.

Buildings designed as morpho-ecologies are intended to functionally exhibit internal environmental balance, such as that of termite mounds, a key example of homeostatic architecture created through the process of self-organization. This much is made clear by Menges's article "Manufacturing Performance" from 2008 (Figure 1.8), in which "form, material, structure,

FIGURE 1.8. Complete internal plaster cast of the main ventilation channels in a termite mound, circa 2002. Courtesy of J. Scott Turner. By continually moving around dirt particles that make up the mound, termites maintain homeostatic temperature and carbon dioxide levels within the mound. Architects uphold termite architecture as the epitome of self-organized, environmentally sensitive construction. Ironically, this plaster cast shows a "freeze-frame" moment (the sort that architects can build) of an ecological system that only works well as an ongoing responsive process.

and performance are understood as inherently related and integral aspects of the manufacturing and construction process."[61] Menges describes the research of Freeform Construction, led by Rupert Soar at the Civil and Building Engineering Department at Loughborough University, to design new material structures for additive manufacturing. Soar and his students learned from the "high-level integration of system morphology and function" demonstrated by termite mound architecture. They traveled to Namibia to cast termite mounds in plaster in order to have a negative-space model (filling the tunnels with plaster and then washing away the soil) that they could incrementally slice and scan, in order to re-create a virtual 3-D model in the computer. They used this model to study how the material properties and structure functioned homeostatically to regulate temperature, water vapor, oxygen, and carbon dioxide in the face of environmental conditions. Termite mound architecture is not static, but changes with the seasons and even on a daily basis based on the continual action of the termites to remove and redeposit soil particles in new locations. This process is a "closed-loop, self-organised process driven by positive feedback phenomena, including pheromone dispersal known as stigmergy, acoustic signaling, response to perturbation and the related interactions between countless termites, and partly directed by differential concentration of respiratory gases in larger fields, or negative feedback, within the mound." They found that a "colony-level performance such as ventilation appears to be the synergetic effect of integrating two energy sources: the external wind pressure and the internal metabolism-induced buoyancy. . . . The effect is a dynamic interaction of all variables leading to a complex permeability map over the mound skin."[62]

One expert on homeostasis in Namibian termite architecture is the biologist J. Scott Turner, professor at the State University of New York's College of Environmental Science and Forestry. As one of the photos on his website of Turner at a Namibian mound was taken by Rupert Soar, it is clear that they have worked together.[63] Turner's book *The Tinkerer's Accomplice: How Design Emerges from Life Itself* (2007) opens with a chapter on termites but moves on to many other examples of homeostasis in the biological world. Menges invited Turner to contribute to the special issue of *AD* that he guest-edited in 2012. Turner's article, titled "Evolutionary Architecture? Some Perspectives from Biological Design," describes the homeostatic actions of osteocytes (bone cells), actions that are similar to those of termites. Osteocytes monitor the strains that bone receives, and continuously remodel bone structure based on these strains. Some cells (the osteoclasts) "bulldoze" bone calcium away from the areas where it is too thick for the smaller stresses received in that location, while others (osteoblasts) are bricklayers, cementing it down where the bone needs thickening. Through this process, the bone retains its own optimal structure, what Turner calls its "sweet spot," given its previous environmental conditions. It is an environmentally responsive architecture, and not one dictated by genes, Turner is clear to point out. He does so to specifically take issue with architects' ongoing promotion of gene-centric discourses when, in many examples of biological functioning, gene–environment interactions with strong emphasis on the environment offer the best explanations for behavior.

Turner writes, "Architects seek to create environments that are equable to the inhabitants of their creations. There are many ways to do this, but the way living nature does it is through the operational, bottom-up striving for comfort that is implicit in homeostasis. This means that living design is not specified or imposed," such as through gene regulation, "but emerges from self-created structures that are dynamically responsive to the inhabitants' comfort: bones are well designed because the osteocytes strive to provide themselves a comfortable environment."[64] As bone provides the "morpho-ecology" of the osteocytes, so buildings designed with these principles are the "morpho-ecologies" of humans, except . . . for the slight flaw in the analogy. For obvious reasons, humans do not continually bulldoze and bricklay the same building on a daily basis to match environmental conditions. For this reason, Soar imagines that "once the technology has matured" thousands of robotic devices will "collaborate in ongoing swarm construction processes driven by continual adjustments to individually sensed internal and external conditions." Note that again we are faced with problems in the definition of "self-organization" with regard to what the "self" is in relation to the components. Is "self-organizing" heterogeneous "morpho-ecological" architecture meant to be inhabited by humans, or by robotic devices, which happened to be programmed, a "top-down" action, by humans?

Hensel and Menges state repeatedly that architecture that is designed and built to the principles of morpho-ecologies will demonstrate what they call "advanced sustainability," owing to how it "links the performance capacity of material systems with environmental modulation and the resulting provisions and opportunities for inhabitation."[65] In 2006, Hensel described how computational biologists can model a plant's growth in relation to its particular environment, including "gravity, tropism, contact between various elements of a plant structure and contact with obstacles." This technique of "modeling environmentally sensitive growth" offers architects "a method and toolset in which design preferences are embedded within a parametric setup . . . simultaneously informed by a specific environmental and material context," leading to "an advanced take on sustainability."[66] Hensel and Menges clearly dislike the "currently prevailing approach to sustainability."[67] They claim that most efforts toward sustainability today are done to "serve either mere public-relations and fund-raising purposes, or boil down to an ever greater division of exterior and interior space through ever thicker thermal insulation combined with reductions in energy use of electrical heating, cooling, ventilation, and air-conditioning devices."[68] This characterization harks to an ongoing debate within the architectural discipline of the roles that aesthetics, innovation, and cultural expression should play in relation to "green" building practices, with those who criticize the "prevailing approach to sustainability" perceiving and branding themselves as striving for higher aims. Hensel does, however, make it clear that he understands that solar energy technologies (photovoltaics) that rely on silicon "require a highly energy-intensive production process" and are not very efficient.[69] Recognition of this fact is rare among most architects interested in sustainability.

Unfortunately, though, Hensel and Menges do not make clear how morpho-ecologies are in fact sustainable, much less how they demonstrate "advanced

FIGURE 1.9. FAZ Pavilion, by Achim Menges, Steffen Reichert, and Scheffler + Partner, Frankfurt, Germany, 2010. The honey-combed panels of this thin plywood pavilion passively open and close in response to humidity levels in the environment, owing to the hygroscopic properties of wood.

sustainability." Is it that a morpho-ecological building should respond to its environment homeostatically, since all parts have been designed parametrically to inform the others? Having this type of associative modeling at work in the in silico design process is not the same as having it work in real time in the ongoing functioning of a building. Menges, with his collaborators and students, builds wooden pavilions that are responsive to humidity, owing to the hygroscopic properties of wood. Thin wooden components bend or straighten depending upon weather conditions, causing the surfaces to open and close (Figures 1.9 and 1.10), modulating the interior environment.[70] While this is an interesting approach to design for educational purposes and for the design of pavilions—which are really large-scale sculptures that permit temporary occupation—it is not a sound approach to the design of buildings that need to be inhabited comfortably regardless of weather conditions. For wood to be responsive to humidity it cannot be sealed, which is what protects it from weathering and biodegrading. Few people or companies would invest their money into an unfinished wooden building whose walls open and close based upon humidity (and not, also, temperature). However, it is not at all surprising that the Centre Pompidou commissioned Menges and Steffen Reichert's piece *HygroScope: Meteorosensitive Morphology* for its permanent collection.

To get environmentally responsive architecture in line with the model that Menges and Hensel propose, it seems that morpho-ecological architects would need to follow Soar's perennial robotic deconstruction and construction process, which would make for an interesting, albeit distracting, work environment. Or, more practically, they would need to equip buildings with numerous sensors and motors—such as how Weinstock envisions future cities—to dynamically integrate, regulate, and possibly even move parts of a building. This latter approach is already being used today by architects to turn off lights in empty spaces and to move louvers on the exterior of buildings to function

FIGURE 1.10. *HygroScope: Meteorosensitive Morphology,* by Achim Menges with Steffen Reichert, Achim Menges Architect BDA, Institute for Computational Design and Transsolar Climate Engineering. Centre Pompidou, Paris, 2012. The *HygroScope*'s meteorosensitive morphology responds to changes in the Parisian weather, which is simulated in a display case that serves as a virtual connection between outdoor conditions and the interior of the Centre Pompidou, where it is in the permanent collection.

as screens making shade in response to the angle and intensity of the sun. These two general approaches, however, are becoming standard approaches in sustainable architecture, and they are energy-intensive propositions, if not so much during the operational life of a building then in the life cycle of all the materials and products that go into the building in the first place. What

Hensel notes for photovoltaic silicon-based technologies is just as true for any device built with silicon-based microprocessors (see the discussion of this at the end of chapter 2).

A further problem with their calling morpho-ecologies sustainable is that their definition of the "ecology" part is so incredibly narrow. Helen Castle, in her editorial preface to Hensel and Menges's guest-edited special issue of *AD* titled "Versatility and Vicissitude" (2008), claims that the guest editors "make us think about the word 'ecology' from afresh, as 'the relationship between an organism and its environment.'"[71] Her definition of ecology is not new at all. What is "fresh" is how Hensel and Menges limit its range of applicability only to humans and their buildings. This move, I think, robs them of a credible claim to promoting environmental sustainability, since generally most people do not define the environment or ecology as a building but rather as the larger world around and including buildings that is increasingly losing species diversity. To even come close to living up to their claim of sustainability, they would have to select materials and modes of design and production that (1) rely on abundant rather than increasingly rare earth materials, (2) have low amounts of embedded energy in their life cycles, and (3) emit low levels of pollution in their production and use, such that overall their use does little harm to other species. These criteria are possible to achieve in tandem with strong considerations of architectural aesthetics and cultural expression. While the work of the Scarcity and Creativity Studio that Hensel worked with at the Oslo School of Architecture and Design is in line with these criteria, most of the projects proposed by OCEAN are not focused on these issues. Parametric design and CAM production fall short of these standards in many regards, for computers and computer-aided manufacturing tools are built using rare earth materials and millions of high-embedded-energy silicon-based transistors, combined to form microprocessors and integrated circuits.

One of the most common verbs that Hensel and Menges use is "instrumentalise," by which they mean to make useful and formatted for computational instruments rather than its other meanings as to make important or to employ or use. This is because digital technologies are fundamental to parametric design, which aligns with the general trend today toward "big data." For example, one technique that Menges uses to optimize the performance of wooden designs is to laser-cut out the "structurally dispensable earlywood" cells in the wood being used to lighten the load but maintain performance in the final structure. To do this, he conducts a finite element structural analysis and digitally scans every piece of wood to be used: "An algorithmic procedure then isolates the earlywood and latewood regions, comparing this data with the structural analysis data and determining, depending on stress intensity, the cut pattern for a laser that subsequently erases the dispensable earlywood."[72] He also mentions that some logging companies have begun using X-ray tomography to scan each tree they cut down to find its irregularities or "defects" with regard to "morphology, grain structure, and anatomical features," in order to decide how to best use each tree. Menges wishes these data were saved and shared, staying with the wood from the tree as it moves through the consumption cycle, becoming part of the product when one purchases wood for a particular use. While the foregoing steps to lighten the wood are already data-heavy, the data on the post-laser-cut wood is then integrated with the other parameters of the pavilion's design and manufacture, an even bigger-data process.

Without having known the precise location of each earlywood cell or possessing the capacity to remove each one with a laser-cutter, humans have been building successful and beautiful structures with wood for millennia. Similarly, the hygroscopic properties of unfinished wood have not changed during this time. The tiny amount of "performance optimization" regarding how wood responds within a particular design obtained through these methods pales in comparison to the giant amount of "instrumentalisation" that makes it possible. How much do we really gain from transitioning to this mode of design and construction, in relation to the energy and materials used to get there? Hensel is aware of passive low-tech building strategies used throughout history in many different cultures to mitigate temperatures in order to create spaces comfortable for human habitation.[73] In his article "Performance-Oriented Design Precursors and Potentials" (2008), he explores three themes with past precedent in "vernacular architecture" that he thinks bear new potential: "functional building elements with regards to the articulated surface; heterogeneous spatial arrangements facilitating varied microclimates and gradient thresholds that in turn are related to dynamic modes of habitation; and bodies in space with their own energy signature."[74] He references the modulating properties for light, heat, air, and visibility of different types of Islamic screen walls, made of wood or stone, which are semipermeable, perforated, even filigreed, as he imagines morpho-ecological architecture should be. He mentions vernacular designs that consider sun position in winter versus summer, including courtyards, porches, overhangs, loggias, or the practice in mountain climates of Europe of sleeping above the barn to make use of the heat of the animals. These are relatively low-tech solutions, even if making them took considerable time and human labor. He correctly states that to cover all the historical precedents for environmental modulation "would vastly exceed the scope of this article." With his collaborators at SEA, they conducted airflow digital analysis and rapid prototype models to help visualize the environmental temperature and airflow properties of fifteen vernacular structures, exhibited in 2014 in Oslo as *Architectural History from a Performance Perspective*.[75]

Yet, Hensel conducts his very brief historical and vernacular survey for one reason: "The question is how such strategies can be updated and *instrumentalised* with regard to the dynamic relationships between subject, object, and environment and towards a critical spatial paradigm."[76] As demonstrated in the exhibition models, he proposes using "thermal imaging, digital analysis of environmental conditions, analysis of material behaviour, and so on as critical design parameters."[77] Why do we need these data when we already know so much about the properties of different materials and spaces and have so many different building strategies that offer environmental modulation and heterogeneous microclimatic spaces? If we walked into those vernacular spaces, we would immediately feel the environmental modulation caused by the material and construction strategies. In other words, what do we gain from instrumentalizing these vernacular analog construction techniques, turning their properties into big data, apart from the ability to then use these data in other digital design operations? Parametric design does far more to push the economic growth of digital technologies and the use of energy and materials to create these technologies, as well as the use of machines to replace skilled human labor, than it does to produce "sustainable" architecture. The "advanced" take on sustainability surely refers not to attaining a new height of sustainable achievement, but rather to their dependence on "advanced" technologies. Beautiful and culturally expressive design is possible regardless of whether one chooses the low-tech rather than the high-tech approach.

Hensel has considered alternate approaches, though, including the creation of new materials and energy sources using the tools of synthetic biology. He calls this approach a "literal biological paradigm for architectural design" and claims that it moves consideration of both biology and architecture down to the molecular scale.[78] "The composite material organisation of biological structures is typically morphologically and functionally defined across a minimum of eight scales of magnitude, ranging from the nano- to the macro-scale," he writes. "While inherent functionality is scale dependent, it is nevertheless interrelated and interdependent across scales of magnitude. It is, in effect, nonlinear: the whole is more than the sum of its parts." He credits this emergence to the "central role . . . played by processes of self-organisation."[79] He cites different efforts in "synthetic-life research" that are working at this molecular scale—both branches of synthetic biology, the first known as protocell or origin of life research, and the other pursuing the engineering of novel life forms or biologically produced materials.[80] Hensel describes the criteria of "real life" established by biologist Tibor Gánti's *The Principles of Life* (1971). These include, among other properties, the need for containment yet with a semipermeable membrane (somewhat like termite mound surfaces and morpho-ecology in architecture), metabolism (the processing of energy and materials through the semipermeable barrier), homeostasis, and an "information-carrying subsystem" that he credits as the source of heredity and evolution. Hensel and Menges envision that "bottom-up" biochemistry of the sort occurring in synthetic biology may become part of the material practice of architecture, as well as potentially offer a new source of energy through "artificial photosynthesis," which ideally would function more efficiently and with far less embedded energy than photovoltaics.[81]

More recently, Hensel has taken an interest in local constructions, not vernacular architecture per se but rather recent architect-designed structures that are place-based, situated to their environment, using local materials and cultural values. The projects that interest him are similar to those done in the

Scarcity and Creativity Studio, which is not surprising given that he and its current director, Christian Hermansen Cordua, guest-edited the issue of *AD* on "Constructions: An Experimental Approach to Intensely Local Architectures" (2015) that explores these structures. As he and Menges dislike homogeneity in modern architectural design and environments and propose its replacement by heterogeneous architecture, so, too, does this new interest of Hensel's in local architectures stress the values espoused by morpho-ecology. Rather than the homogeneity of modernism, local architectures built today challenge the homogeneity of globalization, and it is this that captures Hensel's attention. Such interest can thus be fit loosely into his ongoing fascination with self-organization, interpreted here socially: individual architects, in distinct locations and cultures, building distinctly to meet local needs, which together add heterogeneity or plurality into modes of contemporary design in the face of increasingly homogeneous globalization.

Menges, too, has another separate research trajectory related loosely, in both a literal and conceptual sense, to self-organization. Through a number of different projects over the years, and particularly with his former student Karola Dierichs at the Institute for Computational Design, he has pursued the study of aggregate forms referred to also as "granular morphologies."[82] This is a component-based approach to the creation of structures; yet as the word "granular" implies, the components are unattached to one another. Rather, through careful computational design, their shapes allow them to loosely "grab" other components, being held in place through friction and gravity rather than through actual connectors. Furthermore, rather than "self-" organizing or assembling, they are poured out in a stream on top of one another, either by human hands or by a six-axis industrial robot (Figures 1.11 and 1.12). The resulting forms behave very much like sand or other granular materials in nature, which can function both in stable forms like a solid or flow as a liquid, depending on environmental conditions. These structures are therefore very environmentally responsive and can form different types of patterns.

In fact, the topic of granular pattern formation was explored by physicist and science writer Philip Ball, whom Menges invited to contribute in 2012 to the same issue of *AD* as J. Scott Turner; their articles ran back to back. Ball wrote on "Pattern Formation in Nature: Physical Constraints and Self-Organising Characteristics." In addition to discussing the patterns of granular substances like sand and sand dunes, he described the geometries of different rock formations, oscillating patterns formed by chemical reactions (such as the famous Belousov–Zhabotinsky oscillation), and Turing patterns that make for stripes and spots on animals' coats.[83] These are oft-cited examples of self-organization in complexity theory, to which Ball returns at the end. "There is—despite aspirations to the contrary—no universal theory of pattern formation in nature," he asserts. For example, consider the aforementioned dividing cells as templates, and other modes of reproduction (i.e., component iteration) that do not fit into the definition of self-organization but do make

FIGURE 1.11. *Aggregate Architectures,* by Karola Dierichs, Institute for Computational Design, University of Stuttgart, 2011. A six-axis industrial robot pours out loose components into prespecified shapes. Owing to the components' morphological design, gravity and surface tension hold them together to create the architectural form.

for pattern. Similarly, some scientists consider structures such as beehives and termite mounds to be self-assembled rather than self-organized—the behavior of the insects might be self-organized, but the structure itself remains behind if the colony moves and is therefore self-assembled. In other words, as Ball asserts, patterns arise in different ways.

FIGURE 1.12. *Aggregate Architectures,* by Karola Dierichs, Institute for Computational Design, University of Stuttgart, 2014. By varying component morphologies, materials, or placement location, designers can create differentiated heterogeneous aggregate systems that perform to different capacities in different environments.

"Nonetheless," Ball writes, "it has proved possible to identify many common principles." These include "the universality of certain basic forms (hexagons, stripes, hierarchical branches, fractal shapes, spirals), the importance of non-equilibrium growth processes, the balance or to-and-fro between conflicting driving forces, and the existence of sharp thresholds of driving force that produce global changes in the pattern." His aside earlier in the article—"despite aspirations to the contrary"—challenges those like Weinstock who hold self-organization and emergence as a theory of everything. Yet, many who espouse complexity theory less vigilantly than Weinstock, including scientists, might still consider the principles that Ball subsequently lists to fall under complexity theory's purview. This flexibility in interpretation about the origins of pattern formation, the different modes by which it arises, and the relation of pattern formation overall to self-organization and to complexity contributes to the ease by which architectural features and design approaches are interpreted as self-organizing or emergent. It also contributes to confusion for those trying to unravel just what self-organizing architecture is and to understand just why its rhetoric is so prevalent now.

Why Self-Organizing and Emergent Architecture Now?

Architects have perennially looked to nature as a source of inspiration for architectural forms. Since theories of evolution became prominent at the end of the nineteenth century, architects have used its variants as rationales for different approaches to design. In *Eugenic Design,* I described some of the ways that modern architects from the 1890s to the 1940s applied aspects of the evolutionary theories of Jean-Baptiste Lamarck, Charles Darwin, Ernst Haeckel, and Herbert Spencer to creating the founding tenets of architectural modernism (e.g., "form follows function" and the prohibition on ornament). More broadly, evolutionary theories affected how broad swaths of the American public viewed race, class, gender, disability, "progress," and "civilization." In many ways, streamline design embodied the ideals of eugenics, which was an extension of evolutionary theory using Mendel's laws in order to argue not for natural selection but for rational selection—man's ability to direct or design evolution. After the war in the 1950s, with the discovery of the structure of DNA as the "code of life" and the rise of cybernetics and complexity theory, some architects immediately took note. Gordon Pask, John Frazer, Christopher Alexander, and others linked self-organization and systems thinking to evolutionary and genetic programming, an approach cemented by John Holland's pioneering work in computer science. (For a brief history of the historical intersections of the rise of cybernetics, complexity theory, and generative architecture, see the Appendix.)

Complexity theory has grown in its breadth of application and popularity since its inception. Because it encompasses the dynamics of complex biological systems including development and evolution, it is not surprising that architects have appropriated its theories to explain and justify the development and evolution of generative architecture. This continued appropriation of evolutionary theories in architecture serves the purpose of removing some of the responsibility for design choices from architects as their approaches become naturalized and venerated through associations with science. For generative architects, this removal of agency is compounded because it occurs not just through this naturalization process but also through the use of computers to generate design solutions that an architect may never have considered. Although the first generation of parametric designers often used the passive voice to describe how generative designs arose, current practitioners are owning up to their primary role and responsibility as designers, as the theme of "design agency" for the 2014 conference of the Association for Computer Aided Design in Architecture showed. The use of complexism in generative architecture has opened the door to other pretenses besides just the denial of full responsibility. These include the possibilities of integrating the idea of the "avant-garde" to recast sustainability as "advanced sustainability"; appearing antimodernist when in some ways applications of the ideas of self-organization closely mimic tactics in modernism; discounting the role of energy, materials, labor, and the full life cycle because emphasis is directed to self-organization and biomimicry; and, finally, appearing to be "bottom-up," that is, democratic, while owing greater conceptual allegiance to the dominance of hierarchies. Each of these pretenses are addressed in turn, below.

Historically, evolutionary assumptions offered a scientific-seeming foundation for the art historical idea of the "avant-garde," a concept still prevalent in architecture today that tends to apply to those architects using the most "advanced" technologies. Because of generative architecture's reliance on computational design and manufacture, "starchitects" working in the generative vein have seized the opportunity for recognition. But because the broader architectural discipline is very concerned about its contributory role to environmental damage and climate change, the need to align parametricism with natural processes in light of the broader "sustainable design" movement becomes obvious.[84] Perhaps in this context, then, Hensel and Hermansen Cordua recently celebrated Rural Studio and other non-vernacular contemporary architects working with local materials in local conditions by interpreting them as examples of heterogeneous morpho-ecological design that counteract the homogeneity of globalization, even if their approaches are more low-tech.[85] Whereas the sustainable approaches of Rural Studio are obvious—reuse of local materials, low-cost structures, socially equitable function—the sustainability of parametricism is more dubious. Hensel and Menges's strategy to rename it "advanced sustainability" for its alignment with complexity's march toward ever greater complexity which, according to Weinstock, throughputs ever higher amounts of energy and information, is a savvy ploy. For the production of advanced technologies does in fact entail high amounts of energy, even if during the building's use the amount of energy consumed seems acceptable. Thus, complexity theory seemingly justifies advanced technologies; it is also, of course, "natural."[86] Things that are natural must be sustainable, or . . . the reasoning must go something like that. In modernist versions of evolutionary architecture, the teleology pointed toward "progress," which included hygiene, efficiency, and "advances" in "civilization," interpreted usually as white, technologically advanced cultures. In our current version, the teleology points toward higher energy use and information throughput (big data) in order to make things that we actually made quite well in earlier eras (even "morpho-ecologically") without advanced technologies.

Although current promoters of self-organization, emergence, and complexity, including those in architecture, often align philosophically with materialism and the abolition of the nature/culture divide, in some ways their modes of aligning today's "cultural" practices with "nature" harks back to modernist practices when the nature/culture divide ran strong. This is one intended reference of my title *Toward a Living Architecture?* which points to Le Corbusier's foundational creed *Towards a New Architecture* (1923) but with less certitude of the future. White modernists often considered ethnic "others" and their arts to be "primitive," which implied a closeness to and even alliance with nature, a prioritization of intuition, a lack of rationality, a heightened sexuality, and in general an unevolved simplicity. Since modernists conceived of themselves and their lifestyles in dichotomous relation to the "primitive"—as "civilized," rational, inhibited, complex, and lacking vitality—they appropriated facets of "primitive" cultures seen as natural into modern artistic production as a means of rejuvenation or revitalization. In similar fashion, many scholars in different disciplines who rely on digital technologies for their research (which, as a humanist, I classify as cultural production) are appropriating self-organization and the naturalizing tendencies of complexism to seemingly make complex products and processes seem "natural" or "materialist." In the strain of generative architecture seeking "bottom-up" design using either the techniques of protocell or engineering synthetic biology, the longing for the primitive hut arising out of the earth is undeniable—and undeniably modernist.[87]

To make this point clearer and to offer a cautionary example, one architect at the Bartlett School of Architecture in London described to me a photograph of a Dogon settlement on the Bandiagara Escarpment in Mali as "self-organized architecture" (Figure 1.13). The photo appears in Bernard Rudofsky's classic book *Architecture without Architects* (1964), along with many other images of vernacular architecture, some of which exhibit fractal forms. When pressed to explain why he characterized the Dogon settlement as "self-organized," he offered a counterexample: James Gibb's architecture in London after the Great Fire, which had to conform to new building laws instilled "top-down" by officials hoping to prevent such calamity in the future. When asked how "top-down" laws in London functioned any differently from building principles passed down to each generation of builders in Dogon culture—meaning, both exemplify "top-down" human decisions made for certain reasons, passed on to others to affect design-and-build choices—he seemed to not understand the question. My background is in material culture studies, where architecture begins with small a, a bit like how Rudofsky considers it in his book. The Bartlett professor's background is in "Architecture" proper, so to speak, and perhaps that accounts for our different views.

My fear was that this professor assumed that an African culture was "naturally" self-organized—as in, assuming that as under primitivism, its people *are* nature, building the way termites build mounds, and not only because the profession of architect presumably did not exist when the settlement was built, as implied by Rudofsky in his book title.[88] His interpretation of the Dogon settlement as "self-organized architecture" clearly differs from the approaches of parametric designers (of which he is one)—and, again, not just because most parametric designers go to school or pass an exam to become professionals in the field. Perhaps Rupert Soar's robot termites building the architecture of the future might function as he imagined the Dogon did. But this farfetched example points to the main differences that seem to be invisible to parametricists: their self-externalizing positioning, their "top-down" role in programming, their use of advanced digital technologies—computers and robots—as opposed to local soil and thatch (the latter point made because of material and energetic differences between Dogon and parametric buildings).

FIGURE 1.13. Photographs of the village at the foot of the Bandiagara cliff, by Marcel Griaule, Mission Dakar-Djibouti—Trajet en Pays Dogon, 1931. PP0031320 and PP0031213.1 © Musée du Quai Branly—Jacques Chirac, Dist. RMN-Grand Palais / Art Resource, N.Y. These images appear in Bernard Rudofsky, *Architecture without Architects* (New York: Museum of Modern Art, 1964), 40–41. The repetition of architectural forms in this Dogon village, when viewed from different perspectives, visually resembles "self-organizing" patterns in inorganic and organic natural forms. But such an interpretation of human cultural production robs its creators of agency and intention. Doing so with African tribal cultural production repeats the problematic assumptions so rife in modernist "primitivism."

I would argue that *neither* the Dogon settlement nor parametric architecture is "self-organized."

Rather, parametric designers appropriate a theory of natural pattern formation and assumed progression of order toward greater complexity, and apply it to architecture. The architects are not the components—in the position of the termites, or as he may have imagined, the Dogon—that are self-organizing. Rather, they are designing components "top-down" to supposedly "self-organize." Yet again, the process of construction is seemingly invisible to parametricists as well. The components have to be assembled by architects and builders' hands, or put together or poured out by robots; they do not assemble on their own. Even designer Skylar Tibbit's self-assembling designs (Figure 2.1), in which components connect through being shaken or being buffeted in a turbulent fluid, or open through the force of gravity while falling from a helicopter, are not "self-assembling."[89] Humans have to build the structures and shake them or place them in a turbulent tank, or fly them up and drop them or, even worse, build robots and drones to do this, all requiring large amounts of energy and materials. I say even worse with regard to drone and robots because I do not subscribe to the elimination of human labor through energy- and material-intensive technologies. Human labor is powered by food, not jet fuel, and many humans are unemployed, having been harshly expelled by our complex economy, as Saskia Sassen clearly points out in *Expulsions: Brutality and Complexity in the Global Economy.*[90]

Calling such designs "self-organizing" or "self-assembling" effectively obscures the necessary fact of energy, labor, laborers, and tools to create these structures. Could one say that a Gothic cathedral of the twelfth century, or a brick palace of the eighteenth century—to intentionally pick examples from Western architectural history—"self-organized"? After all, in these buildings, "local" components—brick and stone, some with differentiation—join together to form the "regional" structure of walls, which produce the emergent properties of protection from the elements, glorious echoes, and the capacity to carry a roof. Together, walls plus the roof form the "global" structure of the building, which has the emergent properties of being able to host large gatherings of people playing music and feasting and transmitting power and authority to the person who paid to build the structure in the first place. If the answer is yes to the question about cathedrals or palaces "self-organizing," then I opine that, like Weinstock's *The Architecture of Emergence,* such a view is historicist revisionism. Weinstock might say no, not revisionism nor historicist at all; everything has self-organized, so cathedrals did just as much as urban information technology systems will. Again, if the answer is yes, then clearly the "self" in "self-organization" does not mean anything at all. We could just call it "organization," which in fact might then prompt us to ask about who organized it if whatever is organized is a work of cultural production. After all, buildings have often been designed using components of some sort. Including the "self," though, contributes to the demolition of culture into nature. But if the answer is no, cathedrals and palaces did not "self-organize," then what is the difference in agency, top-downness and bottom-upness, in how a cathedral or palace was built compared to a parametric building? Differences in tools of production do not a "self" make.

Similarly, the appearance of pattern does not "self-organization" make. Pattern formation can be generated "top-down" or "bottom-up" or through some combination of these approaches; it can also be generated by using different methods. "Top-down" designers can generate "bottom-up" patterns in a computer. Self-organizing termites may "self-assemble" a termite mound, but humans or robots using digital technologies intentionally assemble a parametric building, and not in the same way that termites do. When applying the definition of self-organization to generative architecture, always ask: What is the component and is the component itself the agent making the interactions, or is something outside the component forcing it to interact? I do not accept that generative architects are the lowest-level components without a central control, who happen to follow some preordained rules using only local information without reference to the global, to interact with computers to then make the next higher level of components, printing out repeating elements that happen to need assembling by forces external to themselves. In other words, I do not accept the inevitability or naturalism of parametric design. Rather, I think companies are choosing to develop, produce, and profit from digital technologies; architects are choosing to buy and use them as well as choosing to theorize how they are using them according to the most current scientific paradigm and ideology, as a means of branding their work. Architects also control the scripting. Because these choices are made, alternate choices are also possible. There is nothing inevitable about the "advance" of digital technologies, although I agree with promoters of complexity that digital technologies consume large amounts of energy in their production and consumption. Herein lies the rub.

This is, in fact, a problem with "biomimicry," a word that aptly describes the approaches of Weinstock, Hensel, and Menges. EmTech's Biomimicry studio establishes that the term means the adaptation of and integration into technology of solutions to problems solved by biological organisms. In other words, see how "nature" solves a problem, and then adapt that solution to a new technology or technological approach that addresses a similar problem faced by humans. No consideration of the life cycle of the new technology was ever mentioned at EmTech when I was there in 2011 or in most publications. Biomimicry has no definitional requirement to be sustainable, although it is often presumed that if one mimics a natural solution, it will de facto be more sustainable than a solution that does not mimic nature. Weinstock, Hensel, and Menges are taking principles commonly assumed to be natural (complexity theory) and applying them to advanced technologies to arrive at new approaches with very little discussion of life cycle factors.

For this reason, it is important to apply Stephen Helmreich's concept of "athwart theory" to complexism, for it encourages us to consider theory not just for its ideational roles but also for its material environmental effects. With regard to complexism, athwart theory helps us parse the differences between systems in different domains (cultural, social, economic, physical, biological, meteorological, etc.). Systems theory aims to encompass all systemic properties and processes regardless of domain; Weinstock reiterates this tenet that "the concepts and principles or organisation . . . are independent of the domain of any one particular system."[91] His writing reflects this principle in that he often does not clearly distinguish whether a word like "morphogenesis" refers to computational, architectural, or biological processes, leaving the reader to guess or assume it does not make a difference. Yet when we examine the material environmental effects of different systems and the life cycles of common materials and processes used in different domains, it becomes immediately obvious that all domains are not equivalent. Without interpreting it through the lens of athwart theory, complexism can direct our attention away from domain differences, say, the materials and energy consumed and the off-gassing produced by a plant compared to that of a building, since both are complex systems operating according to the same principles. To miss these differences are oversights with serious environmental consequences.

The final pretense I see interwoven in some of the rhetoric of "self-organization" in generative architecture is that parametric design is somehow more democratic than previous modes of architecture. Many people interpret "bottom-up" to mean democratic; this democratic quality, if it exists, is blithely assumed to be beneficial and positive. It is easy for many people to forget that democracies pass laws that are discriminatory and damaging (consider the involuntary sterilization laws enacted while eugenics was in vogue), and that democracies promote economic policies that harm millions of people. Think of the effects of economic deregulation and free trade agreements in our ever-globalizing world, per Sassen's arguments in *Expulsions*. By overlooking all the "top-down" decisions and actions that inhere to the processes of parametric design, it may be possible to imagine, perhaps, that they are only "bottom-up." Yet, self-organization does not insist that all components are created equal, and in fact, its espousal of hierarchy and assemblies imply very strongly that they will not be. In general, Weinstock, Hensel, and Menges do not fall for this common mistake of assuming that "bottom-up" de facto equals "democratic." Hensel and Menges, though, do promote the idea of democratic architecture through heterogeneous space, in the sense that people have the freedom to inhabit different zones based on different moods and needs, to choose according to their own liking.[92] Hensel also states that computer-automated design and manufacturing technologies are making design more affordable "for those less fortunate than the richest man in the known world, the Shah of Persia." Hensel used the music auditorium built for the shah in the seventeenth century as one of his historical precursors to performance-oriented design.[93] Another proponent of self-organization and parametric design, however, Patrik Schumacher, fully supports the increasing privatization of architecture and urban spaces that has been proceeding apace under neoliberal economic globalization. It is thus informative to compare Schumacher's vision with Hensel's and Menges's to see the ways that he uses complexism to argue in favor of a competing aesthetic and economic agenda.

In his recent guest-edited issue of *AD* called "Parametricism 2.0: Rethinking Architecture's Agenda for the 21st Century" (2016), Schumacher's article "Hegemonic Parametricism Delivers a Market-Based Order" opens with a very clear declaration: "Parametricism 2.0 makes urbanism and urban order compatible with the neo-liberal re-emergence of market processes."[94] His theory is based on the current mode of evolutionary economics that relies on self-organization to naturalize laissez-faire capitalism. "The market process is an evolutionary one that operates via mutation (trial and error), selection (via profit versus loss), and reproduction (via imitation)," he writes. "It is self-correcting and self-regulating, leading to a self-organised order." He states that there has been a "vacuum left by state planning," and proposes instead that "'private planning'" fill the gap. He defines the latter as "a process whereby private development corporations or consortiums unify larger development areas within a coherent, market-controlled urban business strategy."[95] Yet, over the last two decades or so that this deregulated economic model has been driving urban development around the world, this process has not, in Schumacher's opinion, led to "spatio-morphological" "legibility," which he intends to provide with parametricism. Rather, urban zones have grown willy-nilly—in good laissez-faire fashion—into what he labels "garbage spill urbanism." He uses this strongly derogative term to refer to the "disorienting visual chaos" of a cacophony of styles that, ironically, appear all over the world in urban zones as "'ugly' environments without identity," or what he also describes as "white noise sameness."[96]

Schumacher's use of the language of complex biological and physical systems is adept and multilayered. He describes his vision of the new parametric urbanism as a "multi-species ecology," appropriating not only the language of complex systems and sustainability but also the most recent posthumanist feminist theory. Schumacher is not referring to nonhuman species at all but rather is using "multi-species" analogically. By this term he means that buildings, designed by different architects but all using parametric design, will each be like a new species: "Parametricism envisions the build-up of a densely layered urban environment via differentiated, rule-based architectural interventions that are designed via scripts that form new architectural subsystems, just like a new species settles into a natural environment."[97] No mention is made of the loss of actual species diversity in monolithic concrete urban environments (Figure 1.14). "Only Parametricism has the capacity to combine an increase in complexity with a simultaneous increase in order," he asserts, owing to "principles of rule-based differentiation and multi-system correlation."[98] He coins what he calls "architecture's entropy law: all gains in terms of design freedom and versatility have been achieved at the expense of urban and architectural order." In response, parametricism "inaugurates a new phase of architectural negentropy."[99] He thus implies that freedom is incontestable but

FIGURE 1.14. Kartal–Pendik masterplan for Istanbul, Turkey, by Zaha Hadid Architects, 2006 proposal. The swooping, streamlined, monolithic parametric design has been interpreted recently by Patrik Schumacher as the only appropriate stylistic manifestation suited to the global privatization of urban "public" spaces.

so is "order" according to his own streamlined universalist approach, which he unabashedly desires to be "hegemonic."

Schumacher's use of the terminology of complexity—self-organization, chaos, white noise, rule-based, entropy and negentropy, et cetera—reveals his deep allegiance to complexism as his ideological bottom line, one he uses to bolster his self-proclaimed superiority. "Parametricism is manifestly superior to all other architectural styles still pandered and pursued," he writes in an audaciously self-promoting statement. "This implies that it should sweep the market and put an end to the current pluralism that resulted from the crisis of Modernism, and that has been going on for far too long due to ideological inertia." With "current pluralism" he is directly referring to postmodernism and deconstructivism in architecture, but when he discussed this topic at The Politics of Parametricism symposium in 2014, he pointed to images of downtowns with historic buildings accrued over a century and not just since the 1980s. He proposes to replace such areas using masterplans that he and Zaha Hadid designed for cities such as Istanbul that aim to tear down and rebuild these zones monolithically, using swooping curved topologies to create new business districts and high-end residential development with cultural and tourist amenities. Schumacher concludes his *AD* article with a statement that veers toward architectural proto-fascism: "This plurality of styles must make way for a universal—hegemonic—Parametricism that allows architecture to once more have a vital, decisive, transformative impact on the built environment, just as Modernism had done in the twentieth century."[100]

This echo of the rhetoric of the 1930s is reified by Schumacher's aesthetic preferences, as his version of parametric design is less component-based and more streamlined than most other generative architecture.[101] Just as streamline designers re-formed what they considered to be "defective" ornamental designs, bringing all outstanding and protruding parts into line, Schumacher proposes the same ideal for urban makeovers. The similarities run even deeper than the surface, though. In streamlining, the new material of plastic was partially to blame for all the curves, since it was much easier to remove curved forms from molds, and more comfortable on the hands as well. Today, however, it is NURBS (nonuniform rational basis spline) software and 3-D printers that encourage the abundance of curvature. Again, like Raymond Loewy in his evolution charts (Figure I.2), Schumacher points to social and scientific evolution as the force transforming designs to the streamline, when in fact the designers are the ones effecting this change. And, although Walter Dorwin Teague claimed that the scope of a designer's reach was "everything from a match to a city," no streamline designers were ever able to transform a whole city because streamlining came of age during the Great Depression.[102] The "smooth flow" of streamline design thus resonated as much with restoring economic "flow" through the sale of consumer goods as it did with eugenic concerns about the "flow" of bodies, both internally in terms of digestion and externally in terms of the "flood" of immigrants into the nation.[103] Now, Schumacher is potentially in a position to rebuild large zones of old cities funded by the "flow" of neoliberal capital. It is as if the aerodynamics of streamlining has been replaced with the fluid dynamics of cargo ships and capital, and the resulting aesthetic is remarkably the same.

To elaborate further the potentially dangerous modernist terrain on which Schumacher's version of parametricism treads under the aegis of self-organization and complexity, the economics and politics of today are both different from and similar to the 1920s and 1930s when eugenic design flourished. The global recession of 2008 is consistently referred to in the media as "the worst financial crisis since the Great Depression."[104] Historical precedent shows that economic hardship has a way of turning national politics inward, as is being demonstrated by the Brexit vote in the United Kingdom and Trumpism in the United States. This distrust of pluralism at large is not directed only at architectural diversity in what Schumacher calls "garbage spill urbanism," but in the public realm is targeting ethnic diversity. His rhetoric of garbage echoes 1930s declarations of certain groups of people as "waste," which implies both disposability as well as a need to begin cleaning. National political movements are again voicing strong restrictions against immigration after a period of heightened immigration, which was exactly the case with the eugenic nationalism of the 1920s that effectively closed U.S. doors for over forty years. Furthermore, Schumacher interprets complexity theory as a rationale for instilling hegemonic order to what he sees as cities in the midst of chaos. Complexity theorists actually often say that the most interesting patterns arise when systems are on the edge of disarray, but clearly Schumacher does not like the pattern he perceives and chooses to label as "white noise sameness." In this light, Hensel's and Hermansen Cordua's celebration of designed-and-built localism as exemplary of a rich global heterogeneity (aka differentiation) in complexity seems a benign, even beneficial, interpretation of complexity in contrast to Schumacher's.

This last comparison between Hensel's and Schumacher's use of complexity theory to argue for opposite ends—Hensel's opposition to the homogeneity of modernism and support for stylistic heterogeneity/differentiation, Schumacher's favoring of modernism and hegemonic homogeneity/order—demonstrates how flexible complexism is as an ideology. The same thing can be seen in the fact that Weinstock uses complexity theory to dismiss sustainability whereas Hensel and Menges argue in favor of an "advanced sustainability" based on complexity. When the same paradigm can be used to justify and naturalize positions at either end of a spectrum—be it aesthetic, environmental, economic, social, or political—that is the clearest indicator it is functioning ideologically. Such was the case with eugenics.[105] That both eugenics and complexism happen to be scientific paradigms lends that much more power and authority to their application in other realms, especially when they become so widely accepted as popular science that many people readily believe arguments based on their rhetoric. Streamlining, after all, was based on natural principles from current science: the physics of fluid and air dynamics, the teardrop shape of a drop of liquid falling, the evolution and intentional breeding of streamlined animals to increase their speed in the competition for survival of the fittest. In light of this historical comparison, parametricism and more broadly generative architecture appear far less innovative for their attempts to instill natural vitality into design through mimicking: the physics of nonlinear dynamics, the fractal forms of branching, the genetics of morphogenetic development and evolution, the engineering of new and "improved" forms through synthetic biology. Emergence and self-organization are everywhere, as shown by the Boulder Beer Company's recent release of "Emergent White IPA."[106] Take care not to drink emergence down too quickly, as occurred, figuratively speaking, with eugenics and streamline design in the 1920s and 1930s and possibly now with the idolization of complexism and generative architecture.

CHAPTER 2

MATERIAL COMPUTATION

These terms in current usage in architecture, engineering, and the sciences—material computation, natural computation, biocomputation, and biomolecular computation—are ambiguous about their subject or object, about what is being computed or doing the computing and whether components are interacting of their own agency or being designed to act according to scripted rules.[1] This same ambiguity pertains to self-organization, not only because the above terms describe processes often categorized as self-organizing but also because a similar vagueness surrounds self-organizing components' agency, the identity of the "self," and the origin of the rules supposedly being followed. These ambiguities may bother few scholars and in fact may even serve as a stimulus for research. For example, the interdisciplinary journal *Natural Computing* defines the term as "computational processes observed in nature, and human-designed computing inspired by nature," which might also be called biomimicry.[2] The cross-fertilization of ideas between the natural and computer sciences undoubtedly sparks interesting and productive research questions and new methodological approaches to understanding. Furthermore, an increasing number of scholars subscribe to what is called nano-bio-info-cogno (or NBIC) technological convergence, which is based on the idea that at root, all things are computational and that technologies using computational tools (information technologies) across the physical, biological, and cognitive realms will bring these disciplines much closer together. From this perspective, "natural computing" makes computing seem, well, natural—meaning commonplace and everyday—in addition to pervasive across the material world.

Yet, one major goal of this book is to demystify the rhetoric of complexity in generative architecture in order to ascertain when in fact architects are talking about biology and when they are talking about computation or architecture. This is because significant disciplinary as well as energetic, material, and environmental differences exist between these domains. This is not done to promote a return to disciplinary isolation, for that would limit the kinds of questions scholars tackle that produce knowledge and change. The goal is to make visible the differences that the rhetoric masks so that architecture students and anyone who cares about the environment can make educated, conscious choices about the approaches and technologies they support. Additionally, in our interdisciplinary world, words that are spelled the same or sound similar often carry different meanings that in any specific instance depend on the discourses and meanings of the field in which they appear. "Natural computation" is not necessarily the same thing as "material computation," nor as "biocomputation," "biomolecular computation," and "programming matter." In general, "natural computation" is used by physicists and complexity theorists, "material computation" by generative architect Achim Menges and his circle, "biocomputation" by generative architect David Benjamin and his synthetic biologist collaborator Fernan Federici, "biomolecular computation" by interdisciplinary computer scientists with biologists and engineers, and "programming matter" by designer Neri Oxman along with materials scientists and synthetic biologists.

The difference between the two interpretations of "natural computing" offered by the journal of the same name—as technologies mimicking nature and as nature computing itself—is significant, and it points to a key issue with all these related phrases. It also is the reason for this chapter. In the former, computer-based technologies are doing the computing with analogous processes to natural systems; note that digital technology is the subject that is doing, as directed by humans. In the latter, natural systems are just being themselves, without hardware or software, and we just describe their normal processes as "computing." Nature, living and nonliving, is the subject of the doing. Humans are differentiated from nature here not because humans are not natural or are not animals, but because humans are the audience reading this book who can choose to alter their actions based on what they learn. Furthermore, nonhuman nature does not make digital technological hardware and software without human direction and provision of parts. A materialist philosopher might take issue with my differentiation of these, saying it is all matter so why distinguish whether living, nonliving, hardly processed, or many-times-processed by humans? I distinguish because human processing of matter requires energy and materials and produces environmental waste and pollution, much of it seriously harmful. Since architecture is responsible for a significant amount of environmental damage, to hide the differences between what is heavily processed by humans (technology) and what is minimally processed (nature) does a disservice to humanity and other species. I therefore strive to distinguish biology from architecture from computation to clarify which materials and productions processes are being promoted. The chapter concludes with an elucidation of the materiality of computation—a short description of the life cycle of digital technologies, as generalized by a transistor, microprocessor, and personal computer, along with their embedded energy, wastes, and pollution.

Material Computation

Since the early 2000s, Menges's research has focused on the material performance of building materials. Although architects have a lengthy history of using computers in their practice and generative architects have been increasingly pursuing parametric design for the last fifteen years, few have considered the materials from which buildings are made as anything but subsidiary to processes of digital design. Computers have been used to aid in the production of geometric form and structure, to calculate engineering loads for particular known materials under different forces, and to integrate such features as architectural program and cost in multi-objective optimizations. Menges and others, like Open Source Architecture's Aaron Sprecher at McGill University's LIPHE (Laboratory for Integrated Prototyping and Hybrid Environments), are forging the paths to add to these the development of computational approaches to integrate microscale material properties and related building-scale performance capacities as "generative drivers in design computation."[3] For example, LIPHE is developing new optimization models for the robotic production of large-scale prototypes that integrate "material and physical behaviours within simultaneous design and operative decision-making."[4] For Menges's approach, at the outset one of the parameters factored into the digital design process is information about materials in order that its potential can inform possible outcomes along the way, including component geometry, the manufacturing process—laser-cutter for 2-D materials, or computer numerically controlled (CNC) or additive manufacturing for 3-D ones—and the structure's assembly logic. All of these are interrelated, as Menges aptly demonstrates through his numerous experimentations with wood (Figures 1.9 and 1.10).

Wood has inherent material properties that many industrially produced architectural materials do not have. The latter are quite homogenous in their composition, either at the level of molecular structure (steel and glass) or in terms of the uniformity of aggregate distribution in a composite such as brick, concrete, or plaster. Wood, however, is a biological composite composed primarily of cellulose and lignin, built up through yearly accretions of different kinds of cells with different chemical makeups in layered arrangements. The tissue that forms early in the annual growth cycle is referred to as earlywood, and that which comes later in the season, latewood.[5] This tissue differentiation leads to the property of wood known as anisotropy, which means it has different capacities when measured and cut in different directions. Wood is also irregular, growing with different branching developments based on the specific environmental context of the tree relative to the local availability of sunlight. Furthermore, because wood is elastic, when it is cut in consideration of the grain (either parallel to or cross-grain), different amounts of bending curvature become possible owing to its anisotropic nature. Thickness of the cut of wood also affects its bendability, with thin sheets bending more readily than thicker pieces. These lend themselves to different tools for manufacturing: laser-cutters for thin flat sheets and robotic CNC milling for thicker beams. Bending of wood can also be triggered post-construction by the presence of humidity, as its cells retain their hygroscopic capacity to absorb water from the atmosphere long after the tree has been cut down.[6] Finally, hardwoods and softwoods have distinct properties and structural capacities, with hardwoods being preferred in contexts that require the greatest structural strength.[7]

Wood is increasingly a material of choice for many architects and builders owing to what Menges calls its "environmental virtues." He notes its biological source and the fact that the growth of trees is powered by the sun through photosynthesis, producing oxygen after absorbing carbon dioxide from the atmosphere. Overall, wood possesses a very low embodied energy and imparts a "positive carbon footprint," even in consideration of "today's heavily industrial wood processing." "The production of a panel of a given compressive strength in wood requires 500 times less energy than in steel. Thus wood is one of the very few highly energy-efficient, naturally renewable and fully recyclable building materials we currently have at our disposal," Menges writes.[8] The climate impact of its use is therefore far superior to that of steel, despite the extra effort it takes to understand the properties and maximize the performance of each piece of wood.[9] Additionally, use of wood for its hygroscopic and anisotropic properties to open and close panels based on humidity further offers what Menges calls "climate responsiveness in architecture." This avoids all technological equipment (e.g., sensors, motors) to move building parts, relying instead on the "no-tech capacity already fully embedded in the material itself."[10] Unfortunately, the latter capacity depends on the wood remaining unsealed.

For all the above reasons, in order to input information about all these properties of wood and their effects on performance, geometry, manufacturing, and assembly, each unique piece of wood to be used in a structure requires digital analysis, owing to its species and individual cellular properties, irregularities, grain, cut, and thickness. One of Menges's initial forays into digitizing each piece of wood for integration into generative design was at the Microstructural Manipulations studio he led at the Harvard Graduate School of Design in 2009. Menges and his students experimented with removing part of the earlywood to lessen the mass and lighten the load. To do this, they scanned each piece of wood to be used, conducted finite element structural analysis on it to ascertain the load on each piece, ran an algorithm on the scan to identify the earlywood regions as distinct from the latewood, and then laser-cut away much of the earlywood. The final structural outcomes confirmed their hypothesis that earlywood plays an insignificant structural role in wood's performance capacity and therefore can be technically eliminated. Menges's research has led him to conclude that "conceiving the microscale of the material make-up, and the macroscale of the material system as continuums of reciprocal relations opens up a vast search space for design, as most materials are complex and display non-linear behaviour when exposed to dynamic environmental influences and forces," such as gravity, wind, and humidity. "Computation allows navigating and discovering unknown points within this search space, and thus enables an exploratory design process of unfolding material-specific gestalt and related performative capacity."[11]

Thus, the most basic meaning that Menges imparts to his oft-used term "material computation" refers directly to this mode of integrating digital information about materiality at the outset of a parametric design undertaking, in order to fully integrate material identity, capacity, and performance into all aspects of the design process. This is the title he gave to his guest-edited issue of *AD* in 2012, "Material Computation," which integrates quotes from scholars familiar with complexity theory that imply alternate interpretations of "material computation" from what Menges usually means. For example, Menges's introductory essay to the issue opens with this quote from architectural theorist Sanford Kwinter. "No computer on earth can match the processing power of even the most simple natural system, be it of water molecules on a warm rock, a rudimentary enzyme system, or the movement of leaves in the wind." Switching notions of "computation," he continues, "the most powerful and challenging use of the computer . . . is in learning how to make a simple organization model that is intrinsic about a more complex, infinitely entailed organization."[12]

Menges, too, repeats this alternate meaning, which is much closer to "natural computation" of the physical and complexity science variety. "Computation, in its basic meaning, refers to the processing of information. Material has the capacity to compute. Long before the much discussed appearance of truly biotic architecture will actually be realised, the conjoining of machine and material computation potentially has significant and unprecedented consequences for design and the future of our built environment," he writes. Note that here he clearly differentiates machine computation from material computation, while still conjoining them as if domain differences are not a barrier. More often than not, though, he simply uses the term "material" computation to refer to either, which leads to ambiguity, making it seem like he is talking about nature when he is not. "In architecture," he continues, "computation provides a powerful agency for both informing the design process through specific material behaviour and characteristics," using his usual meaning, "and in turn informing the organisation of matter and material across multiple scales based on feedback with the environment," using the alternate meaning.[13] He links the latter to both inorganic and organic processes in nature. "Physical computation is at the very core of the emergence of natural systems and forms," he writes, referencing self-organization. He describes how evolutionary biologists are now beginning to integrate physical forces into their theories: "It seems that the more we know about the genetic code the better we understand the importance of physical processes of material self-organisation and structuring in morphogenesis." Since he invited physicist and complexity writer Philip Ball to contribute to the issue, he summarizes Ball's contribution: "Ball introduces a range of pattern formations in both living and nonliving nature, and explains how they can be surprisingly similar because they are driven by analogical processes of simple, local material interactions, which he describes as a form of physical computation that gives rise to material self-organisation and emergent structures and behaviours."[14] Throughout the issue, other contributors also use this terminology of natural or physical computing. Michael Weinstock and Toni Kotnik state that "materials have the inherent ability to 'compute' efficient forms," and Karola Dierichs, with Menges as collaborator on her study of aggregate architecture, repeats this, writing that "aggregates can physically and continuously re-compute structural and spatial characteristics."[15]

One architectural means of modeling material computation apart from digital methods is through what Frei Otto, Menges, and others after Otto refer to as physical "form-finding." Form-finding entails the use of physical models—physical in the sense of tangible and not digital, and physical in the sense of physics, pertaining to load under the force of gravity. Classic examples of physical form-finding are Spanish architect Antoni Gaudí's upside-down hanging models that he used to "compute" the curvatures of his highly original, tree-inspired arches at the Sagrada Familia church in Barcelona. Gaudí tied strings or chains of appropriate length to one another in the same pattern so that the lines of force would be distributed through the stone arches in the cathedral, and weighted each string appropriately with the proportional load each arch would carry. The precise catenary curves that the model "found," despite being upside down relative to the cathedral's upward orientation, indicated the form that would be structurally sound when built right-side up.[16] Otto, who directed the Institute for Lightweight Structures at the University of Stuttgart where Menges is now, specialized in lightweight membrane and cable tension structures and developed techniques for form-finding in tension systems. "In order for a membrane to be in tension and thus structurally active," Michael Hensel and Menges write, "there needs to be equilibrium of tensile forces throughout the system. . . . Membrane systems must be form-found, utilising the self-organisational behaviour of membranes under extrinsic influences."[17]

The processes of modeling used by many architectural students today demonstrate both physical and digital form-finding, which for membrane systems occurs through "means of dynamic relaxation." "Dynamic relaxation is a finite element method involving a digital mesh that settles into an equilibrium state through iterative calculations based on the specific elasticity and material properties of the membrane, combined with the designation of boundary points and related forces," Hensel and Menges explain.[18] Software for finite element analysis of both tension and compression structures made of different materials used today are ANSYS and Strand 7, both of which were taught during the introductory term in 2011 at EmTech. The back-and-forth iteration between physical modeling and digital form-finding is fundamental to techniques of generative design, and both are referred to by the term "material computation."

"Material computation" is also used by Menges and Dierichs regarding aggregate architecture, whose granular components are not connected to one another at all except through friction and gravity (Figures 1.11 and 1.12). "Whereas assembly seeks control on the level of connections between fixed elements, aggregation focuses on the overall system behaviour resulting from the interaction of loose elements," Dierichs and Menges write. "In contrast to assembly systems, aggregates materially compute their overall constructional configuration and shape as spatiotemporal behavioural patterns, with an equal ability for both: the stable character of a solid material and the rapid reconfigurability of a fluid."[19] They refer to using both "material and machine computation," the latter taken from the field of geo-engineering that has developed software to simulate granulate behavior.[20] "Computation denotes . . . the processing and gathering of information. . . . Material and machine computation are based on a common computational model, of information input, information processing and information output," they write. "Material computation thus denotes methods where a physical substance is set to produce data on the system in question. The computation is based on the innate capacities of the material itself." In contrast, "machine computation describes methods using a specifically developed algorithm that can be executed by a machine, such as a personal computer."[21]

Dierichs and Menges note that architecture throughout time typically has been "one of the most permanent and stable forms of human production. As a consequence it is commonly conceived as precisely planned, fully defined and ordered in stable assemblies of material elements." Surely this is due to its function of sheltering and protecting rather than threatening human life. However, perceived stability, they claim, is an illusion, for over time, buildings succumb to entropy and decay, sometimes even quite rapidly if humans are the agents demolishing them before rebuilding. They believe this cycle is accelerating although they do not say exactly why; perhaps it is due to the ongoing pursuit of economic growth through land development and redevelopment, perhaps to shoddier construction techniques in recent times with faster building decay or perhaps to increasing cycles of complexity shifting through collapses and reorganization toward higher complexity.

That Dierichs and Menges may be thinking about complexity theory as a primary motivation for researching aggregate architectures is evidenced by a number of factors. First, aggregates do offer a very tangible realization of shifts between stability and instability, equilibrium and nonequilibrium, as forces shift their state from as if solid to as if liquid, a quality undesirable for human habitation. They provide a clear visual analogy of phase or state-space change, far more easily than does stable habitable architecture. Second, they reference the idea of "self-organised criticality," which in complexity theory refers to systems that mathematically have an attractor to a critical point that triggers a phase transition. The concept originated in 1987 with a paper published in *Physical Review Letters* that used as a key example a model of the changing form of sandpiles, which slowly accrete and then, reaching the critical point, transform to an avalanche.[22] Dierichs and Menges intentionally integrate this potential for self-organized criticality into their aggregate designs through either "strategically program[ing it] into the system during the initial pouring process," or inducing it at a later stage. They can design these points of self-organized criticality into the system because they are designing the components and can vary their geometries and how they "grab" one another, and because they are pouring these out with a six-axis industrial robot that can precisely deposit particular components in particular paths. They do this to "trigger the transformations from one spatial condition, structural state, and environmental performance to another." "A certain area in the aggregate might be modulated to a certain effect in quite a controlled manner, yet this interaction can trigger more emergent phenomena in the wider aggregate field."[23] Thus, stability is only temporary in aggregate architectures, implying that if one were to use this technique for habitable structures, the occupants would just have to go with the flow. This is obviously a dangerous proposition that runs counter to the primary goal of habitation, so a designation as sculpture or pure research seems more appropriate than does architecture at this point. In this case, the allure of complexity theory is clearly so strong that it has become the attractor, pulling architects away from consideration of the primary function of architecture.

Dierichs and Menges also utilize another term related to material computation to refer to their design process for aggregate architecture, one that evokes the work of generative designers Skylar Tibbits and Neri Oxman, both at the Massachusetts Institute of Technology (MIT). All four at times talk of "programming matter," which might be thought of as the next step after material computation and machine computation. If we know how material physically computes itself (e.g., how components grab and pack and stack), and if our computational tools can precisely manufacture and pour these components in exact spatial locations, then we have the resultant capacity to design and develop "specific material behaviour through the calibration" of components at the macroscale or of particles and molecules at the microscales. Dierichs and Menges refer to aggregate architecture therefore as "programmed macromatter," although they hope that "in the future, particles could, however, also be produced through a process of self-organisation based on physical behaviour similar to that of snow crystals."[24] Both Tibbits and Oxman contributed articles to Menges's issue "Material Computation," with Oxman's explicitly titled "Programming Matter."

In it, Oxman argues for a new method of material science and design that is very similar to the aggregate architectures approach except that she seems to hope for bonds to connect the different substances laid down robotically. She describes how nature does not often produce homogenous materials, but rather produces "functionally graded materials" that together produce different properties at different scales. She also states that in nature, "it is often quite challenging to distinguish between structural and functional materials, as most biological materials such as wood, sponge, and bone can be both structural (supporting the branches of a tree or the body) and functional (pumping water up to the leaves or storing energy), with different scales for these different roles."[25] She calls attention to the anisotropy of wood, which is a functionally graded material. "In the fields of material science and engineering, the concept of anisotropy is tightly linked to a material's microstructure defined by its grain growth patterns and fibre orientation," she writes. "Functionally graded digital fabrication . . . enables dynamically mixing and varying the ratios of component materials in complex 3-D distributions in order to produce continuous gradients in 3-D fabricated objects." This approach "expands the potential of prototyping, since the varying of properties allows for optimisation of material properties relative to their structural and functional performance, and for formal expressions directly and materially informed by environmental stimuli."[26] She intends to use this organizational technique at the macro-level as a "design strategy leading away from digital form-finding to trait-finding and the potential programming of physical matter."[27]

In contrast to Oxman, Tibbits's design work in this area focuses not on the design of materials but rather on the design of components that "self-assemble" under extrinsically imposed forces. His aim is the transformation of the outdated construction industry using a method that he thinks will work across many scales, from the biological to the "largest of infrastructures."[28] In contrast to the old established method of "taking raw materials, sending them through a machine or process that is inherently fighting tolerances, errors, and energy consumption to arrive at a desired product, we should be directly embedding assembly information into raw materials, then watching as the materials assemble themselves. This process is self-assembly and it is the future of construction," he asserts.[29] He identifies self-assembly as the construction method of biology "from our body's proteins and DNA to cell replication and regeneration," adding that it contributes to the capacities for "self-repair for longevity, self-replication for reproduction, and growing or mutating new structures." Relying on digital design and fabrication and "smarter systems of assembly" will permit us to "build structures more adaptable to the current demands of our society and environment." "These new possibilities of assembly must rely on smarter parts, not more complex machines," he writes. "This is self-assembly where our parts build themselves and we design with forces, material properties and states, where construction looks more like computer science or biology rather than sledgehammers and welders."[30]

Tibbits's recipe for a design of self-assembly includes "four simple ingredients: 1) simple assembly sequences; 2) programmable parts; 3) force or energy of activation; and 4) error correction and redundancy." He uses DNA as an example of the first, which requires components that respond to simple instructional algorithms like "on/off, left/right/up/down, etc." He wants these algorithms to be able to "construct any desired 3-D structure. Luckily, through algorithms like Hamiltonian paths and Euler tours (various ways to draw a single line through an arbitrary set of points), it has been demonstrated that any given 1-D, 2-D or 3-D geometry can be described by a single sequence or folded line."[31] The second ingredient builds on the first. "Just as DNA has base pairs, or proteins have discrete amino acids with unique shapes, attractions, and rotation angles, we need to design systems with simple yet smartly discrete (and finite) elements. These parts should be able to have at least two states and should correspond to the instruction sequences; for example, on/off or left/right/up/down, etc." As these parts aggregate and interconnect, "every joint should be able to freely switch between states depending on each step in the instructions. This means we are looking to build structures from simple switches; each switch can be activated to change from one state to another depending on its placement or relationship to an external condition."[32] His goal of programming parts, therefore, is accomplished by embedding into the parts their own instructions for assembly. He quotes Neil Gershenfeld of MIT's Center for Bits and Atoms: "The medium is quite literally its message, internally carrying instructions on its own assembly. Such programmable materials are remote from modern manufacturing practices, but they are all around us."[33]

Consider, for example, Tibbits's piece *Logic Matter,* whose component design allows the addition of more components to different faces in order to build the form in different ways; this process is accomplished by human hands, which are included in some of the published pictures of the system.[34] The units work "*hand-in-hand* with the user to store assembly information, build and compute on next moves, check previous moves, and assemble digital discrete structures in 3-D." What is described as a collaborative process here between humans and components subsequently is described as a component-directed process: the components "inform the user to act upon them, or actually generate [their] own sequence of instructions for the next build."[35] A process with reversed agency is at work in Tibbits's *Biased Chains,* which like the Euler tour can fold from a one-dimensional chain into a three-dimensional structure "simply through the act of shaking."[36] "Once the sequence of units is assembled, the user simply shakes the chain, adding stochastic movement and energy that automatically switches each of the units into the correct orientation to successfully build rigid structures." Although he states that this system utilizes "passive energy . . . effectively letting the materials build themselves," this can only be taken as true if it is from the perspective of the units or the chain. Things "self-assemble" only through the addition of external force, in this case, a human being—or, he proposes in his conclusion, an earthquake—actively shaking the designed components.[37] Similarly, in Tibbits's more recent project *Fluid Assembly: Chairs* (2014), done at MIT's Self-Assembly Lab, unique components dropped into a tank of turbulent water self-assembled into a chair over a seven-hour period, utilizing the energy from the water's propulsion to move and jostle until they found their correct places to attach (Figure 2.1). Without the energy injected into the tank, however, such self-assembly is highly unlikely.

Tibbits calls these forces the "muscles of the system," and while he hopes that "our industries should ultimately be moving towards sustainable and energy-producing, rather than energy-consuming, systems," he notes that robots rely on electricity to power their motors and gears. His list of "passive" energy sources for "self-assembly" include "heat and expansion/contraction of materials, fluids and capillary action or hydraulics, pneumatics, gravity, wind resistance, shaking, pre- and post-tension or compression members, springs, and a plethora of other opportunities."[38] His idea of passive energy sources

FIGURE 2.1. *Fluid Assembly: Chair,* by MIT's Self-Assembly Lab with Baily Zuniga, Carrie McKnelly, Athina Papadopoulou, and Skylar Tibbits in collaboration with Arthur Olson and Autodesk Inc., funded in part by MIT's International Design Center, 2014. This project entailed the design of uniquely differentiated parts that fit only one place in the final chair. Over seven hours, turbulent water in an aquarium jostled the parts until they joined together into the structure. Tibbits refers to this as "autonomous assembly" and states that it "points towards an opportunity to self-assemble arbitrarily complex differentiated structures from furniture to components, electronics/devices, or other unique structures."

for component deployment therefore excludes the energy involved in getting the components into the context where these "passive" forces can then do their work, for example, getting component assemblies in place to drop them from helicopters so that they arrive on the ground as three-dimensional "disaster relief" structures. This evasion of the broader systemic forces at work is a strategy common to many industries and designers who want their systems to seem more sustainable than they are, if considered from a broader perspective of their life cycle. In a related manner, Tibbits's fourth ingredient calling for building with "redundancy and interconnectedness" as a means of "error correction" demands more materials and more components, which would matter less if his components were biological rather than synthetic ones produced using advanced digital technologies. Perhaps, ultimately, biological components are his goal, for he sees our future as "one where our structures build themselves, can compute and adapt on demand, and where assembly looks more like biological processes than construction sites."[39] If so, it is a goal shared by others working in the area of generative architecture but at the more biological and "genetic" end addressed in the second half of this book, such as those collaborating with synthetic biologists as Benjamin. It is to Benjamin and Federici's concept of "biocomputing" that we now turn in our exploration of material computation.

Architectural Biocomputing and Scientific Biomolecular Computing

In 2011, funded by a collaborative grant from the National Science Foundation of the United States and the Engineering and Physical Science Research Council of the United Kingdom, Benjamin teamed up with synthetic biologist Federici—formerly at Cambridge University for his doctoral work, now director of the Synthetic Biology Lab at Pontificia Universidad Católica in Chile—as part of the Synthetic Aesthetics research program. This program paired artists, designers, and architects with scientists and social scientists to investigate how cross-disciplinary alliances and shared methodologies might help reconceive the potentials of the new science of synthetic biology before its methods and questions become entrenched in the older habits of other disciplines. Federici's research at Cambridge focused on patterning in complex systems, particularly Turing patterns which produce spots and stripes on animals. He is an expert image-maker of biological patterning using confocal microscopy, which he and Benjamin used for their study. Benjamin, on the other hand, is an expert scripter, adept in the use of a variety of generative approaches, as well as the 2014 winner of the Museum of Modern Art's PS-1 Young Architects Program for his sustainable structure built from mushroom mycelium and corn stalks (Figure I.3).[40]

Benjamin and Federici titled their project "Bio Logic" when they published it in *Synthetic Aesthetics: Investigating Synthetic Biology's Designs on Nature* (2014).[41] This title resonates with their term "biocomputing," which reads both ways like "material computation" and "natural computation." It refers to ways that biological materials and organisms compute structure and form, as well as to ways that computers can be used to model, simulate, and explore biological processes. The field of engineering synthetic biology (referred to here as engineering synbio) bridges both of these meanings. It uses computers to design DNA strings that are produced synthetically, or alternately, one can order "biobricks" that already have a particular known DNA sequence that computes a particular function.[42] After scientists insert this into bacterial cells (the most frequent choice) that then incorporate and replicate the DNA sequence, the resulting cells ideally demonstrate the desired function.[43] So, computers analyze and design the sequences that the cells then compute into particular outcomes. Furthermore, the rhetoric of engineering synbio metaphorically conceives of cells as computers and DNA sequences as strings of information, to the extent that synthetic biologists model their disciplinary approach on the circuitry of electrical, mechanical, and computer engineering. A cell is called a "chassis" that carries "devices" made up of genetic "circuits." The meanings of "biocomputing" therefore are multilayered, conceptual, and procedural, as well as having the ability for either biology or computers or both to perform the act of computing.

As Benjamin and Federici's project title and the term "Biocomputing" imply, the duo chose to use the tools of both disciplines to attempt to discern the "bio logic" of plant xylem structure and pattern. "The process of pattern formation in xylem cells can be seen as a 'morphogenetic' program—it renders form (structural support) in response to the physical conditions of the environment. . . . This process lacks any external guidance for construction and depends on local molecular interactions," they state, referencing self-organization. They therefore view the "morphogenetic program of xylem pattern generation" as a "biological design program" that they aim to uncover in order to make it useful to designers.[44] In essence, they were in search of the presumed biological algorithm for the structure of xylem formation.

Benjamin and Federici began with actual biological samples, slicing the vascular tissue of an artichoke stalk into numerous thin, relatively 2-D, slices that Federici photographed. These images were then loaded into architectural software by Benjamin and layered in order to digitally re-create the 3-D form of the original plant tissue. They then conducted experiments using differently shaped nonvascular cells of a transgenic strain of *Aradopsis thaliana,* adding a chemical that induced the overall formation of the xylem pattern but using the differently shaped cells of this species. The slicing and photographic and virtual reconstruction processes were repeated. Benjamin then compared the two virtual models and used the software application Eureqa to derive the mathematical equation common to both sets of data from the virtual reconstructions. They then used that equation to generate new structural forms in different boundary conditions, in essence using the biological algorithm—assumed to be the same as the derived mathematical equation—as a tool for novel designs.[45] Finally, they attempted to scale this equation-based pattern to actual architectural scale, although in this case that amounted to the scale of 3-D printed models and virtual "full size" renderings. Benjamin found that what may be "optimal" in nature to the particular context of the growing plant may be "suboptimal" for architecture at a much larger scale. In such a suboptimal situation, generative approaches using optimization can evolve the biological forms into ones suited to the needs and scale of architecture.[46]

Benjamin and Federici's experiments demonstrate both meanings of "biocomputing" and presumably point to a deep process at work in biology and computation that is responsible for the generation of form and structure. Like Jenny Sabin and Peter Lloyd Jones, they dismiss the superficiality of the type of biomimicry that merely represents biological forms in architecture—say, in the structure and patterns of a facade or floor plan. Rather, they aim to discover the presumed algorithms at the root of form generation and integrate their process and principles into resultant designs. Sabin and Jones refer to this process as "biosynthesis," Federici and Benjamin as "biocomputing." For both, it is process that matters, encoded as algorithm, rather than the creation of particular organic-looking shapes. In this sense, their approaches have moved beyond the formalist focus of early twenty-first-century generative architecture.

For clarification, it is important to briefly compare Benjamin and Federici's biocomputing to "biomolecular computing." While this may serve to allay confusion for those who come across the latter term in other contexts, it may also just add to the interdisciplinary mash-up that most of these terms reflect. It may even spark new approaches for architects and designers as aspects of "biomolecular computing" resemble projects already discussed in the material computation section. Furthermore, biomolecular computing–based design projects have recently been included in highly visible design exhibitions, pointing to the likelihood of further cross-disciplinary developments.

In 2007, Pengcheng Fu of the Department of Molecular Biosciences and Bioengineering at the University of Hawaii, Manoa, published a review of the field he calls "biomolecular computing." He describes it as an interdisciplinary venture at the intersection of engineering, biological science, and computer science, also known as "biocomputing," "molecular computation," and "DNA computation."[47] As early as 1959, theoretical physicist Richard Feynman proposed the idea that "single molecules or atoms could be used to construct computer components." This idea was developed further since the 1990s into techniques using DNA to store information and perform computational tasks and even to solve difficult and classic mathematical problems like a "seven-node instance of Directed Hamiltonian Path (DHP) problem," otherwise known as the "Traveling Salesman problem."[48] "Many properties that biological organisms often possess are highly desirable for computer systems and computational tasks, such as a high degree of autonomy, parallelism, self-assembly, and even self-repair functions," Fu writes. His comment indicates the hope of scientists working in this area to improve the performance of and create new systems for computational tasks using biological organisms. As the last section in this chapter shows, the current approach to constructing computers has serious environmental consequences. So, the possibility in the future of having biologically based or biological computers could perhaps remedy the industry's current damaging environmental effects, depending on the rest of its infrastructure. It may also raise ongoing difficult ethical questions about manipulating living organisms for human tasks, but this of course is not new.

Fu describes some of the different accomplishments using DNA to solve both complicated mathematical search problems and arithmetic problems. DNA here is not performing a genetic role inside of a cell, but rather it is simply a string of four molecules that bind to one another selectively. Scientists design these strings of A, C, T, and G molecules so that they function combinatorially to create multifaceted structures with numerous vertices and edges, with embedded path directionality.[49] When Leonard Adleman solved the Traveling Salesman problem in 1994, he discovered significant advantages of using DNA over traditional silicon-based computing.[50] "The advantages of Adleman's method were that massive parallelism and super information contents were achieved. The reactions contained approximately 3×10^{13} copies of each oligo," referring to the DNA strings, "resulting in about 10^{14} strand hybridization encounters in the first step alone. In these terms, the DNA computation was a thousand-fold faster than the instruction cycle of a supercomputer," Fu writes. Adleman also found that the information storage density of DNA was "billions of times denser than that of the media such as videotapes that require 101^2 nm^3 to store one bit. In other terms, one micromole of nucleotides as DNA polymer can store about two gigabytes of information," leading to DNA's use as a database. "Lastly, Adleman noted that the energy requirement for enzyme-based DNA computing is low: one ATP pyrophosphate cleavage per ligation that gives an efficiency of approximately 2×10^{19} operations per joule. By comparison, supercomputers of that time performed roughly 10^9 operations per joule."[51]

Describing a design strategy that sounds very similar to that of Tibbits, Fu elaborates on the use of biomolecular computation in self-assembling systems. "Parallel computation can be enhanced by [a] self-assembling process where information is encoded in DNA tiles. Using sticky-end associations, a large number of DNA tiles can be self-assembled," a procedure referred to as the "Wang tiles" or "Wang dominoes" after Hao Wang's work from 1961. "Wang tiles are a set of rectangles with each edge so coded (for example, by color) that they can assemble into a larger unit, but only with homologously coded edges together. It was shown mathematically that by barring rotation and reflection, any set of such tiles could only assemble to cover a plane in a finite pattern that was aperiodic, *i.e.*, the pattern was not repeated," such as occurs with Penrose tiling. Aperiodic tiling differs from periodically repeating patterns such as those that form crystal structures. "It was further shown mathematically that the assembly of a set of Wang tiles into a unique lattice was analogous to the solving of a particular problem by the archetypal computer, known as a Turing machine," Fu recounts. "In other words, self assembly of DNA materials with the architecture of Wang tiles may be used for computation, based on the logical equivalence between DNA sticky ends and Wang tile edges."[52]

Fu cites the work of Paul Rothemund, senior research professor in neural systems and computer science at the California University of Technology, whose work curator Paola Antonelli included in *Design and the Elastic Mind* at the Museum of Modern Art in 2008. Rothemund designed DNA sequences to fold into decorative triangular and snowflake patterns and smiley faces, in essence using DNA as a material for artistic representation. The wall text at the exhibition contextualized Rothemund's work as an example of self-organization that could lead to a new approach for architecture being built from the nanoscale using "bottom-up" techniques.[53] Clearly, DNA can be used to create two-dimensional patterns (drawing smiley faces) as well as three-dimensional structures (Adleman's work). As the wall text vaguely implied, will architects then want to design self-assembling buildings using DNA as the structural material? This question brings us back to the scaling problem that Benjamin and Federici touch on, but in even murkier terrain since they were working with plant xylem structures that actually do hold up plants owing to combinations of cellulose and lignin rather than just the nanoscale molecular bonds of DNA. Furthermore, the amount of time it would take to assemble a DNA- or molecule-based building would be enormous if biomolecular computing experiments stand as a relevant example. Such a ridiculous proposition would surely stem from the ongoing deep and widespread fanaticism with

DNA as a semimystical "code of life" rather than from any known structural properties of this molecule for architectural purposes.[54]

Fu describes the drawbacks of biomolecular computation—namely, they are onetime calculations that require lengthy setup, are very slow to process, and are prone to error. He writes, "Typically, implementation of an algorithm to solve a computational problem itself may take several days or even weeks. When a new initial condition needs to be tested, the same period of time is required for another run of calculation. Therefore, it is inconvenient and expensive to implement the biocomputing experiments which require repeated improvement processes."[55] Fu hopes that research in synthetic biology can remedy some of these problems, although an article from 2015, "Computing with Synthetic Protocells," states that "protoputing" (add that term to the growing list at the start of this chapter) can produce only one machine and solve one problem at a time.[56] Yet, architects' and designers' interests may still be piqued; some certainly are already fascinated with "protocell" architecture. After all, one of Benjamin's graduate students in his Architecture BioSynthesis studio at Columbia University's Graduate School of Architecture, Planning, and Preservation, Mike Robitz, proposed "a future where microorganisms take over the role of data storage in place of computers." Robitz's project, called *Googol Puddles,* was featured by curator William Myers in the recent exhibition and catalog *BioDesign: Nature, Science, Creativity* (2012). Myers also included the *Bioencryption* project that also uses DNA as a data storage and encryption device, designed by the student team from the School of Life Sciences, Chinese University of Hong Kong, which won the gold medal in 2010 at the International Genetically Engineered Machine competition.[57]

Natural Computation and Computational Mechanics

The foregoing examples of material computation, programming matter, biocomputing, biomolecular computing, and protoputing demonstrate different interpretations and techniques of computing at play in the broader arena of generative architecture and the scientific disciplines on which it draws. We began with how materials compute their own structures and forms at both the micro- and macroscales, for Menges is interested in fully integrating digital information about material structure and behavior into parametric design. This means of course that he is in turn using computers to materialize architectural structures. He and Dierichs move that process up one notch, so to speak, exploring not how materials like wood or metal compute at the cellular or molecular level, but rather how components and aggregate architectures compute in the face of changing environmental dynamics in relation to points of self-organized criticality. Oxman shifts the discourse to the computationally designed and manufactured production of new, functionally graded composite materials, whose anisotropic composition and layering should permit new structural performances that are designed into them at the outset. Like Menges and Dierichs, then, Tibbits moves Oxman's process up a step to the design of components (and not the materials making up the components) whose "self-assembly" method and resultant 3-D structure is incorporated into their morphology at the very start. In turn, Benjamin and Federici focus more on methods to discern biological structure and form generation in order to make this process useful to architects. By digitally comparing data taken from two living samples—xylem formation in artichokes and induced xylem formation in *Arabidopsis*—they derived an equation that they believe mathematically expresses the common biological growth pattern or structure. Biomolecular computing, on the other hand, is not biological at all in terms of involving living cells. Rather, it uses the common biological molecule DNA that has particular binding properties, arranged into 2-D or 3-D forms, to solve mathematical problems. Molecules in pre-protocells, which are also not living, function similarly in "protoputing."

Of the above approaches, the closest to what physicists and complexity scientists call "natural computation" is the growth of the plants in Benjamin and Federici's study and the first approach of Menges, who focuses on the material functioning of cut wood.[58] Wood after all is a biologically produced material and carries in its structure the expression of the nonlinear dynamics through which it was formed. This can be seen as a form of memory, which is a characteristic of nonlinear dynamic systems to which information theory can be applied, as argued in 2001 by physicists and mathematicians James Crutchfield and David Feldman.[59] Crutchfield defines natural computation as "how nature stores and processes information"; the memory that he and Feldman refer to is the storage of information. To this Crutchfield adds, "How nature is structured is how nature computes." He then links these two theorems by defining "Structure = Information + Computation."[60] The difficult process of "detecting randomness and pattern" or structure that "many domains face" translates into a need to measure "intrinsic computation in processes" and ascertain new "insights into how nature computes," he writes.[61]

What follows, therefore, is a brief overview of how Crutchfield explains the core concepts and history of theories of complex dynamical systems, both through accessible publications and in his graduate course on Natural Computation and Self-Organization (NCASO) taught at UC Davis. These stand in contrast to the general terminological critique offered in the introductory chapter to this book with reference to ideological complexism, although those general comments still pertain. From this overview, it becomes readily apparent that tools used by a UC Davis and Santa Fe Institute physicist and mathematician to characterize complexity, structure, and natural computation are not the same ones as those referenced by generative architects. The contrast illuminates the differences in approach taken by those in different disciplines and adds layers of depth to even the superficial differences suggested by terms like "natural computation" and "material computation." These differences matter because they point out the mostly rhetorical role that complexity theory currently plays in generative architecture. If architects are truly serious about understanding the dynamics of complex systems in order to make use of the ways in which order is produced in natural systems for design purposes, this approach offers intriguing possibilities despite its difficult and time-consuming nature for those unfamiliar with it. While the benefits of having architectural structures that move or grow—or in other words, actually behave as complex biological systems—are debatable, processes that occur within and around the contexts of buildings certainly do exhibit complex behaviors. A short summary of Crutchfield's course then suggests novel means for understanding complex dynamical systems for those working in generative architecture and design. On the other hand, if architects primarily want to mimic natural geometries, this level of understanding of a system's dynamics is likely extraneous.

Crutchfield relies on dynamical systems theory, information theory, and a technique he has developed known as computational mechanics. Together, these three offer means to ascertain and measure both dynamical structure and chaos. In his 2012 article in *Nature Physics,* "Between Order and Chaos," Crutchfield connects the dots between these approaches while summarizing some of the key tenets of complexity theory viewed through the lens of their historical development. "We know that complexity arises in a middle ground—often at the order–disorder border," he states, which is the systemic zone in which pattern or structure often becomes most interesting. "Natural systems that evolve with and learn from interaction with their immediate environment exhibit both structural order and dynamical chaos." Crutchfield posits that "order is the foundation of communication between elements at any level of organization, whether that refers to a population of neurons, bees, or humans. For an organism order is the distillation of regularities abstracted from observations." But, a "completely ordered universe . . . would be dead. Chaos is necessary for life." Natural systems, therefore, "balance order and chaos" and "move to the interface between predictability and uncertainty. The result is increased structural complexity" that "often appears as a change in a system's intrinsic computational capability." "How can lifeless and disorganized matter exhibit such a drive [toward increased structural and computational capacity]? . . . The dynamics of chaos, the appearance of pattern and organization, and the complexity quantified by computation will be inseparable components in [this question's] resolution," he writes.[62]

Crutchfield's NCASO course, in which I participated during the Winter and Spring semesters of 2012, offers tools for understanding the structure of complex systems with which architects are not familiar, to my knowledge. Although Benjamin and Federici attempted to ascertain a correlational mathematical expression of the xylem formation process through comparing data from two slightly different systems, Crutchfield's process depends on careful observation and data taken from only one system's process over a period of time. Depending on the care taken in deciding how to appropriately extract information/data from the system (this takes learning and experience), the data can reveal the system's memory (stored information), pattern and structure (statistical complexity), and its amount of randomness (entropy). Through using the tools of computational mechanics, this information can be modeled into what Crutchfield calls an epsilon-machine that shows the state space of the dynamical system and the probability of transitions between the states.

The course begins with dynamical systems theory. "A dynamical system consists of two parts: the notions of a state (the essential information about a system) and a dynamic (a rule that describes how the state evolves with time). The evolution can be visualized in a state space, an abstract construct whose coordinates are the components of the state."[63] Using mathematician Steven Strogatz's book *Nonlinear Dynamics and Chaos: With Applications to Physics, Biology, Chemistry, and Engineering* (2001), the course covers mathematical models and maps of different dimensional types of nonlinear systems—their attractors, basins of attraction, and bifurcation sequences.[64] Some one-dimensional systems like radioactive decay are attracted to a fixed point. Two-dimensional systems, like a pendulum or a heartbeat, exhibit periodicity and move around a limit cycle—a two-dimensional loop on a graph—or a fixed point. Some three-dimensional systems are drawn to the shape of tori or limit cycles or fixed points, while other 3-D systems like weather exhibit very complex behaviors that graph to what is called a chaotic or strange attractor, the Lorenz attractor being the first one discovered. In these latter kinds of systems, "microscopic perturbations are amplified to affect macroscopic behavior."[65] Chaotic systems' graphs and maps reveal a folding and bending within the system's state space. "The process of stretching and folding happens repeatedly, creating folds within folds ad infinitum. A chaotic attractor is, in other words, a fractal: an object that reveals more detail as it is increasingly magnified," Crutchfield describes. He compares it to placing a drop of food color onto a mound of bread dough, and kneading it twenty times. The dough visualizes what happens to trajectories within the state space as the food color is "stretched to more than a million times its original length." How does one tell just how chaotic a system is? "A measure of chaos is the 'entropy' of the motion, which roughly speaking is the average rate of stretching and folding, or the average rate at which information is produced."[66]

As the latter suggests with its references to entropy and to information, Claude Shannon's information and communication theory has proved integral for scientists' measuring of complex systems. Complex systems exhibit both ordered and disordered behavior; ordered behavior produces pattern and structure, whereas disordered behavior is random. Pattern and structure contain a certain amount of predictability that is measured by probability (i.e., how likely is something to happen?); randomness and disorder do not. "The outcome of an observation of a random system is unexpected," Crutchfield writes. "We are surprised at the next measurement. That surprise gives us information about the system. We must keep observing the system to see how it is evolving. This insight about the connection between randomness and surprise was made operational, and formed the basis of the modern theory of communication, by Shannon in the 1940s."[67]

Shannon quantifies information through its amount of surprise. "Given a source of random events and their probabilities," writes Crutchfield, "Shannon defined a particular event's degree of surprise as the negative logarithm of its probability." An event that is certain to happen has no surprise and therefore provides no information (zero bits). Yet, one that may or may not happen or happens with a particular probability of frequency does, and using Shannon's definition one may quantify just how much information it contains (up to the maximum of one bit).[68] Shannon also demonstrated that "the averaged uncertainty," what he referred to as the "source entropy rate," "is a fundamental property . . . that determines how compressible an information source's outcomes are."[69] Shannon then extended this to define communication, the transmission of information from one source to another, which often entails noise. A transmission of information may or may not become corrupted. After developing the concept of mutual information, he stated that if the mutual information is zero, then the communication channel completely failed to communicate the information from its source to its end. But if "what goes in, comes out," then "the mutual information is the largest possible." Furthermore, "The maximum input–output mutual information, over all possible input sources, characterizes the channel itself and is called the channel capacity." The most important takeaway, however, that Crutchfield identifies is Shannon's realization that "as long as a (potentially noisy) channel's capacity . . . is larger than the information's source entropy rate . . . there is a way to encode the incoming messages such that they can be transmitted error free. Thus, information and how it is communicated were given firm foundation," Crutchfield explains.[70]

Two processes of communication exist in complex dynamic systems and their study. The first is the system's own process of communication using its stored information from the past to compute its future by moving through its state spaces with certain amounts of randomness and predictability. The second is the process of the observer of the system, who uses instruments to extract data to ascertain the amount of randomness and structure in its history in order to communicate to someone else a model of the system (Figure 2.2).[71] Information and communications theories thus offer means by which to measure a system's communication. "Shannon entropy . . . gives the source's intrinsic randomness" in bits per symbol extracted from the system. A measure known as "statistical complexity," on the other hand, represented as $C\mu$, "measures degrees of structural organization."[72] Yet, it is the technique of computational mechanics, which adds to the tools and concepts of statistical mechanics, that "lets us directly address the issues of pattern, structure, and organization. . . . In essence, from either empirical data or from a probabilistic description of behavior, it shows how to infer a model of the hidden process that generated the observed behavior. This representation—the ε-machine," Cosma Shalizi and Crutchfield write, "captures the patterns and regularities in the observations in a way that reflects the causal structure of the process. With this model in hand, one can extrapolate beyond the original observations to predict future behavior," provided one can synchronize themselves to the system. They summarize, "ε-machines themselves reveal, in a very direct

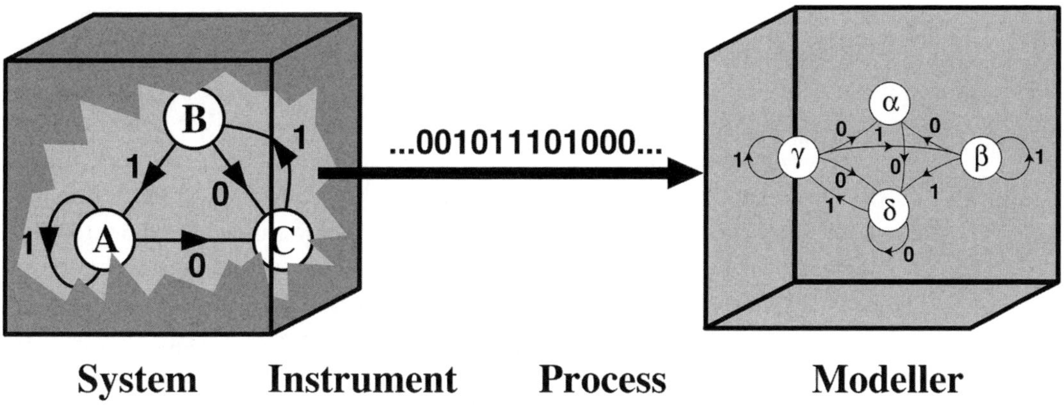

FIGURE 2.2. The Learning Channel, by James Crutchfield. A view of the scientific approach to modeling complex, dynamic phenomena that are observed only indirectly through inaccurate instruments. Inspired by Claude Shannon's communication channel: *(Left)* The states and dynamic of the system of interest are accessed indirectly through an instrument that translates measurements of the system state to a time series of discrete symbols (process). *(Right)* From the process, the modeler builds a representation of the system's hidden states and dynamics. © 1994 James P. Crutchfield.

way, how information is stored in the process, and how that stored information is transformed by new inputs and by the passage of time. This, and not using computers for simulations and numerical calculations, is what makes computational mechanics 'computational,' in the sense of 'computation theoretic,'" they explain.[73] It is also why computational mechanics becomes a primary tool for elucidating "natural computation."

Crutchfield requires students to conduct an original research project for his course. This entails picking a system (either temporal, spatiotemporal, network dynamical, or statistical mechanical), analyzing its informational and computational properties, and relating these to the system's organization and behavior. In other words, students are asked to use the tools of the two-quarter course to attempt to measure and model a chosen system's dynamic behavior as it moves probabilistically between states. I chose to study a biological system to which I was introduced just months before, in the Fall 2011 semester, when I was studying emergent architecture at EmTech. I did so to see what could be gained from studying a single system from different disciplinary approaches: those of architecture, physics, plant biology, and complexity using dynamical systems theory, information theory, and computational mechanics.

In the Biomimicry Studio at EmTech, my team had been assigned the topic of "tendrils" to research for inspiration for architectural design. The studio work was rapid-fire, with the expectation to begin physical and digital modeling by the third day; the whole studio was only a couple of weeks long. Because I had access to UC Davis's library database even though I was in London, in light of the fact that the AA's library did not have access to scientific journal databases, I found and printed about thirty scientific articles that explained the current state of knowledge about tendril coiling. My group members—Marina Konstantatou of Greece, Giancarlo Torpiano of Malta, and Chun-Feng Liu of China—and I divided them up to read, since we presumed we actually needed to know scientifically how and why tendrils coil. Very quickly, however, we learned that the tutors did not expect this. In fact, they discouraged it, for no time existed to truly understand the biological system. Rather, we were supposed to extract geometric formal knowledge about how tendrils likely coiled and then model this and use it to innovate a new architectural outcome. Although EmTech's Weinstock professes deep interest in modeling architecture on the mathematical processes of emergence, in this case we were pushed to reduce a very complex scientific process into a very simple formula. This reductionism is symptomatic across much of the practice of generative architecture and stems from its historical development out of the formalism of postmodernism, beginning with Greg Lynn's emphasis on developing new means to overwhelmingly formalist ends. Those who truly engage with biological scientific processes in the practice of generative architecture—such as Jenny Sabin, Peter Lloyd Jones, Benjamin, and Federici—are rare. Yet, without my having been present at EmTech as a student–observer–critic and based solely on Weinstock's writings, I would have missed the extent of EmTech's biological reductionism.

We therefore put the scientific articles aside and came up with a principle that described tendril coiling. Because tendrils grow and coil along the length of their growth, our principle was Extend + Twist + Bend. Together, these three actions produce a coil. We modeled this physically and digitally in different ways, using Python coding in Grasshopper and Kangaroo with Rhino—notice the menagerie that is the zoo of "evolutionary" architectural software. Although our group did not fully succeed in developing a solid and innovative application of this process for architecture, in hindsight we joked among ourselves that we designed the tendril structure that sculptor Anish Kapoor designed and built with engineer Cecil Balmond of Arup just a few months later for the London Olympic Observation Tower, known as *Orbit* (Figure 2.3). We actually had thought of the possibility of creating a large structure in the shape of a tendril but had dismissed it as the shallowest sort of aesthetic biomimicry.

Selecting tendril coiling for the research project for Crutchfield's course in April 2012 was fortuitous since the passionflower vine in my garden was growing rapidly. In looking at the vine, I realized that many tendrils coil without wrapping around anything at all. Coiling evolved to allow vines to "parasitically" climb on other plants and structures using the foreign object as the support for the vine's own growth. The patterns of the "free coils"—those unattached to anything—demonstrated both order/structure and randomness, showing common traits but also differences, with almost every one being unique (Figures 2.4 and 2.5). This suggested that tools for measuring randomness and structure could potentially offer insight into the system of coiling dynamics. With my tutor and project partner Paul Riechers, we chose which instruments to use and how to extract the tendrils' data and history

FIGURE 2.3. *Orbit,* by Anish Kapoor, 2012. Steel, height 115 meters, Queen Elizabeth Park, London. Photograph Dave Morgan; copyright Anish Kapoor.

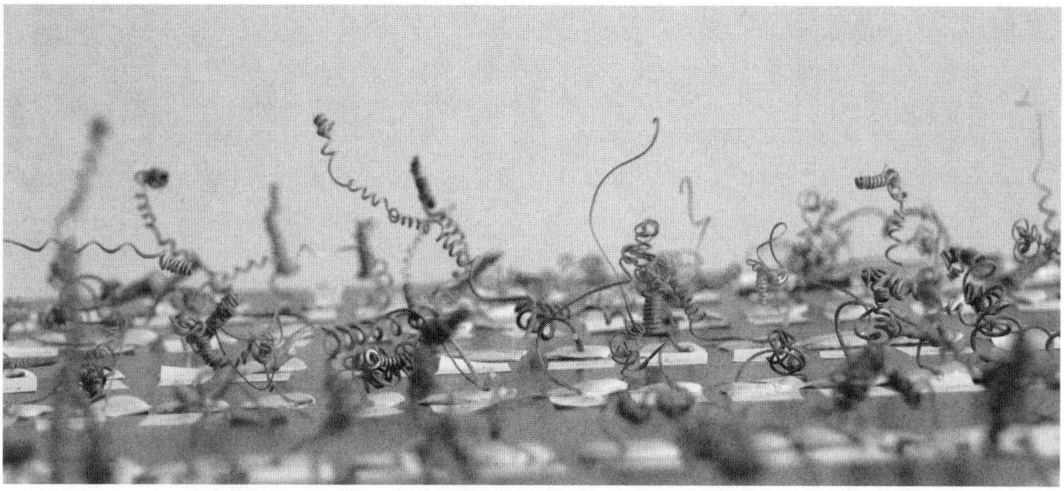

FIGURE 2.4. Nonlinear dynamics of passionflower tendril free coiling, by Christina Cogdell with Paul Riechers, 2012. Photograph by the author.

in order to decode and model their dynamics. This time, I delved thoroughly into the literature of tendril coiling because we were determined to integrate biological knowledge into our interdisciplinary model.

To Riechers's and my great surprise, not a single article that we could find addressed the topic of free-coiling tendrils. Additionally, the biochemical and biophysical explanations for how tendrils coil seem very incomplete, leaving many questions unanswered. Finally, of the articles that do exist about contact coiling, in which both ends of the tendril are affixed, the few that explore nonlinear dynamics all rely on the same mechanical model: Kirchoff's equations for finite rods with intrinsic curvature at equilibria in minimal energy state. These use Kirchoff's equations to explain "perversions"—places where the coil shifts its handedness—in uniform helical coils. This model bears no obvious relevance to the process of untethered coiling—coiling without contact in open air—that produces an astonishing variety of morphologies contrary to what would happen if there were a minimal energy state to which all coiling tends. We posited that coiling likely occurs by the same process in both free and fixed coils. Therefore, better understanding the process of free coiling potentially could transform knowledge of the contact coiling process as well.

Our study therefore attempted to integrate biochemical, biophysical, mathematical, and computational models in order to elucidate the complex stochastic dynamics of tendril free coiling. First, from reading all the scientific literature but without doing any experimentation, I derived a hypothetical biochemical and biophysical model for how tendrils coil. Paul and I wanted a model of the biological process to express using mathematical equations so that we could simulate coiling based upon this model in silico to see whether it seemed plausible. We chose to apply Turing's reaction-diffusion model that has been used to study morphogenetic patterning in plants, particularly for modeling the plant hormone auxin's role as a regulatory gradient, although in root hairs

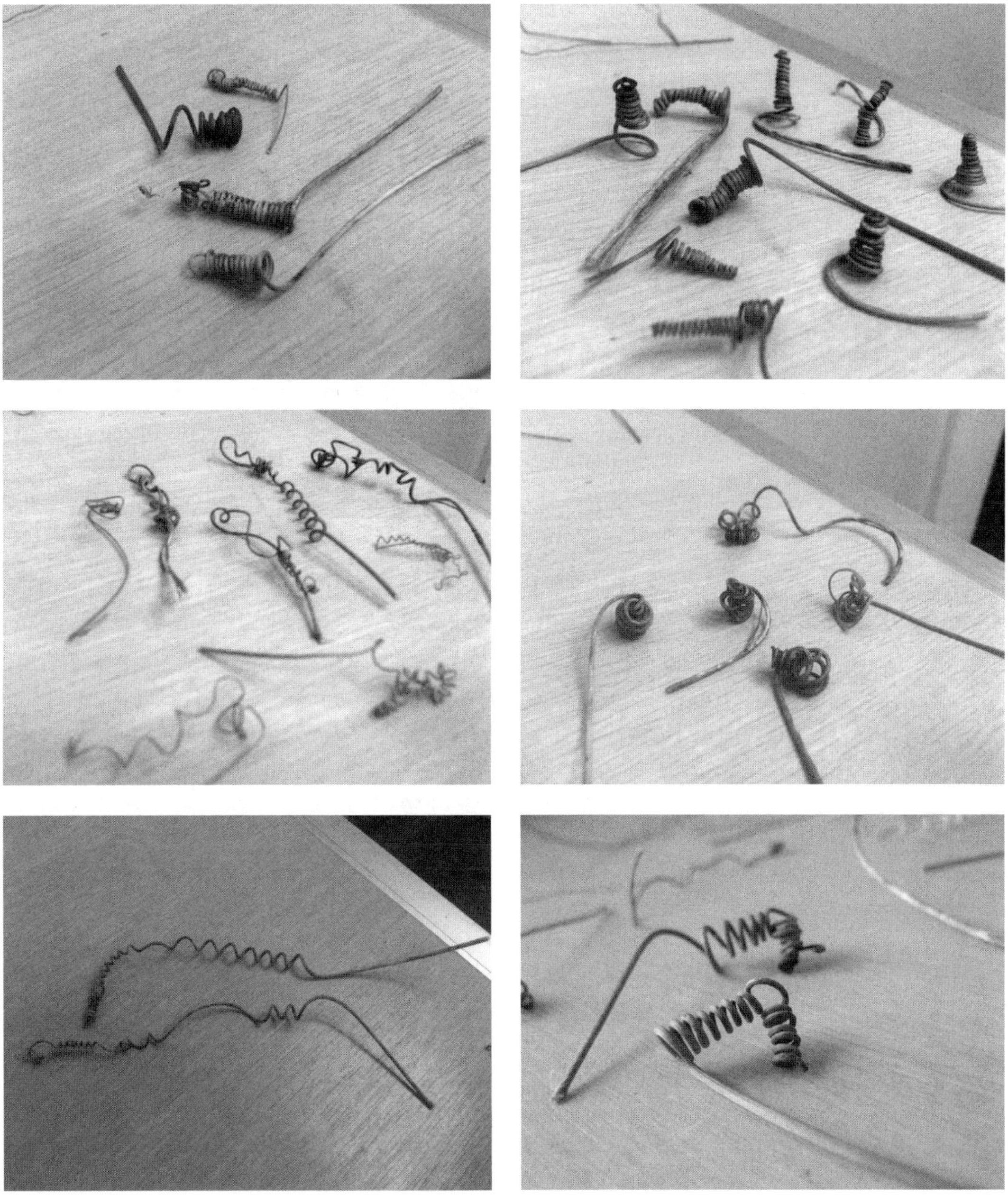

FIGURE 2.5. Nonlinear dynamics of passionflower tendril free coiling, typical free-coiling patterns showing both structure and randomness, by Christina Cogdell with Paul Riechers, 2012. Photographs by the author.

rather than tendrils.[74] Auxin is often characterized as a self-regulating, self-organizing morphogen, one whose differential gradients across tissues trigger different gene responses, including those whose products in turn can inhibit auxin: hence the term often used in tandem with "reaction-diffusion," which is "activation-inhibition." We posited auxin-gradient-induced cell elongation on the convex side of the tendril, combined with lignin-gradient-inhibited gelatinous-fiber (g-fiber) cell contraction on the concave side. We also assumed multidirectional coiling, as passionflower tendrils can coil both to the left and the right. Multidirectional coiling tendrils are contact-sensitive on all sides and can reverse the handedness (left or right, counterclockwise or clockwise direction) of the coiling at any time. We hypothesized that this is based on the location of which cells are active at any given time in relation to those that were active just prior. (G-fiber cells exist in roughly cylindrical form running up and down through the length of the tendril.) Our model presumed approximately a one-third circumferential active g-fiber contact zone, opposite of which active cell elongation occurs owing to a high auxin gradient. Riechers then worked on expressing this model mathematically for computational simulation.

Next, using the statistical methods of information theory and computational mechanics, we analyzed the morphologies of over five hundred free coils in order to measure their randomness (Shannon entropy) and structure (complexity) and determine correlated traits through mutual information analysis, with the hope of achieving an intelligible epsilon-machine minimal model of coiling dynamics.[75] Specifically, using discrete five-millimeter increments, we measured: the changing diameter (of the loops in the increment); periodicity (number of loops per increment); handedness (whether loops turned clockwise or counterclockwise, viewed from the perspective of the cut end); "pervertedness" (which occurs when it shifts handedness); angular axis rotation (when the line made through the center points of the coils turns away from an imagined center line axis from its linear start at its tip); and self-contact status (if a coil touches itself) along the length of each tendril. These six characteristics are sufficient to basically re-create the structure of any coil from the measurements we took. Then, from our 3,389 measurements—representing over seventeen meters in total coil length—we compiled a data string addressing all six of these dimensions. Next, we analyzed this string using the tools of computational mechanics, generating and interpreting Markov chains and Shannon entropies that modeled states and the probabilities of transition between them for each of the variables, as well as the mutual information of the variables in combination with one another.

While we strove to achieve enough clarity from our data to create an epsilon-machine modeling the dynamics of tendril free coiling, owing to the fact that we had six variables in our analysis, a successful epsilon-machine was out of our reach. To get closer to this goal, we would need to use what is known as "optimal causal inference" in order to minimize the noise in our data so as to be able to see the structure beneath the noise.[76] We did, however, learn about the difficulty of processes of multidimensional analysis. Usually, computational dynamics and chaos modeling work with three dimensions, not six; each additional dimension adds complicating factors.[77] Despite not arriving at a successful epsilon-machine, we did discover interesting facts about patterns of tendril free coiling, particularly at the tips and bases of the tendrils. For the tips, we found high degrees of correlation between diameter and periodicity; we also found that 28 percent of tendril tips have a perversion. This disproves what many scholars who are experts in tendrils believe: that free coils *never* have perversions at all, unless they were in contact with something and got their perversion and then somehow broke free again to become a "free coil." In fact, a majority of free coils—57.4 percent—in our sample have a perversion somewhere in their coil. The pattern of how a coil ends, where it opens up toward the base of the tendril that attaches to the vine, is much more predictable than the pattern at the tip. Coils end with large diameters and small periodicities and are more often than not turning in a left-handed direction.

Riechers's and my interdisciplinary tendril study remains unfinished and unpublished, not owing to infeasibility or lack of rigor or contribution, but simply to time and other obligations. The latter interrupted the computational modeling process, both in terms of moving forward toward an epsilon-machine using computational mechanics and in terms of simulating tendril coiling in silico based on the hypothetical biological model and corresponding mathematical equation. Our goal was ultimately to compare the proximity of the data from our computational model's virtual tendrils—analyzed for the same six variables—to real tendril dynamics. It is worthwhile to summarize our approach here in order to communicate some of the methodologies used by complexity scientists to model nonlinear system dynamics. The amount of time and specialization demanded by truly interdisciplinary research often causes practitioners in one discipline to simply rely on the tools and conceptual apparatus with which they are already familiar. Architects wanting to mimic only the mechanical process of tendril coiling can therefore resort to Extend + Twist + Bend if they so choose. But if architects truly want to understand and integrate the dynamics of biological systems into architecture—especially if they imagine buildings will be living organisms in the future—then they need to team up with scientists to garner the depth and breadth of knowledge that is available for this task.

The Materiality of Silicon-Based Digital Computation

This chapter on material and natural computation ends with a short summary of the materiality of computers: the diminishing reserves of material substances from which they are made, the high embodied energy in transistors and integrated circuit chips that are integral to digital technologies today, and the loss of these materials and the pollution of their end-of-life disposal process. Conducting full life cycle assessments (LCAs) with numerical analyses is a difficult and unwieldy process, one that involves many subjective decisions about where to draw the boundary around what one considers to be the system associated with production of the product. Furthermore, in a product as complicated as a computer with so many different parts, each part must be analyzed and included in the overall assessment. For this reason, the most recent LCA of a personal computer dates to 2004, indicating a need for this to be updated as many facets of the process have changed since then.[78] Certainly, other general LCAs more recently have focused on computer parts, for example the display screens or the transistors going into integrated circuit chips.[79] This summary therefore combines this information into a short overview. Because so much of generative architecture and, increasingly, nearly every major facet of our global economy relies on these technologies, it is crucial to understand their material and energetic sources and environmental impacts.

LCAs consider three related types of inputs and outputs involved in the life cycle of any product. The first examines raw materials at every step of the way, beginning with where these are taken from the earth and how they are processed. The second entails cumulative embodied energy, which includes the mass and type of materials used to provide the power; note that energy consumed in operational use of the product is often a very small portion of the overall embodied energy. Finally, LCAs examine all the outputs—not just the useful products but also all the wastes released and environmental pollution associated with the full life cycle. This latter portion often includes the health risks facing workers who produce the product. Additionally, for each of the three main categories—materials, energy, and waste and pollution—every one of the six major facets of the life cycle is considered. Generally, these six include the acquisition of raw materials, manufacturing and production, transportation and distribution to stores and users, operational use and maintenance, recycling if possible, and management of it as waste.

The most basic building block of any digital technology is a silicon wafer transistor. Although the marketing text and imagery of companies like Intel imply that common beach sand is the source of silicon for transistor and integrated circuit manufacture, in fact it is not.[80] Only very pure quartzite can be used as the starting point for polysilicon. Also referred to as just "poly," polysilicon is the name for the material that is produced after purifying small particles of quartzite, which is primarily composed of silicon dioxide. Poly is then altered to make silicon wafers. The creation of poly involves a multistep process. First, add twice as much coal as quartzite—the carbon combines with oxygen to release carbon dioxide, leaving pure silicon.[81] Second, add large amounts of hydrochloric acid to produce the gas trichlorosilane, which effectively removes the "impurities of iron, aluminum, and boron." Finally, add hydrogen gas to turn the silicon into poly, which is then melted down at high temperatures and exposed either to boron or phosphorous and then turned into a crystal ingot that is cut to make wafers.[82]

Quartzite is a metamorphic rock made from seriously heating up sandstone deep in the earth's crust. While it is mined around the world—Africa's Great Rift Valley, Australia, Wisconsin, and the Appalachian region of North Carolina, as well as various locations in Europe—it is a much more limited natural resource than beach sand; for example, in 2009 one ton of quartzite from Spruce River, North Carolina, was selling for $50,000.[83] Its mining also devastates local landscapes, leaving behind large piles of rock debris and dust after removing the soil and plants. Although quartzite can sometimes begin as nearly 99 percent pure silicon, "nine-nines" (99.9999999 percent) level of purity is necessary for transistors today, and the number of nines has been steadily increasing. This incredible level of purity has been described by geologist Michael Welland, citing a Dow Corning scientist, like this: "Imagine stringing tennis balls from the Earth to the moon, and wanting them all to be yellow. . . . This would take about 5.91 billion tennis balls. For the color coding to be of semiconductor quality, 'you could only tolerate two, maybe three that were orange.' . . . For solar cells, which are slightly less demanding . . . 'you could tolerate five or six orange balls.'"[84]

This level of purity is also the primary reason for the high amount of energy that goes into creating transistors, for it is not only the poly that must be extremely pure but also all the other chemicals used in the process.[85] According to the research of UC Davis engineering students Riyaz Merchant, Madison Crain, and Felix Le, the energy expended on the manufacturing and production of transistors accounts for 92 percent of the total embodied energy of its life cycle.[86] This high level of cleanliness is even a requirement of the facility in which transistors and circuits are produced, which uses special ventilation systems to create as close to a particulate-free space as possible. This is made difficult by the presence of workers and the fact that as the poly ingot is cut as much as 50 percent of it is lost as dust.[87] The wafers themselves are therefore further protected, moving through the facility in "front-opening unified pods" as they undergo the rest of the production process. This pod-enclosure system also protects workers from the deadly chemicals used throughout the process, including nitric and hydrofluoric acid.[88] Once the poly ingot is sliced, these wafers are physically and chemically buffed and then etched using photolithography. This involves covering parts of the wafer while doping it with chemicals—bases and acids, to remove or build up layers—and repeating this process many times. This creates the channels for different component function. A transistor is finished with aluminum and gold wiring at the terminals. Yet of all those made, as many as 40 percent are found to be defective before they leave the factory.[89]

Incredibly, putting over a billion transistors together creates only one of today's microprocessors or integrated circuit chips that is approximately the size of a fingernail.[90] That is not a typo. According to Moore's law, the number of transistors on a chip doubles every year, although owing to the physical properties of materials and the laws of physics this cannot continue indefinitely. This shrinking process, which is accompanied by even greater purity requirements, exponentially increases the amounts of energy embedded in this most basic part of today's digital technologies. This is because as a general rule, extremely low-entropy highly organized forms of matter require very large amounts of energy to produce since they are "fabricated using relatively high entropy starting materials."[91] Physicist Eric Williams demonstrates this by stating, "Secondary inputs of fossil fuels to manufacture a chip total 600 times its weight, high compared to a factor of 1–2 for an automobile or refrigerator."[92] Along with Robert Ayres and Miriam Heller in 2002, Williams surveyed the energy and materials used in the production of a 32MB DRAM microchip, much of which comes from the process of making its many transistors, explained above using more recent information. They point out that often purification of materials is "routinely overlooked in most life cycle assessments." In other words, system boundaries are drawn narrowly around the already purified materials used in a process in order to omit the high amount of energy entailed in that part of their production.[93]

Although chips allow computers to process information using binary code, many other materials and a significant amount of energy goes into the life cycle of a personal computer. Rather than six hundred times greater mass of energy used to produce compared to product final weight, computers only require about eleven times the total amount. In his 2004 study, Williams found that "the total energy and fossil fuels used in producing a desktop computer with 17-in. CRT monitor are estimated at 6400 megajoules (MJ) and 260 kg, respectively."[94] His calculations, however, do not take into account the energy, materials, and waste that accompanies parts and wholes of computers as they travel around the globe during assembly, retail, use, and then disassembly. This is a significant oversight. UC Berkeley environmental policy researcher Alastair Iles writes that "computers are designed in the US, Europe, and Japan" but manufactured in China, Mexico, Taiwan, and Singapore by companies that purchase components like chips and other materials made from a number of different regions. These components are "produced with materials extracted from Africa and Australia": "New computers are then shipped to markets worldwide. Similarly, recycling chains have become transnational, stretching from industrial nations to developing countries." A computer purchased in California, say, upon its useful life's end—usually after only three to five years—goes first to a local electronics disposal zone and from there to a port city like Seattle or Los Angeles. It is then sold to "foreign traders" who arrange for its disassembly journey, which often ends in China, India, and Pakistan. Via ship, it travels first to a "regional hub such as Dubai"; traders then "sell machines to dealers in India or China, sometimes routing them through the Philippines or Indonesia to evade customs scrutiny. These dealers then disassemble machines and distribute parts to specialized recycling workshops in urban centers and rural villages."[95]

Iles is concerned about environmental justice and focuses on the economic, health, and environmental inequalities facing workers involved in computer disassembly and recycling. Remember that those involved in manufacturing chips are protected by working in super clean environments; the toxic chip materials, as they are being added, are isolated in front-opening unified pods. These precautions do not exist for those involved in disassembly. Many parts used in computers combine toxic and harmless materials together in such a way that they cannot be taken apart; they are not even labeled to warn of the hazard. This means that as workers remove parts of computers, they inevitably contact toxic materials. "Hands, aided by basic tools such as chisels, saws, hammers, pliers, and screwdrivers, are the primary technologies in use. In India, circuit boards are sometimes smashed against rocks or with hammers to dislodge their lead solder and metals, and to free semiconductor chips," Iles writes. "In China, monitors are crushed to extract the copper yokes, breaking the heavily lead-contaminated CRT glass into fragments that are thrown away into water or land."[96] He estimates that millions of workers in China, and over a million in India, are exposed to these conditions and contend with high respiratory disease rates, groundwater pollution, and pay of approximately $1.50 a day (2004 rates).[97] He summarizes the environmental effect of global outsourcing as relocating pollution caused by both manufacturing and recycling phases to Asia and other parts of the world that participate in the toxic aspects of the computer life cycle.[98]

Many people within the industry and beyond argue that the amount of greenhouse gases released into the atmosphere through the production of chips and computers will be offset by savings in greenhouse gas release owing to changes in lifestyle in which people drive and fly less because they use digital technologies.[99] While this claim is debatable (in fact, many experts dispute it), it has no direct bearing on another problem associated with digital technologies: the waning supplies of materials that go into digital device production. A few studies from 2012, presented at the optimistically titled Electronics Goes Green conference, address these shortages directly since companies and national consortiums are beginning to be concerned about this situation. Although a computer can comprise up to two thousand parts, the main parts produced using "critical metals" are the printed circuit board (PCB), liquid crystal display (LCD) monitor, battery pack, hard disk drive, and optical drive.[100] These parts contain significant amounts of cobalt, germanium, gallium, gold, indium, platinum group metals, silver, and rare earth metals including neodymium and tantalum. Critical metals were identified by a European Union study by the Raw Materials Initiative, which surveyed "the economic importance and supply risk of 41 materials," with those in the direst situation being labeled as "critical."[101] Given that approximately 275 million personal computers were shipped during 2015, not to mention other digital devices, a number of questions then arise.[102]

For these critical metals, how many reserves are there and how long are these predicted to last? One study has estimated the number of years left given recent consumption rates, finding between ten and fifty years for antimony (approximately ten), indium (approximately twelve), silver (approximately eighteen), and tantalum (approximately forty-five).[103] These reserves are divided equally between China and a number of other countries, including the United States, the Commonwealth of Independent States (formerly Russia), India, Australia, and others. Because China controls the global export of rare earth metals, it has been carefully monitoring exports to keep prices high. High prices stimulate the exploration and discovery of new or deeper reserves, which ironically can cause the apparent number of reserves to "increase" despite the fact that we are rapidly decreasing what are finite supplies.[104] Yet these further explorations and extractions are powered by fossil-fuel-driven equipment that releases carbon dioxide into the atmosphere; the rarer a metal is, the more carbon dioxide is released in its acquisition.[105]

What about substituting other metals for the ones that are running out? German industrial ecologist Mario Schmidt notes a number of factors that limit this possibility. He explains that "there are no separate mines for many metals"; rather, many metals are "mined as by-products of 'Major Metals.'" Thus, just because some critical metals are in short supply does not mean that it is easy to just extract more of them, since their extraction is subsidiary. Furthermore, "there are very few deposits of enriched ores worth mining, for the physical frequency of elements in the earth's crust says nothing about whether they can be mined cost-efficiently." Lastly, "if one metal is to be replaced by another, it will need to have similar properties, and generally it is obtained from the same source," he writes. He gives the example of lead, banned for use in solders, which can possibly be "replaced by tin, silver, indium or bismuth, but the latter three are by-products of lead mining. As less lead was mined as a result of the ban, the pressure of price on the other metals increased."[106]

Since the foregoing options are limited, we then ask whether we are recycling the critical metals we have already extracted in order to maintain their useful supply. Unfortunately, the answer for the most part is no. A study from 2012 based on the recycling of computers in Germany—where more stringent requirements and precautions exist in the recycling industry than in India or China—found that "the only metals under study that are partly recovered from the devices are cobalt, gold, silver, and palladium. All other critical metals show losses of 100% distributed over collection, pre-treatment, and final treatment" (Table 2.1).[107] In fact, many metals are recycled hardly at all, as Smit and colleagues show. This returns us to the problem that all the parts in a computer are not designed for disassembly and the fact that many of the parts using critical metals are so tiny that they cannot be easily salvaged by hand using rudimentary tools. Until these materials become so expensive and scarce that industries and nations decide to regulate their design and reuse, or until fossil fuels become so expensive that it is no longer economically viable to extract deeper sources of rare earth materials and pour so much energy into chip manufacturing and shipping parts around the world, the situation is unlikely to change. As Kris de Decker aptly summarizes, "Digital technology is a product of cheap energy."[108] So is generative architecture, despite the fact that its landmark constructions are incredibly expensive.

Clearly, the example of the digital industry suggests an unsustainable trend, and yet this industrial infrastructure is endemic to all major sectors today, not just generative architecture. Riechers hopes, perhaps optimistically, that products designed to "self-organize" may allow a more energy-efficient road to production. He argues that since scientists have seen materials compute, with guided design scientists and designers can influence this innate capacity to harness useful computation for design and manufacturing. Similarly, he envisions systems that can self-disassemble after a product's useful life in order to return precious resources to further utility. For designers to approach these admirable goals, they will have to seriously collaborate with complexity scientists. Riechers sees this as a necessary future design paradigm, and

Metal	Content in all laptops sold in Germany in 2010 (tons)	Losses during collection (%)	Losses during pretreatment (%)	Losses during final treatment (%)	Recovery in Germany (tons)
Cobalt (Co)	461.31	—	20	4	177
Neodymium (Nd)	15.16	—	100	100	0
Tantalum (Ta)	12.06	—	100	5	0
Silver (Ag)	3.11	—	70	5	0.443
Praseodymium (Pr)	1.94	—	100	100	0
Gold (Au)	0.74	—	70	5	0.105
Dysprosium (Dy)	0.43	—	100	100	0
Indium (In)	0.29	—	20	100	0
Palladium (Pd)	0.28	50	70	5	0.04
Platinum (Pt)	0.028	—	100	5	0
Yttrium (Y)	0.012	—	40	100	0
Gallium (Ga)	0.01	—	40	100	0
Gadolinium (Gd)	0.0048	—	40	100	0
Cerium (Ce)	0.00069	—	40	100	0
Europium (Eu)	0.00028	—	40	100	0
Lanthanum (La)	0.00008	—	40	100	0
Terbium (Tb)	0.00003	—	40	100	0

TABLE 2.1. Critical raw material potentials in laptops and losses from the collection and treatment systems currently used in Germany, by Matthias Buchert, Andreas Manhart, Daniel Bleher, and Detlef Pingel. From "Recycling Critical Raw Materials from Waste Electronic Equipment," Institute for Applied Ecology, Darmstadt, Germany, February 24, 2012. Only cobalt, silver, gold, and palladium are partially recovered to feed back into the industrial cycle.

at least in rhetoric and principle, if not in actual method thus far, generative architects agree. This chapter has demonstrated that choices of method matter significantly, beginning first and foremost with generative architecture's reliance on environmentally devastating and finite digital technologies. Generative architects' choice to use terms that mimic a core complexity concept—natural computation—as listed at the beginning of this chapter, reveals the deep ideological influence of complexism in the conceptual framing of their pursuits. Yet, the environmental effects stand as corollaries to this choice, as Stefan Helmreich's "athwart theory" poignantly reveals.[109] The same applies to Riechers's hope, for the road to learn how to design things so that they "self-organize" and "self-disassemble" is paved with two parts coal to one part quartzite plus the earth's dwindling supply of critical metals.

CHAPTER 3

MORPHOGENESIS AND EVOLUTIONARY COMPUTATION

Morphology is not only a study of material things and of the forms of material things, but has its dynamical aspect, under which we deal with the interpretation, in terms of force, of the operations of energy. . . . We want to see how . . . the forms of living things, and of the parts of living things, can be explained by physical considerations, and to realize that in general no organic forms exist save such as are in conformity with physical and mathematical laws.

D'Arcy Thompson, *On Growth and Form* (1917)

On the centennial of the publication of his classic *On Growth and Form,* D'Arcy Thompson's words appropriately open this chapter on morphogenesis and evolution in biology, computation, and generative architecture. Whereas morphology is the study of forms, morphogenesis is the process of creating three-dimensional forms in organic or inorganic materials; some use the word to also refer to the generation of two-dimensional patterns. Many theorists consider both pattern and morphogenesis as emergent from processes of self-organization. In this light, they have garnered significant recent attention from complexity scientists, for example, physicist Philip Ball's three-part series *Nature's Patterns: A Tapestry in Three Parts (Shapes, Flow,* and *Branches)* (2009). In biology specifically, morphogenesis refers to the process by which an embryo or seed grows and transforms its shape as the organism matures into adulthood. Thompson's lengthy tome expounds the mathematical basis of many natural forms and posits the evolutionary relatedness of species whose morphologies can be mathematically transformed through deformation one into the other. Discontented with natural selection as the sole means for explaining evolutionary diversity, Thompson focused on the roles that physical forces play in shaping morphological change over time, both on the small scale in terms of an individual organism's development and growth, referred to as ontogeny, and over the long temporal scale in evolution, referred to as phylogeny.

Although Thompson's groundbreaking work was not well received by fellow scientists in his own time, it has gained an immense appeal in the last twenty years for generative architects interested in designing organically inspired and parametrically based architectural forms that function under physical load. For example, Achim Menges and Sean Ahlquist include excerpts of Thompson's book in their coedited *Computational Design Thinking* (2011). Their introduction to the selected portions explains that Thompson's work establishes "two fundamental branches of a conceptual framework for computational geometry: parametrics and homologies. A parametric equation is defined as a constant equation in which relational parameters vary," they write. "It results in producing *families* of products where each instance will always carry a particular commonness with others. Thompson defines these embedded relationships as homologies."[1] Similarly, Michael Weinstock, Jenny Sabin, and Peter Lloyd Jones have recently required students to read chapters from *On Growth and Form* as well. In 1917, Thompson completed his mathematical computations by hand, but owing to the mathematical nature of architectural form generation and the strong emphases on biological analogies and evolutionary computation in generative architecture, the importance of his writings to generative architecture now is not surprising.

The differences in historical context, however, in terms of the scientific knowledge of biological morphogenesis in the first decades of the twentieth century compared to those of the twenty-first, as well as in the intervening century, reveal significant theoretical changes in morphogenesis and evolutionary biology during this period. These changes pertain directly to some current computational approaches in generative architecture. Yet despite this being so, the assumption that therefore computational approaches in generative architecture accurately mirror those of biology is false. Two current experts in evolutionary computation, Sanjeev Kumar and Peter Bentley, state this clearly: "Talk to any evolutionary biologist and they'll tell you that the standard genetic algorithm (GA) does not resemble natural evolution very closely. . . . Should you have the courage to talk to a developmental biologist, you'll have an even worse ear-bashing."[2] Evolutionary computation—the theoretical and technical intermediary between biology and architecture—bears far more relevance to computer science pursuits of artificial intelligence and artificial life than it does to biology.

This chapter therefore introduces major developments in theories of biological morphogenesis and evolution from D'Arcy Thompson's lifetime to the present, in order to critically analyze their transformations into the fields of evolutionary computation and generative architecture. After a brief overview of late nineteenth- and early twentieth-century ideas about evolution, eugenics, and genetics, it addresses the historical and conceptual overlaps between theories in biology and computer science, explaining when computation began to draw on theories of biological morphogenesis and evolution. It then explores the obverse: the conceptual shift that occurred when we began to conceive of biological development and evolution themselves as computational processes. The chapter goes on to focus on the three major developments in evolutionary theory from the mid-twentieth century onward that have inspired techniques of evolutionary computation. In turn, two of these have been adopted by and innovated on by generative architects, while the architectural potential of the third has yet to be fully developed.

The first is the neo-Darwinian modern evolutionary synthesis of the mid- to late twentieth century, arising concurrently with the rise of population genetics, the discovery of DNA in the early 1950s, and the central dogma of molecular biology. Second is the recent theory known as "evo-devo" (short for evolutionary developmental biology) from the late twentieth to early twenty-first centuries. Evo-devo arose from the results of DNA sequencing considered in tandem with experimentation that revealed a common set of "homeotic genes" integral to morphogenetic development that are shared by very distantly related organisms. The third entails recent theories of epigenetics and the roles of epigenetic processes in developmental systems biology and evolution. Epigenetic processes are environmentally responsive, affect gene regulation, and pose a second short-term line of heredity. For these reasons, some scientists consider epigenetics to offer a new Lamarckian addition to accepted Darwinian evolutionary ideas of environmental adaptation and natural selection. Generative architects rely primarily on neo-Darwinian computational design techniques. Only a few have adapted ideas from evo-devo, notably Michael Weinstock, Achim Menges, and possibly Aaron Sprecher and his team on the Evo DeVO Project at the Laboratory for Integrated Prototyping and Hybrid Environments at McGill University.[3] Only one—John Frazer—has developed and used epigenetic algorithms, amazingly as early as the 1990s, although in their essay published in *The Gen(H)ome Project* (2006) Jones and Helene Furjàn call for greater interest in epigenetic approaches.[4] The chapter concludes with an analysis of the implications of architects' choices to use these theoretical models, with thoughts about why recent theories of evo-devo and epigenetics may matter for generative architecture going forward.

Historical Overview to the Mid-Twentieth Century

In the conclusion to his book, Thompson notes that despite the numerous decades since Charles Darwin's publication of *On the Origin of Species* (1859), scientists still had not figured out how to explain the apparent gaps in the evolutionary phylogenetic tree. These could be small—such as the changes causing species differentiation—or large—such as breaks in the observable chain of evolutionary relatedness. Thompson does not accomplish this either, and in fact all but ignores chemical aspects of morphogenesis; he simply accepts discontinuity as a mathematical and evolutionary fact. Many others, though, in Thompson's time and since, have worked very hard to discover what Darwin failed to explain despite the title of his book: the actual origin of new species, and therefore the sources of species' change over time. New traits and new species might be naturally selected, but how variation arises in the first place was not known. Darwin's own flawed theory of pangenesis was based on aspects of

Lamarckism, the ideas of French biologist Jean-Baptiste Lamarck that posited evolutionary change through the inheritance of acquired characters. Habitual behaviors enacted throughout an organism's life were absorbed into its adult form and essence and subsequently passed on to its offspring. In this way, Lamarckism proposed the processes of morphogenetic development over a lifetime, coupled to environment, as the guiding force of evolution writ large. An alternate late nineteenth-century theory put forward by German biologist Ernst Haeckel also linked organismal ontogeny to phylogenetic development overall. Haeckel observed that during embryonic development, different species' embryos resembled one another at different phases of development. Accordingly, he proposed the now-refuted theory of recapitulation, which posited that the development of an individual organism recapitulates the entire phylogenetic evolution that came before and led up to that particular species.[5]

Other biological theories in the late nineteenth century, however, seemingly contradicted those of Lamarck and Haeckel. The work of German evolutionary biologist August Weismann, for example, in the 1880s and 1890s established the differentiation of sex or "germ" cells from somatic cells (i.e., those cells in the body that bear no obvious relation to reproduction but just carry out other bodily functions). Although formerly Weismann had accepted facets of Lamarckism, his theory of the separation of the "germ" and the "soma" put an end to Lamarckism in many people's minds, for it proposed that influence only flowed one way—from the germ cells to the somatic cells—rather than also, as Lamarckism suggested, from changes in somatic cells into the germ cells for ongoing inheritance. Lamarckism continued to be debated in some scientific circles throughout the twentieth century and is experiencing a revival and transformation today owing to increasing knowledge of epigenetics.[6] But for the most part owing to Weismannism, in addition to the rediscovery of Gregor Mendel's theory of inheritance based on invisible "factors" carrying dominant or recessive traits that appeared with mathematical predictability, early twentieth-century scientists pursued alternate routes of inquiry into inheritance. These led first to eugenics ("to have good genes," coined by Englishman Francis Galton in the 1880s) and then to the development of modern genetics. One result of this shift was that theories of evolution slowly decoupled from those of biological development and morphogenesis, leading to the establishment of these as subfields that largely pursued independent research until the end of the twentieth century, when evo-devo began to rejoin them.

It is in this roughly sketched context, then, that Thompson published *On Growth and Form,* which entered the academic biological scene as an outlier both for its emphasis on physical forces and mathematics as well as for its approach conjoining morphogenesis to evolution. In 1917, eugenicists on both sides of the Atlantic were busy applying principles derived from Mendelism and long-established agricultural breeding practices to attempt to control human evolution toward "betterment," using "rational selection" enacted through social and political policies on reproduction rather than natural selection. They presumed a biological basis for physical, mental, moral, and social human traits, without knowing what the seat and source of inheritance was. They conducted broad-scale research on patterns of inherited traits using family studies and fitter family contests at state and world's fairs, creating a large U.S. databank in the fireproof vaults of the Eugenics Record Office in Cold Spring Harbor, New York.[7]

At the same time, other scientists were attempting to uncover the source of heredity in germ cells. British biologist William Bateson first described this pursuit using the word "genetics" in 1905, which fit well with the words "eugenics," "pangenes," and "genes," the second being proposed by botanist Hugo de Vries, based on Darwin's word "pangenesis," then shortened to "genes" by Wilhelm Johannsen in 1909. In the early twentieth century, de Vries published *The Mutation Theory* that, in contrast to Darwin's ideas of gradual change, posited the possibility of abrupt changes in inheritance. This theory inspired American embryologist Thomas Hunt Morgan to investigate physical mutations in fruit flies and patterns of mutation inheritance through breeding experiments. The results led him and his colleagues to posit *The Mechanism of Mendelian Heredity* (1915), that mutations are heritable and that inheritance and sex factors reside on chromosomes in germ cells. It was not until the discovery of the molecular composition of deoxyribonucleic acid—DNA—and its double-helical structure, published in 1953, that geneticists felt confident that they had located the presumed root source of inheritance for which they had long been looking. That Francis Crick and James Watson described DNA as an information "code," however, reveals a mid-century shift in the framework for considering biological processes, one influenced by developments in the 1940s in information theory, digital computation, and code-cracking from World War II.[8]

In fact, Alan Turing, the eminent British code-cracker and one of the founders of digital computation, had proposed at the outset of the computer's invention something like the obverse: that "evolution could be used as a metaphor for problem solving."[9] At the beginning of the formation of theories and techniques of digital computation, Turing envisioned the potential of evolutionary computation; thus began the conceptual overlaps between theories of biological morphogenesis and evolution and theories of computation. Philip Ball recounts that as a schoolboy, Turing had read Thompson's *On Growth and Form* and had been fascinated by the problem of biological morphogenesis for many years prior to his prescient essay "The Chemical Basis of Morphogenesis," published in 1952.[10] In his essay—and similar to Thompson's brief discussion of the same topic in *On Growth and Form*—Turing mentions the puzzle of symmetry breaking for the development of biological forms: "An embryo in its spherical blastula has spherical symmetry, or if there are any deviations from perfect symmetry, they cannot be regarded as of any particular importance. . . . But a system which has spherical symmetry, and whose state is changing because of chemical reactions and diffusion, will remain spherically symmetrical for ever. . . . It certainly cannot result in an organism such as a horse, which is not spherically symmetrical."[11] Ball describes the fundamental quandary: "How, without any outside disturbance, can the spherically symmetrical ball of cells turn into one that is less than spherically symmetric, with its cells differentiated to follow distinct developmental paths?"[12]

Turing posited a process of reaction and diffusion of autocatalytic chemicals that in developing tissues could trigger gene action based on threshold levels of chemical gradients. He chose to call these chemicals "morphogens" owing to his faith in their certain role in morphogenesis, even though he had few specificities in mind about what types of chemicals might perform this function.[13] Because in autocatalysis the amount of chemical or morphogen generated depends on the amount that is already present, "this kind of feedback can lead to instabilities that amplify small, random fluctuations and, under certain constraints, turn them into persistent oscillations."[14] Turing worked out the equations for this process by hand, all the while wishing he had a digital computer, for a hypothetical two-dimensional sheet of cells and concluded that such a reaction-diffusion process might be responsible for the stationary "dappled" patterns that appear on animal skins, as well as for gastrulation and plant phyllotaxis.[15] Twenty years later, German scientists Hans Meinhardt and Alfred Gierer revisited Turing's proposition; to it, they added an inhibitory element alongside the activating one, calling theirs an "activator-inhibitor scheme" (these are now recognized as one class of reaction-diffusion processes). The result of this addition is the production of stationary patterns such as spots and stripes, which are now often referred to as "Turing patterns."[16]

Owing to both the precociousness of Turing's ideas about evolutionary computation and morphogenesis and his inability to develop them further due to his untimely death, other thinkers are credited with founding techniques of evolutionary computation in the late 1950s. It was not until John Holland's work in the 1960s and his publication of the technique of genetic algorithms in *Adaptation in Natural and Artificial Systems* (1975) that the field became more widely known and began to be firmly established. In their 2015 *Nature* publication, computer scientists Agoston Eiben and Jim Smith recount that "although initially considerable skepticism surrounded evolutionary algorithms, over the past 20 years evolutionary computation has grown to become a major field in computational intelligence." They include in the field "historical members: genetic algorithms, evolution strategies, evolutionary programming, and genetic programming; and younger siblings, such as differential evolution and particle swarm optimization."[17] They document the widespread success of evolutionary computation for multi-objective problem solving in general, typically for up to ten objectives.[18] Computer scientist Melanie Mitchell in 1996 described the value of genetic algorithms and evolutionary computation for biologists as allowing "scientists to perform experiments that would not be possible in the real world," "accelerating processes of biological evolution *in silico*," and simulating "phenomena that are difficult or impossible to capture and analyze in a set of equations."[19] But Eiben and Smith make it clear that biological theories of evolution and methods of evolutionary computation are

	Natural evolution	Evolutionary algorithms
Fitness	Observed quantity: a posteriori effect of selection and reproduction ("in the eye of the observer")	Predefined a priori quantity that drives selection and reproduction
Selection	Complex multifactor force based on environmental conditions, other individuals of the same species, and those of other species (predators). Viability is tested continually; reproducibility is tested at discrete times.	Randomized operator with selection probabilities based on given fitness values. Survivor selection and parent selection both happen at discrete times.
Genotype-phenotype mapping	Highly complex biochemical and developmental process influenced by the environment	Typically a simple mathematical transformation or parametricized procedure. A few systems use generative and developmental genotype-phenotype maps.
Variation	Offspring are created from one (asexual reproduction) or two parents (sexual reproduction). Horizontal gene transfer can accumulate genes from more individuals.	Unconstrained vertical gene transfer. Offspring may be generated from any number of parents: one, two, or many.
Execution	Parallel, decentralized execution; birth and death events are not synchronized	Typically centralized with synchronized birth and death.
Population	Spatial embedding implies structured populations. Population size varies according to the relative number of birth and death events. Populations can and do go extinct.	Typically unstructured and panmictic (all individuals are potential partners). Population size is usually kept constant by synchronizing time and number of birth and death events.

FIGURE 3.1. Main differences between natural evolution and evolutionary algorithms, by Agoston Eiben and Jim Smith. In "From Evolutionary Computation to the Evolution of Things," *Nature* 521 (May 28, 2015): 478.

only superficially related (Figure 3.1). The successes they recount using techniques of evolutionary computation (e.g., NASA spacecraft antenna design, pharmacology, and robotics) lie far afield from biology.[20]

If the primary impact of evolutionary computation is on complex multi-objective problem-solving in general, and if it bears more relevance to artificial intelligence and artificial life than to biology, why did Turing and others consider biological evolution to be a potentially useful metaphor for computational problem solving? Mitchell describes evolution as "a method of searching among an enormous number of possibilities for 'solutions.' In biology the enormous set of possibilities is the set of possible genetic sequences," she writes (an oversimplified statement, to say the least), "and the desired 'solutions' are highly fit organisms. . . . The fitness criteria continually change as creatures evolve, so evolution is searching a constantly changing set of possibilities. Searching for solutions in the face of changing conditions is precisely what is required for adaptive computer programs," she explains. She further describes evolution as a "massively parallel search method: rather than work on one species at a time, evolution tests and changes millions of species in parallel." Note that her verbiage positions evolution as an active agent or force and not as simply a passive result. Lastly, she finds the rules of evolution to be remarkably simple—"species evolve by means of random variation (via mutation, recombination, and other operators), followed by natural selection in which the fittest tend to survive and reproduce, thus propagating their genetic material to future generations."[21] As will be shown below, the rules of evolution, as she calls them, are now considered to be far more complex than she describes. Mitchell's version of the rules reflects neo-Darwinian evolutionary principles of the mid-twentieth century and does not include recent revisions and additions.

Mitchell goes so far as to suggest that evolutionary computation has a "largely unexplored but potentially interesting side," which is that "by explicitly modeling evolution as a computer program, we explicitly cast evolution as a computational process."[22] Just a few years after she suggested this, historians of science Lily Kay, in *Who Wrote the Book of Life? A History of the Genetic Code* (2000), and David Depew, in his essay recounting how organisms came to be seen as "digital printouts," traced the interesting historical development of how biology came to be viewed as computational.[23] After physicist Erwin Schrödinger's assertion in 1944 of a "code-script" at the root of life, and James Watson and Francis Crick's casting of DNA as an information code in 1953, work in genetics throughout the ensuing two decades focused on "decoding 'the code of codes.'"[24] Scientists worked hard to ascertain which nucleotide sequences make which proteins, as viewed under the rubric of Crick's "Central Dogma of Molecular Biology," first pronounced in 1958.[25] The central dogma emphasized that "information" from the "code" only flows one way: from DNA to RNA to proteins. Similar to information theory, communication down a line, and computer programming, the "code" was conceived of as a linear sequence of letters: A, C, T, U, and G. "They are, of course, not letters at all," Depew writes, "any more than amino acids are words or proteins sentences. They are merely chemicals with a certain specificities [*sic*] for bonding with other chemicals."[26]

Even at this point, however, Depew notes that the use of information theory as a framework for "unraveling the DNA–RNA–protein relationship" was not the same as the "notion that an organism is a readout from something like a computer program," for during the 1960s and 1970s, "computers and computer programs were not yet widely known."[27] He credits the shift to fully considering organisms using a "digital tropology"—seeing them as "digital printouts" from a "genetic program"—to stem from the influence of a few specific publications in the 1980s and 1990s. These are Richard Dawkins's *The Blind Watchmaker* (1986) and *Climbing Mount Improbable* (1998), and Daniel Dennett's *Darwin's Dangerous Idea* (1995), which posits an "algorithmic" view of natural selection. "In these works the assimilation of genetic programs to computer programs—and in particular to so-called genetic algorithms that mimic the sheep-and-goats process of natural selection, in which only adapted combinations of genes are allowed to 'reproduce,'" he writes, "is presented as a way of adumbrating, protecting, and even empirically confirming [Dawkins's] selfish gene hypothesis, which was first put forward without any analogy to computational software or hardware."[28]

Thus, Dawkins's and Dennett's interpretations of biological evolution and genes around the turn of the twenty-first century came to be tinged by evolutionary computational approaches, specifically that of genetic algorithms, in which "inefficient combinations are programmatically weeded out by a recursive decision procedure."[29] Depew notes the resonance of these interpretations of genes, evolution, and natural selection with biologically deterministic "quasi-eugenic" approaches prior to the war.[30] And while genetic algorithms are structured on mid-twentieth-century neo-Darwinian principles, they do not reflect the statistical considerations of variability proffered by population genetics from that time. Depew, whose specialty is the history of changing views of Darwinism, emphatically concludes, "As widespread as digital imagery of the gene now is among both expert and popular audiences, it is nonetheless a markedly imprecise representation of the relationship between genes and traits. Even if we insist on seeing the relationship between nucleic acids and protein as a coded and programmed one," he asserts, "still *there is no 'machine language'—no binary system of zeros and ones—lurking beneath the correlation between the base pairs of nucleic acids and proteins.*"[31]

After Depew's essay from 2003, another historian of science, Hallam Stevens, picked up the story of the transference of ideas from computation to biology where Depew left it. Over the next decade, biological organisms came to be viewed as comprising numerous networks: "gene regulatory networks, protein interaction networks, cell-signaling networks, metabolic networks, and ecological networks."[32] Stevens identifies a network as being made of up "objects" viewed as "nodes," connected to one another by "edges," combined into a "web." He points to the widespread growth across domains of digital technologies, which are linked in networks, as the source of this new conceptual mode of seeing relationships, including relationships between "objects" in biological organisms. Because biological networks "do not consist of stable physical links between fixed entities," because their links are always changing, and because the "objects that are supposed to be connected are not always the same objects," he asserts that "the idea of a 'biological network' is therefore a kind of fiction."[33] Yet, this fictional mode of seeing and thinking about biological processes undoubtedly contributes to a general view of biological organisms as computational entities. As Depew writes, "This rhetoric celebrates the cyborgian notion that there is no distinction in principle between organisms and machines that can be programmed to perform various tasks."[34] Additionally, within the field of engineering synthetic biology (hereafter engineering synbio), the consideration of genes as "standard biological parts" arranged into "circuits" (conceived as being like both electronic and digital circuits), and from circuits into "devices," further reinforces this mode of thought. That much biological research is now done sitting at computers rather than in experimental laboratories only heightens this perception.[35] When biology and evolution are viewed from this perspective, the current pursuit by some of nano-bio-info-cogno (aka NBIC) convergence seemingly gains plausibility simply through pervasive metaphorical overlaps between, in this case, biology and computation.

Undoubtedly, prominent discourses in generative architecture build on these overlapping metaphors between biology and evolutionary computation, in contrast to their actual disjunctions. One of the founding texts of generative architecture, John Frazer's *An Evolutionary Architecture* (1995), asserts, "Our description of an architectural concept in coded form is analogous to the genetic code-script of nature."[36] Alternately, Alberto Estévez, in his essay "Biomorphic Architecture," states his aim to fuse "cybernetic–digital resources with genetics, to continuously join the zeros and ones from the architectural drawing with those from the robotized manipulation of DNA, in order to organize the necessary genetic information that governs a habitable living being's natural growth."[37] Frazer clearly recognizes that his approach to architecture relies on a biological analogy, but Estévez believes in a more literal correlation. Even so, statements like theirs stem from a view of biological processes heavily influenced by methods of evolutionary computation, as Depew shows.

In the interdisciplinary cross-borrowing between biology, computer science, and generative architecture—despite the aforementioned shortcomings lost in translation between biology and computation—generative architecture still lags furthest behind in adapting its theories and techniques to current ideas of biological development and evolution. As will be discussed below in the summaries of the three major modes of evolutionary theory and programming since the mid-twentieth century, computer scientists have modeled new, roughly analogical approaches to current understandings of evolutionary developmental biology and epigenetics. These are referred to as computational development or evolutionary developmental systems, and epigenetic algorithms. Yet, in the field of generative architecture, only Weinstock and Menges promote adapting basic neo-Darwinian approaches into scripting for generative architecture with the aim of integrating some features of individual "embryonic development" in tandem with population evolution.[38] Apart from this, however, the scientific biological sources that Menges cites remain squarely in mid-twentieth-century neo-Darwinism and his approach is heavily neo-Darwinian, similar to most other generative architects who publish on uses of evolutionary computation or genetic algorithms.[39] The next three sections, therefore, trace the theoretical shifts with regard to morphogenesis and evolution in biology, computer science, and generative architecture, beginning with adherence to the neo-Darwinian modern synthesis and the central dogma of molecular biology, on which most genetic algorithms are based.

Mid-Twentieth-Century Neo-Darwinian Evolutionary Theories

The term "neo-Darwinism" was created by George Romanes in 1895 to join Darwin's idea of natural selection to Weismann's theory of the separation of "germ" cells from somatic cells (referred to as the Weismann barrier). Darwin himself believed that change occurred gradually through a blending process affected by an organism's actions in its environment. Romanes's term, therefore, distinguished neo-Darwinism of the late nineteenth century as a theory that upheld natural selection while also asserting that germ cells were the seat of heredity, unaffected by an organism's actions or the environment in which an organism lived. Yet, in the 1940s, the term was revived and reinterpreted once again, this time to include knowledge from the previous four decades of research on Mendelian genetics, including ideas from the rise of population genetics in the 1930s. The latter asserted that genetic variation across populations played an important role in evolution overall; it established the population, rather than the individual, as the primary unit for academic evolutionary study since heredity can vary far more between individuals than between populations. Although phenotypes were considered the unit of natural selection, genes were seen as the source for variation and change over time, with changes due to mutations and sexual recombination.

Also referred to as the modern evolutionary synthesis or just the modern synthesis based on the title of Julian Huxley's book *Evolution: The Modern Synthesis* (1942), neo-Darwinism became the reigning evolutionary theory for the duration of the twentieth century.[40] Historians of science Depew and Bruce Weber, in their masterful book *Darwinism Evolving* (1995), describe the modern synthesis as a synthesis of a few different sorts. It not only brought together the ideas mentioned above (Darwin + Weismann + Mendel + population genetics), but also synthesized ideas from different fields of biology, including genetics, morphology, and paleontology, among others. It worked to reconcile microevolution—evolution on the scale of genetic change—with macroevolution—evolution on the scale visible in the paleontological record. Depew and Weber describe the modern synthesis as "more like a treaty than a theory," for it was intended to define acceptable research areas in evolutionary biology by excluding contrary voices whose opinions challenged aspects of the synthesis.[41]

Watson and Crick's publication of the structure of DNA in 1953 kick-started the field of molecular biology in earnest. Crick's assertion in the late 1950s of the central dogma of molecular biology played an influential role in establishing the kinds of questions to be asked, and it quickly became an integral feature in neo-Darwinian thought. The ensuing research focused almost exclusively on seemingly linear molecular processes, with many scientists turning a blind eye to the complexity of cellular interactions.[42] The first task was deciphering which sequences make which proteins, with the twenty amino acids produced by sequences referred to as codons becoming known by 1965.[43] It had been presumed from the work of George Beadle and Edward Tatum published in 1941 that one gene made one enzyme. This idea shifted in the 1950s to one gene, one protein—since enzymes are only one type of protein—and then to one gene, one polypeptide—since some proteins consist of multiple polypeptides and it was learned that a gene could encode a single polypeptide.[44]

These phrases followed an earlier reductionist assumption prominent in eugenics that one gene makes one trait. While this may be true for a simple trait such as eye color, of which there are few, it is certainly not true for most other complex traits. Ongoing research focused almost exclusively on the sequences known to code for polypeptides and proteins, those referred to as "genes," with the rest of the DNA in the genome considered inconsequential and named "junk DNA" as early as 1960.[45] During the 1970s and 1980s, challenges to the central dogma were voiced from respected scientists, but they were largely considered anomalies rather than revealing fundamental theoretical problems. These eventually culminated in a reconfiguration of evolutionary theory under the influence of epigenetics in the late twentieth century. Yet, for the most part, the gene-centered reductionism of the central dogma was reinforced further by the writings of evolutionary biologist Richard Dawkins. His "selfish gene theory" in the late 1970s and 1980s all but shifted the unit of natural selection to the gene, with the phenotype viewed primarily as just a carrier that exists for the duplication and propagation of genes.[46]

Thus, when computer scientists were first inventing evolutionary computation including genetic algorithms in the 1960s, they did so within the context of neo-Darwinian evolutionary theory.[47] Dawkins's emphasis on genetic reductionism simply tightened the fit with the version of evolution implemented in genetic algorithms, which Mitchell considers to have been created "in the spirit of analogy with real biology."[48] In her summary of the biological terminology borrowed by this branch of computation, she offers a quick summary of neo-Darwinian concepts, which is useful not only because computer scientists saw neo-Darwinism this way but also because they reflect broader popular understandings of evolutionary theory. "All living organisms consist of cells, and each cell contains the same set of one or more *chromosomes*—strings of DNA—that serve as a 'blueprint' for the organism," she begins. "A chromosome can be conceptually divided into *genes*—functional blocks of DNA, each of which encodes a particular protein."[49] Note the focus only on what is considered "functional" DNA, in contrast to "junk DNA" which is completely omitted, just as it largely was in twentieth-century molecular biology; note also the assertion that each gene codes for one particular protein. This oversimplification is then further oversimplified: "Very roughly, one can think of a gene as encoding a *trait,* such as eye color. The different possible 'settings' for a trait (e.g., blue, brown, hazel) are called *alleles,*" whose statistical variance in populations was being analyzed by population geneticists. "Each gene is located at a particular *locus* (position) on the chromosome," she asserts, noting that "many organisms have multiple chromosomes in each cell. The complete collection of genetic material (all chromosomes taken together) is called the organism's *genome.*"[50] Note again that since she earlier defined a chromosome as being divided conceptually into genes without "junk DNA," that this definition of the genome can be read as only consisting of "genes" that make up chromosomes. In fact, this was the assumption of the Human Genome Project (HGP) at the end of the twentieth century, which was conceived of and implemented under the neo-Darwinian framework. The Human Genome Project only decoded 1.2 percent of the full genetic material on our twenty-three pairs of chromosomes, ignoring the other 98.8 percent, yet its name specifies this tiny portion as "the" human "genome."

Many of these statements, and more to follow, now read more as faulty assumptions owing to their having been overturned or seriously revised by scientific research in the last couple of decades. It is important to state them here since this is the fundamental biological theory that genetic algorithms reflect, which in turn are broadcast by many generative architects. Mitchell describes the *genotype* as "the particular set of genes contained in a genome" (again, ignoring everything but genes), stating that "the genotype gives rise, under fetal and later development, to the organism's *phenotype*—its physical and mental characteristics, such as eye color, height, brain size, and intelligence."[51] By creating this list, starting with eye color (which was previously used in her explanation to define a trait), all entities in the list by implication read as if they are traits determined by genes, since the genotype gives rise to them, without any environmental interaction or sociocultural factors being mentioned. She notes that organisms with paired chromosomes (usually owing to sexual reproduction) are referred to as *"diploid,"* while those "whose chromosomes are unpaired are called *haploid*."[52] *Recombination* (or *crossover*) occurs in sexual reproduction for diploid organisms, and this plus *mutation* offer the two sources of genetic variation between generations. Her definition of mutation states that "single nucleotides (elementary bits of DNA) are changed from parent to offspring, the changes often resulting from copying errors." Finally, "the *fitness* of an organism is typically defined as the probability that the organism will live to reproduce *(viability)* or as a function of the number of offspring the organism has *(fertility)*."[53] Note that it is only within the arena of determining fitness that the environment has any role in this conception of evolution, although Mitchell does not specifically mention the environment as a factor in natural selection so strong is her focus on gene centrism. It is also far more difficult to include environmental factors in computational processes, as this demands that "the environment" be reduced to a few qualities that are numerically quantifiable and from which data are continually gleaned.

After explaining the biological terminology, Mitchell summarizes how these terms (the ones she italicizes) are integrated into the structure of genetic algorithms. "The term *chromosome* typically refers to a candidate solution to a problem, often encoded as a bit string. The 'genes' are either single bits or short blocks of adjacent bits that encode a particular element of a candidate solution," she writes, offering as an example "in the context of multiparameter function optimization the bits encoding a particular parameter might be considered to be a gene." Since most genetic algorithms "employ haploid individuals" and therefore computationally simplify the process by omitting sexual reproduction and just crossing over between single chromosomes, variation comes through crossover combined with mutation: "Mutation consists of flipping the bit at a randomly chosen locus (or, for larger alphabets,

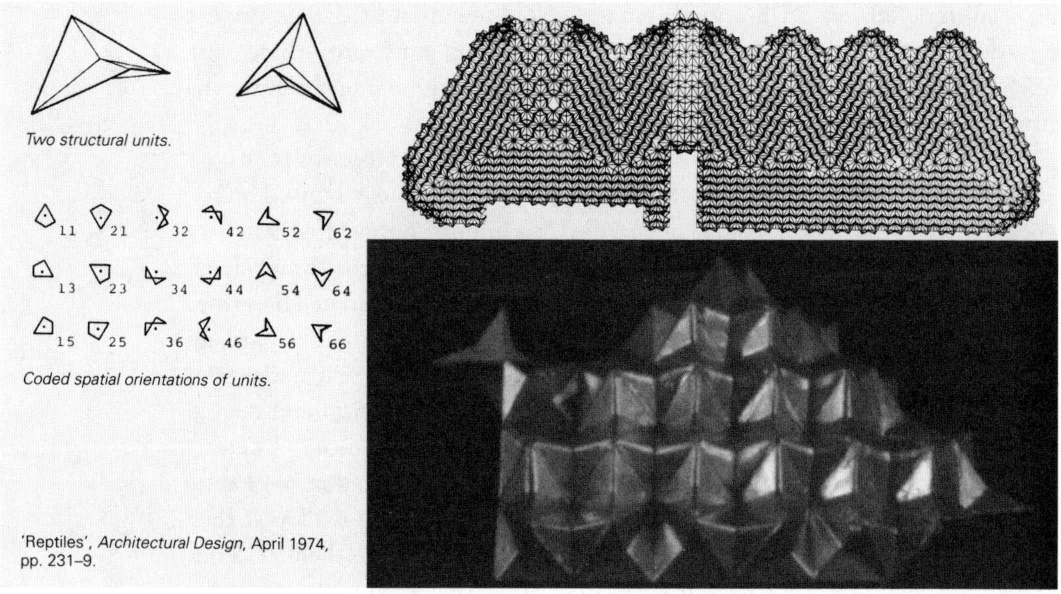

FIGURE 3.2. Reptile structural system computer drawings and sculpture, by John Frazer, 1974. Beginning with computationally described "seeds" that fit together in multiple ways to create structural systems, Frazer then designed an undulating roof structure from these seeds that he printed out two-dimensionally and built by hand three-dimensionally.

replacing the symbol at a randomly chosen locus with a randomly chosen new symbol)." These algorithms most often work only with genotypes; "often there is no notion of 'phenotype' in the context of GAs, although more recently," she notes, "many workers have experimented with GAs in which there is both a genotypic level and a phenotypic level (e.g., the bit-string encoding of a neural network and the neural network itself)."[54] The omission of the phenotype could only be seen as *almost* justifiable if the algorithm is based on Dawkins's extreme genetic reductionism, where the phenotype really only matters to sustain the genotype. It is certainly an omission that Kumar and Bentley realize would qualify for an "ear bashing" from a developmental biologist, since it omits the developmental stage completely and reduces an organism to only a string of information. This is obviously the ultimate "digital tropology," as Depew calls it.[55]

Architects' descriptions of genetic algorithms vary little from what Mitchell describes, although some of their terminology offers a clearer description of how genetic algorithms often function eugenically. John Frazer was arguably the first to use adaptive learning processes to find digital design solutions, as well as the first in 1968 to digitally print a coded two-dimensional architectural rendering of a roof structural design; his three-dimensional sculptural model had to be made by hand (Figure 3.2).[56] He "evolved" column designs beginning in 1973 using Donald Michie's OXO method, but after discovering Holland's genetic algorithms he began using these techniques in the late 1980s.[57] His important publication *An Evolutionary Architecture* from 1995 de-

FIGURE 3.3. Interior girders at Yokohama Port Terminal, Yokohama, Japan. Building designed by Foreign Office Architects (Farshid Moussavi and Alejandro Zaera-Polo), 1995–2002. Photograph by blanco teko (CC by NC 2.0). The unique girder structure of the ceiling, covered with panels here, was likely "evolved" using genetic algorithms.

scribes the technique of GAs, as well as a technique on evolving "biomorphs" put forward by Dawkins in *The Blind Watchmaker.*[58] The same year, Foreign Office Architects (FOA, consisting of Farshid Moussavi and Alejandro Zaera-Polo) designed a building that won the famous competition for the Yokohama Port Terminal in Japan. Over the next seven years as it was completed, it likely became the first building constructed integrating features designed using genetic algorithms (Figure 3.3). Possibly for this reason, the Museum of Modern Art in New York acquired documentation of the project for their permanent collection.[59]

FOA's use of genetic algorithms as part of their design process is strongly hinted at by the title of the 2003 exhibition featuring their work at the Institute of Contemporary Art (ICA) in London, *Foreign Office Architects: Breeding Architecture.* This exhibition was accompanied by a book, *Phylogenesis: FOA's Ark,* that further reinforces the predominant neo-Darwinian evolutionary theme. In their opening essay to the book, Moussavi and Zaera-Polo describe their practice as a "phylogenetic process in which seeds proliferate in time across different environments, generating differentiated but consistent

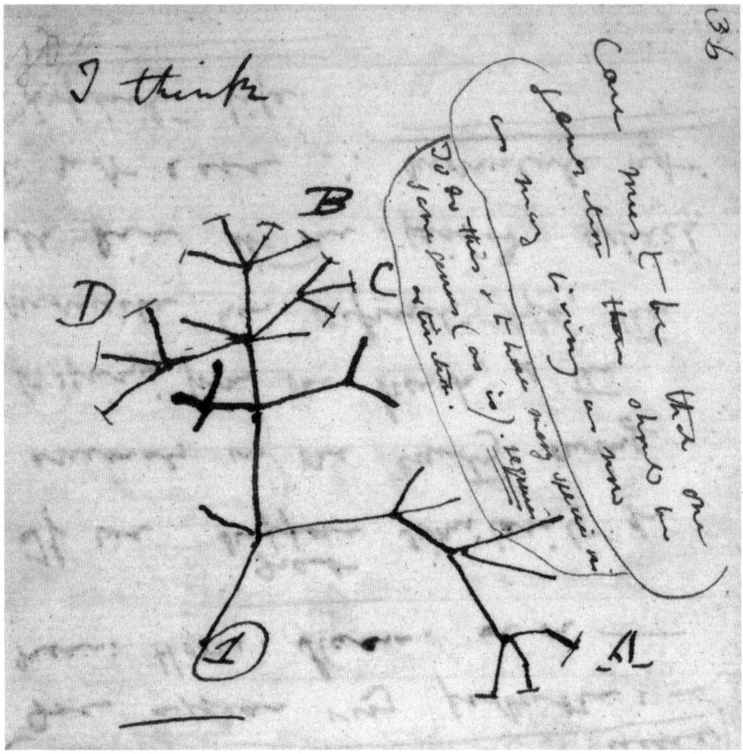

FIGURE 3.4. Sketch of the tree of life, by Charles Darwin from his notebooks, 1837. Tree_of_Life.tif (DAR.121, p. 36), reproduced by kind permission of the Syndics of Cambridge University Library. The tree has one trunk that branches successively outward; this structure is built on only vertical generational hereditary transmission (in contrast to the evolutionary web or net, in Plate 5, which includes horizontal gene transfer).

organisms." They create a classification scheme for analyzing the "families" and "species" of buildings created by their practice's "genetic potentials," also described as "a DNA of our practice."[60] From this classification system, they construct a phylogenetic tree (Plate 3) that resembles Darwin's famous evolutionary tree sketch from 1857, of which a more formal version appeared as the sole image in *On the Origin of Species* (1859) (Figure 3.4). They describe how stylistic and functional aspects "compete" against one another to result in "improved" designs: "This is not a simple bottom-up generation; it also requires a certain consistency that operates top-down from a practice's genetic potentials. Just as with horses and wines, there is a process in which successful traits are selected through experimentation and evolved by registering the results."[61] "Top-down" intervention in breeding to select particular traits for design improvements is otherwise known as eugenics, despite the fact that some restrict usage of this term to refer only to humans, not to plants and animals.

Just a few months after the *Breeding Architecture* exhibition closed at the ICA, Weinstock published his first description of genetic algorithms for use in "morphogenetic" architectural design. In his 2004 article "Morphogenesis and the Mathematics of Emergence," he described Holland's technique of designing adaptive processes in artificial systems using genetic algorithms. "Genetic algorithms initiate and maintain a population of computational individuals, each of which has a genotype and a phenotype," he explains, showing already a difference from Mitchell's description in 1996 that mentioned only the beginnings of experimentation with having phenotypes. Through simulated sexual reproduction and crossover plus mutation, "varied offspring are generated until they fill the population. All parents are discarded, and the process is iterated for as many generations as are required to produce a population that has among it a range of suitable individuals to satisfy the fitness criteria."[62] In a 2010 publication he added to this description, retroactively imposing neo-Darwinian principles into Darwin's own mind. Weinstock mistakenly asserts, "In Darwin's view variations are random, small modifications or changes in the organism that occur naturally in reproduction through the generations. Random variation produces the raw material of variant forms, and natural selection acts as the force that chooses the forms that survive."[63] He elaborates, again referring to neo-Darwinism (instead of Darwin's own Lamarckian-influenced views): "Changes arise in the genome by mutation, often as 'copy errors' during transcription, when the sequence may be shuffled or some modules repeated by mutation." Finally, he mentions implementation of "the kill strategy," which decides "how many if any of the parent individuals survive into the next generation, and how many individuals are bred from."[64] Weinstock's explicit mention of discarding and killing parent individuals is unique; usually descriptions of GAs find ways around so clearly describing this integral yet metaphorically and historically unsettling part of the process.

Consider these two examples. The first is an online tutorial website about genetic algorithms, created in 1998 and maintained by computer scientist Marek Obitko, that has been referenced by graduate students in David Benjamin's Columbia University Graduate School of Architecture, Planning, and Preservation studios.[65] While Obitko repeats Mitchell's description of the biological background almost verbatim without citing her, nowhere does he mention killing. He simply emphasizes selection of the fittest using the principles of "elitism," a term with clear eugenic resonance.[66] Similarly, Keith Besserud and Josh Ingram (previously Joshua Cotten), of BlackBox SOM, presented a paper titled "Architectural Genomics" at the Association of Computer Aided Design in Architecture (ACADIA) conference in 2008. In their description of a genetic algorithm for the selection portion, they simply state, "Test the fitness of the designs that are generated from each genome" against the established "fitness function" parameters. Then, "identify the top performers; these will become the selection pool for the next generation."[67]

Besserud and Ingram's talk focused on a hypothetical architectural example that used the algorithm to find "the optimal shape" for a "300-meter tower (subject to a handful of geometric constraints) in order to maximize incident solar radiation on the skin of the building" (Figure 3.5): "The working assumption was that this form would best suit the deployment of photovoltaic panels to collect solar radiation."[68] In general, features that architects want to "optimize" include "construction cost, structural efficiency, carbon footprint, daylighting quality, acoustic quality, programmatic compliance, view quality, etc. Basically any parameter that exerts an influence on the execution of the design intent is eligible to become the metric of the fitness function," they

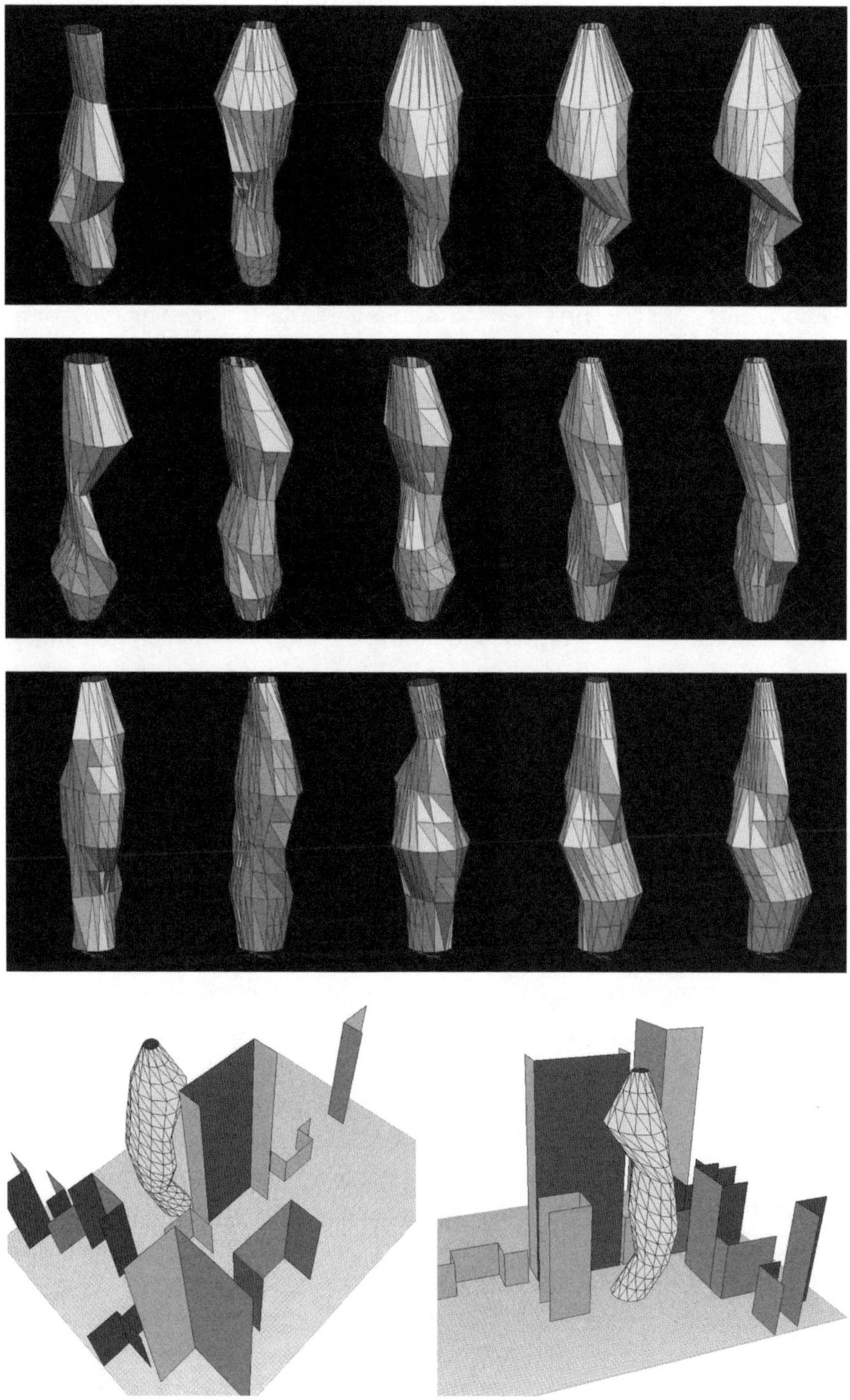

FIGURE 3.5. Architectural genomics, by Keith Besserud and Joshua Ingram (formerly Joshua Cotten), ACADIA conference proceedings, 2008. The hypothetical "Evolution of Tower Form with No Adjacent Context" shows five solutions across generations (iterative cycles) evolved by the computer, as produced in three different runs of the algorithm, presented to the architects to select. "Views of the Tower . . . Positioned within Context" shows the three-hundred-foot-tall tower design virtually placed in relation to adjacent structures. The designs were optimized to maximize "incident solar radiation on the skin of the building" to suit the "deployment of photovoltaic panels to collect solar radiation."

write, so long as it is numerically quantifiable and automatable into the program. When two criteria for optimization conflict with one another in a multi-objective optimization problem, one way they resolve the dilemma is by using "penalty functions" whereby particular fitness scores are marked down by how poorly they meet the other criteria.[69] They also mention the pragmatic aspect of computation time for consideration of how one establishes a fitness function, for "the speed of the fitness function is the single most influential factor in the efficiency of the GA," they state. "It is not uncommon for a GA to have to run tens of thousands of iterations to reach convergence. Even if it takes just a few seconds to complete a simulation and analysis iteration, the total optimization process could take many days to reach convergence."[70]

As the images of their hypothetical example reveal, for architectural GAs a morphological phenotype is required for visual evaluation by the designer. Additionally, as will become more apparent in the following section on evo-devo, environmental features are also important to integrate into the algorithmic process as a context within which building parameters can be optimized through fitness assessment. This is so not only for aesthetic reasons, which factor heavily into design, but also for functional reasons, as surrounding buildings for a skyscraper may have glass surfaces that reflect light and heat, thereby affecting calculations for the structure being designed.[71] Despite the necessity of having a phenotype and including some features of the environment, architectural GAs are still heavily gene-centric. Visual phenotypes simply exist as digital visualizations of their underlying genetic code, which is designed at the outset to include various morphological and behavioral features. In other words, their structure reflects an underlying genetic determinism. This coding basically follows the "one gene, one trait" framework despite this rarely being the case biologically. Such genetic reductionism permits designers and scientists to minimize the true biological complexity of organisms in order to make "design" seem achievable.

That GAs are more eugenic than neo-Darwinian is revealed by a few other factors. First, in mid-century neo-Darwinism, population genetics valued genetic diversity as a variability that protects a population in the context of environmental change. But in GAs, fitness criteria and discarding or killing of parent individuals moves potential diversity ever closer to the fitness criteria. In other words, "genes" dubbed unsuccessful are omitted rather than preserved. This is akin to "dysgenics," the negative counterpart of eugenics historically that strove to remove "bad genes" from the population through policies of reproductive sterilization. Furthermore, perhaps through the influence of repeated use of methods of evolutionary computation, the meaning of natural selection as Darwin intended begins to get lost. GAs carry a teleology, goals toward which their evolution aims that are set by the designer; Darwinian evolution does not. This replacement of Darwinian natural selection with eugenic "rational selection" is apparent in Weinstock's thinking. He confusingly writes, "Darwin argued that just as humans breed living organisms by unnatural selection, organizing systematic changes in them, so wild organisms themselves are changed by natural selection." His use of "just as" and "so" equate human rational selection with natural selection. Furthermore, he believes that this process in nature tends toward ever-greater success, the "eu" part of eugenics: "Successful organisms will survive the fierce competition and have greater breeding success and, in turn, their offspring will have greater reproductive success," he states.[72] Certainly there is no guarantee of this in nature. Computer scientists Eiben and Smith at least separate the two types of selection, even while embracing the eugenic version. "From a historical perspective," they write, "humans have had two roles in evolution. Just like any other species, humans are the product of, and are subject to, evolution. But for millennia . . . people have also actively influenced the course of evolution in other species—by choosing which plants or animals should survive or mate." Without being clear whether they are talking about biology or computers, they declare, "Together with the increased understanding of the genetic mechanisms behind evolution, this brought about the opportunity to become active masters of evolutionary processes that are fully designed and executed by human experimenters 'from above.'"[73] Note that they do not hide the "top-down" approach of GAs behind the "bottom-up" rhetoric of self-organization, unlike generative architects who imply that "bottom-up" self-organization is at work in methods of evolutionary computation that generate architectural designs.

These two examples clearly reveal the tendency of gene-centric neo-Darwinism toward what Depew calls "quasi-eugenics." I would go further and simply state that GAs should be renamed eugenic algorithms (EuAs). At least in the computational realm, this would make their eugenic assumptions clear. Yet in the realm of biology, owing to the prevalence of digital tropology, its implications are murkier while tending in the same direction, as engineering synbio demonstrates. As Depew states, digital tropology of living organisms "gives the impression that the evolutionary process is more orderly, more programmatic, more oriented towards adaptive efficiency than the main line of Darwinism has hitherto assumed. This effect is rhetorically enforced by projection of the language of engineering design onto the statistical process of natural process." Accordingly, "Dennett even speaks of natural selection as a 'designer.'"[74] When evolution is designed, it becomes eugenics, since we tend to design for "what seems to us" improvement. I assert this in *Eugenic Design,* quoting Charles Davenport, the father of American eugenics, from 1930: "When we understand the processes directing contemporary evolution we will be in a position to work actively toward the acceleration of these processes and especially to direct them in what seems to us the best way."[75]

Within neo-Darwinian molecular biology and in GAs, owing to a number of factors, morphogenesis did not play a major role in the dominant research agenda or model of evolution. In part this was due to gene-centrism, the emphasis on random mutation and sexual selection as the primary avenues of change, the influence of the central dogma and its one-way flow of information and action that outlawed Lamarckian environmental influences on heredity, and the minimization of the phenotype under followers of Dawkins. Within developmental biology, of course, the study of morphogenesis continued, but evolutionary theorists and computer scientists were not paying close attention to that arena as an influence on their considerations.[76] Some realizations from scientific experiments that later, in hindsight, have been interpreted as potential challenges to the central dogma, were at the time of their discovery interpreted and accommodated within the dogma's framework. For example, in the late 1950s, Frenchmen François Jacob and Jacques Monod discovered that the bacteria *E. coli* changed its genetic response to producing certain proteins depending on whether a food source was present in the environment. This could be seen as environment-triggered gene action with information flow moving in the wrong direction, from the environment to DNA rather than the other way around. Jacob and Monod, however, theorized the existence of "regulatory genes"—genes that function as a switch to turn on or off another gene that produces a protein. The regulatory gene is "off" so long as a "repressor protein" is bound to it, but in the face of particular environments, that repressor protein may release itself from the regulatory gene, in effect turning the gene "on," which then triggers the protein-producing gene. Historian of science Evelyn Fox Keller writes that Jacob and Monod's theory maintained the central dogma in the face of this challenge, by conceiving of the genome still as made up only of "genes" that matter—some of which happened to be "structural (i.e., responsible for the production of a protein that performs a structural role in the cell), while others did the work of regulating the structural genes. In this way, the Central Dogma held, with genetic information still located in gene sequences, and the study of genetics still the study of genes."[77]

Other evidence contrary to the dogma accrued as mounting challenges. For one, Barbara McClintock had discovered "jumping genes," referred to now as transposable DNA, which are DNA sequences that move "from one area of the chromosome to another and could even reposition themselves on another chromosome." Although she discovered this in the late 1940s, she was so criticized that she stopped work on this topic in the early 1950s and only was validated twenty years later when other scientists verified her research. She received a Nobel Prize for it in 1983. According to Depew and Weber, "The transposition of genes from one site on a chromosome to another is possible because specific enzymes can recognize transposons, can cut or cleave the DNA at an appropriate spot, and then can reinsert the gene(s) that are attached to the transposon at another site on the same or a different chromosome."[78] In other words, genes do not have only one locus, as Mitchell stated: "When this occurs, changes are observed in the phenotype, even though there is no change in the gene itself, and no substitution of an alternative allele."[79] Around the time that McClintock's work was beginning to be recognized, Howard Temin discovered that viruses can penetrate organisms' genomes through the process of reverse transcription. By using an enzyme encoded by their own RNA, they can reverse-transcribe their own RNA into "complementary DNA" (cDNA) that the host organism then integrates into its own genome. This discovery forced Francis Crick, in a rebuttal published in *Nature* (1970), to "clarify" that the central dogma "has been misunderstood" in order to integrate reverse transcription into the dogma.

Results of these experiments and others, along with the development of technologies that could sequence DNA in the 1980s and 1990s when the Human Genome Project began, led to new knowledge of gene sequences and gene actions in many different organisms. Some of these proved to be instrumental in developmental morphogenesis. Furthermore, when the results of the HGP were announced in 2003 revealing that humans only had around thirty thousand genes (remember, only 1.2 percent was decoded) instead of the eighty thousand predicted by Francis Collins, director of the HGP, scientists had to quickly rethink many of their long-standing assumptions about the relationship between biological complexity and genetic complexity. (The estimated number is now around nineteen thousand.)[80] Together, these developments transformed evolutionary theory into a new synthesis that came to be known as evo-devo in 2000, although it took until 2005 and the publication of Sean Carroll's *Endless Forms Most Beautiful: The New Science of Evo Devo* to become popular knowledge.[81] Thus, when John Frazer wrote in 1995 that "there is so far no general developed science of morphology, although the generation of form is fundamental to the creation of natural and all designed artefacts. Science is still searching for a theory of explanation, architecture for a theory of generation," he was correct.[82] However, he would soon have access to a very solid theory for biological form generation that both scientists and architects could begin to explore.

Turn-of-the-Millennium Evo-Devo

Because the major discoveries that led to the theory of evo-devo were genetic rather than epigenetic and came from the study of higher organisms (fruit flies, then mice, frogs, worms, insects, cows, and humans), evo-devo is considered by many scientists to fit within the neo-Darwinian framework as a revised synthesis.[83] In the 1980s, when the first full decoding of the genomes ("genes" only) of many organisms allowed their comparison with one another, scientists were shocked to find major similarities in genetic sequences across very evolutionarily distant organisms.[84] They named this shared sequence the "homeobox," which shortens to *Hox* genes, and named the proteins produced by this region the "homeodomain."[85] Incredibly, these similarities occur in the genes that scientists knew contributed to body plan organization and organismal development.[86] Virtually overnight considering how many decades had passed, morphogenesis reentered the stage of evolutionary drama, and earlier embryological evidence such as that which had led Haeckel to his misguided theory of recapitulation could be seen in a new light.

Centuries of observation of living organisms had revealed a number of physical similarities across phyla. Many animals have homologous parts in different species that are basically the "same structure . . . modified in different ways," for example, the segmented bone structure of human arms, mice forelimbs, bat wings, and dolphin flippers.[87] Other similarities are more general; for example, insects and animals have modular parts repeated in sequence, whether segmented sections of an insect like an ant or repeating vertebrae down the spine of a mammal.[88] Different types of organisms also share symmetry and broken symmetry, with left and right sides or radial segments mirroring each other, say, but front and back sides showing differences.[89] Some of these broken symmetries occur along axes of polarity (much like the axes of the three dimensions); for animals that walk on four legs, these run from head to tail, top to bottom, and from center out to appendages (imagine left to right, like a splayed-out animal).[90] The discovery of genetic similarities suggested that the visual correlations of animal morphology might be traceable to a common root related to morphogenesis. This idea radically departed from previous notions of gradual genetic change over a very long time via random mutation and sexual recombination. Such notions had led scientists to assume that greater biological complexity required the existence of many more genes, such as Collins had predicted for the human genome. As Carroll states, "No biologist had even the foggiest notion that such similarities could exist between genes of such different animals."[91] The discovery of the homeobox made sense out of the otherwise shockingly few numbers of protein-coding genes that genome-decoding projects had revealed different species possess, along with their similarities.

Scientists therefore implemented visualization strategies in order to literally see the processes of gene activation across different cell lines during embryonic development, beginning with the fruit fly but also in other species for comparison. To determine which early cells in embryo formation became later cell lines associated with different parts of the body, they inserted colored dye into early cells and then observed the location of daughter cells carrying that color dye in later development.[92] To follow the activation of the *Hox* genes and the homeodomain—also referred to as the "tool-kit proteins" since the homeobox was viewed as a tool kit shared across species—they used techniques of fluorescent tagging and fluorescent microscopy to create images of developing embryos that reveal which tool-kit proteins are active, when, and where (Plate 4). These methods produced amazing discoveries for they revealed that the order in which *Hox* genes appear in the homeobox sequence is the order in which they are expressed in biological development across most species: "This meant that the depth of similarity between different animals extended not just to the sequence of the genes, but to their organization in clusters and how they were used in embryos. . . . The implications were stunning. Disparate animals were built using not just the same kinds of tools, but indeed, the very same genes!"[93]

Furthermore, like the *lac* operon model whereby a protein binds to or releases from a regulatory gene that then switches on or off another gene, tool-kit proteins appeared in a sequence that "prefigured" subsequent organization

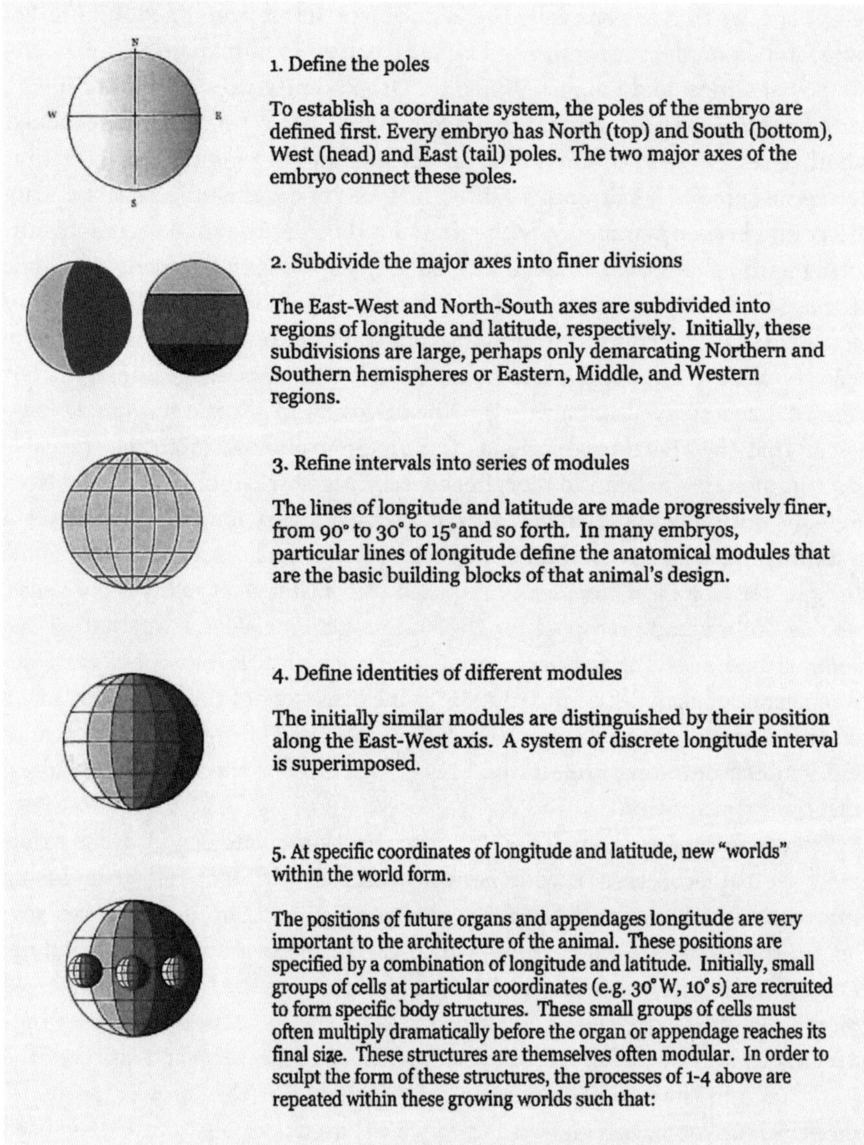

and production of different parts of an organism in development. In other words, *Hox* genes function as regulatory genes for other gene action. Philip Ball describes them as "mere *routers*, like train-line signals, the effects of which depend on precisely when and where in the developmental process they get switched on."[94] All of this enabled scientists to create both "fate maps" of development for particular organisms and an overall general theory of morphogenetic development (Figure 3.6).[95] And similar to how Turing had hypothesized decades earlier that secreted morphogens might be responsible for embryonic symmetry breaking, scientists found that "organizer" cells and "zones of polarizing activity" were responsible for developments at particular

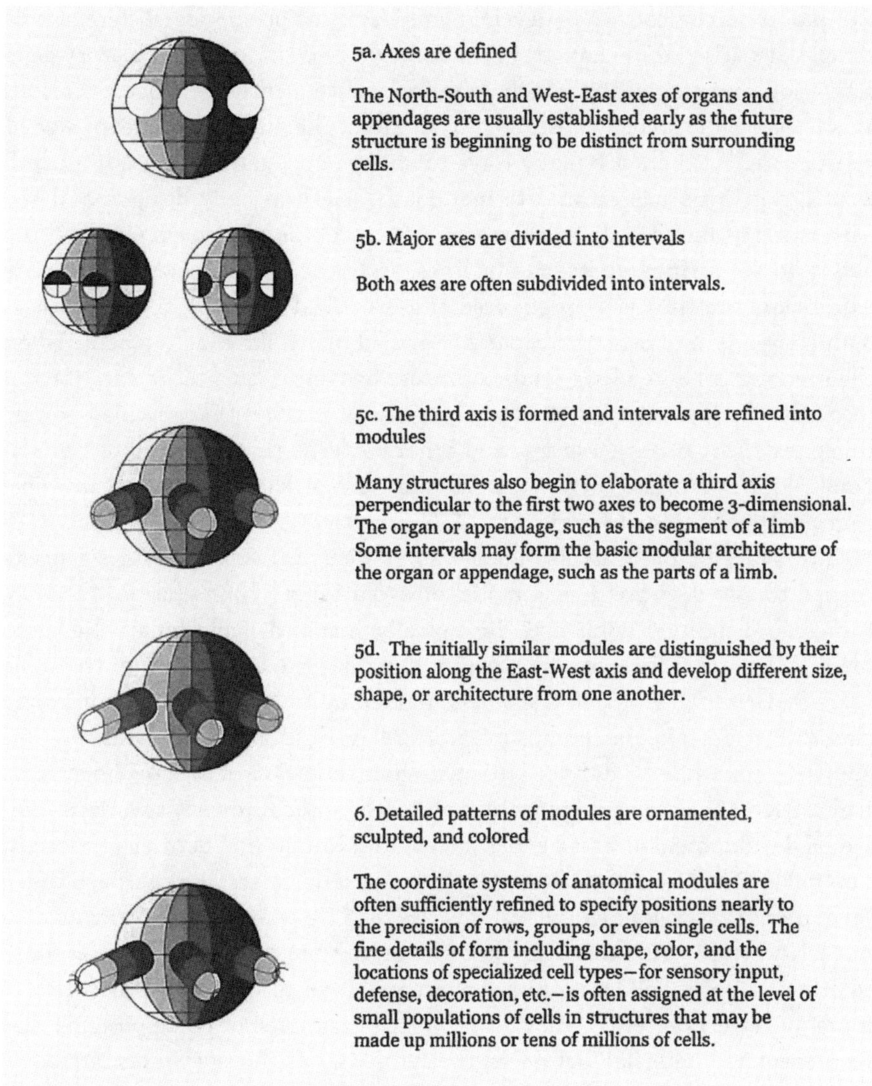

FIGURE 3.6. Diagram of the general logic of embryo geography, from Sean Carroll, *Endless Forms Most Beautiful: The New Science of Evo Devo* (New York: Norton, 2005), 92–93.

locations and stages.[96] For example, the tool-kit protein sonic hedgehog (Shh, based on the humorous naming of a gene) can function as a secreted morphogen that diffuses and triggers gene action at a distance from its source.[97] Further experimentation over the last decade aimed at identifying morphogens has revealed a number of proteins that may function as Turing thought in morphogenesis.[98]

The resulting major change in evolutionary theory shifted the presumed origin of biological complexity away from assumptions of gene mutation and number and onto the role of the homeobox and gene regulation. "The development of form depends upon the turning on and off of genes at different times and places in the course of development," and major species' differences in complexity arise from changes in the location and timing of regulatory gene activation and changes in which genes are subsequently switched on or off. This is especially so for "those genes that affect the number, shape, or size of a structure."[99] "There are many ways to change how genes are used," Carroll writes, and "this has created tremendous variety in body designs and the patterning of individual structures."[100] This revelation has been elating. "The ability to see stripes, spots, bands, lines, and other patterns of tool kit gene expression that precisely prefigured the organization of embryos into segments, organs, and other body parts provided many 'Eureka!' moments when the role of a gene in a long studied process became exquisitely clear," Carroll recounts. "Stripes that foreshadowed segments, patches that revealed powerful zones of organizing activity, and other patterns that marked positions of bones, joints, muscles, organs, limbs, etc.—all of these connected invisible genes to the making of visible forms."[101]

Two years before Carroll's book was published, two computer scientists turned to evo-devo for a new model of evolutionary computation. In 2003, Kumar and Bentley published "Biologically Inspired Evolutionary Development," a longer version of which begins their coedited anthology of the same year, *On Growth, Form, and Computers,* named in honor of D'Arcy Thompson's classic. Evo-devo made Thompson's work relevant in a new way and to a new audience, for while he did not anticipate homeobox genes or morphogens, he had argued that the same physical and mathematical forces at work in individual development affected evolution overall. Kumar and Bentley proposed a new field named "computational development" and created an approach called "evolutionary developmental systems" (EDS). "Development is controlled by our DNA," they write, reflecting knowledge of homeobox genes. "In response to proteins, genes will be expressed or repressed, resulting in the production of more (or fewer) proteins." They acknowledge that some of these proteins may be present as "maternal factors" in the cytoplasm of the egg that is fertilized, but that others are produced by DNA in the developing embryo: "The chain-reaction of activation and suppression both within the cell and within other nearby cells through signaling proteins and cell receptors, causes the complex processes of cellular differentiation, pattern formation, morphogenesis, and growth."[102] In this way, gene regulation triggered by protein signals affects other gene action.

Kumar and Bentley acknowledge some deficiencies in their model in comparison with biological knowledge. For example, they write, "Currently, the EDS's underlying genetic model assumes a 'one gene, one protein' simplification rule (despite biology's ability to construct multiple proteins); this aids in the analysis of resulting genetic regulatory networks. To this end, the activation of a single gene in the EDS results in the transcription of a single protein."[103] Other oversimplifications are not acknowledged, however, such as their statement that "the only function of genes is to specify proteins"; in fact, some genes do not code for proteins but function as regulatory elements.[104]

For example, *Hox* genes are referred to as regulatory or transcription factor genes, although some drop the word "gene" and refer to "cis-regulatory elements," leaving the word "gene" for functional protein-producing regions.[105] This problem of terminology and understanding has compounded since 2003; scientists even more recently are acknowledging that the definition of a gene is very much in question. In 2008 a *New York Times* story by Carl Zimmer, "Now: The Rest of the Genome," opens by narrating that bioinformatician Sonja Prohaska, of the University of Leipzig, tried to not say the word "gene" for a day owing to the need for scientists working in this area to completely rethink its meaning, based on "too many exceptions to the conventional rules for genes."[106]

With reference to the biological accuracy of the EDS model, however, the only reason that variations from or oversimplifications of biology matter depends on for what the model is being used and by whom. If it is being used by biologists in conjunction with computer scientists to complete experiments in silico, then biologists can ascertain whether the model suits their needs and uses. If like GAs, EDS is another general problem-solving tool that opens up new modes of solution—say, ways to evaluate and integrate functional "phenotypic" features in the short or long term in the initial evolution of a solution—then it will likely be adopted as a preferable design strategy. For the purposes of this chapter, however, it matters only that generative architects understand that, like GAs, EDS does not actually mirror biological process, no matter how complicated it is. And compared to GAs, EDS is complicated, but nowhere so much as actual cellular, much less organismal, processes.

The basic design of EDS utilizes three main components: proteins, genes, and cells. Cells offer an isospatial element, allowing proteins to diffuse between neighboring cells in virtual 3-D space (one cell is surrounded by twelve others). Different proteins are generated at certain rates, and decay and diffuse at certain rates, and they are also tagged with levels of strength of interaction and inhibition. This design is roughly analogous to diffusing morphogens or to processes of gene regulation associated with transcription factors, such as in the *lac* operon. Each cell has two genomes, the first of which holds all the information about each protein, and the second of which "describes the architecture of the genome to be used for development." "It describes which proteins are to play a part in the regulation of different genes" and is the primary genome "employed by each cell for development."[107] Each gene in the genome has two parts, a cis-regulatory element that precedes and regulates the gene that follows, and proteins that bind to and release from the cis-regulatory element to trigger gene action. Each cell has a cell membrane that functions as a sensor "in the form of surface receptors able to detect the presence of certain molecules within the environment." "Cells resemble multitasking agents, able to carry out a range of behaviours. For example, cells are able to multiply, differentiate, and die."[108] Cells are tracked as "current" or "new," with a heavy infusion of proteins provided to new cells. Around all these "developmental" aspects of their program is wrapped an "evolutionary" GA that "represents the driving force of the system." It provides "genotypes for development," tasks or functions against which genotypes are measured for success or failure, and a way to measure the fitness also of "individuals."[109] EDS is only one approach to computational development, as is shown by the essays in Kumar and Bentley's anthology *On Growth, Form, and Computers,* which combines writings by development and evolutionary biologists alongside those by computer scientists.

The usefulness of EDS to generative architecture is not readily apparent. In 2010, when Weinstock described his own approach to integrating a developmental factor into GAs as a means to add an aspect of evo-devo to his basic neo-Darwinian method in computational architectural morphogenesis, he was possibly not aware of Kumar and Bentley's work or else could not see its relevance to architecture. "The use of evolutionary algorithms has been quite limited in architectural design, and algorithms that combine both growth (embryological developments) and evolution (operating on the genome) over multiple generations have not yet been successfully produced," he writes.[110] Weinstock's method focuses on including a homeobox into a GA, where the homeobox genes act "on the axes and subdivisions of the 'bodyplan'" in a mode very similar to the general theory of morphogenesis mapped out by Sean Carroll in *Endless Forms Most Beautiful* (Figure 3.6).[111] "The earlier that 'mutation' or changes to the regulatory set are applied in the growth sequence," Weinstock explains, "the greater the effect is on the completed or adult form. Random mutation applied to the homeobox produces changes in the number, size, and shape of each of the subdivisions of the 'bodyplan.'"[112] By altering the amount of mutation "in different segments of individual form" and "by constraining the differentiation of axial growth across the population," he writes, "very significant differences in populations and individuals are produced."[113] He induces "environmental pressures" onto populations through applying, for example, "constraints on the total amount of surface 'material' available for the whole generation. The interaction of environmental constraints and population strategies are also amplified or inhibited by the kill strategy."[114]

Apart from Weinstock, Menges and Sprecher are two of the very few architects who publish references to evo-devo when describing their evolutionary computational approaches.[115] Menges finds that "the underlying principles of morphogenesis present relevant concepts for the development of generative design." This includes both the "ontogenetic aspects" and the phylogenetic ones, which are related because of the long-term conservation of the homeobox across species. Together, development plus evolution "provide a conceptual framework for an understanding of computational design as variable processes of algorithmic development and formation, whereby adaptation is driven by the interaction with internal and external influences."[116] Menges explicitly mentions the role of the external environment as a factor in architectural natural selection, including such environmental qualities as gravity and load, "climatic factors like solar radiation, wind, and natural light," thermal loading, cross-ventilation, amount of outdoor covered space, and connectivity between spaces, considered in relation to "overall build volume and floor area."[117]

This suits two student projects he discusses, which are case studies exploring the role of evolutionary computation in architecture at different scales. The first addresses the design of "spatial envelope morphologies" for a building in which form and energy performance due to climate and site are linked, and the second uses evolutionary computation to design "urban block morphologies" to lower overall energy use as considered for the interaction between a number of structural units on the block, not just one building. Processes involved the creation of different "evolutionary operators" in the algorithm, including: a "ranking operator" to determine "an individual's overall fitness"; a "selection operator" to determine the "preferred individuals for reproduction and creation of offspring for the next generation"; an "intermediate recombination operator" that "allows offspring variables"; and an "embryology operator." "The embryology operator initiates the growth of individuals through a series of subdivisions and the assignment of characteristics to the resulting volumes based on five sets of genes. The embryology operator developed for this project requires a special chromosome order of the gene sequence controlling the spatial subdivision"; it functions similar to the homeobox.[118]

As Weinstock's and Menges's methods both demonstrate, evo-devo is adapted for use in architectural evolutionary computation as a means of providing an order of development and greater structural variety only during the design phase of creating a solution. The temporal aspects of organismal development—which, as we shall see shortly, depend very much on environmental inputs—are constricted in generative architecture to an in silico prefinalization realm. Actual buildings are dissimilar from biological organisms in that their "development" in material form is simply a process of construction of a finalized design—the "adult" form selected by the architect as the design. The building itself does not undergo material morphogenesis or development or growth, unless you count a later addition or renovation as "morphogenesis," which would be a trite analogy. Some parts in some buildings can move to alter its shape between pre-set ranges of possibilities, or sensors can affect the behavior of different functional systems. But there is no actual phase remotely analogous in the architectural realm to what occurs in the development of biological organisms. This drives home the point that even the use of a more current evolutionary model—that of evo-devo—on top of earlier neo-Darwinian views brings architecture no closer to actual biology. However, because some architects claim to want to grow living buildings—not just in silico but in actuality, using cells as building material or organisms as buildings—understanding the state of current biological knowledge of cellular processes, organismal development, and evolutionary theory is important for evaluating the likelihood of their visions being realized.

Epigenetics and Evolutionary Theory

This last section briefly introduces many exciting discoveries from microbiology and epigenetics. Together these have prompted some serious rethinking of some of the fundamental assumptions of Darwinian and neo-Darwinian evolutionary theory regardless of the version of "synthesis."[119] Darwin's theory was based on observation of higher eukaryotic organisms—plants and animals—and did not factor in microbiological processes of prokaryotes, including archaea and bacteria. A comprehensive theory of evolution, however, should account for both so that all living organisms are included. This means that evolutionary theory needs to accommodate the capacity of microbial organisms to swap genes with each other through processes of horizontal gene transfer (HGT, also called lateral gene transfer) (Plate 5).[120] While this 2005 diagram from Cold Spring Harbor Laboratory shows the reconfiguration of the microbial phylogenetic tree into a net, scientists are debating the mounting evidence that bacteria also swap genes with plants and animals, and not just through viral vectors.[121] The most obvious example stems from Lynn Margulis and Dorion Sagan's now-accepted theory of endosymbiosis, which posits that eukaryotic cells arose from the engulfing of one prokaryotic cell by another. This resulted in eukaryotic cells that in animals have mitochondria, and in plants, chloroplasts. DNA sequencing has revealed that in fact the DNA inside mitochondria and chloroplasts is bacterial DNA, and in eukaryotic cell functioning, mitochondrial DNA interacts with the DNA in the nucleus.[122] One recent study has found bacterial genomes integrated into human somatic cell genomes in certain tissues, which reveals not only that humans are "multispecies" or "polygenomic" beings—both genetically and in the fact that bacteria constitute 90 percent of the cells in our bodies—but also that despite the widely accepted generalization, every cell in the body does not absolutely carry the exactly same genome.[123] These types of findings from microbiology contributed to articles published in 2009 on the 150th anniversary of *On the Origin of Species* that proclaimed "Darwin Was Wrong" and argued that the idea of the "Tree of Life" demands serious reconfiguration.[124]

While knowledge of microbial gene-swapping processes is causing reconfigurations of the phylogenetic tree, rapid increases in knowledge of environmentally responsive gene regulation via epigenetic processes are transforming our understanding of both development and heredity. The word "epigenetics" was created by Conrad Waddington in 1942 as "the study of processes by which the genotype gives rise to the phenotype."[125] By this definition, morphogenesis and biological development, and what we now understand as significant aspects of the homeobox and evo-devo, clearly fit within Waddington's epigenetics. Yet Michel Morange and others working in the history and research of epigenetics since Waddington recount that over the subsequent decades, interpretations of both genetics and epigenetics have shifted. One key example of this already cited pertains to the discovery by Jacob and Monod of the *lac* operon model and their choice to describe transcription factors that function as a genetic switch as involving "regulatory *genes*" and being part of a "*genetic* program."[126] Because the *lac* operon is triggered by the presence of particular food sources in the surrounding environment, it could also have been interpreted as information flowing from the environment through proteins to

DNA—in other words, as a challenge to the central dogma and as a clear example of epigenetics. Morange shows that just before Jacob's discovery of the operon in 1961, Jacob had worked on a topic related to "mobile genetic elements" (MGEs, or in French, *episomes*). MGEs are McClintock's "jumping genes" (also referred to as gene transposition), which she felt to be "the main mechanism controlling gene expression through differentiation and development," and therefore decidedly epigenetic in Waddington's sense.[127] Morange argues that Jacob therefore could have interpreted the operon as epigenetic, but instead, chose to only characterize the process as a genetic one, hypothesizing the existence of "regulatory genes," when before, only "genes" that made "functional" or "structural" proteins for use in other cellular functions were considered "genes."[128] Morange states that other scientists have interpreted the results of biological experimentation similarly, following Jacob and Monod's precedent, to the extent that "epigenetics, as defined by Waddington," has been made "an integral part of genetics."[129]

Other respected scientists, however, interpret both environmentally triggered gene regulation and gene transposition—which is aided by changes in genome architecture, its structural configuration, and compaction in chromosomes—to be fully epigenetic processes. "Epi-" means "over," "above," or "beyond"—hence, beyond the gene. These processes affect gene function and result in a changed cellular and even a changed organismal phenotype, despite the "fact" that the genes in all cells are generally presumed to be the same. The processes are therefore beyond the gene. Yet, since the definition of a "gene" has become very much in question, what is properly "genetic" versus "epigenetic" is perhaps even murkier than it was before. Scientists today often use this definition for epigenetics: "the study of changes in gene function that are mitotically and/or meiotically heritable and that do not entail a change in DNA sequence."[130]

This definition calls attention to a number of interesting features. First, through its reference to mitosis, which is the process of cell division, it shows that changes in gene function, despite cells having the same DNA sequence, occur in cell differentiation. As stem cells in morphogenesis assume particular identities as skin or liver or muscle tissue cells, these identities are heritable from cell to cell in subsequent cell lines, with the stability of cell identity in the line maintained through epigenetic processes. Second, through its reference to meiosis, which is the process in organisms that sexually reproduce by which "germ" or sex cells are created containing only half the chromosomal material as somatic cells, it shows that changes in gene function are heritable across generations of organisms through sexual reproduction despite there being no change in the DNA of the genome (Plate 6). For example, both flowers in this image are toadflax, *Linaria vulgaris*, but when Carl Linnaeus discovered the second one, he was sure it was a new species, since the second has five petals and radiant symmetry but the first has a different petal formation and bilateral symmetry. Genetic sequencing, however, reveals that both flowers share the same genome. In 1999, scientists learned that the remarkable phenotypic difference is due to a change in methylation on one gene, which they called an epimutation.[131] DNA methylation is an epigenetic process whereby a small methyl group (CH3) attaches to some nucleotide bases of DNA, often cytosine (C, of A, T, C, G). Methylation can be a global pattern across the genome, one that changes during the process of development, and it affects gene regulation, often preventing transcription, by serving as one method of chromatin marking.[132] Chromatin is what makes up chromosomes; in addition to DNA, it includes RNA proteins and other molecules, and in eukaryotes, specific proteins known as histones. Histones help compact chromosomes into tightly wound structures, thereby shaping the architecture of chromosomes, which can be different both in the same cell at different times of its life and in different cell types.[133] These architectural differences affect gene transcription and therefore can and do alter the functioning of cells.

The toadflax example and the second part of the definition of epigenetics should make one pause, even miss a breath, for under classic neo-Darwinism based on Weismannism, the only form of heredity passed from organism to organism resides in the genome. Even with the most recent definition of genome after the close of the Human Genome Project, which can refer to *all* the DNA on the chromosomes, the existence of two visibly different phenotypes arising from the same genotype does not fit our usual understanding of heredity.[134] Eva Jablonka and Marion Lamb write, "Over two hundred years after Linnaeus's specimen was collected, the peloric [radially symmetrical regular variant] form of *Linaria* was still growing in the same region."[135] This shows that epigenetic processes form a second line of heredity that can be very stable. Clearly, at least this second line of heredity, and maybe even two or three others as Jablonka and Lamb argue, exists in addition to that of the genome and plays a role in evolutionary processes.

Some aspects of epigenetic heredity are clearly sensitive to and affected by the environment, even by a mother's behavior in diet and habits during pregnancy and early development of her offspring.[136] One pathbreaking study on this topic was conducted by geneticist Emma Whitelaw and her colleagues in 1999, where they found that a genetically identical strain of mice of the "agouti" type produced differently colored offspring, but the color of the coat of the offspring depended on and followed that of the mother despite *all* the mice having the same genome.[137] The correlation with the mother's coat color stemmed from sharing the same methylation pattern as her, revealing continuity from generation to generation in methylation heredity. Methylation patterns, however, can be affected by stress, chemical exposures, the mother's diet (which can change the color of the coat of her offspring), or her behavior, for example, a lack of maternal care (e.g., mother rats who do not lick their young offspring).[138] Thus, a number of scientists are calling for recognition of a new form of Lamarckism in addition to changing neo-Darwinian ideals, for it is clear that behaviors and environmental effects can produce heritable epigenetic patterns that affect traits in offspring, with these patterns lasting for as few as four generations but sometimes for many more.[139] For this reason, epigenetic mechanisms are viewed as a relatively short-term form of heredity that is responsive to environmental or behavioral changes.

Although modern epigenetics research began in the mid-1970s and picked up in the 1980s, since the Human Genome Project an explosion of research on epigenetic processes has occurred.[140] Adrian Bird in *Nature* describes 2006–7 as a watershed year, with over 2,500 articles and even a new journal being devoted to epigenetics.[141] Two major sequencing projects by international consortia followed the HGP to begin to fill in the huge gaps and numerous questions left by its results. The first was the ENCODE project (Encyclopedia of DNA Elements), which ran from 2003 to 2012 and decoded the other 98.8 percent of the human genome.[142] Although scientists are still debating their interpretations, the results have undoubtedly transformed knowledge of the genome's complexity and only added to the identity crisis of the "gene." It is now certain that one gene can make many proteins, that genes frequently splice and recombine with other genes to make proteins, and that different cells can use the same gene to make different proteins. Therefore, a "gene" is no longer a stretch of DNA at one location that codes for one protein.[143] Furthermore, what previously was known as "junk DNA" is now known to be pervasively transcribed, producing noncoding RNA (ncRNA) that is heavily involved in genetic regulation at many levels. Noncoding RNA plays a role in mediating between "chromatin marks and gene expression" and between other gene regulatory systems, including leading proteins to places they need to be in order to lay down methylation patterns. "The take-home message would seem to be clear," Keller writes. "Genetics is not just about genes and what they code for. . . . All of this requires coordination of an order of complexity only now beginning to be appreciated. And it is now believed that the ncRNA transcripts of the remaining 98–99 percent of the genome are central to this process."[144]

Concurrently with the ENCODE Project, the National Institutes of Health (NIH) in the United States and the International Human Epigenome Consortium began creating databases from deciphering the sequences of "normal" and "abnormal" human epigenomes, focusing on "methylation, histone modifications, chromatin accessibility, and RNA transcripts."[145] Epigenome projects are unlike the HGP or ENCODE, both of which worked with the so-called human genome—meaning, the sequence of DNA as statistically averaged across those humans sampled, which is presumed to be the same in all cells. Because epigenetic processes are responsible for cellular differentiation into different cell lines and tissues and organs, in order to understand "normal" and "abnormal" epigenetic structures, each tissue type requires multiple samplings and study. The NIH project is therefore targeting "stem cells and primary *ex vivo* tissues . . . to represent the normal counterparts of tissues and organ systems frequently involved in human disease."[146]

Yet, all involved are certain that the investment of time and money to accomplish this huge task is worthwhile because of the numbers of diseases that we are learning are associated with epigenetic differences.[147] As early as the 1980s, cancer researchers noticed that cell genomes in some types of tumors are abnormally methylated. Other epigenetic mechanisms such as the action of prions—proteins that have taken an alternate structural conformation that then convert other proteins to their structure—play a role in Creutzfeldt–Jacob disease and mad cow disease.[148] Researchers are expecting to find numerous overlaps between epigenetic mechanisms and many other diseases. Apart from the pursuit of knowledge about human health, agricultural and biotechnological industries are also seriously delving into epigenetics owing to the connectivity of life and biological processes and the fact that epigenetics offers a second line of heredity, one actively involved with the first. Epigenetic marks also affect processes involved in cloning and genetic engineering, which scientists discovered when inserting a gene resulted in producing an opposite effect from their intent, or when cell lines that were engineered reverted to their former state because the inserted genes were silenced epigenetically.[149]

Given the powerful role that epigenetics plays in development and evolution, as Jablonka and Lamb argue, and its recognition by scientists as "some of the most exciting contemporary biology" and "a revolutionary new science" as Bird stated in 2007, it is not surprising that computer scientists in the field of evolutionary computation are adapting it for new algorithmic approaches. Bird's article "Perceptions of Epigenetics" inspired Sathish Periyasamy, William Alexander Gray, and Peter Kille to create the Epigenetic Algorithm (EGA) the following year. The authors base their interpretation of epigenetics on Robin Holliday's definition as "the mechanism of spatial and temporal control of gene activity during the development of complex organisms." Their system attempts to integrate biomolecular "intra-generational adaptive mechanisms . . . to self-organize various activities in biological cells." They refer to epigenetic processes such as "gene silencing, bookmarking, paramutation, reprogramming, position effect, and a few other mechanisms."[150] They state that their EGA "aims to bridge the gap between phenotype-to-genotype representations, considers Lamarckian properties, and builds decentralized, highly parallel, self-adapting, coevolving, and agent-based models." They hope that it will aid in cancer research. Yet, owing to the structuring of their model based on a combination of terminologies and approaches from evolutionary computation, swarm intelligence, epigenetics, and autopoeisis, it is quite difficult to follow. Nonetheless, a few points deserve mention.

Autopoiesis was coined by biologists Humberto Maturana and Francisco Varela in 1973 to describe the self-maintaining and self-reproducing properties of the cell as the basic unit of life. Some today, including Periyasamy, use it as a synonym for self-organization, though this is quite an inexact translation. Interpreting biology through the lens of autopoiesis, Periyasamy and his colleagues describe biology as being organized into "strata": "The lowest level entities of the organization are the atoms which form the next higher level entity biomolecules. Biomolecules self-organize via covalent and non-covalent interactions in space and time to form the cells as next higher level entities." Here, they refer to cells coming into existence through protocells as if this is known, when more accurately, protocells are still hypothesized as

Conceptual category	20th century of the gene	21st century of the genome
Dominant scientific perspective	Reductionism	Complex systems
Fundamental mode of biological operation	Mechanical	Cybernetic
Central focus of hereditary theory	Genes as units of inheritance and function	Genomes as interactive information systems
Genome organization metaphor	Beads on a string	Computer operating system
Sources of inherited novelty	Localized mutations altering one gene at a time due to physico-chemical insults or replication errors	Epigenetic modifications and rearrangement of genomic subsystems by internal natural genetic engineering functions
Evolutionary processes	Background random mutation and natural selection of small increases in fitness; cells passive	Crisis-induced, non-random, genome-wide rearrangements leading to novel genome system architectures; cells actively engineering their DNA

FIGURE 3.7. Genome organization and reorganization in evolution: formatting for computation and function. From James Shapiro, "Genome Organization and Reorganization in Evolution: Formatting for Computation and Function," in "From Epigenesis to Epigenetics: The Genome in Context," special issue of *Annals of the New York Academy of Sciences*, ed. Linda van Speybroeck, Gertrudis Van de Vijver, and Dani De Waele, 981 (December 2002): 113.

an origin of life theory since no scientist has yet created a protocell.[151] "The cells form the unicellular and multicellular organisms which are considered as the unit of selection. Finally the organisms and their interactions with nature form the biosphere."[152] Like Weinstock, they mistake natural selection in biological evolution as aiming for improvement, likely owing to their immersion in the field of evolutionary computation. They state, "Evolution is an optimization process, where the aim is to improve the ability of a biological system to survive in a dynamically changing and competitive environment."[153] Although they acknowledge that biological "structures are not optimized," they assert that "they are on the verge of approaching it."[154] Along these lines, they state that their algorithm "is one of many . . . that could be developed to optimize the internal organization of autonomous systems."[155]

Nature without human interference is not an optimization system; it seems likely that their language is pointing to ideas of a eugenic ideal type rather than Darwinian natural selection as we have understood it. However, owing to the fact that some facets of epigenetics have been interpreted as active strategies for environmental adaptation by cells and organisms, it is possible to interpret their use of "optimization" with regard to their epigenetic algorithm in this light. Microbiologist James Shapiro posits that "natural genetic engineering," rather than random mutation, should be seen as the dominant twenty-first-century mode by which novelty arises and evolution changes (Figure 3.7).[156] Shapiro is not just referencing horizontal gene transfer but predominantly bases his idea of "natural genetic engineering" on "epigenetic modifications and rearrangement of genomic subsystems" that result in gene silencing, activation, or alternative uses and functions, often in direct response to the environment. If cells and organisms are actively adapting themselves to their environment, then what is the point, the "goal," of their adaptive processes? Biologist J. Scott Turner, in his 2012 article in *AD*, argues that their "goal" is homeostasis, which he interprets as seeking comfort—or rephrased, that comfort is produced through natural processes of homeostasis.[157] Yet, Periyasamy and his colleagues do not cite Shapiro or Turner for this more nuanced interpretation of "optimization" in terms of goal-directed adaptation by cells and organisms themselves.

An Evolutionary Architecture?

Whether, and how, epigenetic algorithms matter to biologists or generative architects is for them to determine. Only John Frazer references "epigenetic algorithms," and he did so in 1995, which is very early considering that knowledge of epigenetics has become mainstream only in the twenty-first century. In *An Evolutionary Architecture,* he describes some general features of his model for evolutionary architecture: "The environment has a significant effect on the epigenetic development of the seed. . . . It has been emphasized . . . that DNA does not describe the phenotype, but constitutes *instructions that describe the process of building the phenotype.*" The materials produced and assembled by this process "are all responsive to the environment as it proceeds, capable of modifying in response to conditions such as the availability of foodstuffs, and so on. . . . The rules are constant, but the outcome varies according to materials or environmental conditions."[158] Some of Frazer's and his students' projects in this vein were realized as interactive installations in the mid-1990s that took cues from and responded to observers and qualities of the environment, which fits his biological analogy of epigenetic environmental responsiveness. Although Jones and Furjàn do not discuss epigenetic algorithms per se, in 2006 they proposed the need for them: "An epigenetic approach to design, then, suggests that complex feedback relations with the environment must be front-ended and generative. Code is no longer everything, context matters." They suggest integrating the "dynamic forces and flows" between the building and its environment in feedback loops, including "flows of matter, air, heat, light, moisture, sound, but also infrastructural flows of energy, information, capital, transportation, and so on." Their list begins to get at the complexity of the environment, to which we could add other social factors, chemical inputs, other species and their needs, and so forth. Yet in order to do so, if one wants to treat epigenetics as a careful analogy, then all these variable conditions need conversion to data and real-time feedback with development, not just a onetime statistical summary for the design phase of the process.[159]

Frazer mentions the possibility of moving from analogy to reality, in which case it is not epigenetic algorithms but epigenetic processes themselves that become exceedingly important. "Our longer-term goal lies in trying to incorporate the building process literally into the model, or perhaps the model into the very materials for building, so that the resultant structures are self-constructing. This may be achievable by either molecular engineering," he imagines, or "by the application of nanotechnology, or perhaps by the genetic engineering of plant forms or living organisms to produce forms appropriate for human habitation as an extended phenotype." Frazer is not alone in this vision, but follows in a tradition of architects from previous decades before he was writing. "Frei Otto has suggested growing structures," and "[Rudolph] Doernach and [William] Katavolos imagined organic structures erected from chemical reactions," he writes. "Alvy Ray Smith envisaged buildings growing from single brick-eggs. Charles Jencks referred to scenes from 'Barbarella' showing the emergence of human and vegetable forms," and "the final issue of the *Archigram* magazine contained a packet of seeds from David Greene." Yet, in the short term, he writes, "the prospect of growing buildings seems unlikely, but self-assembly may be achievable."[160] Since 1995, his voice has been joined by others whose ideas are discussed in the last two chapters of this book.

The foundation laid here, though, as an entrée to this discussion, begins to hint at the scope and complexity of the challenges to be faced by those hoping for this future. This chapter has examined how closely techniques in generative architecture mirror recent advances in biology. In doing so, it has shown that the most useful, or perhaps just the most used, approaches thus far in generative architecture are neo-Darwinian ones structured on outdated, faulty assumptions about biological processes and evolution, at least from today's vantage. Of all the theories from D'Arcy Thompson's lifetime to the present, the neo-Darwinian period was also the most divorced from actual morphogenesis and knowledge of developmental biology. This is an ironic choice for use then as a model for architectural morphogenesis, or perhaps it is just a pragmatic choice since neo-Darwinism and neo-Darwinian evolutionary computation are the simplest and most reductive models of them all. For those generative architects who do not aim to grow living buildings but are primarily interested in the "instrumentalisation" of architecture, Eiben and Smith recognize the usefulness of evolutionary computation as a tool for the "evolution of things." "Recent developments in rapid fabrication technologies (3D printing) and ever smaller and more powerful robotic platforms mean that evolutionary computing is now starting to make the next major transition to the automated creation of physical artefacts and 'smart' objects," they write.[161] Clearly, generative architects are already aware of this, as this has been a primary motivator for shifting to techniques of generative design in order to enhance compatibility of and develop new methods of digital design and fabrication.

Yet, given the lack of congruence between evolutionary algorithms from natural evolution as summarized by Eiben and Smith (Figure 3.1), generative architects at the very least should refrain from rhetorically positioning their approaches as biological and should be explicit about the computational thrust of their methods. Although Kumar and Bentley's EDS or any version of an epigenetic algorithm may need adapting for architectural purposes, use of these approaches or even just adoption of their terminology would make architects appear far more knowledgeable about contemporary scientific and computer scientific theories than they currently are. Of course, this is a poor reason to adopt such language, especially if such adoption is unaccompanied by curiosity about and acquisition of current biological knowledge. However, should architects want to actually collaborate with contemporary scientists—as is the case in the next chapter, about Jenny Sabin and Peter Lloyd Jones's establishing of LabStudio—then they must become fluent in current biological terminology and theory.

One major challenge facing contemporary biologists and computer scientists that is directly relevant to generative architecture is the difficulty of describing, quantifying, and integrating "the environment" into models of biological functions at the cellular or organismal levels. The framework in biology and medicine has moved away from gene-centrism toward gene–environment interactions. If one is to use current computational methods and draw on the big data of genetics for statistical correlations with epigenetic markers and environmental phenomena affecting bodies, then one needs the capacity to acquire, codify, and search environmental data that pertains to the issue one is investigating. Such is the focus of Sara Shostak and Margot Moinester's article "The Missing Piece of the Puzzle? Measuring the Environment in the Postgenomic Moment" (2015), which compares the new field of exposomics with approaches in sociology and epidemiology examining "neighborhood effects on health."[162] Exposomics aims to track data on environmental exposures that are known triggers of epigenetic response by focusing on the internal environment of a body—say, molecular markers from toxic encounters correlated by one's zip code, diet, smoking, stress, et cetera.[163]

Architects who have read Michelle Murphy's *Sick Building Syndrome and the Problem of Uncertainty* (2006) and who understand epigenetics might ask themselves about the possible epigenetic health effects of their building materials and construction methods on the health of buildings' occupants.[164] But the point of developing more useful methods of identifying and quantifying "the environment" in architecture is actually broader than this. If we play along with the idea that a building is an organism, and we are trying to generate an appropriate design solution either in silico pre-construction or model a building through its lifetime, then we need much better ways of integrating "the environment" into our models. Besserud and Ingram, in "Architectural Genomics," describe the need for all parameters in evolutionary computation to be both quantifiable and automatable.[165] Menges mentions the importance of designing a building or a block of buildings in relation to environmental factors. Gravity/load, solar angle, thermal gain, wind speed and direction, and cross-ventilation are just a small percentage of all the possible environmental features one might want to consider and include; more surface the closer one looks. Perhaps Menges and Hensel's narrow definition of "morpho-ecologies" as simply humans and the buildings they occupy is a strategic oversimplification. This is because actually considering the broader ecological impact of buildings on the environment—both local and immediate, and through the life cycle of building materials—is a huge big-data task. It is also a task not limited to physical qualities like gravity, force, and heat, but also chemical, biological, and ecological impacts. Although D'Arcy Thompson avoided chemistry and focused only on physics and mathematics in his theory of biological growth and form, it would be overly reductive and irresponsible for generative architects to continue now to do so.

CHAPTER 4

CONTEXT MATTERS
LabStudio and Biosynthesis

The work of LabStudio—a collaboration between architect Jenny Sabin and molecular and cell biologist Peter Lloyd Jones begun in 2006 at the University of Pennsylvania—differs significantly from that of most generative architects.[1] Until David Benjamin collaborated with synthetic biologist Fernan Federici in 2010, Sabin and Jones were the only generative architect–scientist duo doing serious biomedical scientific research. Other technological and conceptual differences from neo-Darwinian generative architecture as usual begin to be revealed by a compelling high-tech image made by Jones in 2005: a photomicrograph of a rat's smooth muscle cell engineered to fluoresce in different colors so that its constituent parts glow vividly in red, green, and blue (Plate 7).[2] It shows red striated actin filaments penetrating both the blue nucleus housing the cell's DNA and the green dotted cloud of the extracellular matrix (ECM, or just matrix) located outside the cell's cytoskeleton. This image offers a stunning reframing—precisely because of its contextualization—of popular views of DNA that imagine the molecule in isolation (Figure 4.1).

These popular conceptualizations stem from Rosalind Franklin and Ray Gosling's well-known X-ray diffraction image of sodium deoxyribose nucleate

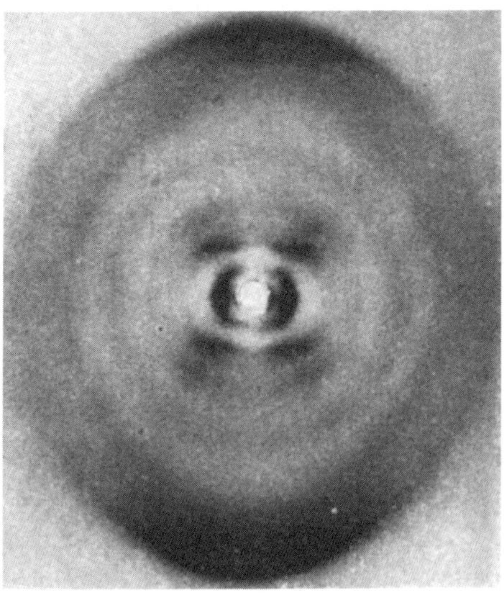

FIGURE 4.1. Photograph 51, X-ray diffraction image of deoxyribose nucleate, 1952, by Rosalind Franklin and Ray Gosling. In Franklin and Gosling, "Molecular Configuration in Sodium Thymonucleate," *Nature* 171, no. 4356 (April 1953): 740. This image reveals the double-helical structure of DNA, as famously claimed in *Nature* by Francis Crick and James Watson in April 1953.

from 1952, which first revealed DNA's molecular helical formation precisely by chemically and visually isolating DNA in a nebulous space.[3] Their image belies the tools, techniques of analysis, and disciplinary focus of the then-burgeoning field of molecular biology, which shaped Francis Crick's powerful yet flawed central dogma (1958) and recently reached its popular climax in the completion of the Human Genome Project (2003). Indicating the ongoing widespread popularity of this neo-Darwinian conception in the late 2000s, the recent advertising campaigns for Sony's high-definition HDNA and Pearl Izumi's cycling products, along with Pandora's Music Genome Project, feed into our ongoing cultural preoccupation with DNA as the source of built-in quality and personalization. The marketing of all these make use of the double helix, and Pearl Izumi claims to offer a "genetically engineered fit." This sort of "genetic engineering" arises most likely from the use of genetic algorithms as a computational problem-solving design tool rather than from use of scientific biotechnologies. However, as this distinction may not be obvious to the general public, such campaigns serve to reinforce popular belief today in the primary biological efficacy of "genes" and DNA.

Over fifty years after our obsession with DNA began, Jones presents us with perhaps a new iconic image, one also made using the most recent technologies but which hones in on current research interests in cell and matrix biology. Its frame intentionally encompasses the broader context, the microenvironment within which DNA exists and functions in living organisms—namely, the cell and its extracellular matrix.[4] Similar to previous isolations of DNA molecules, cells and their matrices can be extracted from an organism and kept alive in a sterile laboratory in the presence of nutrient gel. In nature, however, their broader systemic context continues to expand outward into tissues, organs, organisms, and so on up the scale. Jones's image therefore references systems biology yet still draws a tight boundary, one that freeze-frames a living moving cell into a fixed measurable form. Importantly, the image visibly captures the actin filaments that function as structural supports and signaling pathways and permeate zones previous scientists conceptualized as borders—that is, the edge of the nucleus and the edge of the cell. In so doing, it illuminates the integrated and extensive architectural and communication tensegrity system that scientists now theorize functions epigenetically to regulate gene expression and stabilize cell and tissue identity, homeostasis, and morphology.[5]

Jones created this image soon after meeting Sabin, when he and his colleagues were researching the biochemical processes involved in the systemic responses of the extracellular matrix and vascular smooth muscle cells after injury. In general, Jones's scientific research focused on the morphogenetic functions of homeobox genes and epigenetic processes in cells, their matrix, and tissues during the onset of vascular and breast tissue development and disease. It therefore offers an apt example and extension of the theoretical issues raised in the previous chapter under the headings of evo-devo and epigenetics. Sabin and Jones met in 2005 at the University of Pennsylvania when Jones saw a sign and out of curiosity walked into the first annual conference of the Nonlinear Systems Organization (NLSO). As a cell and molecular biologist who worked on nonlinear biological systems and had always possessed an interest in architecture and design, he wondered what architects meeting under the aegis of the NLSO were discussing. The NLSO was begun by Cecil Balmond, a Penn professor, structural engineer, and architect; for many years, Balmond directed the Advanced Geometry Unit of the international engineering firm Arup, which has led the world in the construction of geometrically complex structures. Sabin, who had been a graduate student at Penn before becoming a lecturer there, had studied with Balmond and pursued her own work in complex geometric architextile design. She was (and is) an expert scripter and participant with the SmartGeometry Group who had also studied biology and art as an undergraduate.[6] It did not take long for her and Jones to decide to collaborate, founding LabStudio in 2006 and coteaching the seminar/studio Nonlinear Systems Biology and Design beginning in the summer of 2007.

During the years that Sabin and Jones were both at Penn, LabStudio's research and teaching focused on the multiscalar, interconnective architectures of nonlinear biological systems. The biomedical aspects of their collaboration fit within the research agenda of Jones's lab at the Institute for Medicine and Engineering (IME), but they reached out to scientists and graduate students in other fields to join their cross-disciplinary explorations. For example, materials scientist Shu Yang, whose lab focuses on nanoscale materials, has written grants with Sabin and Jones, and continues to work with Sabin on one project funded by the National Science Foundation (NSF). Mathematician Robert Ghrist guest-lectured on Euler transformations of topological structures. And between 2008 and 2009, graduate students from architecture, molecular biology, biophysics, mathematics, and pharmacology teamed up in their course. In general, the collaboration aimed to merge their approaches—the intuitive, computational, spatial skills of Sabin with the theoretical and technical biomedical laboratory expertise of Jones—to devise new ways of seeing, thinking, and modeling cell and tissue morphogenesis under "normal" and "pathological" conditions. One deliverable they worked toward was developing novel diagnostic tools for patients with pulmonary arterial hypertension using computational analysis to identify "personalized signatures" of cell architectures, motility, and grouping patterns.[7]

This chapter therefore offers an overview of their collaboration, focusing particularly on 2008 to 2009, when I was in residence at Penn as a postdoctoral scholar participating in their studio seminar and studying their partnership. Because so much happens pedagogically in studio that is not published and available later to scholars to understand, the best way to learn about contemporary teaching and research methods is to actively participate. The chapter opens with a discussion of Mina Bissell's and Jones's scientific research on the morphogenesis of cell and tissue architecture in order to demonstrate the relation of their work to theoretical developments in developmental biology, homeobox gene functioning, and epigenetics. It then explores how LabStudio extended this research into a bold, innovative, cross-disciplinary teaching and research initiative, one that produced creative work aiming to bridge the nano- with the macroscales in visualization and prototyping. It concludes with a brief overview of Sabin's recent work, part of which extends the research begun with LabStudio at Penn in Jones's lab into an NSF-funded project exploring nanoscale building-skin materials.

Morphogenesis of Cell and Tissue Architecture

In the mid-1980s, Harvard cell biologist Donald Ingber along with his Yale doctoral mentor, James Jamieson, first proposed that cells function as "tensegrity structures," a term coined by designer and architect Buckminster Fuller to describe his approach to designing geodesic domes.[8] Tensegrity combines "tension" with "integrity" and refers to structures "that gained their stability or integrity through a pervasive *tensional* force." Fuller's domes and Kenneth Snelson's sculptures demonstrate the means by which prestressed struts, or struts connected with cables, that are interconnected using tension allow local forces to be distributed across the entire structure. Extending this to cells, Ingber and Jamieson hypothesized that tensegrity functioned in cells at many hierarchical levels, from the bonds in molecules up to the structure of the nucleus to the filament bundles in cellular cytoplasm (like actin) to the architecture of the cell overall. "This concept may seem obvious now to those familiar with modern day cell biology," Ingber and colleagues write, "but it was heretical when it was first proposed because most scientists viewed the living cell as a membrane surrounding a viscous cytoplasm with a nucleus floating at the center."[9] Jones's image clearly shows the architectural struts of the cell—actin filaments that combine structural and signaling properties and even extend beyond the cell membrane to connect it to the matrix. The radical implication is that cell position and shape in context is dynamically affected by a cell's connections with the matrix and other contiguous cells, resulting in the fact that cell architecture—shape, configuration, nucleus position, et cetera—affects gene regulation and cell functioning.[10]

Similar to the architecture of buildings, cells exist within contexts where physical forces matter significantly; structural collapse or major architectural changes can signal disease. These forces include not just the force of gravity but also those generated by osmotic pressure, cell-on-cell pressure within limited space, and forces of motion from energy expenditure as cells and organisms move. (One hundred years later, D'Arcy Thompson's mode of thought reenters, mainstage.) Ingber and colleagues, in their recent review "Tensegrity, Cellular Biophysics, and the Mechanics of Living Systems" (2014), survey developments in the new field of "mechanobiology that centers on how cells control their mechanical properties, and how physical forces regulate cellular biochemical responses, a process that is known as mechanotransduction."[11] Cells are affected by tensional, compression, and shear forces, and their "tensional prestress" serves as a "critical governor of cell mechanics and function." Another way of describing this is to say that tissue architecture affects cell and tissue homeostasis. This is the approach of Jones's postdoctoral mentor, Mina Bissell of Lawrence Berkeley National Laboratory, and her colleagues, who study breast cancer.[12] Transformations of tissue architecture under the onset of cancer are usually pathological. So, in contrast to J. Scott Turner's description of homeostasis as the pursuit of comfort, here architectural changes link to discomfort and disease.[13]

This drives home a very important point about morphogenesis. Although biological morphogenesis most commonly refers to the development of an embryo into its early and adult phenotypic forms, morphogenesis is actually a continual process that stops only at death. Cell or tissue architecture is simply another way of referring to cell or tissue morphology. Almost all cells perpetually repeat the process of dividing and then dying throughout the tissues and organs of a body, to the extent that the three-dimensional architectural structures they compose and the functions they perform are actively maintained through time. In some cases, such as the development of breast tissue in puberty and the changes that it undergoes in pregnancy and menopause, major morphogenetic changes occur in adulthood rather than as an embryo and developing fetus and child. Similarly, when tissues are damaged from injuries, morphogenesis is reinitiated to rebuild tissue architecture.

For these reasons, Bissell's research on breast tissue architectural changes during cancer has revealed crucial information that is relevant to morphogenesis overall, one factor of which is the central role played by the matrix. Because the matrix is produced by cells but remains external to them in tissues, its effects on cell morphology and gene regulation are characterized as epigenetic. In 1997, Bissell and her colleagues published a landmark study demonstrating the role of the matrix as the dominant factor affecting whether the morphology of malignant cancerous human breast cells was pathological (i.e., cancerous) or normal (Plate 8).[14] In the image, all cells possess the genes for breast cancer, but what changes is the matrix environment in which they are grown and placed. The first image shows the morphology of cancerous cells grown in a healthy normal matrix environment; note the spherical shape with central void. The second shows the malignant morphology that appeared when the matrix was changed. The third reveals a reversion back to the normal morphology from the malignant morphology that occurred when it was placed back into a normal matrix environment. Thus, changing the matrix causes malignant breast cancer cells to produce the malignant morphology, but it can also cause malignant cells to revert to the normal morphology. Based on this study, Bissell claims that "tissue phenotype [architecture] is dominant over the cellular genotype," which is a radical counter to neo-Darwinian assumptions. She states, "When you have the form, the function comes. So form and function are related dynamically and reciprocally," a concept she refers to as "dynamic reciprocity."[15] This could function well as an updated biologically based mantra for generative architecture, one like Louis Sullivan's "form follows function" under modernism. The importance of cell and tissue architecture for Bissell is demonstrated by her innovation of growing cell and tissue cultures in three-dimensional flasks of Matrigel, rather than on flat petri dishes, as the spatial volume allows cells to reproduce as if they were in a body and assume the architecture they choose, rather than an architecture dictated by the experimental context.[16]

Following from his work with Bissell, Jones's research at Penn investigated the normal and pathological morphogenesis of pulmonary vascular and breast tissues. In the morphogenesis of both tissues, the homeobox gene referred to as Prx1 functions as a transcription factor. In 2003, Jones and his colleagues showed that Prx1 induces the production of the matrix protein tenascin-C (TN-C) and also promotes the migration ("motility") of fibroblast cells to the site of injuries; fibroblasts produce collagen and the extracellular matrix, and so are crucial for rebuilding tissue architecture in the healing of wounds.[17] The following year, they found that Prx1 affects cellular differentiation of fetal lung mesodermal cells into endothelial cells that, in turn, can incorporate into vascular networks.[18] When Jones began collaborating with Sabin, he was exploring the role of TN-C in the release of adhered vascular smooth muscle cells from their matrix at time of injury in order to allow them to move to the wounded area. TN-C also plays a role in pulmonary vascular disease, particularly lung arterial hypertension, as well as in breast cancer, as Jones's lab has shown.[19] These examples and the published articles reveal that cellular and tissue interactions entailing homeobox genes and epigenetic processes are exquisitely complex, with details being ascertained as best as possible only through very careful experimentation. Alternately put, the theoretical developments presented in the previous chapter are grounded in the slow, painstaking, laboratory-based research of scientists like Sean Carroll, Bissell, and Jones.

LabStudio's Research and Teaching Collaboration, 2008–9

Jones, who now directs the Emergent Design + Creative Technologies in Medicine program at Jefferson Medical College in Philadelphia, introduced the Penn graduate architecture seminar Nonlinear Systems Biology and Design in the Fall 2008 semester with his image showing the tensegrity structure of the cell in relation to its matrix (Plate 7). Cotaught with Sabin (currently leading the Sabin Design Lab at Cornell), the seminar grew out of their research collaboration. The epigraph for the studio seminar brief clearly states the importance of computer modeling for scientific research into the dynamic networking behavior of complex biological systems: "The objective of Systems Biology [can be] defined as understanding network behavior, and in particular, their dynamic aspects, which requires the utilization of modeling tightly linked to experiment."[20] This statement is corroborated by the accompanying images on the brief, which show digitally designed and manufactured models made by Sabin based on experiments in Jones's lab that show the changing shapes of breast tissue morphogenesis under cancer (when the matrix contains tenascin-C) (Plate 9). The syllabus thus used Sabin and Jones's own research methods as the model for ways that their course would tackle the study of nonlinear systems biology and design.

These images were published in the paper that Sabin and Jones presented that fall at the annual conference of the Association for Computer Aided Design in Architecture in Minneapolis, titled Silicon + Skin: Biological Processes and Computation. Their paper addressed their collaborative study of breast cancer morphogenesis under the title "Nonlinear Systems Biology and Design: Surface Design." For this research, Jones and his assistants grew human mammary epithelial cells in 3-D volumes filled with Matrigel. The "normal" form of mammary epithelial cells is in spherical form with a central void (the far-right image), which is referred to as an "acini" and is where milk forms. By altering the amount of tenascin-C in the matrix environment, they transformed normal form into cancerous tumorigenesis (the second image from the left). Blue fluorescence marks the nuclei of each cell in both in vitro tissue formations (top, second image from right), whereas green marks the border of the tissue where the matrix surrounds the tissue. After Jones's lab sliced the in vitro three-dimensional tissue into very thin Z-stack layers and digitally scanned these to the computer, Sabin then relayered them into an in silico virtual 3-D tissue. To do this, she scripted algorithms that computationally analyzed and then re-created the geometries of both normal and pathological forms. She then created 3-D-printed models in composito of a size to hold in one's hand for the lab to study.

Our seminar began with Jones offering the first lecture, which critiqued gene-centrism and the shortcomings of the highly linear central dogma. Sabin and Jones's ACADIA paper expressed the same point of view: "The fashionable ideology of ultra-Darwinism, which reduces organisms to little more than machines for the replication of DNA, is gradually being replaced by a more holistic trajectory in which life is considered to depend upon complex interactions that occur within cells, organisms, and with their micro- and macroenvironment through time and space." His second lecture introduced epigenetics so we could have a context for understanding matrix biology and the experiments that were to be used as the initial exploratory content for the studio projects. He used Mina Bissell's question for this: "If all somatic cells in a body have the same genome, then what makes your nose tissue remain a nose, and your liver tissue a liver?" As Bissell explains, it is the matrix that epigenetically stabilizes or destabilizes different cell identities.[21] At the time, Jones was reading Eva Jablonka and Marion Lamb's pathbreaking book *Evolution in Four Dimensions: Genetic, Epigenetic, Behavioral, and Symbolic Variation in the History of Life* (2006), which he recommended to the class. Together these two lectures set the primary course theme, one that is just as relevant to architecture as to biology: How does environment (context) specify form, function, and structure? What is the nature of the dynamic reciprocity between these?

Sabin's lectures clarified the difference between biomimicry and biosynthesis; she and Jones prefer the latter to distinguish their approach, which focuses on the nonlinear processes of complex biological systems. (It has no relation to synthetic biology.) Cutting-edge biomimetic designs had just been featured at the Museum of Modern Art's exhibition *Design and the Elastic Mind* (2008), including the 2005 Daimler AG / Mercedes-Benz *Bionic Car* design by Peter Pfeiffer based on the skeletal structure of a boxfish. Yet, Sabin characterized biomimetic design as a relatively quick, goal-oriented approach in which designers and architects directly copy natural forms or adapt aspects of them into useful technologies. Biosynthesis, as they use it, refers to the processes underlying form-generation in the development of biological systems; in their much slower, open-ended research driven by the pace of laboratory experimentation, they were seeking to uncover these processes.

Sabin offered tooling and scripting sessions on the program Generative Components in between lectures and readings that explored topics from architectural history, philosophy, evo-devo, self-organization, cell mechanics, algorithmic design, mathematical topology, and nanofabrication. Three themes offered a framework for the research projects, which focused on patterns in the architectural aspects of cell and tissue morphologies—patterns in the deep and surface structures of cells ("surface design"), in their architecture during cell movement ("motility"), and in their grouping habits ("networking"). "By immersing oneself in complex biological design problems, and abstracting the inherent relationships of these models into code-driven parametric and associative models," Sabin writes, "it is possible to gain new insights into how nature deals with design issues that feature pattern formation, part-to-whole relationships, complexity, and emergent behavior. Perhaps architects might learn from these biological models such that architecture acquires 'tissueness' or 'cellness' and is not merely 'cell- or tissue-like.'"[22] The class approached these topics from the theoretical starting point that complex biological systems demonstrate self-organization informed by nonlinear processes entailing feedback between the many participants at different hierarchical levels—genes, cytoplasm, matrix, tissues, organs, organisms, and environmental contextual inputs. Sabin and Jones also were committed to working both in Jones's biomedical laboratory where the 3D-printer was housed and in the computer labs at Penn Design so that students would become well versed in both environments and the sets of skills each requires.

Early in the semester, students were grouped into interdisciplinary teams—ideally, each group had at least one architecture and one molecular or cell biology graduate student—who were assigned a term project focusing on either cell surface design, motility, or networking. For each topic area, Sabin and Jones provided video recordings and still photo documentation of experiments they had conducted in preparation before the course began. The images captured the different behaviors of a particular type of cell related either to breast cancer or pulmonary arterial hypertension, both diseases studied by Jones's lab, in different environments. For example, teams studying cell motility worked with vascular smooth muscle cells in a two-dimensional matrix environment that either had native or denatured collagen. The surface design teams examining the shapes of cells moving over time on a two-dimensional surface studied breast epithelial cells in a matrix environment with or without TN-C. Those studying cell networking patterns examined pulmonary endothelial cells in a uniform matrix environment; some of the endothelial cells had the homeobox gene Prx1 knocked out, while others had the gene present. Prx1 affects the production of TN-C, which allows cells to connect to their environment and communicate with one another; in its absence cells did not network in clusters, but with it present they clustered directionally. Based on these initial starting points, teams were asked to carefully analyze the visual data for their topic utilizing both computational and experimental scientific tools and processes, in order to pursue ideas and questions of organization and process that might be relevant to unlocking reasons behind the patterns presented. All teams were required to demonstrate the results of their research using 3-D-printed forms for their final projects.

Although student projects from the Fall 2008 course did not result in publications, the work of graduate students biologist Mathieu Tamby and architect Erica Savig (who finished her Ph.D. in 2016 at Stanford University's School of Medicine in Cancer Biology) from the previous year resulted in conference presentations.[23] Yet, regardless of whether such high professional accomplishments resulted from a one-semester studio (which is a tall order), the most valuable contribution of the LabStudio teaching collaboration was introducing students to the concepts, terminologies, and methods from different academic disciplines. Together, these different disciplinary viewpoints offer the potential of unique insights into structural design processes, whether biological or inorganic, whether nano- or macroscale. Being forced to collaborate with students in these other fields—in addition to being expected to bring oneself up to speed on whatever biological or architectural concepts one was not familiar with before the course—prepared students for future collaborative research using a systems-thinking approach. Complex systems do not fit into one discipline, nor do the types of complex problems facing our world today. Funding organizations such as the NSF are now eliciting calls for proposals from teams representing multiple disciplines, offering only one obvious instance that the direction of advanced research is moving toward such collaborations. It is precisely one of these NSF grants that has funded the ongoing work of Sabin as a principal investigator (PI), along with architect and technician Andrew Lucia and other co-PIs: materials scientist Shu Yang (Penn), engineers Nader Engheta and Jan Van der Spiegel (Penn), and matrix biologist Kaori Ihida-Stansbury (in Jones's former lab at the Penn IME).

Scaling Up: From the Nano to the Macro

An important facet of the LabStudio collaboration has been the production of human-scale models of nano- or microscale material formations from scientific laboratory research. When Sabin first printed out the models of normal and malignant tissue morphologies of breast cancer and scientists at Jones's lab held them in their hands, they remarked on the difference of perspective and insight offered by experiencing cell and tissue architecture at the new scale. Sabin, whose creative practice specializes in even larger-scale architextile installations, decided to scale up further. In the summer of 2008 along with a number of assistants, she connected seventy-five thousand zip ties into a room-sized installation that modeled the interconnected forces between cells in the formation of branching vascular tissue morphogenesis. Called *Branching Morphogenesis,* the installation consisted of five interconnected layers hanging ceiling to floor (3.5 meters tall, 4.5 meters wide) that one could walk into and through so as to surround oneself with the structure (Plate 10). Sabin writes, "The project investigates part-to-whole relationships revealed during the generation of branched structures formed in real-time by interacting lung endothelial cells placed within a 3D matrix environment. The installation materializes five slices in time that capture the force network exerted by interacting vascular cells upon their matrix environment."[24] The piece won first place in the 2009 International Science and Engineering Visualization Challenge, earning a spot on the cover of *Science* magazine.[25]

Cellular networking also inspired Sabin's *PolyThread Knitted Textile Pavilion,* another room-sized work commissioned for the 2016 exhibition *Beauty: The Cooper Hewitt Design Triennial* (Plate 11).[26] This piece was brought to life, so to speak, by light and shadow in a manner similar to Philip Beesley's *Hylozoic* works that move and rustle in response to human motion and heat (Plates 2 and 14).[27] Yet, whereas Beesley's work integrates tiny sensors into his installations, Sabin's thread simply responds to light by virtue of its material composition.[28] The pavilion absorbed colored light from the room as well as sunlight and transmitted it across the threaded network, which would respond to shadows made by the presence of visitors. The digitally knitted textile was tensioned through its connection to a freestanding fiberglass tubing edge, which metaphorically functions as the extracellular matrix around the edge of a tissue. (Compare with the green-fluorescing matrix edge of the pathological breast cancer tissue morphology, top and second from the right in Plate 9.) Thus, although in this pavilion the tube functions visually more like a hoop onto which one knits, Sabin was surely referencing cell and matrix networks as tensegrity structures.

Network structure even informs Sabin's digital curriculum vitae, which clearly shows the interconnectivity between her research, teaching, private practice, and work with industries (Figure 4.2). She created this practice diagram in 2008 using the program Generative Components, meaning that the image is an associative visual model of a scripted code and not a surface diagram created with a graphics application. Visually, it compares beautifully with the "net of life" diagram of the microbial phylogenetic network influenced by horizontal gene transfer (Plate 5). Sabin's process reflects her deep theoretical commitment to nonlinear complex adaptive systems, rather than a gene-centric linear focus, as the biological model for her work. Compare it as well to the practice diagram by Foreign Office Architects (FOA) from *Breeding Architecture* (Plate 3). In Sabin's, you can trace multiple paths from any one

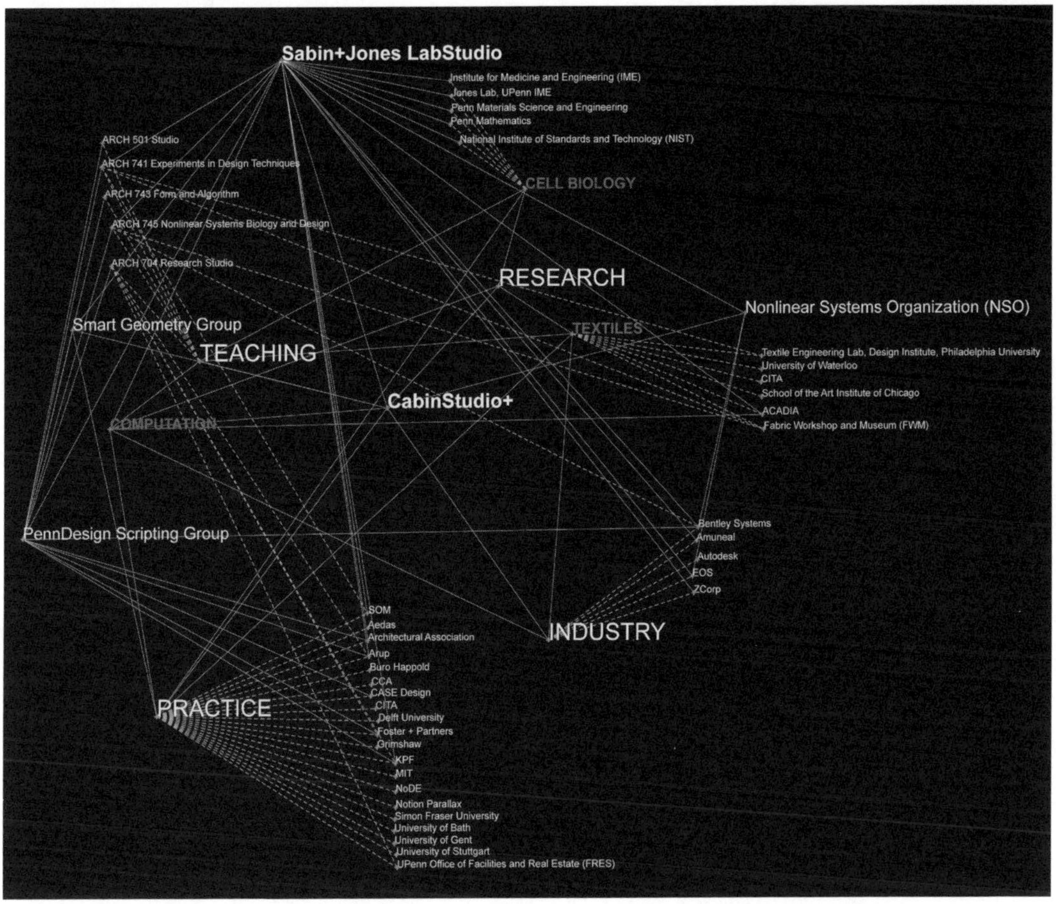

FIGURE 4.2. Jenny Sabin practice diagram, digital curriculum vitae created in Generative Components, 2008. Courtesy Jenny Sabin. In lieu of the normal linear text to be read on paper, this CV reveals the multiple connections and crossovers between different facets of her architectural practice, teaching, research, and work for industry. The overall effect is of a web. (For comparison, see Plate 5; for contrast, see Plate 3 and Figure 3.4.)

point to any other, with the implication that they influence and transform the others in dynamic fashion. FOA's is purely linear, where all phenotypic traits are defined by their firm's "design DNA" despite different expressions conforming to different projects' programmatic and site-specific needs. Sabin and Jones summarize this profound difference particularly well by describing that in their collaborative research, "by placing the cell, tissue, or organism, rather than the gene at the center of life, a different perspective on the construction and dynamics of organismal architecture is beginning to emerge."[29]

Sabin's ongoing project funded by the NSF, referred to as *eSkin,* tackles an even more ambitious form of modeling from the nano- to the macroscale. Along with her current collaborators (Lucia, Yang, Engheta, Van der Spiegel, and Ihida-Stansbury), she is striving to create an aesthetically interesting, passively responsive, new building skin using nanofabrication. In other words, the goal of the project is not to model from the nano to the macro, but actually to develop and construct the innovative building skin. Yet, owing to hurdles they are encountering along the way in their collaboration and development, modeling has become an integral part of the process. Currently, substrates created through nanofabrication are limited to about four inches square.[30] This means that simulation must be used in order to understand how this wavelength-filtering material might function optically if applied on the scale of a building facade. In the process of attempting this simulation, Sabin, Lucia, and Simin Wang realized that currently available software does not offer the capacities they need, so they have written their own tools to this end. Unfortunately, because the computational memory required for this task is impossibly high, they have also had to innovate alternate prototyping modes for ascertaining the visual effects, which change depending on the angle from which one views the material.[31] In this regard, the computational limitations they face are similar to those tackled by Michael Hansmeyer and Benjamin Dillenburger in the creation of *Digital Grotesque II* (2017).[32]

True to Sabin's ongoing interest in nonlinear systems biology and design, the nanomaterials they are working with "exhibit nuanced nonlinear behavior as a product of their nano and micro scale geometric structures, such as angle and wavelength dependent properties."[33] When she and her colleagues applied for the NSF Emerging Frontiers in Research and Innovation (EFRI) program Science in Energy and Environmental Design (SEED) in 2010, Jones was still at Penn and was part of the original grant. One feature of the proposal uses knowledge gained from studying the nonlinear networking behavior of human smooth muscle cells with their extracellular matrix as a model for biomimetic (or, in their words, biosynthesis-derived) design of the building skin. This project is thus an ambitious extension of the research begun in LabStudio. "This project represents a unique avant-garde model for sustainable and ecological design via the fusion of the architectural design studio with laboratory-based scientific research," they write. "In turn, this project benefits a diverse range of science and technologies, including the construction of energy efficient and aesthetic building skins and materials."[34] The full name of their grant proposal—"Energy Minimization via Multi-Scalar Architecture: From Cell Contractility to Sensing Materials to Adaptive Building Skins"—states the goals clearly. Aiming overall for energy minimization through the use of nanofabricated architectural materials, they hope to use cell behavior as a biomimetic model for adaptive building skins that respond contextually to the environment using sensors. Sabin prefers to not use the word "biomimetic," though. "Generative design techniques emerge with references to natural systems," she writes, "not as mimicry but as transdisciplinary translation of flexibility, adaptation, growth, and complexity into realms of architectural manifestation." Continuing, with reference to the idea of self-organization, she states, "The material world that this type of research interrogates reveals examples of nonlinear fabrication and self-assembly at the surface, and at deeper cultural and structural levels."[35]

Although *eSkin* is still in process and future publications will reveal more

PLATE 1. *Victimless Leather: A Prototype of Stitch-less Jacket Grown in a Technoscientific "Body,"* by Oron Catts and Ionat Zurr, Tissue Culture and Art Project, 2004. This living, two-inch-tall jacket, created using processes of tissue engineering by seeding mouse cells onto a jacket-shaped scaffold and growing it in a bioreactor, was on display at the Museum of Modern Art in *Design and the Elastic Mind* exhibition (2008).

PLATE 2. *Hylozoic Ground,* by Philip Beesley, at the Venice Biennale, 2010. Image by Philip Beesley. Olive oil and water in this glass vessel, along with other trace chemicals and small infusions of Venice seawater and carbon dioxide exhaled by visitors to the installation, form pre-protocells.

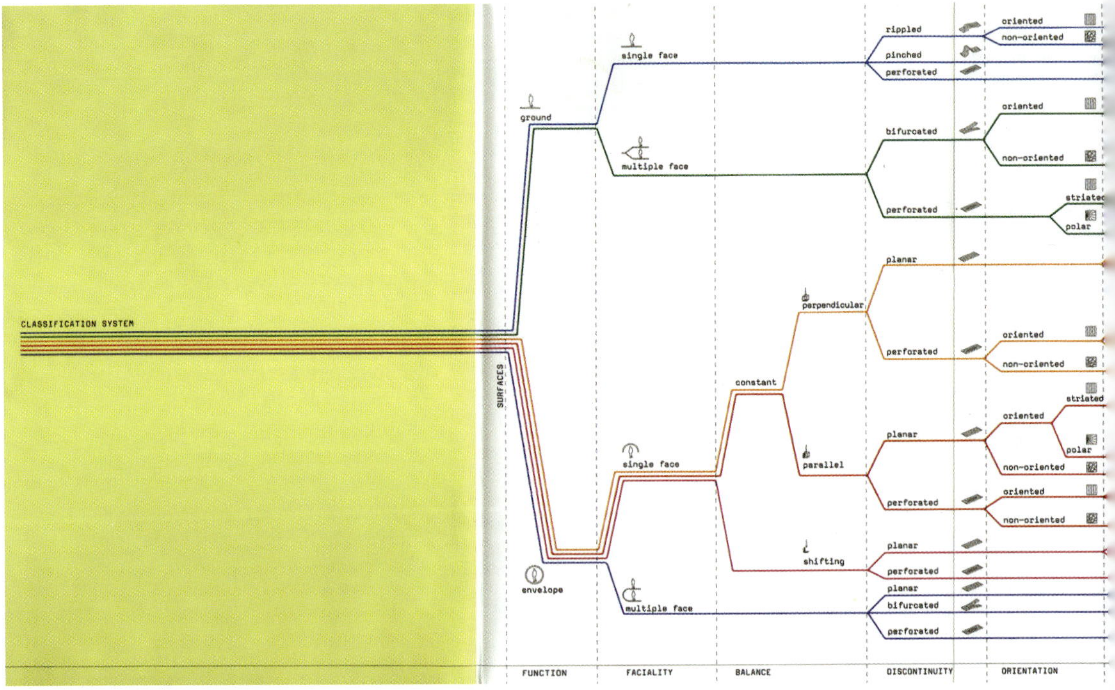

PLATE 3. FOA's phylogenetic tree diagram, inserted at the back of Michael Kubo and Albert Ferre in collaboration with Moussavi and Zaera-Polo, eds., *Phylogenesis: FOA's Ark* (Barcelona: Actar, 2003). This diagram of FOA's architectural practice is based on the same conceptual and linear branching structure as Darwin's tree of life (Figure 3.4).

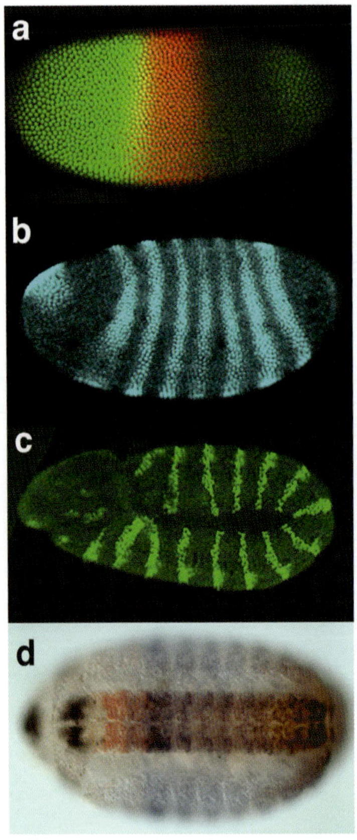

PLATE 4. Fluorescing "tool-kit proteins" made by *hox* genes reveal future segmentation and growth in the development of a fruit fly. Photographs by Jim Langeland and Steve Paddock, courtesy of Sean Carroll, University of Wisconsin–Madison. By engineering cells in a fruit fly embryo to fluoresce under UV light when certain proteins made by particular *hox* genes are present during development, Carroll and his lab could visually see these genes in action.

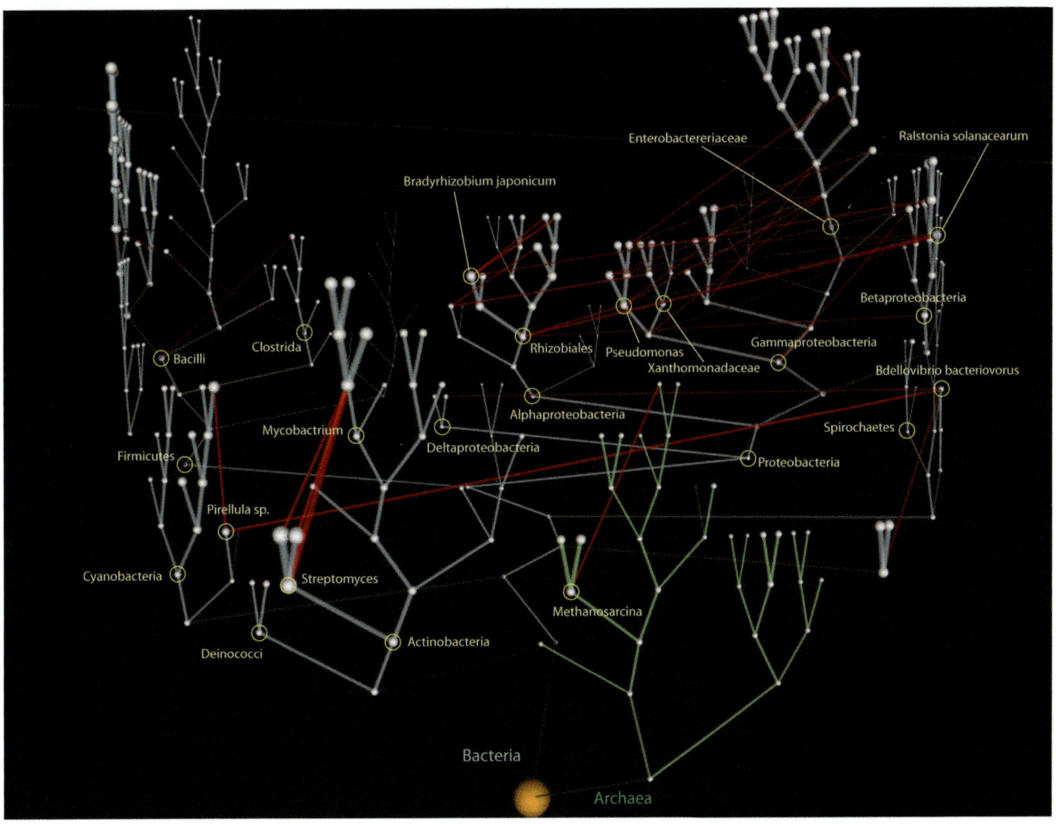

PLATE 5. Horizontal gene transfer reconfigures the microbial tree of life into a net of life, by Victor Kunin, Leon Goldovsky, Nikos Darzentas, and Christos Ouzounis. From "The Net of Life: Reconstructing the Microbial Phylogenetic Network," *Genome Research* 15 (2005): 954–59, available at http://genome.cshlp.org/content/15/7/954.full. Color key: bacteria = cyan, archaea = green, horizontal gene transfer (HGT) = red.

PLATE 6. Two toadflax flowers, *Linaria vulgaris,* both have the same genome, yet the one on the right has five separated petals and radial symmetry whereas the one on the left has five combined in a different tubular form and bilateral symmetry. One gene in the yellow five-petaled phenotype has a distinct methyl cap; this epigenetic marker is external to the DNA and is hereditary. Photographs by Enrico Coen, provided by the John Innes Centre, Norwich, United Kingdom.

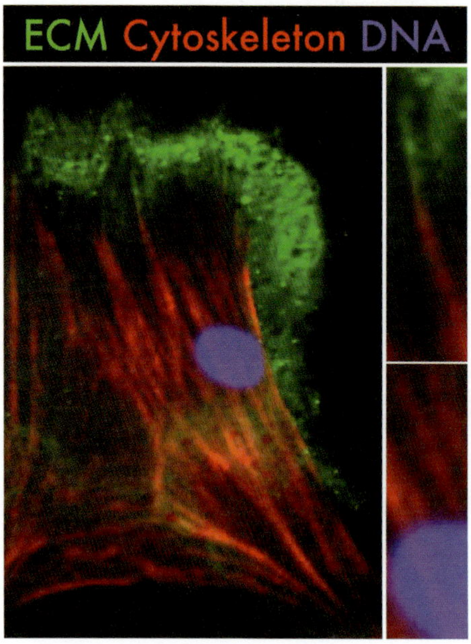

PLATE 7. Photomicrograph of fluorescing smooth muscle cell with striated actin filaments (red) connecting nucleic DNA (blue) to the extracellular matrix (green), by Peter Lloyd Jones, 2005. From Agne Taraseviciute, Benjamin Vincent, Pepper Schedin, and Peter Lloyd Jones, "Quantitative Analysis of Three-Dimensional Human Mammary Epithelial Tissue Architecture Reveals a Role for Tenascin-C in Regulating c-Met Function," *American Journal of Pathology* 176, no. 2 (February 2010): 827–38.

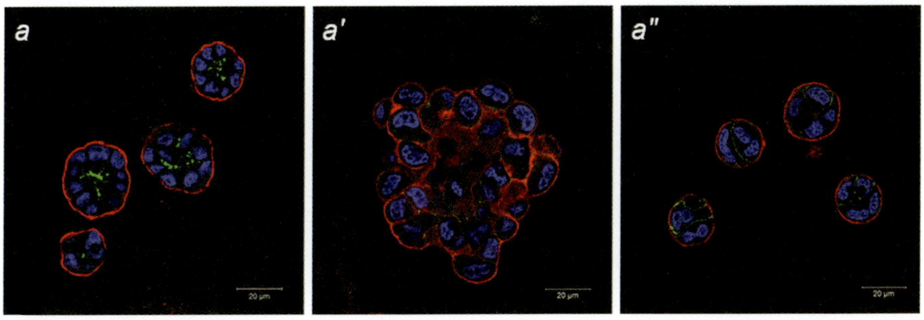

PLATE 8. Normal (a), malignant (a′) and reverted (a″) morphologies of malignant breast cancer cells, where the changes in morphology are not changes in whether the cells possess genes for breast cancer (all of them do), but changes in the chemical makeup of the extracellular matrix. Changing the matrix causes malignant breast cancer cells to produce the malignant morphology, but it can also cause malignant cells to revert to the normal morphology. Images by Cyrus Ghajar and Jamie Inman. From Valerie Weaver, O. W. Petersen, F. Wang, C. A. Larabell, P. Briand, C. Damsky, and Mina Bissell, "Reversion of the Malignant Phenotype of Human Breast Cells in Three-Dimensional Culture and In Vivo by Integrin Blocking Antibodies," *Journal of Cell Biology* 137, no. 1 (April 7, 1997): 238.

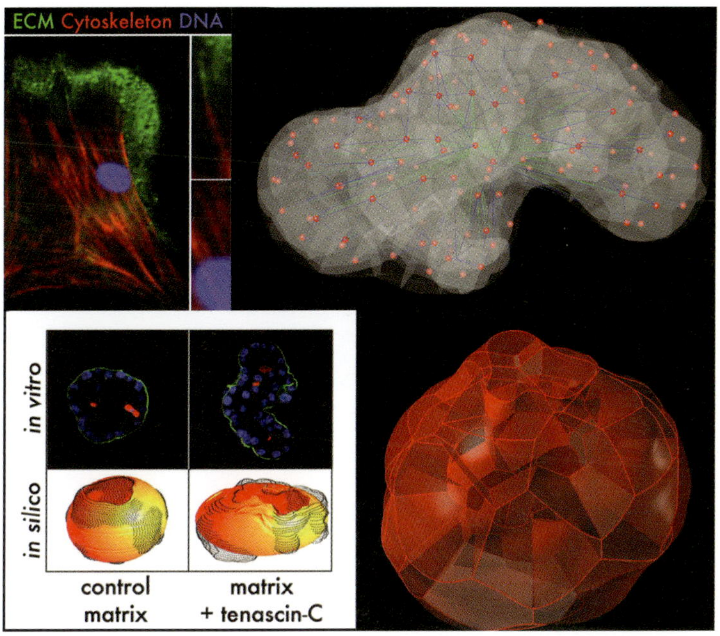

PLATE 9. Images from Peter Lloyd Jones and Jenny Sabin's syllabus for ARCH 745: Nonlinear Systems Biology and Design, Fall 2008, University of Pennsylvania, demonstrate their process of computational modeling of pathological and normal tissue morphologies in breast cancer. See Agne Taraseviciute, Benjamin Vincent, Pepper Schedin, and Peter Lloyd Jones, "Quantitative Analysis of Three-Dimensional Human Mammary Epithelial Tissue Architecture Reveals a Role for Tenascin-C in Regulating c-Met Function," *American Journal of Pathology* 176, no. 2 (February 2010): 827–38; and Sabin and Jones, "Nonlinear Systems Biology and Design: Surface Design" in *Silicon + Skin: Biological Processes and Computation,* ed. Andrew Kudless, Neri Oxman, and Marc Swackhamer (Morrisville, N.C.: Lulu Press, 2008), 54–65.

PLATE 10. *Branching Morphogenesis,* SIGGRAPH 2008, Design and Computation Galleries; Design Team: Sabin+Jones LabStudio; Jenny E. Sabin and Andrew Lucia in collaboration with Peter Lloyd Jones and Jones Lab members. Special thanks to Annette Fierro for critical commentary. Production Team: Dwight Engel, Matthew Lake, Austin McInerny, Marta Moran, Misako Murata, Jones Lab members. Image courtesy Jenny E. Sabin. This large-scale hanging textile installation, created out of 75,000 red and white zip-ties, illustrates the forces in lung tissue "exerted by interacting vascular cells upon their matrix environment."

PLATE 11. *PolyThread Knitted Textile Pavilion,* commissioned by Cooper Hewitt Smithsonian Design Museum for *Beauty: The Cooper Hewitt Design Triennial,* 2016. Images courtesy of Jenny Sabin, Matt Flynn, and William Staffeld. Compare with Sabin and Jones's images of cells in their matrix environment (shown in Plate 9, bottom left in vitro images). Here, the hooplike border visually references the extracellular matrix, while the cellular architextile made of thread that glows response to light within its borders shows tissue morphology.

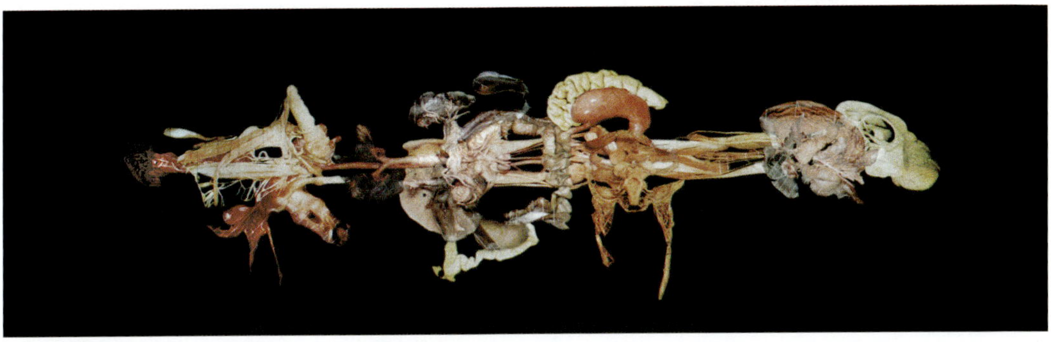

PLATE 12. *Synthetic Neoplasm,* by Marcos Cruz, 1998, described as a "collage of human organs showing the inner side of a synthetic neoplasm."

PLATE 13. *Genetic Barcelona Pavilion* (2007), by Alberto T. Estévez (with Marina Serer), in *Genetic Architectures III: New Bio and Digital Techniques,* ed. Estévez (Santa Fe, N.M.: SITES Books / ESARQ-UIC, 2009), 20. Photograph by Alberto T. Estévez. Mies van der Rohe's Barcelona Pavilion (1929) is remade most likely using polyfoam board, marble, chicken breast, and toothpicks, to demonstrate the possibilities of living "genetic architectures."

PLATE 14. *Hylozoic Ground,* by Philip Beesley, at the Venice Biennale, 2010. Image by Philip Beesley. The person in the center-right provides a sense of scale to this interactive sculpture that moves in response to motion in the room. Pre-protocell glass vessels (shown in Plate 2) are interspersed within these interwoven, pieced, acrylic forms.

information than currently published articles offer, the current descriptions of the project raise a number of questions that need to be addressed. While Sabin and her colleagues claim to be minimizing energy through the creation of an efficient, sustainable, and ecological building skin, the fact that it is a nanofabricated material instantly makes this seem problematic. The two current publications on the project do not address how it will minimize energy, much less state from which material the final product is intended to be constructed; the current prototype is made from polydimethylsiloxane. In general, however, nanomaterials and nanofabrication require a high embedded energy in life cycle analyses. This finding is verified by a recent article coauthored by the director of the Center for Life Cycle Analysis at Columbia University, Vasilis Fthenakis, and an environmental research scientist at the Ford Research and Innovation Center, Hyung Chul Kim. They examined twenty-two life cycle analyses of nanotech products since 2011, ranging from "nano-materials, coatings, photovoltaic devices, and fabrication technologies. The reviewed LCA studies indicate that nano-materials have higher cradle-to-gate energy demand per functional unit, and thus higher global warming impact than their conventional counterparts. . . . This is mainly attributed to the fact that nano-materials involve an energy intensive synthesis process, or additional mechanical process to reduce particle size," they write.[36] Their findings contrast those of the studies they reviewed, however, which argued that the "cradle-to-grave energy demand and global warming impact from nano-technologies in a device level is lower than from conventional technologies." This is due to the fact that "nano-materials are typically used in a small amount to improve functionality and the upgraded functionality offers more energy efficient operation of the device."[37] If one were to produce nanomaterials on the scale of a building, it is highly likely that this would entail a huge investment of energy in the production process, which is an integral part of the life cycle. Other questions concern the types of sensors to be used, which are also not specified. Most sensors function within a digital computational network, yet Sabin and her colleagues are proposing to create a "passively responsive" skin. Given that the early simulation processes of the optical effects were impossible because of the amount of computational memory involved, one would hope that the final product would require little to no energy for its responsive attributes. (Sabin cites another NSF EFRI SEED grant recipient, Maria-Paz Gutierrez, director of the BIOMS research center at UC Berkeley, whose "breathing membrane manages multiple functions through zero energy input" using "an array of pores and apertures.")[38] Finally, the ways in which cellular responses to their matrix are affecting the design of the nanoscale material or its performance goals are unstated and not obvious.

Apart from *eSkin,* Sabin's other installations (*Branching Morphogenesis, PolyThread,* and others in the *Poly* series or works visible on her website) face a similar critique as the works of Achim Menges and Beesley. Undoubtedly, the work of all three is very smart, visually stunning, even breathtaking, and in different ways highly innovative. As sculpture, interior architecture elements, or design, the works generate a powerful presence and affect. But in relation to architecture, the pavilions and installations function more as pure research or as prototypes with yet-uncertain applications in the creation of habitable structures. One of the goals shared by all three is to inspire new modes of thought about the materials and processes that can be used in the conception, design, fabrication, and function of architecture. For each, this entails the use of advanced digital technologies at almost every level of production, apart from the hand-assembly required for most of the final products. Yet, the ways in which their works are "environmentally responsive"—to humidity, light, or human motion and heat—are predicated on very narrow definitions of what counts as an environment, much less as an "ecology." Sabin and her colleagues' use of the word "ecological," with regard to *eSkin,* seems to resonate more with Menges's "morpho-ecologies" than Sabin's theoretically current knowledge of systems biology and biological complexity would suggest. Systems do not end with humans and their buildings; as life cycle analyses show, that is just the start of the process.

But in many other ways, Sabin's work and that of LabStudio stand out as radically different from the work of most other generative architects. LabStudio's niche within the field of generative architecture derives from Sabin and Jones's fundamental adherence to biological theories that prioritize context and connectivity, not genes, as the primary determinants of form and function. While genes are indispensable for living forms, they did not evolve and do not exist in isolation from their contexts: the genome and epigenome, cells, extracellular matrices, tissues, organs, other organisms, and the forces and substances in an organism's external environment. Rather, these four-dimensional contextual "layers" are systemically networked throughout development and maintenance of morphological form and function. This stance—favoring context as primary—positions LabStudio theoretically far beyond the neo-Darwinian central dogma and differentiates their work from that of most other generative architects.

Furthermore, Sabin and Jones began LabStudio by studying real biological morphogenesis in cells affected by breast cancer or pulmonary arterial hypertension. Their in vitro experiments simulated as closely as possible in a laboratory three-dimensional in vivo conditions. Sabin wrote the algorithms for modeling these in silico and printing them in composito, making biological tissue architecture visible and tactile to human eyes and hands. This type of lab experimentation is completely unfamiliar to most generative architects. Furthermore, Sabin does not rely on genetic algorithms or evolutionary computation for form generation but rather writes her own algorithms, often using Generative Components. These allow her to interpret the geometry of specific biological morphologies: development, cellular growth and proliferation, tissue architectures and their transformations over time via mechanical forces into different shapes. LabStudio's understanding of architectural structure and morphogenesis is particularly broad and deep, spanning biological and cultural architectural realms. Furthermore, it has had implications for new understandings of health and disease, although with Jones now being more involved with design and less involved with scientific laboratory research, the collaboration has shifted into new domains.

Finally, LabStudio's work shows that an even deeper interdisciplinary alliance is in the process of being forged by researchers who are seriously interested in the function and architecture of complex biological and environmental systems. The NSF EFRI SEED call for proposals signals a broader shift occurring as funding organizations recognize the need for different types of minds, trained in different disciplines, to work together to solve the crises we face and to innovate new strategies of conceptualization and not just problem-solving.[39] A 2009 story from the *Penn Gazette* boldly stated that LabStudio's "unusual partnership" may "rewrite the rules of biomedical research," a summation that along with the article's title—"An Architect Walks into the Lab"—hinted that the collaboration may lend more to biomedicine than it does to architecture. Yet the obverse—that science may transform architecture through such inventions as the potential creation of energy-minimizing "intelligent skins," new tensegrity constructions, or mobile skeletal structures that allow buildings to change shape (should that be deemed necessary)—alludes to the ways architects are also using scientific research and development to rethink the potential of their practice.

CHAPTER 5

GROWING LIVING BUILDINGS

Tissue and Genetic Engineering in Architecture and Design

Growing living buildings can be accomplished in different ways, entailing variables of size, speed, species, cost, technology, vulnerability, and ethics. For example, over the last few centuries, the Khasi tribe in Meghalaya, India, have coaxed the roots of ficus trees to grow into bridges over a local river. Roots and branches can just as easily be grown into the form of habitable structures, as imagined by Mitchell Joachim, Lara Greden, and Javier Arbona in their *Fab Tree Hab* (Figure 5.1).[1] Curator William Myers included both of these examples in *BioDesign: Nature, Science, Creativity* (2012), along with other works of arborsculpture—*baubotanik* in German—shaped into architectural forms, and urban buildings constructed to allow plants to grow over their exteriors and roofs.[2] While the arborsculpture approach is slow, quite inexpensive, and can be relatively unintrusive as far as human manipulation of other species, it clearly is not new, even in terms of being promoted by prominent designers. In 1970, counterculture guru Stewart Brand wrote, "Live dwellings? How soon? Houses of living vegetable tissue. The walls take up your CO2 and return oxygen. They grow or diminish to accommodate your family changes. Add a piece of the kitchen wall to the stew pot. House as friend. Dweller and dwelling domesticate each other. Society for the prevention of cruelty to structures."[3]

Brand clearly hopes the process of residing in a live shelter might help domesticate humans, who have a tendency to abuse other living creatures. This theme is also central to the work of artists Oron Catts and Ionat Zurr, whose *Victimless Leather* two-inch-tall living "leather" jacket, created out of mouse cells using tissue engineering, was also featured in *BioDesign*.[4] While the artists have created and shown this piece many times for different exhibitions, its 2008 version at the Museum of Modern Art's *Design and the Elastic Mind* sparked much admiration and controversy. Partway into the exhibition, the coat's sleeve started separating as cells grew out of control and clogged the

FIGURE 5.1. *Fab Tree Hab,* by Terreform ONE, 2008. Courtesy of Mitchell Joachim, Lara Greden, and Javier Arbona. To create these homes, (relatively) fast-growing trees would be sculpted around a removable and reusable structural scaffold. This designed process, somewhat ironically in contrast to how trees grow on their own without scaffolds, results in very similar structures, lending a green twist to familiar suburban sameness.

system, so curator Paola Antonelli decided to pull the plug on the peristaltic pump and kill the coat. "Museum Kills Live Exhibit" stated the title of the *New York Times* coverage afterward; the story missed the obvious irony that the piece was thus no longer "victimless" (Plate 1).[5]

Although a jacket is not architecture, nor a two-inch-tall anything habitable by humans, the work of Catts and Zurr has been elevated to the status of "prototype" by some generative architects who want to use advancing biotechnologies—particularly tissue and genetic engineering—to design and grow living buildings. For example, Marcos Cruz and Steve Pike at the Bartlett School of Architecture, University College London, for their coedited issue of *AD,* "Neoplasmatic Design" (2008), adopted "the broader definition of artists/researchers Oron Catts and Ionat Zurr, for neoplasm as a 'semi-living entity.'"[6] In the issue, they ask, "How are designers going to understand design when it implies notions of programming, control, and maintenance of cellular structures that grow, evolve, and eventually mutate?"[7] "Ultimately," Cruz asserts, flesh-based designs such as Catts and Zurr's work and the gamepods visualized in David Cronenberg's *eXistenZ* "launch a very important debate on how we will face the prospect of a semi-living architecture."[8] For the most part, arborsculpture and "green" buildings with plants covering them do not interest generative architects. The former is likely too low-tech, requiring no "associative modeling" or computer automated manufacturing, although *Fab Tree Hab* would entail CAD/CAM design of the scaffold on which to shape the growth of the tree. The other approach of green walls or roofs perhaps seems too staid for the way it readily upholds the separation of nature and culture, with plants superficially covering an architectural structure. The rhetoric of generative architecture tends toward collapsing, not reifying, these boundaries. Both approaches may even be too botanical; Catts and Zurr's work and tissue engineering of the sort discussed by generative architects, like the fleshy blobs that Cruz calls "Synthetic Neoplasms," involve animal cells and tissues (Plate 12). There is no discussion by generative architects of whether a clientele exists that wants to live inside animalish structures. Regardless of the reasons for Catts and Zurr's work being considered an architectural prototype, it is featured in books by generative architects and twice they have published in the primary journal promoting the movement, *AD,* in 2008 and 2013.[9] Catts has lectured at the Bartlett School of Architecture at the invitation of Cruz, who asked him to explain how to use biotechnologies like tissue engineering to grow living architecture.[10]

That architects continue to imagine the possibility of tissue-engineered living buildings reveals a number of rather embarrassing facts. First, it demonstrates either how shallowly they read Catts and Zurr's own writings—even, apparently, the ones in architectural journals—or else, how blindly determined they are to overlook or not address the critique and numerous problems raised by the artists. These include problems of technological production, materiality, sterility, scale, and ethics. At the most basic level, they miss the very visible fact that tissue-engineered entities must grow inside glass jars in a sterile environment. Even the dome that Buckminster Fuller and Shoji Sadao envisioned placing over part of Manhattan in 1960 would not come close to meeting the necessary criteria for tissue-engineered architecture, which also requires a perfusion pump and nutrient fluid suited to scale. In this regard, usually exhibitions featuring Catts and Zurr's work end with *The Killing Ritual,* which simply means that the work is removed from its sterile glass chamber and people are allowed to touch it. Touching is killing, for the bacteria on human hands so damages the tissue that it dies. Could one live in a building without touching it? People cannot be autoclaved before entering their homes. Dennis Dollens's acknowledgment in text of the integral role of the bioreactor in tissue engineering is rare; most generative architects completely bypass this issue. Because most tissues grown for medical purposes are then implanted into a living body, often after growing for months inside a host organism that cultivates it, Dollens assumes something similar would have to happen for architecture: "For this dependent situation to change, for the possibility of an autonomous grown work, enormous medical, scientific, and engineering strides must be made so that the work's tissue can become part of a pre-existing life system."[11] It is only within the context of a living body that animal tissue gains its full functionality, integrating into the body to be kept alive and healthy and to maintain its proper identity owing to epigenetic contextual cues. What existing organism, then, is of a size and kind to function as a host body to maintain tissue-engineered architecture, where the vasculature of the architectural form could integrate with the organism's own?

FIGURE 5.2. Hollwich Kushner (HWKN), still image from the video *Econic Design,* also known as *MEtreePOLIS,* available on YouTube. Genetically engineered kudzu takes Atlanta, in 2108, "off the grid," meaning both the destruction of the modernist grid of cities and skyscrapers and the harvesting of energy from plant photosynthesis, rather than from fossil fuel–powered electric grids.

This hurdle may be insurmountable by those dreaming of this future, prompting them to turn to alternative biotechnologies such as genetic engineering in order to bypass the bioreactor/scale/host–organism problems of tissue engineering. Genetic engineering (as distinct from synthetic biology) involves altering gene sequences in a particular organism's genome with the intent of designing its form, function, or both; feasibility depends on many factors.[12] Owing to the need for animals to develop inside a womb—no incubator or current technology can accomplish the same thing as a womb—engineering plants seem a more likely option.[13] In 2008, Matthias Hollwich and Marc Kushner, of the New York–based architecture studio Hollwich Kushner, imagined something similar to this in their video *Econic Design,* also referred to as *MEtreePOLIS* (Figure 5.2).[14] Rachel Armstrong the same year described "an ideal architecture" as "one that you can plant as a seed having programmed it with all the information it needs to grow itself in an environment where it can organically seek out and connect with the resources that it needs. Through its lifetime it would remain responsive to its surroundings and adjust according to the demands and needs of its human habitants," though how this happens she does not state. "The architecture would be able to reproduce by cloning itself using a germ line structure that offers humans an opportunity to make any necessary genetic adjustments." Like Brand, Armstrong imagines house as friend (or slave?) that submits itself for genetic alterations from its humans when it is cloning itself. "The end of the lifecycle of the architecture would come," she predicts, "when it is no longer responsive to human activity," like a tired toy, and "becomes an inert, skeletal structure, possibly decaying into the ecosystem to be recycled by its progeny."[15] Given that the pursuit of architectural "sustainability" is a primary motivator driving architects' desires to grow living buildings, it is ironic that Armstrong thinks there is only a partial chance that they might decay to be recycled.[16]

This chapter therefore explores the multiple ironies present in the literature in generative architecture on growing living buildings, beginning with the ironies and critiques initially raised by Catts and Zurr. It examines the application of current technologies of tissue and genetic engineering for architectural purposes in order to demonstrate the infeasibility and impracticality of generative architects' visions. Part of its critique stems from architects' reliance on what historian of science David Depew calls "digital tropology," the idea that organisms are just digital printouts from a designed DNA chain. Another part of its critique is due to the complexity of biological systems with regard to new knowledge of morphogenesis and gene regulation through epigenetic mechanisms with implications for the difficulty of control and design of the form and function of cells, tissues, organs, and organisms, in relation to the environment. Although the new gene-editing technology known as CRISPR/Cas9 (from clustered regularly interspaced short palindromic repeats, with Cas9 being a derivative associated protein) is revolutionizing the method, relative accuracy, and cost of genetic engineering, editing DNA alters only one part—albeit an important one—of a very complex interconnected system.[17] And part just comes from common sense. For example, Cruz and Pike use the word "bioterrorism" in one sentence, and in the very next they lament that "architecture continues to be seen as fundamentally removed from such phenomena." They then introduce their guest-edited issue on "Neoplasmatic Design" as arguing in favor of a future with "neo-biological" "semi-living" architecture.[18] Alternately, Cruz devotes pages to imagining medical surgical procedures as a new design technique for altering aesthetics in this type of architecture, but gives barely a single sentence to the much more obvious and serious point that living buildings would require medical interventions for injury and disease, not just "facelifts" and plastic surgery.[19] Given these most basic commonsense critiques in addition to many others, why are generative architects promoting growing living buildings and what are the effects of their pronouncements? The chapter concludes with some thoughts to these questions.

Tissue Engineering in Architecture

Just a few years after scientists Robert Langer and Joseph Vacanti published the article that initiated the field of tissue engineering in medicine in 1993 and the Vacanti brothers grew a cartilage ear on the back of a mouse, Catts and Zurr founded the Tissue Culture and Art Project.[20] Catts was finishing his graduate degree in product design, seeking to implement more "sustainable modes of production."[21] But as he explored the possibilities of tissue engineering for use in design, he and Zurr decided that the best strategy to expose the "very profound ethical and epistemological issues" that the technology presented, especially outside the context of medicine, would be to work as artists rather than as designers; they carried this mind-set into the founding of SymbioticA, their lab and artist residency program at the University of Western Australia in Perth.[22] From the very outset, then, they have been critical of the role of design in alliance with a competitive capitalism and industrial mass production in promoting consumerism and ecological destruction.[23] Yet, owing to the unease they felt in manipulating animal cells and tissues, rather than embrace and promote tissue engineering as a sustainable design material for living products, they chose the road of contestation.[24]

In 2000, they were appointed research fellows at one of the leading research sites in the field, the Tissue Engineering and Organ Fabrication Laboratory at Massachusetts General Hospital of the Harvard Medical School. Here they created their first works that were displayed alive outside of a scientific laboratory at the *Ars Electronica* exhibition. During that year, they produced living works in the forms of worry dolls (McCoy Cell Line) and pig wings (pig bone marrow stem cells differentiated into bone tissue). They became the first to grow in vitro meat using prenatal sheep muscle cells in *Tissue Engineered Steak No. 1* (2000).[25] These initial works matured into a "series of works that dealt, with much irony," Catts and Zurr wrote in *AD* in 2008, "with the 'technologically mediated victimless utopia' that involved the creation of tissue-engineered in vitro meat and leather," the latter referring to *Disembodied Cuisine* (2003) and *Victimless Leather* (2004–8).[26]

Thus, in 2005 when Dennis Dollens, instructor in the Genetic Architectures doctoral program at the Escuela Arquitectura (ESARQ) at the International University of Catalunya in Barcelona, first discussed Catts and Zurr's Pig Wings Project in his book *Digital–Botanic Architecture,* he was an early promoter of their work as an architectural prototype. In his book, which is also one of the early works in the body of literature for generative architecture, he writes, "*The Pig Wings Project* . . . comes closest to modeling a biologically-grown prototypical architecture."[27] Catts had just been interviewed for a *New York Times* piece, and his comment that "these entities we create might become our naturalish companions, our machines, and even our dwellings" caught Dollens's attention.[28] Dollens emailed him and published excerpts of their exchange in his book. Their conversation revealed that the biggest problem facing tissue engineers wanting to create "large-scale" tissues was that of "internal plumbing," meaning the need for vascular tissue inside of other tissue to function as a circulatory system to impart nourishment and remove wastes.[29]

Years later, "large-scale" is actually still very small when the production method is tissue engineering. At the time, Catts and Zurr were using the standard "top-down" process, which entailed seeding living cells onto a handcrafted scaffold made from "biodegradable/bioabsorbable polymers," including polyglycolic acid (PGA), polylactic-co-glycolic acid (PLGA), and poly-4-hydroxybutyrate (P4HB); polylactic acid (PLA) is a common scaffold medium now.[30] The cells proliferate over the scaffold while the scaffold slowly biodegrades inside a sterile bioreactor, which regularly moves in order to impart mechanical forces into the tissue that it needs to experience. Motion also both freshens the contact location of liquid nutrients that diffuse through the tissues and removes the wastes that compile on the exterior of the tissue. Diffusion of oxygen and nutrients only occurs through a maximum depth of one hundred to two hundred micrometers, a distance that limits the thickness of grown tissue. However, more recent innovations in processes of tissue engineering can simulate or create vascular tissues for purposes of circulation.[31] For example, some researchers have used very creative methods to make voids through a tissue that can function as hollow tubes for fluid transmission. One used a "sacrificial" "sugar" or carbohydrate glass that was removed after its insertion; another used a thick gel that later turned to liquid and drained out.[32] Another current technique, printing onto perfusion chips rather than seeding a scaffold, permits thicknesses up to or greater than one centimeter, which David Kolesky and colleagues refer to as "thick vascular tissues."[33] Thus, in the eleven years since the problem of "internal plumbing" was brought to architects' attention by Catts—with scientists in the meantime constantly working on this problem—thickness is possible only to the scale of Catts and Zurr's small living leather jackets.

Shifting one's approach to using recently developed methods of "bottom-up" bioprinting does not solve the problems of vasculature and scale, even though this alternate method sounds as if it aligns better with the methods and rhetoric of generative architects because of its reliance on CAD/CAM technologies and "bottom-up" "self-assembly." Around 2000, scientists began using 3-D printers to print scaffolds onto which to seed cells (the "top-down" method), and by the mid-2000s "bioprinting" began in earnest when scientists began to fill emptied ink cartridges from color 3-D printers with different cell types and matrix materials in order to experiment with what was then called "direct cell writing."[34] Since then, a number of different bioprinting techniques have been invented, each with benefits and drawbacks. While inkjet printing is still used with high precision in cell placement location and high cell viability post-printing, it is relatively slow and works with low-viscosity liquid-based materials that do not hold up well in maintaining voids that are necessary for vasculature circulation. Extrusion-based bioprinting, while being less precise in cell placement and having lower cell viability post-printing (as the forces of extrusion can damage cellular phenotypes), is faster and better at printing thicker materials. These materials include decellularized extracellular matrix, a superb but costly material taken from a former organism's tissues sans cells that maintains its epigenetic cues. It therefore is better for printing voids or porous constructs that can function as vasculature.[35] For both types, the goal of bioprinting is to speed up the process of manufacturing a tissue or organ for transplant by putting the different cell types that tissues have in their correct positions at the outset, using the precision of digital design and manufacture. Although bioprinted tissues still require time in a sterile bioreactor and also months inside a host organism in order to join together into mature functional tissue with developed vasculature, because the cells are printed at the outset instead of dividing on a scaffold after seeding, weeks are saved after the printing process.[36] The time is simply moved beforehand, since cell division still takes time; it is just done before printing rather than afterward.[37]

Thus, in both "top-down" and "bottom-up" tissue engineering, scale is limited by the problem of vasculature as well as by the size of the bioreactor and host organism. Large bioreactors do exist; for example, the largest bioreactor capable of culturing cells in suspension has a volume of twenty cubic meters. Yet, this is used not for creating tissues that need to fuse together with the proper form and function, but rather for culturing cells for use in "labmeat," which is similar to ground beef if cow cells are used. A "run" or "batch" of this size takes four to five weeks of culturing before being ready for chemical cross-linking to form "easily settling aggregates of cells" that can be pressed together and then ground into "minced meat."[38] Clearly, even this approach and scale is not compatible with what architects imagine, since both form and function are integral to architectural and organismal performance. Even if one could print tissue or organ or organism parts modularly in order to fit each part inside the limitations of the bioreactor or host organism, assembling them together after removal from host organisms would require yet another host for them to bond and mature together. This is very far-fetched, but architects like to use 3-D printers modularly and tissue engineers like to think architecturally—for example, imagining the body as a building where workers can repair any part as needed (Figure 5.3), or considering the extracellular matrix as the architectural scaffold for an organ.[39] The latter was proposed by Doris Taylor and her team at the University of Minnesota, who in 2008 invented the process of whole organ decellularization. They removed the cells from a rat's and a pig's heart using a solution that left only the extracellular matrix remaining. They then seeded this "scaffold" or "framework" with new cells and, after a week of keeping the cells alive with a perfusion pump, the cells began to contract and the heart began to beat. They hope to use this process for human organ replacement, seeding decellularized matrices of pig organs with a person's own cells in order to grow a personalized replacement organ.[40]

Taylor's approach reveals a number of very interesting factors at play in how tissue engineering has developed over the previous decade, including not only issues of tissue architecture but also the importance of epigenetic factors in maintaining cell and tissue identity, an issue that is only now beginning to be addressed.[41] In "top-down" tissue engineering where a 3-D-printed scaffold is seeded with cells—be they stem cells or already differentiated cells—these include the shape or architecture of the scaffold itself and the material from which is it made, which is typically a synthetic biodegradable and bioabsorbable material. In the mid-2000s, Wei Sun's laboratory at the Computer-Aided Tissue Engineering (CATE) laboratory at Drexel University began questioning the standard method of creating scaffolds in orthogonal grid patterns, which were commonly used regardless of the needed final shape of the tissue or organ which the tissue was intended to transplant. Sun teamed up with generative architects Mattias del Campo and Sandra Manninger of the Austrian architectural firm SPAN, who at the time were

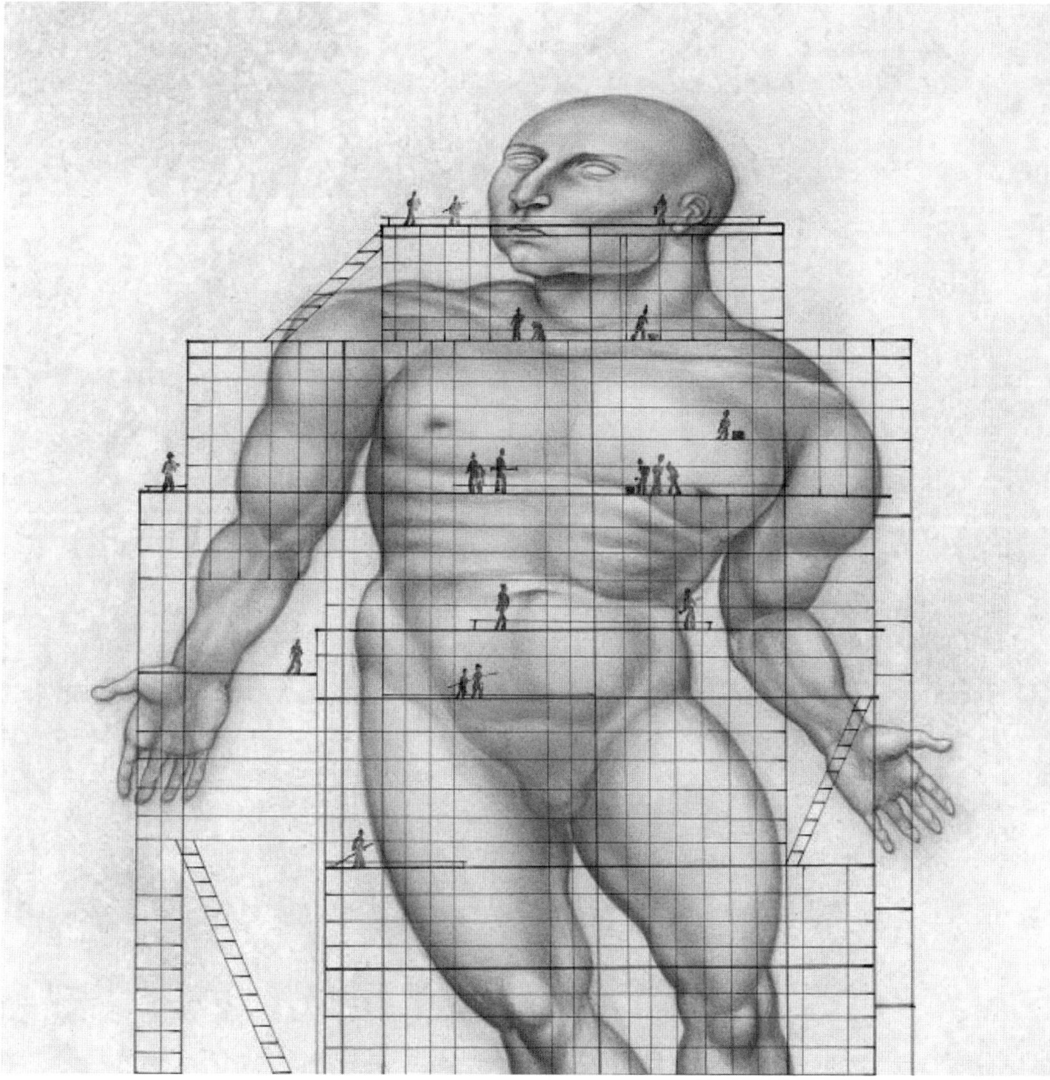

FIGURE 5.3. Illustration for "The Power of Tissue Engineering," by Anita Kuntz. In *Scientific American,* April 1999, 59. © Anita Kuntz. Tissue engineers and matrix biologists both describe tissue using architectural metaphors. The extracellular matrix surrounding cells in a living tissue, or the scaffold onto which cells are seeded in tissue engineering, play structural and functional roles in tissue morphology. While visualizing this idea of the architectural scaffold, this illustration also suggests that bodies can be conceived of as modular with interchangeable parts, in that broken parts can be replaced with newly grown ones.

pursuing their doctoral degrees at the University of Applied Arts in Vienna under the directorship of architect and designer Greg Lynn. Del Campo and Manninger were interested in using their skills in digitally designing complex geometric architectures that could be used as scaffolds that are truer-to-form in tandem with a tissue engineer who could then help them explore the possibilities of using tissue technologies in architecture. They designed complex scaffold architectures and then sent the files to Sun, who 3-D printed them at CATE in 2006 (Figure 5.4).

FIGURE 5.4. Tissue engineering test no. 1, by SPAN (Matias del Campo and Sandra Manninger), rendering, 2006. This model was created by SPAN at a time when they were collaborating with Dr. Wei Chun at his Computer-Aided Tissue Engineering lab at Drexel University. Before this, most scaffolds for tissue engineering were orthogonal, but with the rise of 3-D printing and the ability to model and print complex geometries, new approaches to architectural scaffold design in tissue engineering and tissue-engineered architecture seemed possible.

Two years later, del Campo and Manninger spoke at the ACADIA conference about "Speculations on Tissue Engineering and Architecture," where they explained their hope that in complex generative architecture, since the joints in complex curvilinear panel geometries pose the most difficult construction problems, that "possibilities within the realm of biological *wet* solutions inside the realm of tissue engineering" might exist.[42] They imagine bridging "a gap of a joint with organic matter that can provide the same qualities as normal gaskets used in such cases," and using bioprinting to fabricate "responsive components consisting of heterogeneous materials, each one with a specific quality and entirely sustainable." These would be "ready to grow together as soon as they are on site and provided with the necessary nutrients," with the "main problem" being "the problem of scale and the problem of access to the material." They imagine that these building materials could be "able to regenerate . . . be responsive on [*sic*] environmental conditions . . . provide light by bioluminescence and they can die and decompose. They can transform carbon dioxide into oxygen."[43] As is hopefully clear, the problems are many more than they realize, since they fail to mention sterile glass enclosures, bioreactors, host organisms, connected vasculatures, epigenetic changes, and how cells or tissues would grow together on-site, in addition to scale, access to material, and death, the latter of which they note but, ironically, fail to consider an architectural problem. Additionally, most bioluminescence is so dim to human eyes even in darkness that many challenges face designers hoping to use it for anything other than mood lighting.[44]

At the small scale, though, seeding a synthetic scaffold that at least has the proper tissue architecture, such as something like that designed by del Campo and Manninger for Sun, could possibly improve the time or results for achieving successful tissue function. This is because having correct cellular and tissue morphologies is crucial to their functionality.[45] Even better, if one could use actual extracellular matrix rather than synthetic polymers as media in "bottom-up" bioprinting, as is possible with extrusion-based printers, then the proper epigenetic cues for particular tissue architectures with its different cellular identities would already be present. Since knowledge of what these epigenetic cues are in human tissues—much less, that of other organisms—is only now being researched through the National Institutes of Health Roadmap Epigenomics Mapping Consortium, Taylor's approach to decellularizing whole organs offers an ingenious solution that to a significant degree skirts both problems of proper architecture and epigenetic factors, since the matrix form and functions are already intact.[46] But the ethics and the appeal of using the organs of slaughtered animals for purposes other than medical organ adaptation and transplantation—say, to create care-needing, mortal, semi-living products or architectural gaskets—confounds. Is the appeal due to the presumed "sustainability," as they state, of using living tissues for gaskets in a building that is already made of complex geometric panels—perhaps of titanium or ethylene tetrafluoroethylene? If so, this is tokenism at the very least. The allure more likely is the ability to control and utilize life through processes of industrial production, whether mass or customized. This pursuit depends on a conceptual reductionism of the complexity of living cells, tissue, and organisms into manageable, controllable, instrumentalizable parts. Such mental and capitalist constructs do not, though, affect the actualities of biological complexity.

Catts and Zurr are critical of what they refer to as "the instrumentalisation of life," and they note the irony that "the further life is being instrumentalised, becoming a product for human manipulation, matter—whether living, semi-living, or non-living—is being attributed with vitality and agency."[47] This irony compounds another that pervades all their tissue-engineered pieces, whether attributed with the name "victimless" or not. In tissue-engineered "semi-living" entities, it is not just that the semi-living entity dies—that is, becomes a victim—when it stops having its fluids replaced or is removed from its sterile chamber, but rather that the fluid itself that is its nourishment comes from death. Most nutrient fluid used in tissue engineering consists of about 10 percent fetal calf serum (FCS, also called fetal bovine serum or FBS), which is extracted from pregnant cows just before slaughter through the insertion of a long needle through their body into the amniotic sac.[48] Although serum-free nutrient fluids exist, they are costly and cells do not grow as quickly or effectively in them; therefore, until these conditions change and a serum-free fluid is adopted by the industry, tissue engineering is intimately connected with the cattle industry.

Therefore, claims of tissue-engineered products being "sustainable" or "animal-free" are quite likely misleading. When journalists claim for the production of "synthetic meat" ("labmeat") that "they also do not need to slaughter any cows," and misled ethicists then proclaim that it "stops cruelty for animals" and "is better for the environment. . . . It gets the ethical two thumbs up," they are misspeaking or speaking of which they do not know.[49] Similarly, if one were to wear a coat produced through processes of tissue engineering, one would not be making a more sustainable choice than if one wore a leather jacket for which only one cow, and not also her baby, needs to die. So long as nutrient fluid contains FCS, this is true whether one chooses a coat that is "semi-living"—assuming one could be made at the scale of a human body and kept from dying on contact—or one that is biofabricated but dead. For example, Modern Meadow in New York may have been developing biofabricated leather products from cultured bovine cells grown in a sterile incubator or bioreactor like "labmeat," but then pressed and bonded into "leather" instead of being cooked. In 2015, Suzanne Lee, the company's founder, gave Daniel Grushkin, cofounder of Genspace in New York, a tour of the lab and showed him that they were growing bovine cells. Lee collaborates with Gabor and Andras Forgacs, two of the founders of the company Organovo, a leading tissue and organ bioprinting company in San Diego. While the Modern Meadow website then claimed that they were creating "animal-free" leather without "animals," if they are still using bovine cells and tissue culture processes with nutrient media containing FCS, then their products are not "animal-free" and they are not "unlocking the capabilities of nature to solve our biggest sustainability challenges." Since 2017, however, the company is now using synthetic biology to engineer yeast cells to make collagen, from which they are creating their new material Zoa.[50]

In addition to the instrumentalization of life, Catts and Zurr also are opposed to the use of digital tropology and the "genohype" and "DNA mania" on which it is based. "Life is not a coded program," they write, "and we are not our DNA." They clearly state that DNA on its own outside of a cell cannot produce anything.[51] Even Craig Venter's creation in 2010 of the "first self-replicating synthetic bacterial cell," they point out, relied on a preexisting bacterial cell into which synthetic DNA was inserted.[52] Creating a cell from scratch, much less an organism, is something that protocell researchers have been trying to do for decades. The difficulties of creating viable tissues at "larger scales" even from conglomerations of cells using tissue engineering show how exponentially difficult the dream of creating a "bottom-up" organism from self-organizing molecules is. Yet, this is just the vision hyped by nanotech researcher Paul Rothemund, whose *DNA Origami* (2007) that created happy faces from synthesized DNA was included in MoMA's *Design and the Elastic Mind* exhibition as an example of the beginning of design by "self-organization" and "self-assembly." In his TED talk "Casting Spells with DNA," Rothemund stated, "What we really want to do in the end is to learn how to program self-assembly, so we can build anything, right?" It is as if digital algorithms are the means by which molecules bind and life occurs. "We want to be able to build technological artifacts that are maybe good for the world." (Maybe? Perhaps he means if not good for the world, then good for capitalism?) "We want to learn how to build biological artifacts like people and whales and trees," he asserts, conflating living beings of all sorts with products. "And if it is the case that we can reach that level of complexity—if our ability to program molecules gets to be that good—then that will be truly magic."[53] Catts and Zurr's Pig Wings Project and *Victimless Leather,* which Antonelli killed, were just behind the partitions from Rothemund's work in the exhibition. There, they were being promoted as design, not art, that will help us "take a more responsible attitude toward our environment and curb our destructive consumerism."[54] This is yet another of the ironies, one that was certainly not apparent at the MoMA exhibition: that Catts and Zurr oppose "DNA mania," understand the crucial importance of the cell, and deeply respect the autonomy of other living entities, but that Rothemund seems to think that by programming molecules of which he focuses on DNA, we will be able to build "biological artifacts like people."

Finally, Zurr and Catts early on in their work and publications made it very clear, in their article "Are the Semi-Living Semi-Good or Semi-Evil?" (2003), that the exploitation of living or semi-living beings under the context of capitalist profit-taking and political ideologies of fear based upon "othering" those different from oneself makes them uneasy. "Though looking at the level of compassion to living systems of our own species from different ethnicities, religions, races and class," during times of "increased suspicion and intolerance," "we are worried in regard to these new lives," they write. "The form and the application of our newly acquired knowledge will be determined by the prevailing ideologies that develop and control the technology. . . . When the manipulation of life takes place in an atmosphere of conflict and profit-driven competition, the long-term results might be disquieting."[55] They correctly note that "Darwin's writing on the origin of species stemmed from the economic theories that were developed in the late eighteenth century. Adam Smith's *An Inquiry into the Nature and Causes of the Wealth of Nations,* which was published in 1776, argues for a natural basis for poverty and the need for a free market as a model for progress and innovation."[56]

While Zurr and Catts acknowledge that the competitive theory of capitalism and evolution with survival of the fittest continues, in fact other possibilities exist as well, such as biologist Lynn Margulis's theory of evolution by cooperation. "The nature of the explanations of the mechanisms governing evolutionary principles reflects the dominant ideologies of our society rather than some scientific truth," they write. "The microbiologist Lynn Margulis . . . has offered an alternative emphasis in regard to the evolutionary process. She theorized that some of the greatest leaps in evolutionary development are caused as a result of cooperation and symbiotic relationships."[57] Her theory of endosymbiogenesis as the origin of eukaryotic cells from the merger and cooperation of two prokaryotic cells was in fact the source for their choice of the name SymbioticA.[58] Rather than uphold the "othering" of humans and "other" forms of life or semi-life through instrumentalization and manipulation, they intend to promote cooperation and symbiotic relationships. "Can it be that the basic building blocks of our own bodies, hence the eukaryotic cell, is a result of symbiotic relations between two entities (different bacteria)? Can it be that the origins for our own functioning body are collaborations between the entities we consider to be our enemies?" they ask.[59] The strong suggestion is that the answer is yes.

Genetic Engineering in Architecture

Many of Catts and Zurr's concerns and critiques are equally relevant to practices of genetic engineering and genetically engineered architecture even if the technological hurdles are different. Standard genetic engineering alters gene sequences of an organism's genome either through the addition or removal of DNA using various methods, in order to produce desired alterations to what otherwise functions as generally the same organism. In other words, one is not completely repurposing the organism to function solely as a "workhorse" or "chassis" just to produce a chemical, as is the intent in much synthetic biology. In the recent past, choice of method has depended on whether the organism being engineered is a bacterium, plant, or animal, although now, CRISPR/Cas9 is able to be used for any organism. As the changed genome occurs inside of a single cell to result in an adult organism if it is a plant or an animal, the engineered cell must undergo the process of morphogenesis and growth. Hence, it is common to use stem cells for this process if it is an animal, but since many plant cells are totipotent, almost any plant cell can be used to regenerate an entire plant. If one has the DNA sequence one wants to insert by removing it from another genome including (usually) the desired gene(s) as well as a promoter and terminator for each to mark its transcription, it can be inserted into a cell's cytoplasm using a plasmid or into a cell's nucleus using a viral vector or microinjection. These methods come with greater or lesser precision as to where the genetic material is actually placed. Even with CRISPR/Cas9, although the locational accuracy for gene placement is greatly improved since the binding site for the target gene is clearly specified, studies have shown both on-target and off-target activity. Enough off-target placement occurs that one review from 2016 states, "It would seem inappropriate to suggest that the CRISPR/Cas9 platform *per se* is specific or non-specific" in its locational accuracy, although in general its relative accuracy surpasses that of the previous approaches. Since genome architecture matters, including the tightness of a chromosome's coiling owing to chromatin, histones, and whether methylation is present, placement can affect whether the gene will function as intended; it often does not.[60] To this end, the same review notes that future studies of

CRISPR/Cas9 are "required to understand how chromatin structure and sequence context contribute to target site accessibility, as well as on-target and off-target site recognition." It also mentions using data from ENCODE—the Encyclopedia of DNA Elements, an ongoing study decoding intergenic DNA in different species—and the need for increased data on epigenomes in order to improve methods of genetic engineering toward desired results.[61] This shows the beginnings of acknowledgment in the genetic engineering community of the challenges posed by biological systems complexity.[62]

Thus far, these technical hurdles and the theoretical and methodological implications of this new knowledge have not affected architects' pronouncements in favor of genetically engineered architecture and urbanism. As Hollwich stated in 2009, actual realization of these futuristic architectural visions—no matter how detailed or difficult—is the purview of scientists and engineers.[63] Engineers, after all, lauded the ten-minute video *Econic Design: A New Paradigm for Architecture* (2008) that Hollwich, Kushner, and Hollwich's architecture students at the University of Pennsylvania created in one week for a competition sponsored by the History Channel to offer innovative visions for the future city of Atlanta.[64] The video won the IBM Engineering Innovation award and was featured on both the History Channel and at the 2008 TED conference, whose motto is "Ideas Worth Spreading." Early on, the video establishes the current oil crisis that is prompting a search for high-tech alternative energy solutions. It then walks viewers through the scientific and technological innovations of the next century that culminate in the first urban "biogrid": MEtreePOLIS—Atlanta in 2108—"the city of the future." Genetically engineered kudzu vines take Atlanta "off the grid" (Figure 5.2). They both clean the air by replacing carbon dioxide with oxygen through the process of photosynthesis and serve as "power plants," as the energy from this process is harvested to power the city. The vines therefore offer a "twofer" solution to the current environmental problem that buildings consume 48 percent of the United States' electricity and contribute a similar percentage of greenhouse gases to the atmosphere, a situation whose urgency has prompted recent debates in state and federal congresses across the nation.[65]

Hollwich and Kushner take turns narrating *Econic Design*, their voices matter-of-factly directing us to their vision of a biotech future that at the outset harks back to an idealized, primitive past. "Historically, humanity used to be in harmony with nature," they tell us, admitting that "in our industrial age, we abused nature. Today," however, "we try to create harmony through sustainability. Even as the weather changes, and worldwide resources are depleted, we predict that society won't change its lifestyle to be in harmony with the environment, but rather we will use technology to change nature to be in tune with us."[66] Their sequence begins in 2006 with the scientific publication of "the first complete DNA sequencing of a tree," then shifts to university architectural laboratories that, between 2015 and 2022, develop "econic design" techniques that integrate genetic engineering into architecture, turning it into an "ecological performer." Architectural researchers learn how to grow structures, implement living technologies, use structural materials as nutrients and vice versa, and simulate ecosystems. In 2046, "scientists at MIT" conducting cross-disciplinary research "integrate a photosynthetic protein with a solid-state electronic device, effectively turning [genetically] modified plants into electricity producers." Less than twenty years later, the "National Office of Genomic Research, in collaboration with national universities, patents DNA-manipulated trees that produce consumable electricity. They call them 'power plants' and begin prototype installation nationwide. After five years of growth, the manipulated kudzu vines provide 80 percent of buildings' energy needs." In the interim (2052), "eight years earlier than predicted," "the Arctic Ocean is free of ice"; in 2073, "one hundred years after the oil crisis, OPEC declares worldwide fossil fuel reserves depleted." Planners in Los Angeles—the quintessential city of the automobile and endless expansion of the sprawling urban grid—take the lead by implementing the "sequential erosion of street infrastructure to be replaced by a single layer of [genetically] enhanced biorenewable moss." By 2098, U.S. cities adopt a "natural growth building code that follows the organic model of forests," depicted with actual footage of a real forest at sunset that appears to be superimposed with smog and tinted yellow. The next and final stage jumps ahead ten years to 2108, when kudzu "power plants" have overtaken and obliterated all evidence of actual nature—perhaps better described as "unenhanced" or "first nature"—and the city of Atlanta becomes entirely a "simulated ecosystem." In honor of this accomplishment, the city renames itself "MEtreePOLIS."[67]

Besides Hollwich and Kushner's brief video foray into genetically engineered urbanism, the primary generative architect promoting genetic engineering for architecture is Alberto Estévez. He began and directs what once was the Genetic Architectures doctoral program at ESARQ, Barcelona; now ESARQ offers a master's program in Biodigital Architecture.[68] Through this program and also through three books he has edited and published—*Genetic Architectures* (2003), *Genetic Architectures II* (2005), and *Genetic Architectures III* (2009)—Estévez is well known as the chief promoter of this goal. His books, however, include chapters by many famous generative architects, including among others Michael Weinstock, Evan Douglis, Karl Chu, François Roche, Bernard Cache, Michael Hensel, and Neil Leach. In 2003, he wrote, "Pure utopia or near reality? Buildings whose walls and ceilings grow with their own flesh and skin, or at least with plant textures, which genetics is able to develop, including shining heating coming through the veins delivering the oxygen necessary for breathing. There will be no need for painting and repainting the walls."[69] Referring to Austrian architect Adolf Loos's utopic vision "of his wife's bedroom space being covered in white hair," he predicts that this "may be realizable with genetic architecture. If so, the manipulation would be a mere remake of nature, accomplished without sacrificing any animal," he states, echoing claims of victimlessness that surround tissue-engineered architecture. "Just the opposite," he continues, "by creating the animal! With no creature suffering because of the manipulation. Without obstacles to manipulation. With whatever forms, textures, and colors one may choose. Very long, silky hair in bright silver shades or in iridescent red."[70] Alternately, "with the already existing genetic techniques," one can build "a real toadstool house, a tree house, a whale house," he added in 2005.[71] To be clear, he states, "We have to bear in mind, though, that we are not talking only about virtual reality. . . . Our reference is plain reality."[72]

In contrast to the strategy of sustainability put forward in *Econic Design,* Estévez unabashedly dismisses environmental concerns as passé, conservative, and "preservationist." Referring to environmentalists of the 1970s and 1980s, he states, "The ecologist avant-garde was conservationist at the start of its eternal struggle, but throughout the last decade of the twentieth century there was an evolution and the subject has become more complex. At present, at the start of the twenty-first century, the avant-garde of 'those who actively talk about the environment' . . . have extended such an understanding of nature." The current avant-garde, in which he groups himself, knows "that one can intervene in nature, work 'with' nature, work nature itself, obviously always to improve it, enrich it, and give it greater yield, without preservationist prejudices, that are now obsolete."[73] Earlier, in 2003, he had written, "The model's name, Genetic Architecture, may be misleading, because it has nothing to do with traditional uses of the terms *ecology, environment, context, caring for the environment, sustainability,* and so on." This is because "the new ecologic-environmental architectural design does not imply creating *in* nature but creating *with* nature. What is more, the new architect creates nature itself. Therefore, there is no point in being environmentally friendly since we are about to recreate the environment anew. . . . The architect of the future will no longer direct masons but genetic engineers."[74] Yet, despite his different strategy, his vision is similar to the narrative of *Econic Design.* Both depict the engineered world of the future completely replacing "first nature." "If we apply genetic techniques to the Earth's real vegetation, transforming it into habitable spaces," Estévez writes, as if no "first-nature" habitable spaces would exist, "we could create a real, living, soft and furry 'gencity,' free for all genetic architecture growing throughout the planet. A continuous city, which could embrace the entire world with seamless vegetation," presumably implying everything everywhere would be both urban and vegetated. He casts this as "an era where humans will be capable of effectively using 100 percent of the potential of what we call nature. . . . This is all that we have yet to achieve," he concludes. "Committed architects have the gargantuan duty of improving the real world through architecture. We wish them strength and courage."[75]

Estévez strongly believes that his vision of genetic architecture is possible because he sees both generative architecture and genetic engineering with the blinders of digital topology.[76] It is largely for this reason that the ESARQ Genetic Architectures website is so confusing, since the genetic and the digital are so conflated that one cannot easily ascertain what is being claimed.[77] For example, the website states that their work "is related to the application of genetics to architecture, in an interdisciplinary way, from two points of view: a natural one, using the latest biological technology, and an artificial one, using the latest digital technology."[78] Yet, when I met Estévez in 2010 at the Association for Computer Aided Design in Architecture (ACADIA) conference in New York and asked him which genetic engineers he was working with, he said, "I need one. Do you know any?" Although their brochure claims that students have access to "a digital manufacturing laboratory and a genetics laboratory," no genetics lab is listed on their website under the section "Labs." Estévez does, however, in the 2009 book, include a photo of himself in the "Laboratory of Genetic Architecture," which does show scientific equipment.[79] Yet, neither the curriculum requirements nor the faculty nor the publications coming out of ESARQ reveal a serious biological laboratory–based component of research.[80] This lack of clarity is compounded by Estévez's claims that "the architect, as the geneticist, can now design the software, the DNA chain (artificial or natural), which will produce the built product by itself."[81] It is as if there are no material or systemic differences between scripting a "chain" of zeroes and ones in computer software to generate a building, and synthesizing a DNA molecular sequence that he thinks can produce a "built product by itself," with no mention even of a cell. This is what Catts and Zurr refer to as "genohype" and "DNA mania." Elsewhere Estévez states, "The architect has only to program the chain that will generate everything else."[82] He repeats, again, in slightly different terms, sounding a bit like Rothemund, "Today, one can go beyond the threshold and search at the level of molecular action, even transforming the genetic design, the programming chains that will later generate naturally alive elements automatically."[83]

Perhaps most clearly of all, it is as if he thinks that because both architecture and a DNA sequence, prior to being synthesized, can be described using binary code, that they are basically one and the same: "The only thing remaining is to link the ones and zeros of digital organicism with the ones and zeros that govern the DNA reorganization orders to get them to grow as live buildings: this would be the real *cyber-eco fusion design*."[84] In this, however, his is not too different from an assertion made by del Campo and Manninger concerning tissue-engineered architecture. They write that with regard to creating a tissue-engineered gasket to cover an architectural joint, that "provided the necessary porosity within the material it should be actually possible to close such a gap with organic material, and it is just a question of time till this idea is realized in small scale as a proof of concept. For this proof of concept it comes in handy, that tissue engineering and advanced architecture share some tools, such as 3D printing and advanced animation software." It is as if, because a scaffold can be 3-D printed in a tissue-engineering lab from an architect-designed file, that this is almost viewed as sufficient to create the semi-living proof of concept: "To check the possibilities of communicating via 3D models, the authors sent digital data to the CATE Tissue Engineering Lab to be 3D printed in their lab."[85] Even if Sun were using the CAD/CAM approach of "bottom-up" bioprinting that uses no scaffold at all (he likely is now, since he pioneered direct cell writing in 2008), this is only the very beginning of the process of creating a viable semi-living tissue.

Neither Estévez nor del Campo and Manninger demonstrate in their publications much scientific knowledge at all about the processes they envision using in architecture. Estévez's *Genetic Barcelona Pavilion* (2007) shows this clearly (Plate 13). Are we really supposed to believe that the fleshy substance that is overtaking the small model of this modernist architectural icon is not textured chicken breast propped up by toothpicks, but is actually tissue grown by Estévez and Maria Serer using either tissue-engineered or genetically engineered cell cultures? No cell type is identified; Estévez just describes it as a "soft and edible" genetic reformulation of Mies's famous pavilion.[86] As "genetic architecture," it has very little structural form or function and clearly has not undergone morphogenesis of the developmental sort, which provides skeletal structures, among other things. This demonstrates a serious lack of ability to genetically manipulate living cells into useful architectural forms beyond a "neoplasmatic" blob that needs to be propped up by supports. If instead it is tissue-engineered tissue and is truly in an outdoor environment as shown, rather than in a sterile glass chamber that is not shown, then it is on its deathbed, destined soon for the cooktop or the trash.

Yet Estévez is undeterred from strongly stating the newfound power of the architect as geneticist: "An individual may create so much as an entire race, with an infinite number of small, automatized variations. . . . Architects, creators of races of buildings: that sounds good but strange, with connotations that have nothing to do with architecture."[87] While use of the phrase "races of building" may just be an awkward translation, the fact that he acknowledges that it carries "strange" "connotations" suggests it is not, and that it somehow associates a perception of human "racial" or ethnic difference with the creation of races of genetic architecture. Most other generative architects describe their offspring as families, species, or populations, not as races. Estévez does champion colonialism, imperialism, competition, and survival of the fittest in his writings as if these are evolutionarily instilled "natural" qualities, as is currently proposed by some evolutionary psychologists. For example, in his essay that he characterizes as a "First History of Genetic Architecture," after recounting the architects he considers to be his historical predecessors, he describes a series of recent conflicts between architects battling to win competitions or secure their place in architectural history. "In the end, they are all still fights for survival," he writes, "but ones which the human being establishes with 'bridgeheads' [referring most likely to an architectural success here, a building there, making a mark in history so to speak], without limiting himself to one single hunting ground, as the tiger does. . . . The same yearning that pulled us out of the caves leads us to have a deep-rooted imperialist instinct that if we do not control it, it will finish with our neighbor."[88] Although the language is unclear about whether the neighbor—other architects—triumphs or is done in, Estévez clearly asserts that he accepts having a "deep-rooted imperialist instinct," which aligns with other pro-colonialist assertions he makes.

In the same essay, he asserts that "the first person to dedicate their time to [creating genetic architecture], and who achieves it, will be the Christopher Columbus of the genetic New World. And as with the discovery of America, as it is not something that must be invented—it is simply a question of time and money—the only thing remaining is to find the corresponding Queen Isabella to concede their personal jewels for such an enterprise."[89] He repeats this idea often: "Nowadays the only obstacle is a matter of money"; "It is simply a question of finance."[90]

Given the ravages wrought on the world's first peoples under colonialism over the previous few centuries, as well as the substantial body of literature about postcolonial theory, Estévez's outspoken idolization of a Spanish colonial "hero" as the title to be placed on the first genetic architect comes across as either a poor choice strategically but honest, or else just uninformed. Yet, he is not alone in the context of generative architecture in promoting a competitive colonialist attitude as a fundamental necessity for use of genetic technologies in design. Pike, in his article "Manipulation and Control of Micro-Organic Matter in Architecture," interprets the habits of microorganisms to form colonies as providing "metaphorical parallels with human colonization." "The manner in which these micro-organisms colonise their environment, how they communicate, organize, and negotiate their territory, along with the mechanism and purpose they employ, provide metaphorical parallels with human colonization," he writes. He seemingly misses the difference in agency between bacteria forming colonies themselves using "bottom-up" "self-organization," as is often claimed by promoters of complexism, and humans, "top-down," attacking and colonizing other human beings. To make this unpalatable metaphor based on a "morally sensitive issue" a bit more comfortable, Pike softens it with symbiosis and sustainability: "Valuable lessons regarding symbiotic relations and sustainable systems can be drawn, while touching on the morally sensitive issues of growth manipulation and behaviour control." But without doubt, "the precedent for architects and designers to plunder nature as a resource is firmly established. . . . For the designer to utilize micro-organic material in a meaningful way, with any degree of achievable intent, it is imperative that the material may be manipulated and controlled, as for other traditionally available materials." He continues, "This type of control can only be achieved within closed environments, sealed vessels with filtered transmission between the interior and external conditions. All components must be sterilized and only the desired organisms introduced."[91] Given his metaphor of how this process parallels human colonization, his writing harks back, perhaps unknowingly on his part, to the history of placing tribal peoples into the closed environments of reservations and even to their forced reproductive sterilization.[92]

Colonialism is also referenced in *Econic Design*, although much more subtly and arguably from an oppositional stance.[93] While the video on the surface rather glibly presents biotechnology wedded to architectural and urban design as a natural, environmentally friendly technofix to environmental problems created by Western expansion and industrialization, the narrative can also be read in reverse. The word "technofix" is frequently used by critics with historical consciousness who weigh the persistent, future-focused, utopian rhetoric delivered by those promoting and profiting from new technologies against the negative effects these technologies continue to produce in social, economic, and environmental domains. This latter view runs as an undercurrent in the video in the form of a counter-narrative that critiques the colonialist ideals and technological triumphalism that historically led to our current environmental predicament, with which the video opens.

The architects' choice of kudzu for the "power plants" works double time in a metaphorical role that ultimately undoes the video's unquestionably forward-progressing narrative. Kudzu is a highly invasive nonnative species first brought to the United States from Japan for the 1876 Philadelphia Sesquicentennial Exposition. In the 1930s, it was cultivated by Civilian Conservation Corps workers in the American South as a ground-covering solution intended to halt erosion during the Dust Bowl—erosion instigated in part by industrialized farming techniques. It is currently one of the most unwanted species in the United States for a number of reasons. First, it fails to succumb to the technofix of herbicides. Despite heavy chemical doses, it continues to grow at an inordinate rate of speed over the tops of trees and buildings, much like past colonial powers or contemporary "neocolonial" economic and gene-patenting strategies under globalization.[94] Furthermore, it has huge root tubers that anchor it deep in the soil, an apt metaphor for Western anthropocentrism and imperialist ideologies. Rather than encouraging biodiversity and equality as global agribusiness, gene banks, and pharmaceutical companies working with genetic technologies claim, it subsumes other species completely and has produced "devastating environmental consequences." Its cost, in lost crops and strategies of control, runs close to $500 million annually.[95] The video's imagery reinforces the damaging power of kudzu (Figure 5.2); steroid-studded kudzu vines rip at the vertical grid of twentieth-century skyscrapers, which often function as corporate headquarters. Like many nonnative species introduced through Western colonization and global trade that have overrun species native to local environments, genetically altered kudzu and "enhanced bio-renewable" moss threaten to totally consume "first nature" and the entire urban environment.

The architects' rhetorical descriptions of kudzu's effects bolster this interpretation of a critical metaphorical counter-narrative in the video. Kudzu "feeds off the historic fabric" so that "the old forms and traces of the past become part of a growing organism."[96] "Through this combination," they state, "the past is updated and preserved," yet their imagery shows it in the process of being destroyed—the grid is, in fact, being torn down and replaced by a dubious "biogrid," a concept that functions as an oxymoron. "The surviving twentieth-century buildings," ostensibly those that won out in the cultural struggle of survival of the fittest before genetically engineered kudzu appeared on the scene at least, "have adapted to the biogrid and survive off the energy it provides," assimilating themselves to economic domination and the trickles it provides. Does their term "biogrid" refer to the kudzu, which grows in anything but a grid-like pattern, or rather to the so-called rational ordering and control of nature by Western scientists, architects, and urban planners, symbolized by both the Jeffersonian grid *and* genetic engineering, which has become so endemic and so pervasive as to become invasive?

As Zurr and Catts astutely note and these excerpts and readings demonstrate, the ways in which one interprets the manipulation of life stems from the ideologies one accepts.[97] This holds regardless of whether one sees the world anthropocentrically, perhaps through the lens of capitalism and survival of the fittest interpreted by Spencer and Darwin into evolutionary theory, or one promotes multispecies equality, makes a conscious choice to do one's best not to exploit "the other," and chooses Margulis's evolutionary theory of cooperation and symbiosis. "In many ways we are not smarter than a cell or bacteria," Zurr and Catts write, "and we can learn about our behaviour from the building blocks of our own bodies. The use of collaborative colonies of cells outside of a body is epistemologically and ethically a very relevant artistic expression which forces us to look at human civilization and its shifting rhetoric from an alternative position." Referring to their own work, they state that "learning about communicative cells in a new 'unnatural' environment is like shining a mirror at our own behaviours."[98]

Such self-conscious reflection is largely absent from discourses of generative and genetic architecture, even though Catts and Zurr's work offers the identified prototype. For example, Cruz and Pike in their introduction to Catts and Zurr's article in *AD* describe the work of SymbioticA as "crucial in testing new phenomena and elaborating new vocabulary that articulates the potential of new 'semi-living' conditions, or 'object-beings that evolve in partial life.'"[99] They describe the contribution of their article as being about "how to control, maintain and support living conditions."[100] Yet, in the article, Catts and Zurr state that "the Tissue Culture and Art Project (TC&A) was set up in 1996 to explore, develop, and *critique* the use of tissue technologies for artistic ends," and even more so, for design ends. "There is still the major question *should we go down this path*? This question led to a succession of artistic research projects . . . and a series of works that dealt, *with much irony,* with the 'technologically mediated victimless utopia' that involved the creation of tissue-engineered in-vitro meat and leather." Finally, they declare, "*the intention is not to provide yet another consumer product, but rather to raise questions about the exploitation of other living beings.*"[101] Yet, five years later, since architects continued to invite them to come explain how to grow living buildings, they published in *AD* again. This time, they stated that

> although the initial idea of the semi-livings came from a design perspective, we pursued it as artists in the belief that this position will enable us to *question, critique, and problematise the instrumentalisation and objectification of the semi-living beings* created. As artists, we hope that we have a different "contract" with

society—we ought *to provoke, question, and reveal hypocrisies* through different tactics: whether aesthetic, absurd/ironic, or subtle confrontation. Making our audience uneasy is an outcome of *our own uneasiness*, perusing the very things that *make us uncomfortable*. All we propose to offer are contestable future scenarios that are different from the canon of the contemporary trajectories.[102]

Toward a Living Architecture?

Zurr and Catts acknowledge that "humans are accumulating better control" over technologies associated with evolutionary biological processes, "though not necessarily a better understanding of the long-term results of such interventions."[103] While Zurr and Catts's work is primarily focused on enhancing critical thinking and deep understanding, the architects who want to grow living buildings using biotechnologies seem more intent on hoping that funding will arrive to overcome the technological hurdles. Although artist Eduardo Kac and others have used genetic engineering to cause organisms to glow green when exposed to ultraviolet light by adding the gene for the creation of green fluorescing protein (GFP) into their genome, this is only the most superficial example of genetically engineering animals for design purposes. Architectural visions of furry rooms, presumably of a size suitable for human habitation, imply a scale beyond that of most animals that have evolved on this earth, apart from perhaps the dinosaurs.[104] Plants are the largest organisms on earth and the strongest against gravitational forces owing to their production and integration of lignin. If an animal–plant hybrid is imagined by architects to be the solution that solves both problems of scale and aesthetics—assuming there is a clientele that wants this—architects need to realize how fundamentally different plants and animals are; such is the stuff of science fiction.[105] Even within one organism's genome, engineering a specific quality is a hit-or-miss affair because of the complexity of interactions across many different scales—from the organism with its environment to the ways in which chemicals from those interactions affect epigenetic responses and gene regulation throughout different parts of a body. This complexity of interactions does not just occur at one temporal or spatial point but at all times of development, beginning with morphogenesis, when the complex switches of homeobox gene functioning—when, where, how long they are turned on or off—can establish radically different trajectories of development.[106]

Given these hurdles and the fact that other, worthier problems merit the time, money, and efforts of scientists and architects, why pursue genetic architecture at all when we already have plants that are suitable for shaping into architecture using arborsculpture? Is the allure of a living "sustainable" house that extracts carbon dioxide from the air and returns oxygen—read plant, not animal—really so strong that it trumps problems of architectural disease, death, and bioterrorism, with the economic fallout and loss of shelter that those circumstances imply, especially on the urban scale? Pablo Picasso said, decades ago, "Imagine a house built of flesh—it wouldn't last long."[107] The allure is not making arborsculpted living shelters, since if it were, we would already be making them. Arborsculpture is not being taught at schools featuring generative or genetic architecture. Rather, it seems the allure is to control, manipulate, and instrumentalize life using the most recent computational technologies, for the anthropocentric boost, for the potential profits it proffers, for the cultivation of one's status as avant-garde within one's discipline.

If architects do not understand the science, and if architecture students and the interested public do not know that their professors or architects do not understand the science, then these visions promoting growing living buildings using biotechnology can dupe those who also do not understand the science into thinking that creating architecture using biotechnology is imminently viable, "sustainable," and "victimless" when it is not. That the ideas are promoted through a "potent . . . heady mix of projects, with no real differentiation being made between the visionary, speculative, and built" (as editor Helen Castle said of the "Neoplasmatic Design" issue) further compounds the problem of clear understanding.[108] Many of the projects done under the name of "speculative design," "critical design," or "design for debate" begun by Anthony Dunne and Fiona Raby at the Royal College of Art in the mid-2000s (some were included in "Neoplasmatic Design") tend more to promote the envisioned technologies as inevitable than to actually question the need for them at all. Promoting growing living buildings through biotechnology primarily functions as an avant-garde architectural fetish built on the misconceptions of digital tropology that distracts aspiring architects from the more important work of addressing our current environmental crisis, to which the discipline and practice of architecture has significantly contributed.

CHAPTER 6

"PROTOCELL" ARCHITECTURE AND SYNBIODESIGN

Observations of the natural world and the fossil record have revealed that the most basic form of life is a cell, yet how life comes to be is unknown. Perhaps the holiest grail of all scientific pursuit is to produce life from nonlife. Such is the goal of origin-of-life researchers and those in the field of artificial life who are pursuing the creation of the first "protocell," which would be the first living cell created from the "bottom up."[1] Researchers pursuing this goal combine knowledge of the chemistry of single-celled organisms and the composition of the earth's primordial sea, as ascertained from the geological and fossil record and from studying single-celled organisms today, to try to create a cell from scratch. Their attempts have led to the creation of vesicles, "constructs," and "pre-protocells" (Plate 2), which possess some of the properties of living cells, but thus far no cell with all the properties of life has been created in such a manner (Figure 6.1).[2]

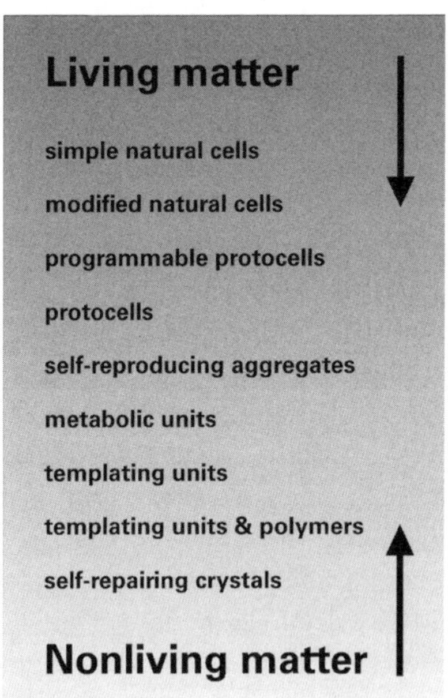

FIGURE 6.1. Diagram of "bottom-up" and "top-down" approaches to synthetic biology, from *Protocells: Bridging Nonliving and Living Matter*, ed. Steen Rasmussen, Mark Bedau, Liaohai Chen, David Deamer, David Krakauer, Norman Packard, and Peter Stadler (Cambridge, Mass.: MIT Press, 2009), xv. Attempts to create life "bottom-up" from nonlife drive the "origin of life" work in the branch of synthetic biology referred to as protocell research. At the same time, engineering synthetic biologists begin with living cells and, "top-down," remove genetic material or replace it with synthetic DNA to try to understand what a "minimal cell" is, or to create programmable protocells that can be designed to produce particular biological materials and outcomes.

Other scientists are pursuing the same problem with an opposite, "top-down" approach. They are taking single-celled organisms and removing their DNA bit by bit (or synthesizing new "minimal" DNA from scratch) to try to understand what a "minimal genome" is that allows the cell to still function with the basic properties of life. In March 2016, Craig Venter and his team at the J. Craig Venter Institute, who also were the first to decode the human genome, succeeded in creating a "minimal cell" with only 473 genes made from synthetic DNA.[3] They believe that this version of the bacteria *Mycoplasma mycoides,* which they named JCVI-syn3.0, offers "a working approximation of a minimal cellular genome, a compromise between small genome size and a workable growth rate for an experimental organism."[4] Note that their approach is gene-centric. They are not removing parts of the cell—for example, features of the membrane, ribosomes, plasmids, or cytoplasm—but instead define a "minimal cell" solely by its having a "minimal genome" but with all the other parts of a prokaryotic cell. Yet, because they are synthesizing the DNA and implanting it into a cell that has had its DNA removed, their techniques and research aiming to create minimal cells in general are classified as part of the relatively new field of synthetic biology, defined as "the attempt to engineer new biological systems."[5] It is hoped by researchers at both ends of this spectrum of synthetic biology that their work will "meet in the middle" and thereby unlock the key to creating life from nonlife.[6]

Although pre-protocells are not biological entities since they are not living cells, they exhibit a number of interesting "programmable" physical and chemical properties that appear lifelike, as architect Rachel Armstrong states.[7] Armstrong promotes the use of pre-protocells from synthetic biology as a means to grow "genuinely sustainable" buildings and cities from the bottom up.[8] She describes pre-protocells as "chemically programmable" because the results are predictable depending on which combination of chemicals one adds to the solution, so long as it is confined to a beaker or other controlled environment. Some of the chemicals that in combination can form pre-protocells, which must always be in water, include olive oil, different metal ions, calcium chloride, sodium hydroxide, ferrofluid solution, and copper sulphate, among others.[9] Pre-protocell properties include the ability to move through liquid, to respond to light and vibration, to cluster together, and to selectively let different materials into and out of their bordering membrane while transforming some of that material into energy. While all of these properties are explainable with insights only from chemistry and physics, Armstrong chooses to interpret these properties using language that imbues them with biological-sounding qualities. First and foremost in this regard, she consistently refers to her creations as "protocells" when they are pre-protocells; this choice leads her followers to think that protocells have already been created. She says that pre-protocells form "populations" and that they have a "metabolism" and secrete "waste," some of which are solid precipitates like calcium carbonate of which limestone is basically constituted.[10]

Armstrong therefore has promoted their use for shoring up the foundations

FIGURE 6.2. *Future Venice* project, underwater droplet formation, computer drawing by Christian Kerrigan, 2009. Here, pre-protocells chemically "programmed" to move into the shadows away from light are shown flocking to the decaying footings beneath Venice's sinking architecture. Here, they are supposed to deposit tiny particles of calcium carbonate onto the piers in order to shore up the city.

of Venice, asserting that the calcium carbonate precipitate will make rotting piers solid again: "The protocell system would be released into the canals, where it would prefer shady areas to sunlight. Protocells would be guided towards the darkened areas under the foundations of the city rather than depositing their material in the light-filled canals, where they would interact with traditional building materials and turn the foundations of Venice into stone."[11] She adds that "at the same time, a limestone-like reef would grow under Venice through the accretion and deposition of minerals" (Figure 6.2). These proclamations, backed up by the fact that she collaborates with scientists in Venice at the European Center for Living Technology who are trying to create protocells, have garnered her notable publicity. Subsequently, she was invited to exhibit her concept at the Canadian Pavilion at the Venice Biennale in 2011 in collaboration with architect Philip Beesley, professor at the University of Waterloo, Ontario. Together, they installed Beesley's piece *Hylozoic Ground* (2011) (Plates 2 and 14), replete with pre-protocell flasks of two types and tubes connecting the flasks to the water in the Venetian Lagoon. As people visited the gallery and exhaled carbon dioxide, the gas was absorbed into the canal water in the tubes; the pre-protocells responded by changing color and "demonstrat[ing] a carbon fixation process where the waste gas was recycled into millimeter-scale building blocks. In this way metabolic materials turned products of human activity into bodily components for the construction of Beesley's giant synthetic 'life form,'" she summarized.[12] To clarify, the "metabolic materials" she refers to are the chemicals in the flasks, and the "bodily components" they produced in the form of millimeter-sized calcium carbonate particles are "bodily" only metaphorically, in the sense that she views Beesley's sculpture as a form of artificial (synthetic) life. These "bodily" components do not "construct" any architectural or structural support in any way for the sculpture; they simply are part of it, in the water inside the flasks.

Although Armstrong and Beesley's work offers the best example of "protocell" architecture/design/sculpture, it demonstrates art–science interdisciplinarity involving only the "bottom-up" protocell-research branch of synthetic biology. As Venter's work demonstrates, the other branch of synthetic biology works with genetically manipulating cells, not only to ascertain a "minimal genome" but also to alter the functional properties of cells in order to have them produce designed outcomes such as the secretion of chemicals useful in other industrial processes. This second "top-down" branch, referred to as engineering synthetic biology (shortened here to engineering synbio), is also attractive to architects and designers who hope to use its techniques to create new bio-based materials or biofabrication methods for design. For example, the work of architect David Benjamin in collaboration with synthetic biologist Fernan Federici, for the Synthetic Aesthetics project and book, aimed to uncover growth algorithms using engineering synbio processes that could then be used for architectural design purposes.[13]

Benjamin does not just envision using synthetic biology for novel conceptual and algorithmic approaches to design, however. According to an interview with William Myers, he is building a compendium Registry of Synthetic Biology Applications to accompany Massachusetts Institute of Technology's Registry of Standard Biological Parts, a repository of "BioBrick" gene sequences created and built through annual iGEM (International Genetically Engineered Machine) competitions. Both of these—MIT's registry and iGEM—were started by synthetic biologist Tom Knight in 2003, and they form core apparatuses for the "top-down" engineering branch of the field. Benjamin's registry would contain puzzles and problems that could potentially be solved using synthetic biology, functioning as a database of future research ideas. He also claims he is working with a major software company to "explore the intersection of architecture, synthetic biology, and computation. We are looking to advance the use of software tools in synthetic biology and we think this might help both experienced synthetic biologists and non-expert designers—architects, artists, material scientists, computer scientists, and all types of students—to improve their capacity to deal with biology."[14]

Benjamin is a principal of the architectural firm The Living, which created the project *Hy-Fi* that won the 2014 Young Architects Program competition at the Museum of Modern Art PS-1 (Figure I.3). The structure was created from bricks made by the biodesign company Ecovative from mushroom mycelia and corn stalks.[15] In this case, as in some of the other design visions described in this chapter as well as in some of Phil Ross's design work using mushroom mycelia, synthetic biology is not actually integrated into the process (Figure I.4).[16] This is because for *Hy-Fi* and Ross's *Walnut Legged Yamanaka McQueen* (2012), it was not a necessary technology to implement the design. But like Benjamin, Ross is researching ways that synthetic biology might be useful in the process of creating designs using mycelia. He has been working in syn-

FIGURE 6.3. *Nanotopia,* by Michael Burton, 2006. In this vision of the future, some people sell their bodies to grow engineered novel aesthetic body parts to be worn by others, in an industry different from surrogacy only in the genetic engineering aspect.

thetic biologist Drew Endy's lab at Stanford University exploring the possibilities. In other biodesign examples included in Myers's book, despite being referenced, synthetic biology is not actually integrated into the design projects because as a technology, engineering synbio is not yet successful enough to be useful in realizing the designer's visions. In these cases—such as Michael Burton's *Nanotopia* for the *Future Farm* project (2006–7) (Figure 6.3) or Alexandra Daisy Ginsberg's *Designing for the Sixth Extinction* (2013–14)—the works function more as speculative design or "design for debate." Yet, despite the fictional nature of the projects, a number of architects and designers express their opinion that synthetic biology should be integrated into architectural and design education to prepare designers for this imminent reality.

This chapter therefore explores the two branches of synthetic biology in relation to the approaches of each, and how some architects and designers envision using these technologies. After introducing the scientific approaches in a bit more detail, it elaborates on and critically analyzes proposals of architects and designers working in this area. It concludes by exploring four themes that run throughout both this chapter as well as the book, therefore serving as a conclusion to both. The first theme is that of complexism and complexity theory, which is engaged by "bottom-up" protocell researchers but largely ignored by "top-down" engineering synthetic biologists. In many ways this makes sense, since the first group is trying to put together materials that can "self-organize" to produce the "emergent property" of life, but the second group is trying to reduce biological complexity to a great extent in order to control it for standardized industrial outputs, or at least to bolster support for the idea that they can. The second theme addresses the lack of clarity in both the language used by generative architects working with pre-protocells and in their visual depictions or material realizations of their ideas. Ambiguity in terminology, like Armstrong's choice to use the word "protocell" to describe what actually are pre-protocells, and ambiguity in visual works that may or may not be created as "design for debate," can produce confusion about the actual reality versus the possibility of the concept or its technology. Third, in engineering synbiodesign (adapting Myers's use of "biodesign") projects especially, ideas of eugenic improvement surface with regularity, so these are reconsidered in relation to the other examples of eugenic thought offered throughout this book. And finally, since "protocell" architects and designers promoting engineering synbio both claim that they pursue these technologies in order to create more "sustainable" solutions, this topic then frames the book's end.

"Top-Down" Engineering SynBio and SynBioDesign

As stated above, synthetic biology as a scientific discipline generally claims two complementary territories of research that are at least partially viewed as different means to a shared goal of trying to ascertain the basic chemical ingredients of life.[17] The first approach, protocell research, combines "nonliving matter" to try to create a living cell from the bottom up. Whether this cell will resemble the simplest single-celled organisms that we know of today, or whether it will be simpler or different, is not clearly specified or even known. But the phrase "minimal cell" is used to describe scientists' aim to achieve life at its most basic level. The second approach, top-down engineering synbio, begins with "living matter." This is a strategic term that not only works to link "living matter" into a continuum with nonliving matter, as the diagram shows. It also works to desensitize readers to the standard process of this branch of the field: genetic manipulation of living organisms. By substituting the word "matter" for "organism," life seemingly becomes less special and less autonomous.

Engineering synbio draws heavily from electrical and computer engineering in its conceptual logic and terminology. For example, designed gene combinations are described as "circuits" that have "toggle switches" and "logic gates"; multiple circuits can be combined into "devices."[18] The design of circuits and devices is thought through using processes of mathematical modeling. Once designed, the circuits or devices are inserted as plasmids into host prokaryotic and eukaryotic cells, often using the processes of transformation through heat shock, polymerase chain reaction, and then gel electrophoresis to ascertain if the transformation was successful.[19] The host cell is referred to as a "chassis" for its sole role of providing the necessary cellular support infrastructure for the inserted gene. In other words, it functions as a "machine" or a "workhorse" to transcribe, translate, and replicate the inserted DNA in order to produce its intended chemical output. The most common chassis by far is the bacteria *Escherichia coli* owing to its quick reproducibility, relative success in being transformed, and known properties from decades of research. In general, bacterial host cells are fed with a sugar-rich nutrient media that offer the energy and supporting molecules necessary for biofabrication. Sometimes, the goal of engineering synbio is not make a chemical product but rather to design a new form of living organism that can perhaps then serve as a chassis—such is the claim of Venter regarding JVCIsyn3.0.

Two other defining features of engineering synbio play a major role in the approach and growth of the field. The first is the use of "standardized parts," introduced by Knight, to design circuits and devices. He named the basic part a "BioBrick," which is a genetic sequence that can serve a standardized function when inserted into another organism. This means that regardless of what organism it is inserted into, it is only qualified to be a BioBrick if in fact it does produce the outcome it is claimed to produce. Owing to the importance and complexity of genome architecture and the interactions that naturally occur within it, say gene-splicing and recombination, however, to always produce the intended output is a tall order. Therefore, a BioBrick can be removed from the registry just as it can be added to it as greater knowledge about the gene sequence is uncovered. Because it is difficult to define what a "gene" is, much less what it is as a "standardized part," definitions of what constitutes a BioBrick have also changed rather consistently.[20] BioBricks were originally housed at MIT and could be accessed and ordered through the Registry for Standard Biological Parts, although owing to growth in the field, other sources now exist.[21] The second major feature, the iGEM competitions, has become the best-known contributing mechanism for adding BioBricks into the registry and recruiting students from around the world to study engineering innovations using synthetic biology.

Interestingly, engineering synthetic biologists describe the history of their field as beginning in the early 1970s, with the discovery of restriction enzymes (what they call "molecular scissors") as "a form of genetic 'cut and paste' in which genes could be removed from one organism and introduced into another."[22] Since at this point much less knowledge about genomes and molecular biology existed in general, "the power of restriction enzymes could not be harnessed much beyond the serendipitous." Without any infrastructure for "an engineering industry, . . . this biotechnology version 1.0" persisted into the 1990s.[23] With increased knowledge of genomics particularly with regard to specific crop species, "genetic engineering" from the 1990s onward introduced genetic modifications that in a "hit or miss" fashion gradually took hold. Engineering synthetic biologists also tend to characterize "biotechnology" or "genetic engineering" as "a disappointment" that "grossly undershot its promise" precisely because it lacks the engineering theoretical basis and methodology of synthetic biology that supposedly would allow standardized outputs.[24] When not characterized as a disappointment, genetic engineering is considered to offer only "bespoke solutions" for individual challenges and not an across-the-board platform for "cut and paste," "drag and drop," or "plug and play" genetic circuit design.[25] The difference between "genetic engineering" and "synthetic biology" is thus characterized as being comparable to the difference between artisan production by hand and mass production at the onset of the Industrial Revolution. Yet, continuing this analogy, both approaches aim for a similar goal even if they end up being realizable on different production and economic scales.[26]

These fine-grained historical distinctions between what the general public may perceive as being part of the same discipline (usually called "genetic engineering" or "biotechnology") reveal strategies of internal posturing among those in synthetic biology. These characterizations of others in their general field serve to distinguish what are significant conceptual distinctions in their approaches in order to hopefully garner financial support from those who can help grow the field of synthetic biology, whether granting agencies or biotech corporations. Within the discourses of generative architecture, earlier publications like Estévez's *Genetic Architectures* series and Antonelli's *Design and the Elastic Mind* refer mostly to genetic engineering without distinguishing it from synthetic biology. Since the publication of Myers's *BioDesign* and *Synthetics Aesthetics,* more designers and architects have begun using the latter term.

Just to be clear, in this book the terms are distinguished by a few factors. Genetic engineering refers to altering DNA sequences in a particular organism's genome in order to affect some aspect of its form or function while generally desiring basically the same organism to result, hopefully with the added features. With regard to architecture, these are envisioned to be large-scale organisms, not single cells, and usually it is the *form* of the organism that is imagined to be changed. Synthetic biology, on the other hand, seems to be less interested in altering the form of an organism and more interested in altering its function. It works primarily with fast-reproducing bacteria and views them as machines that can produce chemicals. The genetic alterations can use synthetic DNA or BioBricks, whether synthesized or extracted from natural DNA. Engineering synthetic biologists speak of their field as the means to the Second Industrial Revolution, one that is bio-based but otherwise envisioned as similar in terms of resulting in new, highly profitable innovations based on consistent, large-scale mass production.

Few of the ideas being put forward as synbiodesign have actually been realized since the scientific field itself is in its "infancy," as its supporters claim, implying a long and successful disciplinary life in the future. Top-down engineering synbio is still trying to garner enough successes to substantiate its methods and frequently exaggerated claims.[27] Synbiodesign pieces therefore usually exist as images or concept prototypes that have been published in books or included in exhibitions.[28] Ginsberg, one of the leaders of the Synthetic Aesthetics project, notes, "It is easy to forget that many of the outputs of the residencies are fictional. Will [Carey] and Wendell [Lim]'s packaging that builds its own contents is a computer-manipulated image, as are many of the images on these pages."[29] A number of works included in these recent exhibitions and publications are from designers in the United Kingdom created in the vein of Anthony Dunne and Fiona Raby's "speculative design," "critical design," or "design for debate." Now, the Design Interactions Department at the Royal College of Art includes synthetic biology as one of its research areas, as well as professors Oron Catts and Ionat Zurr, who are leading the study of "contestable design."[30]

For example, the *Design and the Elastic Mind* exhibition included a section on "Design for Debate" featuring the work of faculty and students from the Design Interactions Department. Two of these were Burton's *Nanotopia* from the *Future Farm* project (2006–7) and *The Race* (2006–7). In the first, he visualizes human bodies transformed through genetic engineering, synthetic biology, nanotechnology, and pharmaceuticals in order to grow novel body parts for harvesting for use by other people, within socioeconomic contexts of inequality that exploit the poor.[31] The second depicts pets engineered to be extra hairy and human fingernails engineered to have cascading ridges so that bacteria can be harbored in the hair and crevices in order to expose overly hygienic "first world" humans living under the legacy of hygienic modern design to more bacteria. If our immunity does not improve, the piece implies, bacteria and other humans and species who live comfortably in dirty, bacteria-rich environments may survive in "the race" (evolutionary competition). Burton's work is thoughtful and more questioning than promoting of the implementation of this new technology for the ways it engages socioeconomic disparity and the injustice of an economic system that encourages those who need money to farm out their bodies, such as for surrogacy. They were also prescient in being created before the recent revelations and new popular scientific knowledge concerning the extent of the human microbiome.

Similarly critical are Ginsberg's essays and her recent creative work *Designing for the Sixth Extinction*. The latter depicts newly created organisms made by synthetic biology—ones that have never existed before—that are designed to "support endangered natural species and ecosystems" in the wild in line with current conservationist efforts, given that "the sixth great extinction in the history of biology is underway." She asks, "If nature is totally industrialised for the benefit of society—which for some is a logical endpoint of synthetic biology—will it still exist for us to save?"[32] Like Catts and Zurr, she is a master of irony. Her publications make clear that rather than reach this point, perhaps more countries should follow Ecuador's lead in granting constitutional rights to nature. Ginsberg quotes Article 71 from Ecuador's constitution, passed by public referendum: "'Nature or Pachamama, where life is reproduced and exists, has the right to exist, persist, maintain, and regenerate its vital cycles, structure, functions, and its processes in evolution.' Ecuador's constitution charges its people not only with protecting nature, but also with the responsibility to 'promote respect towards all the elements that form an ecosystem.'"[33]

Other works of synbiodesign seemingly harbor less criticality toward the aims and means of synthetic biology, serving more as visionary applications of the foreseen technology even if their creators say they intend to provoke debate. For example, Natsai-Audrey Chieza's *Design Fictions*, like Burton's piece, also imagines future bodies as farms; she materializes this vision through the creation of a "very precious, very valuable Genetic First Aid Cabinet." Whereas Burton's text accompanying his piece highlights socioeconomic injustices that may accompany body-farming, Chieza's piece simply validates bodily alterations as precious, valuable, and even common, like do-it-yourself (DIY) sculptural tattoos made from stem-cell alterations. Her website claims that the "project makes us reconsider the role of the designer whose manufacturing process is likely to take place in a laboratory in 2075." Such a statement reads more strongly as an affirmation of the likelihood of this happening rather than as a "reconsideration" or a "debate" about making a choice in the first place not to pursue these technologies for the human body at all.[34]

Both Chieza and Amy Congdon were students in the Textile Futures Program at Central St. Martin's College of Art and Design, London, where designer Suzanne Lee used to teach. Congdon's *Biological Atelier*, like Chieza's work, imagines that "biotechnologically engineered high fashion . . . might be realized one day soon."[35] She imagines "growing objects in the lab from our own cells or those of animals" that could be used for "personalized and renewable fashion." Her images depict bracelets, a brooch, and a collar that are "grown, not made," using "developments in the fields of biotechnology to create materials" such as "cross-species fur" or "ethically-grown" "victimless ivory."[36]

A few designers working at the architectural scale are also promoting the use of synthetic biology. Marin Sawa is another student who passed through the Textiles Future Program who has now earned a Ph.D. from the Energy Futures Lab, Imperial College, London. Her project *Microalgerium* aims to create textiles interwoven with "hybrid algal species" engineered to secrete oil and release ethanol for use architecturally in "everyday spaces" to "prevent and eliminate pollution and waste."[37] Sawa was inspired by Rachel Armstrong's "protocell" research, which Sawa summarizes as work "where an artificial cell was created and programmed with a basic behaviour."[38] The chemical reactions of pre-protocells differ from the top-down approach of genetically engineering hybrid algal species, but Sawa sees both as applications of synbiodesign. She astutely recognizes the current limitations she faces with realizing her project in architectural spaces apart from a laboratory. "We realize that the creation of an engineered biological entity must be contained within the lab and not outside the lab because of its unverified synthetic biohazards to our ecosystem," she states. "The idea of genetically encoding a biological logic of death in the case of unwanted leakage is great," she says, referring to the idea of putting "kill switches" into genetically engineered species released into the wild.[39] "But I think if we were to get new designs of synthetic biology out of the lab, it would be equally interesting and imperative to design secure containment and disposal systems in our physical world as a natural by-product. In this sense, this design tool actually contradicts my interest in creating an open metabolic relationship between 'living' textiles and the rest of the biosphere."[40]

Others, such as Spaniards Eduardo Mayoral Gonzalez and Alberto Estévez, who are less troubled by such difficulties than Sawa is, imagine using trees engineered to bioluminesce to provide nighttime light in urban areas.[41] Bioluminescent light is very dim so this proposal is actually impractical for its proposed purpose, yet the designers do not mention this fact. Lastly, Benjamin has been teaching a studio on synthetic biology and architecture at Columbia University's Graduate School of Architecture, Planning, and Preservation, which has produced a number of interesting student projects included in Myers's *BioDesign* (as were the works of Chieza, Congdon, Sawa, Mayoral Gonzalez, and Estévez). For example, Mike Robitz's project *Googol Puddles* imagines using urban bodies of water to store data information encrypted in the DNA of bacterial organisms living there.[42] Another project, *Algal Filter Machine* by Benjamin, Nathan Williams Smith, Geoff Managh, Mark Smout, and Laura Allen, proposes a system to remove carbon dioxide from urban airways to feed algae designed by synthetic biologists to create biofuels, thereby using algae "acting as engines and filters for the environment simultaneously."[43]

Ginsberg is one of few designers who mention horizontal or lateral gene transfer as something to rightly consider if synthetic biology becomes practiced on a larger scale. Microorganisms, including bacteria, easily swap genes when they are in an environment where they need a function that other nearby bacteria have.[44] Bacteria are the chassis of choice for biofabrication of chemicals that could eventually be used for design purposes, although most designers currently imagine plant or animal cells being manipulated for their designs. However, with the use of bacteria, how will the intended genetic modifications be stabilized, especially if they do their "work" outside the laboratory in the external environment, as imagined?[45] Critics do note the possibility of engineered bacteria evolving—which to most people implies random mutation rather than lateral gene transfer—and so they propose mechanisms such as "kill switches" or "programmed cell death" that can be activated to terminate the engineered species, assuming one knows a problem exists. If engineered bacteria are in the wild, however, such knowledge would be unlikely, and theoretically the engineered genes could swap into a non-engineered bacteria that does not contain a kill switch. Lateral gene transfer thus poses a fundamental problem for synbiodesign of this sort.

"Bottom-Up" "Protocell" Architecture

The protocell branch of synthetic biology focuses on very different questions than does engineering synbio. These concern the definition of life as constituted by criteria on which scientists more or less agree (Figure 6.4). This textbook diagram uses a cell-like circle to frame the "operational functionalities of living systems," which are separated into three separate rectangles with different systemic qualities.[46] This makes the system appear relatively simple, yet each of the three rectangles contains a few different properties, allowing perception or interpretation of the "three" necessities with greater or lesser reductionism. Different scientists do in fact use different criteria to get

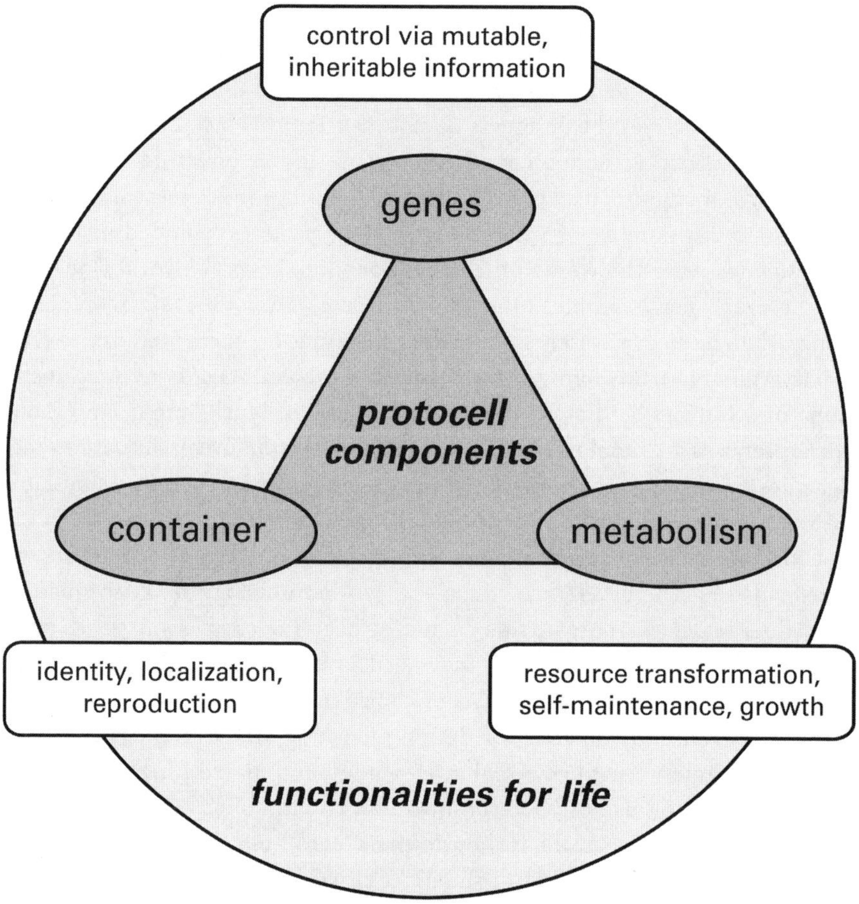

FIGURE 6.4. Diagram showing functionalities for life, from *Protocells: Bridging Nonliving and Living Matter*, ed. Steen Rasmussen, Mark Bedau, Liaohai Chen, David Deamer, David Krakauer, Norman Packard, and Peter Stadler (Cambridge, Mass.: MIT Press, 2009), xiv. According to Tibor Gánti's "chemoton" concept, the minimal criteria for life entail a "chemical supersystem" made up of "a metabolic network" (metabolism), "template replications" (genes), and a "boundary system" (container).

at the essence of life. Some define life using biologists Humberto Maturana and Francisco Varela's concept of "autopoeisis," which focuses on cellular life.[47] Cells are dissipative systems that possess a membrane, a semipermeable boundary that both separates them from and allows a selective connection to their environment. Within this boundary, a cell regenerates all it needs to live by drawing on materials from its environment.[48] Chemist and synthetic biologist Pier Luigi Luisi describes life in fairly technocratic terms as "a factory that makes itself from within." He holds that "a system can be said to be living when it is defined by a semipermeable chemical boundary which encompasses a reaction network that is capable of self-maintenance by a process of self-generation of the system's components from within."[49]

Instead of autopoiesis, others use the "chemoton" concept first proposed by Tibor Gánti: "a minimal living system is a chemical supersystem comprising three systems: a metabolic network, template replication, and a boundary system," where all three systems are "autocatalytic." These are demonstrated in the inner triangle of the diagram as the primary protocell components.[50] Alternately, Frank Harold, a cell biologist, proposes that "architecture is what ultimately distinguishes a living cell from a soup of chemicals of which it is composed"; "how cells generate, maintain, and reproduce their spatial organization is central to any understanding of the living state."[51] Others add to these criteria the need for genetic material (DNA or RNA) and homeostasis.[52] Finally, protocells have been "defined in various ways, ranging from a plausible representation of a hypothetical precursor to the first biological cell, through to the description of a synthetic cell-like entity that contains non–biologically relevant components."[53] The latter is a goal of some synthetic biologists who aim to synthesize novel minimal cells from scratch in order to either not use current living organisms as technological machines or to design a minimal organism most efficiently toward a certain product outcome, without any "extra" stuff that evolution might have provided along the way.[54] A similar move, in this case to create a novel genetic information system (XNA) that could be used an alternative to the A, C, T, and Gs of DNA so as not to interfere with the evolution of organisms with DNA, has been created recently at Cambridge University by Philipp Hollinger, Jason Chin, and others.[55]

The most visible aspect of these characteristics evident in pre-protocells created in laboratories is the membrane bounding the vesicle (Plates 2 and 14). Because this membrane is what isolates the fluid and chemicals inside from the liquid outside, it is fundamental to the creation of a pre-protocell. In theories of evolution, however, the primordial sea is thought to have contained supramolecular chemical aggregates prior to their joining together to form a cell. For example, cell membranes comprise a bilayer of lipids that are made up of fatty acids "with a sufficiently long linear hydrophobic chain," phosphate and glycerol; so, in order for a membrane to form, these constituents must already be present.[56] It is not easy, by the way, to theorize the processes by which all the different chemical constituents came into being in the first place.[57] Although the primordial sea may have contained supramolecular chemical aggregates such as DNA or RNA prior to the formation of the first cell, in the creation of pre-protocells today this material—the source of "template replication," heredity, or "genes"—is not always included. This is because cells have so many important parts that also must "self-assemble" that research into the creation of protocells focuses on understanding each of these different facets. For example, the pre-protocells that Armstrong and Beesley create do not contain any genetic material—at least, this is not stated in the publications describing them. Rather, they are chemical vesicles or constructs that exhibit chemical reactions without having even the three basic features required for life, as defined by Gánti's chemoton concept or by the textbook diagram (Figure 6.4).

Armstrong collaborates with some well-known protocell researchers at the European Center for Living Technology and at the Center for Fundamental

Living Technology (FLinT) in Odense at the University of Southern Denmark. In 2011, when she and Neil Spiller guest-edited an issue of *AD,* titled "Protocell Architecture," she was a visiting research assistant at FLinT, where Martin Hanczyc, Steen Rasmussen, and Mark Bedau are based. Rasmussen is also affiliated with the center in Venice, along with Norman Packard, and both also are connected to the Santa Fe Institute. Together, these scientists have edited the primary textbook on protocells, *Protocells: Bridging Nonliving and Living Matter* (2009), and authored numerous articles, including "Living Technology: Exploiting Life's Principles in Technology" (2010).[58] Hanzyc also published an article in Armstrong and Spiller's "Protocell Architecture" (2011).[59]

Armstrong and these researchers often use the words "living" or "living technology" to describe pre-protocells, which they describe as having the lifelike qualities of being "robust, adaptive, self-repairing, self-optimizing, autonomous, intelligent, and evolvable."[60] "We deem technology to be living if it is powerful and useful precisely because it has the core properties of living systems," they write, "including such properties as the ability to maintain and repair itself, to autonomously act in its own interests, to reproduce, and to evolve adaptively on its own."[61] They predict that "as our technologies increasingly embody such core properties of living systems, they will become increasingly powerful, natural, and sustainable," although why they think the latter two are true is not supported.[62] They state that in the past, humans harnessed oxen and horses as sources of power to do work, although with the invention of the internal combustion engine and the onset of the Carbon Era, animals were replaced by machines.[63] "In the coming technological revolution, the technological systems themselves will become alive or very much more lifelike," they state, "bestowing the advantages of life on the wider sphere of material and technical innovation."[64]

In contrast to Armstrong, in his own publications Beesley more cautiously uses the term "near-living" to refer to the artificial-life qualities of *Hylozoic Ground,* created in collaboration with Armstrong, as well as those qualities present in many of his other responsive and interactive installations.[65] Although his architectural firm is named Living Architecture, his writings make it very clear that his research bridges the domains of architecture loosely defined and "hard" artificial life, which explores physical and material "implementations of lifelike systems" such as those used in robotics.[66] Beesley uses techniques of generative design to create exquisite environments made from tens of thousands of laser-cut acrylic pieces that are connected into meshes, membranes, and webs and suspended from ceilings so that viewers can walk under and through them. The works have what might be called appendages, branches, fronds, and feathers that are embedded with tiny microprocessors, sensors, and lightweight actuators connected into a distributed communication and control system. Together, they function kinetically, moving slowly in response to the presence and motion of people in the room or other factors they are designed to sense.[67] His works often evoke emotional, affective responses in viewers even without the addition of "protocell" flasks; when these are present, they add one more layer—a "wet" one—to the artificial lifelikeness of his work.

In presenting her concept of *Future Venice,* Armstrong communicated her concept not only through the "protocell" flasks in *Hylozoic Ground* but also through talks accompanied by visualizations, still and video, created by Christian Kerrigan, an artist in residence at the Victoria and Albert Museum around 2010 when Armstrong and Hanczyc were discussing protocell research.[68] Armstrong and others describe the mixture that creates pre-protocells, as was demonstrated by the flasks in *Hylozoic Ground,* as "reminiscent of salad dressing."[69] Should large amounts of this actually be dumped into the lagoon, many people might worry about effects equivalent to an oil spill damaging the local ecology. Armstrong asserts that "protocells" form at the interface between the oil and mineral-rich water, but she does not discuss the fact that the lagoon is open water and not a scientifically controlled glass vessel. Currents or variations of the proper chemical composition certainly would hinder this predicted formation, even if the "protocells" are "chemically programmed" to move away from light (Figure 6.2).[70] In fact, a number of Kerrigan's renderings actually depict the opposite of what Armstrong claims will happen (Figures 6.5 and 6.6). They show the canals and lagoon filled with rock formations. Rather than not use his images or explicitly address their critique of her vision, Armstrong publishes them without a hint of recognition.[71] Is her strategy similar to Matthias Hollwich and Marc Kushner's, whose *Econic Design* can also be read two ways, straight and as farce, or is her work meant to be "design for debate"? Is her oil spill in a lagoon equivalent to their use of kudzu, since both are forms of humanly caused environmental devastation that now are being imagined to form the basic infrastructure of a new "sustainable" urbanism?

Armstrong and others following her lead imagine that "protocells" can form a revolutionary sustainable architecture. Paul Preissner, architectural professor at the University of Illinois at Chicago, asserts, "It only takes a few moments to be taken in by the utterly fantastic possibilities protocells offer the world; for example, these real and shapeable life forms promise to grow us limestone faster than limestone. Starting from oil and water and a few more things," he explains, "the resulting calcification suggests a material residue that is not only agreeable, but also useful, essentially giving us the ability (not unlike our novelty plant-imal the Chia Pet) to grow our surrounds—although, instead of sheep or heads of hair, we can think about growing our buildings. Buy some land, mix up some salad dressing, sit back a couple of decades, and then move right in. Wild."[72] Armstrong believes that "ultimately metabolic materials will give rise to a whole new range of architectural forms that could potentially represent the architectural equivalent of the Cambrian Explosion, when according to fossil evidence, most major groups of complex animals suddenly appeared on the earth around 530 million years ago."[73] *Wired* magazine writer Bruce Sterling writes, "I really enjoy that rhetorical way in which Dr. Armstrong 'talks architecture' while saying some of the weirdest stuff

FIGURE 6.5. *Future Venice* project, reef supporting foundations, computer drawing by Christian Kerrigan, 2009. Even the canals between historic buildings fill up with pre-protocell calcium carbonate secretions, threatening gondola tourist activities.

FIGURE 6.6. *Future Venice* project, future Venetian Lagoon, computer drawing by Christian Kerrigan, 2009. Here, pre-protocells that were chemically "programmed" to move away from light into the shadows (Figure 6.2) have apparently lost their way, depositing their tiny calcium carbonate secretions in such large volumes as to begin to infill the Venice Lagoon.

imaginable."[74] Enjoyment is one thing; taking this vision seriously is an entirely different matter. Preissner calls protocell architecture "utterly fantastic" and uses the phrase "to be taken in," implying gullibility. Are we supposed to find these visions credible?

For example, Armstrong seemingly forgets, but then remembers, that human beings do not thrive on living in aqueous environments, or perhaps she just forgets that architecture as a discipline has been and is intended for human occupation. Throughout her various publications, she predicts "protocell" cities of the future as the new sustainable architecture, equipped with "the principles of emergence, bottom-up construction techniques, and self-assembly," albeit necessarily in a wet environment.[75] In contrast to the "traditional architectural approach to meeting the challenges of hostile environments" by creating "the most effective possible barrier between nature and human activity, using durable and inert materials," she prefers the ways that "algae, shellfish, and bacteria have claimed a construction process" within the harsh terrain at the edge of waterways by "accreting, secreting, remoulding, and sculpting the materials of their surroundings to create tailored micro-environments." Human architecture "has worked sufficiently effectively for human development" in the past, she states, "but on an evolutionary time-scale it's not how the most resilient structures persist."[76]

Armstrong rarely acknowledges the need for persistent wet conditions for protocell action as a "design limitation" that requires a "troubleshooting" solution. To remove the necessary protocell "medium" of water from the space presumably occupiable by humans, she proposes at times the "creative design of water removal systems" that would still permit the "feeding" of "computational materials," by which she means the "protocells," referencing complexity science's terminology of "natural computing." One such system could use porous rock to offer structural rigidity to the building while functioning as a water supply for "chemical computers."[77] This might cause one to ask why the protocells are necessary at all, if a stone structure already exits—after all, stone lasts a very long time. To this, Armstrong might reply that "protocells" offer "self-repairing architecture." Since they secrete calcium carbonate—what Preissner refers to as limestone—then presumably if the porous stone started to erode, perhaps owing to constant water motion inside it, the protocells could reinforce it.[78] Yet without water being added, the stone is highly unlikely to erode.

The ambiguity of whether "protocell" architecture is actually imagined to be structural as opposed to just a "self-repairing" surface persists in other examples. Consider, for example, Lisa Iwamoto's contribution to the *AD* issue on protocell architecture, whose title—"Dynamic Array: Protocells as Dynamic Structure"—implies that "protocells" create a structure, albeit a dynamic one.[79] (This raises another interesting question: Is "protocell" architecture motile like water, or stable like limestone?) Yet the caption to the first image in Iwamoto's article states, "Detail view showing aggregation of protocells along lines of structure," calling into question whether the "protocells" are the structure or whether they are *on* it. Iwamoto writes, "A driving concern for Line Array (2010) was how to envision a protocell modality suitable for architecture that could be applied to a range of structural *surface formations.* Protocells are used here as a self-organising structural matrix," but this is surely on the surface of another structure, since she asserts that "protocells" in their aqueous environments have the ability to "circumvent gravitational conditions as well as aggregate without concern for larger-scale, hierarchical structure."[80] Similarly ambiguous about the structural use of "protocells" given the rest of her explanations of "protocell" architecture, Armstrong envisions protocell paint for buildings that she is developing in collaboration with chemist Leroy Cronin at the University of Glasgow. "If buildings were covered in a layer of [protocells], they would act as a sort of smart paint, absorbing carbon dioxide from the atmosphere," she states. "When the building got wet the mineral salt would dissolve, react with the carbon dioxide in the rain, and produce a deposit of mineral carbonate, which would strengthen the bricks." Note the bricks. As "carbon dioxide would be removed from the atmosphere," she asserts, "over time . . . the building would become more robust."[81] Yet elsewhere, she and architectural professor Neil Spiller refer to "protocells" as a "synthetic *surface* ecology."[82]

The contradictions over "protocell" use as structure versus surface deepen when Armstrong attempts to explain how "protocell" architecture is superior to "green building." She claims that her approach is unlike green-bling, or "gling" architecture, which she criticizes for covering buildings with greenery when the building itself, made with the same normal structural materials, keeps "the fundamental unsustainability of modern architectural practices" unchanged.[83] How is this different from using stone as the porous structure of a protocell building or applying protocell paint to a brick building? "Green walls and roofs require constant energy, water, artificial fertilizers, maintenance, and a high upfront cost to create the illusion of a mature and self-sustaining ecosystem," Armstrong argues, adding, "Once installed, these systems are resource-intensive and require daily upkeep from external sources, which effectively outweighs any environmental benefit they offer." One of these benefits is the removal of carbon-dioxide from the atmosphere, the same benefit Armstrong extols for "protocell" architecture, which also requires energy in the form of light, chemical additives, and maintenance, even if the upfront cost of olive oil might be considered to be relatively cheap.[84]

Armstrong states these points explicitly when describing how "protocell" "salad dressing" can replace traditional ready-mix concrete to hold up fence posts. "You take your spade of [new] ready-mix concrete and stir it into a bucket containing a greasy solution, reminiscent of salad dressing. The solution congeals as the chemistry of the concrete is taken up into the protocell droplets, and you pour the mixture into the hole." She describes how "the mixture swells and almost instantly supports the pole with its turgor"; "it now resembles a large lump of jelly. Bubbles start to appear and are quickly turned into a precipitate as the released carbon dioxide from the reaction is absorbed into a solid form." Time passes. "The sun comes out. . . . The world turns, the rain falls, the snow comes. . . . By the end of the year, it is time to add a new protocell material to the base of the post. This is a species of strengthening agent." Yes, "each year, you come back to the post and make an assessment regarding what processes are required for the post to be kept in place, and each year a new protocell species is added."[85] Instead of "gling," she desires a "new kind of biology [insert chemistry] for the built environment that is native to its context and . . . genuinely sustainable. In order for this to happen, the basic materials that underpin this system need to be developed using a bottom-up approach."[86]

What does it mean to use a "bottom-up approach" when humans are the ones developing a chemical system, picking its basic ingredients, and adding the new "protocell species" required each year? A fundamental contradiction in agency is at play here between humans designing something and putting all the parts together and something just making itself through self-assembly. The latter requires all the right materials being proximate to one another in the correct environment, which they would not be now without human design and action. Even if cells formed in the primordial ocean, at this point pre-protocells are being created in laboratories and in artworks by humans thinking very carefully about what molecules are necessary to produce the proper precipitates. This process is no different from what humans have always done—combining materials to produced desired effects—except now owing to the popularity of complexity theory and self-organization, some are strategically calling this "self-assembly" since chemistry happens.

The tiny scale—half of a millimeter—of a pre-protocell just exacerbates the bottom-up architectural problem, although truly building from the bottom up, molecule by molecule, is by definition always going to be very small. Its precipitates are even tinier. Just how much olive oil and mineral additives, floating in (a contained body of) seawater, does it take to "self-assemble" a human-scale building, presumably with rooms inside? How are "protocells" "chemically programmed" to create rooms? "Protocell Architecture" is full of blown-up images of micron-sized "protocells" allowing us to see and imagine this otherwise nearly invisible-to-the-naked-eye future.[87] Cronin describes in his article in the issue, "Defining New Architectural Design Principles with 'Living' Inorganic Materials," how his lab aims "to reduce the fundamental building block of building materials from the centimetre (real bricks, nails, concrete blocks) to the same dimensions as the building blocks of biology and to produce inorganic cells. Imagine the outcomes of establishing such a paradigm," he writes. "Buildings would have a cellular structure with living inorganic components that would allow the entire structure to self-repair, to sense environmental changes, establish a central nervous system, and even use the environment to sequester water, develop solar energy systems, and regulate the atmosphere, internal temperature, and humidity using this decentralized approach." The stratospheric air of his vision is brought back to earth by the caption for an image of a crystal tube that states, "The diameter of the tube is around 0.0001 millimetres."[88] Yet, his own description jumps from the micro to the global scale: "To be useful, to create systems with this degree of sophistication requires a robust chemical library of structures with embedded chemistries that are adaptive, resilient, environmentally compatible, and realisable on a global scale." The word "global" can, of course, be used relatively to speak of the broad limits of a system, as it is in complexity theory and in generative architectural practice. With a slight bit of caution, he adds, "The global deployment of such a fundamentally new building platform, though, should probably not be permitted until we are able to get to grips with the concepts of artificial inorganic 'living technology.'"[89] This could take a while.

Full Circle. Stop.

Synthetic biology is the last scientific field discussed in this book, which has ranged through the founding of complexity theory in relation to cybernetics and its current ideological manifestation in complexism (self-organization, emergence, natural computation), to changing theories of biological evolution, morphogenesis, genetics, and epigenetics, to the applied practices of tissue and genetic engineering and synthetic biology. Fittingly, the two branches of the latter bring us full circle to a few themes that have surfaced multiple times across the different chapters.

This first recurring theme is the pervasive application of complexism, informed by materialism, as a primary interpretive tool for characterizing the processes of the three main systems explored here together: architectural, computational, and biological systems. Complexism provides the language of "bottom-up" versus "top-down." The former is heavily favored now for its convenient and useful connotations of being untainted by human intervention and its connotations of matter having agency. Because the universe consists of energy and matter, which Einstein showed to be equivalent, and matter takes shape in the form of atoms, and because atoms combine into molecules and molecules constitute the physiochemical basis of cells, many scientists and philosophers of science consider life to be an emergent property of the self-organization of matter. Although the sciences of physics and chemistry have thrived under reductionism—the idea that wholes can be broken down into and sufficiently understood and described by their constituent parts—biology is posited by some to be a “special science,” one that cannot be reduced to the laws of physics and chemistry.[90] This debate informs the earliest definition of self-organization by philosopher Immanuel Kant in 1790, who was attempting to identify what separates living organisms from other objects, as well as the degree to which science can help us understand what is unique about living organisms.[91] Thus, the founding of the discipline of biology is intertwined with the philosophy of emergence and its related concept, self-organization. What are now facets of complexity theory are key framing devices by which even disciplines cordon themselves off from one another.

Interestingly, although the bottom-up protocell research branch of synthetic biology embraces complexity theory for its descriptions of self-organization and acquired hierarchies of order and complexity—which seem necessary for the move from self-assembled vesicles to protocells to actual cells, with their spatial architecture, organelles, et cetera—the top-down engineering branch of synthetic biology keeps complexity theory at a distance. This is because the former need the molecules to do the hard work. Scientists can provide the right chemicals in the right environment, but the “life” is going to have to “emerge” through “self-organization” and “self-assembly.” On the other hand, top-down engineering synthetic biologists are striving for control over an already living system; they take living cells and alter their genetic makeup and hope for a precise outcome. The fact that as recently as 2014, students in a synthetic biology course that I took at UC Davis were still being taught the central dogma of molecular biology as the ruling theory, reveals the extent to which theory is put to work to bolster the self-image of an engineer who can control, even if this theory is now known to partially describe only one part of heredity owing to new knowledge of the rest of the genome and epigenetics.[92] Students were also not introduced to epigenetics, the rationale being that synthetic biology is already challenging enough without the addition of another system that complicates it.[93] Critiques of the central dogma as oversimplistic given recent postgenomic discoveries are well recognized among many groups of scientists. Yet, computer scientists and most architects designing genetic algorithms and synthetic biologists engineering organisms still teach the dogma as the primary theory. Its simplicity, without the complications of postgenomics or complex systems interactions, is necessary for a relatively easy theorization of how genetic circuits work. Without this, it becomes much more difficult to uphold the idea that synthetic biology can in fact produce standardized products. If other branches of biology are aware of systemic processes that are environmentally responsive and clearly affect gene regulation and heredity, then the fact that engineering synthetic biologists can willfully ignore this knowledge in order to shore up their nascent discipline simply shows how determined they are.[94]

In contrast to bottom-up approaches that are all the rage, top-down engineering synbio carries associations of a bygone modernist paradigm of control, except for the fact that this paradigm is anything but gone. Scientists working in this field are unabashed about stating their desire to design, engineer, and control. Yet, even beyond the field of synthetic biology, natural or social or economic processes that are cast as "self-organizing" are still targeted for co-optation by scientists, social scientists, economists, and designers. These practitioners either want to predict and profit from the outcomes of these systems or intend to use "self-organization" to generate designed outcomes. This use or control of so-called self-organizing systems produces a problematic agency and fundamental definitional tension, owing to the "self" part. That aspects of the modernist paradigm are alive and well is made clear simply by the engineering mentality of synthetic biology (Figure 6.7). As this comparison of images first put forward by Ginsberg in one of her essays in *Synthetic Aesthetic* shows, the hand of the designer and the pipette referencing a scientist's hand reveal the agency that creates the design, be it Le Corbusier's ideal city *Ville Radieuse* (1930) or JCVIsyn1.0 (2010), the first self-replicating synthetic bacteria cells ever created. Similarly, Patrik Schumacher is not shy about his dislike of postmodern and deconstructivist architecture and favors a return to the control and homogeneity that modernism offered (Figure 1.14).[95] Whereas biologists try to understand living organisms, synthetic biologists want to manipulate and use them. Bottom-up protocell research intends the creation of protocells for use in synthetic biology as artificial cells that can be engineered to produce desired products, as well as for knowledge gained about the creation of life—which after all, if it is achieved, will put humans in a position once occupied by the deities.

The few articles that address facets of complexity theory or systems biology in relation to top-down engineering synbio primarily pertain to the issue of "stochasticity" or "noise" in gene circuits.[96] Gene circuits are mathematically modeled in computers, but when DNA plasmids are actually inserted into an organism, "very often inherent stochasticity of gene expression process strongly influences dynamic behavior of the network."[97] In fact, "stochastic fluctuations (noise) in gene expression can cause members of otherwise genetically identical populations to display drastically different phenotypes." Therefore, "an understanding of the sources of noise and the strategies cells employ to function reliably despite noise is proving to be increasingly important in describing the behavior of natural organisms and will be essential for the engineering of synthetic biological systems."[98] Scientists therefore are exploring different methods to regulate the effects of "noise," for example by designing transcriptional cascades of different lengths that can either "attenuate or amplify phenotypical variations depending on the system's input conditions."[99] It may be that "noise" is due to

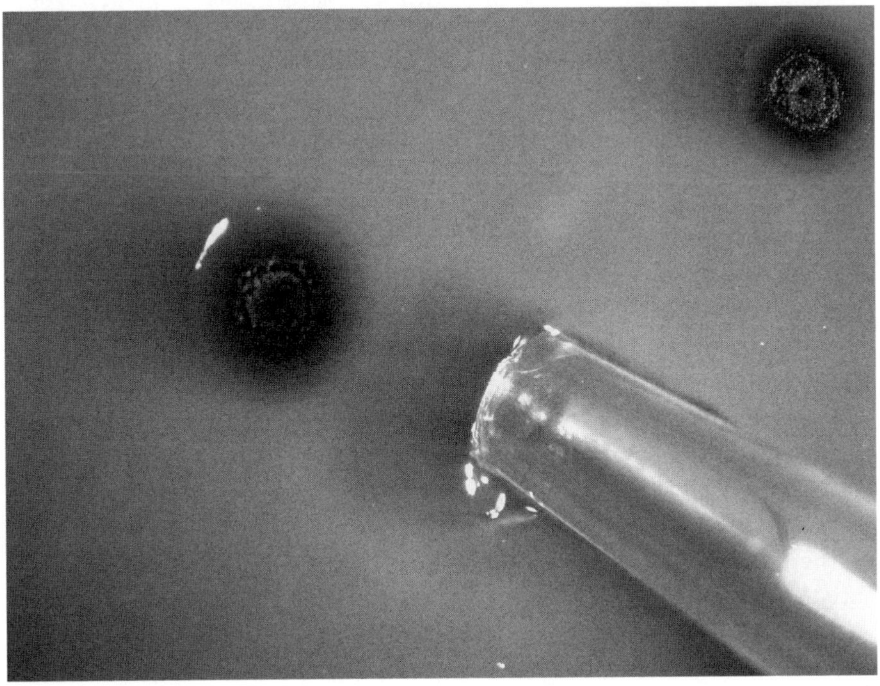

FIGURE 6.7. *Le Corbusier's Hands,* still from Pierre Chenal's film *Architecture d'Aujourd'hui,* 1930, reproduced with permission of the Fondation Le Corbusier, Paris, and Artists Rights Society (ARS), New York / ADACP, © FLC/ARS, 2017; and colonies of the transformed *Mycoplasma mycoides* bacterium, courtesy of J. Craig Venter Institute, 2010. Side-by-side comparison of these two images first published in *Synthetic Aesthetics: Investigating Synthetic Biology's Designs on Nature,* ed. Alexandra Daisy Ginsberg, Jane Calvert, Pablo Schyfter, Alistair Elfick, and Drew Endy (Cambridge, Mass.: MIT Press, 2014), 58. The all-powerful hand of the architect (1930) and handheld instruments of the engineering synthetic biologist (2010) both aim for control over predictable, designed outcomes; hence, this facet of modernism is anything but dead.

epigenetic processes that most assuredly can produce unpredictable phenotypic outcomes in engineered cells.[100]

To phrase this limited use of complexity theory in engineering synbio slightly differently, top-down synthetic biologists draw a narrower boundary around what they see as their "system" than do biologists working in the fields of cell biology or systems biology. Top-down synthetic biologists limit their view primarily to the engineered genetic circuit. They apply complexity theory within the "system" of the genome and the gene circuits they create and, after installation, to its phenotypic expressive variability. They do this instead of, from the outset, integrating elements outside the gene circuit—epigenetic markers such as methylation patterns or other important interactive molecules already present in the "chassis" cell—into their theoretical and mathematical models. As scientists Pengcheng Fu and Cliff Hooker summarize, "Systems biology is inherently a universe in which every 'ome'—genome, transcriptome, proteome, metabolome, interactome, phenome, and so on, is another dimension. We have to reduce this dimensionality through integration in order to comprehend, evaluate, and make use of the information."[101] Or, as biologist Michael Bolker states, "The inherent complexity of biological systems renders any strict calculations impossible and thus poses an enormous challenge to synthetic biology." Because of this, "two alternative strategies have been adopted by synthetic biologists to deal with this problem: (1) Reduction of complexity by applying engineering principles to biology like standardization and modularization and (2) orthogonalization through chemical or biological modification of synthetic cells to prevent genetic interactions with other organisms."[102] Selectively drawing one's boundaries around a system so as to frame it as you need to see it is common practice for many people in both science and daily life. Yet, doing so does not remove the actual interactive relations that extend beyond the edge of the imagined boundary. Narrowly drawing system boundaries just provides a short-term conceptual coping tool. This is as true for how a synthetic biologist chooses to apply complexity theory—either for its concepts of self-organization and emergence, as protocell researchers do, or for its mathematical tools for analyzing stochasticity and contingency, as top-down synthetic biologists do—as it is for how synthetic biologists construct the history of their discipline in order to differentiate it from genetic engineering.

The second recurring theme in both branches of synthetic biology that echoes other instances throughout this book is the potential confusion caused by ambiguities of language and presentation. That Armstrong uses the phrase "protocell architecture" instead of "pre-protocell architecture" offers a prime example since a protocell has not yet been created and is the holy grail of protocell researchers. Granted, Hanczyc, the synthetic biologist with whom she collaborates, also talks misleadingly about pre-protocells that he makes as if they are protocells, or at least "simple protocells."[103] He also uses the present tense in talking about protocells: "Protocells are . . . made in a laboratory. . . . The protocell is motile."[104] (Sometimes, he more modestly uses "protocell-type structure"; this is closer to what other contributors to the *Protocells* textbook use, the term "pre-protocell.")[105] If scientists discuss pre-protocells as if they are protocells, then architects who collaborate with them may possibly be excused, except for the fact that their use of the word "protocells"—not just Armstrong, but others who follow, work with, and promote her—gives readers who do not know better the impression that protocells already exist. This makes her pronouncements seem much more realizable and possible, and gives her vision more respectability, on top of the fact that she collaborates with scientists and is frequently cited as a medical doctor. Outside of synthetic biology, a similar problem occurs with use of the word "victimless" by scientists, journalists, and designers using processes of tissue engineering who either fail to realize or acknowledge that the primary nutrient media used contains FCS from slaughtered calves and cows. A different type of ambiguity in generative architecture occurs from the use of words that sound the same but refer to very different technologies or modes of production. Usually the words or phrases refer to digital modes of production but they sound biological—namely, "gene," "genetic," "genotype," "DNA," "morphogenesis," "phenotype," "organism," "species," and "phylogenesis." Another group of similar sounding terms, some of which confuse subject/object position as to what is computing and what is computed, include "natural computation," "material computation," "biomolecular computation," "biocomputation," "biosynthesis," and "synthetic biology."

The third theme that connects this chapter with the others is the presence of eugenics, although the word itself is never used. Its stand-ins are words such as "optimization," "enhancement," and "improvement" when used in tandem with any technique of genetic engineering. For example, in one "design for debate" project called *Child Force* by Marei Wollersberger that Marcos Cruz and Steve Pike included in "Neoplasmatic Design" (2008), the designer "explored the impact of gene technology and its ensuing ideology in relation to our current move towards heightened surveillance." Anthony Dunne describes her work as a "cautionary tale." Yet in the footnotes of his description of her research process, he writes that Wollersberger consulted "Horst Voithenleitner, psychologist and director of the International Social Service (ISS) in Vienna, about our current understanding of the social role of children and how optimisation of our genetic make-up could impact on this."[106] His use of the phrase "optimisation of our genetic make-up" shows transference of the conceptual coding process of optimization from the digital realm of design into and onto that of our hypothetical human future. Michael Weinstock and computer scientists Sathish Periyasamy, Alex Gray, and Peter Kile make a similar move when they state that optimization is part of actual evolution.[107] The latter three write, "Evolution is an optimization process, where the aim is to improve the ability of a biological system to survive in a dynamically changing and competitive environment."[108]

Top-down synthetic biologists are also proclaiming the imminent creation of "enhanced" human beings through the use of CRISPR/Cas9. These are perhaps the most vociferous and respected proponents of eugenics today.[109] Consider for example the words of Juan Enriquez, who chairs the Genetics Advisory Council at Harvard Medical School, and Steve Gullans, who was a professor there, in their 2015 coauthored book *Evolving Ourselves: How Unnatural Selection and Nonrandom Mutation Are Changing Life on Earth*: "CRISPR can be repurposed to cut, paste, and edit any DNA sequence into or out of any genome quickly and easily, not just bacteria. . . . CRISPR can effectively edit out any harmful DNA sequence (for example, a disease causing gene mutation) and replace it with a beneficial DNA code (a normal non-mutated gene)." Unlike other approaches in genetic engineering "such as gene therapy, which introduce one new gene into a genome with many complex and tedious steps, CRISPR is rapid, large-scale gene-editing technology." They describe this as "transitioning from a mechanical typewriter, having to use Wite-Out, and retyping a word or phrase . . . to having a primitive word-processing program that allows one to swap whole paragraphs or pages in and out," without retyping.[110]

Enriquez and Gullans see CRISPR as an everyday technology, one that DIY biologists and high school kids alike will have access to; the possible uses for it are seemingly limitless. "But by far the most important impact of CRISPR," they write, "will be on the modification and evolution of humans."[111] Though they acknowledge lightheartedly that this might be controversial, they are certain that our "broad ethical debate and education" on this technology will lead us to decide to use it. This pronouncement is similar to how "critical design" urges debate with the same expected outcome.[112] "Reasonably soon we will find a safe way to engineer long-term changes into our descendants. When we choose to do so, we will begin to shape the species according to our own set of instructions and desires," they state. "This is not just unnatural selection altering and shaping what already lives, this is nonrandom mutation rapidly creating and passing on something new. So let's now look at the completely uncontroversial topic of altering future babies."[113] They begin their next chapter, "Unnatural Acts, Designer Babies, and Sex 2.0," with the fact that the United Kingdom in 2015 "may become the first country to allow trans-generational genetic engineering" known as "germ-line engineering," in order to "deal with mitochondrial diseases." In fact, a law was passed in 2015 that "carve[d] out an exception to the prohibition on human inheritable genetic modification in the UK"; it allows "'3-person IVF' techniques without human clinical trials, and with no required follow up of any resulting children."[114] Enriquez and Gullans predict "a tidal wave of genetic upgrades in humans," ranging from ones targeting the brain to those that can make us "Forever Young, Beautiful, and Fearless."[115] These qualities are almost identical to those desired and pursued by American eugenicists in the 1920s and 1930s.[116]

This pursuit of being disease-free, ageless, even evading death, is proposed by Armstrong for "protocell" architecture. She states that "protocell" architecture is "self-healing" and "self-repairing," but fails to explicitly mention though that it can get hurt, wounded, or sick, the necessary precondition demanding these qualities. Throughout the special issue of *AD*, whenever the word "death" is mentioned with regard to "protocells," the sentence negates its presence. "Protocells inherently engage with the principles of design," Armstrong and Spiller write. "They manipulate and can be manipulated to alter matter in their environment, reworking and repositioning this material in time and space—a strategy shared by life to avoid entropy and the decay towards equilibrium, in other words, death. . . . [Protocell architecture] resists the equilibrium since this constitutes death."[117] Realize that "protocells" can only do this if their environment provides the necessary molecules for their ongoing "metabolic" reaction. In essence, then, "protocell" architecture seemingly does not age, repairs and heals itself, and never dies. This is the same future that nano-bio-info-cognitive convergence (NBIC) supporters imagine for the human body, including Armstrong's friend, British sociologist Steve Fuller.

Fuller dedicated his 2011 book *Humanity 2.0: What It Means to Be Human Past, Present, and Future* to Armstrong. Late in 2012, Armstrong and Fuller presented together lectures on "Architecture and Ecology" at the Victoria and Albert Museum in London.[118] In his review of this event for *Architectural Review,* Robert Bottazi states that Armstrong agrees with Fuller's predictions in *Humanity 2.0* that "the role of human beings in a world increasingly governed by convergent nano- and biotechnologies will unavoidably fade for at least three reasons": climate change, technologies that "level out differences between living beings and inorganic matter," and other actors (inorganic and organic) playing a role in designing the environment. "The architect will recede into the background to become more of a designer of systems of interaction rather than fixed objects."[119] As Bottazi mentions, Fuller promotes NBIC convergence, which together will become the tools for designing the future world when humans assume a role akin to a demiurge. Fuller also supports transhumanism, which promotes humans' "evolving into something different, something better" and is serving as a foundation of the new eugenics.[120] In fact, transhumanists cite their forefathers as eugenics supporters Julian Huxley and J. B. S. Haldane. Its Wikipedia page describes transhumanism as "an international and intellectual movement that aims to transform the human condition by developing and creating widely available sophisticated technologies to greatly enhance human intellectual, physical, and psychological capacities."[121] Protocell researchers, who work on the nano-bio portion of this predicted convergence, in the introduction to the textbook *Protocells* state that both the National Science Foundation in the United States and the European Commission "believe that convergent technologies will have a very large socioeconomic impact in the next 25 years."[122]

The similarities between NBIC proponents and less critical synbiodesigners must be highlighted, lest we overlook their common acceptance and prediction of eugenics in the rush to meet the future. For example, Susana Soares's *New Organs of Perception* (2007) and *Genetic Trace* (2007), which were included in *Design and the Elastic Mind,* depict new perceptual organs on the body, such as sensitive whiskers on the eyebrows or comblike tips on fingernails that allow individuals to collect other people's biological data through interpersonal encounters, perhaps for "selective mating."[123] Her website asserts that "genetic screening technologies are enabling parents to design their babies and weed out undesirable diseases." She supports this with quotes by evolutionary psychologist Geoffrey Miller—"Within a few generations market-based genetic technology will eclipse social-sexual selection"—and biologist Kate Douglas—"1,000 years from now, people will be much more beautiful, intelligent, symmetrical, healthy and emotionally stable, thanks to 40 generations of genetic screening."[124] In fact, the United Kingdom passed the Human Fertilisation and Embryology Act (2008) that prevents the implantation of embryos diagnosed with a "serious illness," including "deafness," into a mother's womb.[125] In this case, the parents' desire to "design their babies," as Soares puts it, should they desire a deaf child, is overruled by national law, a situation that repeats and renews the aims of laws passed in many states and nations during the 1920s and 1930s in the name of eugenics.[126]

Similarly, technocratic thinking that was so prevalent in eugenics of the interwar period surfaces today in synbiodesign. Chieza's *Design Fictions* adopts the idea of a body as a farm, which echoes but counters the dystopia of Burton's *Nanotopia* for the *Future Farm* project. Her pieces reflect a broad acceptance of technocratic thinking based on industrial processes, showing humans using DIY genetics to grow new aesthetic or health-giving biological prosthetics that function in part as fashion. Whether human bodies are genetically engineered to be factories to grow body parts viewed as "products" for other humans, or whether humans use other living organisms as factories to grow materials or "products" for ourselves, the underlying approach and action are based on means–ends thinking and a valuation of living bodies as nothing special, therefore just seeing bodies as materiality, matter, "stuff."[127] This "engineering mindset" carries with it corollary industrial assumptions that products/bodies should be "well-designed," engineered, managed, and profited from—or at least something that companies or governments should not be made poorer by, as when politicians argue that women on welfare should be paid to be sterilized.[128] This mode of thought runs deep in synthetic biology today and is fundamental to the principles of NBIC convergence. It is beneath the idea of social control through rational selection, assuming of course that one believes there are social factors that result primarily from genetic bases, an idea that was and is prominent throughout facets of twentieth- and twenty-first-century psychology, sociology, and criminology. Technocratic logic was, according to historian of German eugenics Sheila Weiss and myself, the most fundamental, pernicious, and ethically perverse mode of thought behind eugenics and its policies during the interwar period and beyond, as demonstrated most prominently through its effects in the Holocaust.[129]

The language of controlling evolution is virtually identical between the eugenicists of the interwar period and synthetic biologists today, although the means by which they intend to reach their goals are based on different knowledge bases and scientific methodologies. Both speak of replacing natural selection with "rational selection" (the interwar term) or with "unnatural selection and nonrandom mutation" (the current terms).[130] Between the world wars, "positive eugenics" aimed to increase the population of the "fit" using "race betterment," whereas today, "eugenic algorithms" "optimize" "fitness" according to parameters set by designers. Without obvious historical consciousness spelled out in the choice of name, software named "Eugene" offers synthetic biologists a language for creating "composite devices from collections of parts."[131] In the interwar period, "negative eugenics" minimized the presence of those deemed "unfit" or "dysgenic" through reproductive sterilization. The first state sterilization law was passed in Indiana in 1907, with others added through the 1930s; some state sterilization laws in the United States remained on the books and were actively in practice into the 1980s, with over seventy thousand individuals across the United States being involuntarily sterilized. A few governors have apologized to their state's citizens, but so far only North Carolina has voted to make financial reparations to living victims.[132] Just two years ago, California passed a bill to ban forced sterilizations from occurring in California prisons, precisely in response to it being brought to light that nearly 150 women had been sterilized illegally between 2006 and 2010.[133] Even worse, in the interwar and wartime period, doctors, scientists, politicians, and citizens "removed" the "unfit" using "euthanasia" or outright murder—referring primarily to Germany, as well as to eugenically motivated race-based murders in the United States, mostly across the South. Today, computer scientists design kill strategies in eugenic algorithms while synthetic biologists design kill switches for rogue species.

Along these lines, in *Synthetic Aesthetics* Ginsberg describes a "lease of life" concept for engineered products, which would legally and physically make them finite even if they could still be useful, according to the economically useful idea of planned obsolescence. She recounts how Oxitec Ltd. has designed and engineered a variety of male mosquito (RIDL mosquitoes) "whose progeny are designed to never live. . . . Already on trial in the Cayman Islands and Brazil, factory-grown RIDL mosquitoes are sorted by sex, and then released into the wild by the million." After the mosquitoes mate, their "offspring will never hatch. . . . Mosquitoes are not killed as such; they are just never born. . . . Mosquitoes that never live seem to be good design."[134] Methods such as these, she proposes, "could offer an economic and social safety mechanism beyond the kill switch, as we continue to seek reliable ways to *design a good death for our things*"—such is the source of the word "euthanasia." "While biotechnological obsolescence may become a fact of life and a functional design reality, it also marks the ultimate instrumentalization of life."[135] The lines blur between the past and the present, except for the fact that in the publications on synbiodesign and synthetic biology, the words "eugenics" and "euthanasia" are never used.

This historical amnesia is inexcusable. Does it stem from ignorance, hubris, or both? Regardless of the underlying reason for why this amnesia is so widespread, these continuities of and resonances with eugenics of the past force us to face questions of justice and injustice, including asking who now is wielding

FIGURE 6.8. Using affect to increase empathy in near-living architecture, by Ali-Akbar Samadani, Dana Kulic, and Rob Gorbet. From *Near-Living Architecture: Works in Progress from the Hylozoic Ground Collaboration, 2011–2013,* ed. Philip Beesley (Toronto: Riverside Architectural Press, 2014), 66. The programming of acrylic fronds in Philip Beesley's sculptures (see Plate 14) to mimic human hand gestures is intended to evoke greater affect, empathy, and responsiveness in viewers of the works.

power over "the other," how so, and what and who constitutes "the other." Philip Beesley wisely intended to raise these questions through the works he created for the *Hylozoic* series, including *Hylozoic Ground,* on display in Venice in 2011. The responsive, kinetic environments that hover in space, enveloping humans beneath and between its parts, are intended to make humans perceive themselves as the potential "other" in relation to "near-living" architecture. Beesley's worthy goal is motivated by and intending toward the creation of humility, which is a fabulous position from which to begin facing questions of "othering" and injustice. Yet, efforts by some of his collaborators unfortunately, and perhaps unwittingly, work against Beesley's intent. Dana Kulic, Rob Gorbet, and Ali-Akbar Samadani observed human responses to the sculpture in Venice, literally noting expressions and hand gestures, and then algorithmically scripted these very shapes into the movements of the fronds ("fingers") of later sculptures in the *Hylozoic* series (Figure 6.8). The group wanted to heighten future visitors' experiences by designing the sculpture's actions to produce affect, making humans think that the "near-living" architecture is empathetic and responsive to them when, in fact, the sculpture was simply being created in their own image. What could have been "other"—and would be legitimately "other" were it actually a living organism—has merely become a scripted representation of human beings themselves.[136] Alternatively, Burton's *Nanotopia* (Figure 6.3) addresses these important questions by directing us toward the broader contexts of socioeconomic inequalities within which future practices of human genetic engineering, or NBIC convergent technologies, might occur. What he observes is not much different from how surrogacy is currently being outsourced today. In other words, new technologies often integrate themselves into existing patterns of injustice implemented through political economy, economic production, and socioeconomic stratification. In a very different sense from how Jenny Sabin and Peter Lloyd Jones address it, we return to the idea that "context matters."

The final theme apparent in synthetic biology and throughout the book is the way the technologies discussed here, especially when implemented by generative architects or synbiodesigners, can presumably contribute to "sustainability." In her critical thinking about the potentials and pitfalls of synthetic biology as it is becoming constituted as a field, Ginsberg notes that industrialization and design under the mass production and mass consumption mentality of the twentieth century have both proven themselves unsustainable. They have also demonstrated that the profit models they are allied with tend toward mono-cropping and homogeneity rather than diversity. Synthetic biology touts its foundational role in what promoters are predicting will be the Second Industrial Revolution that permits unabated consumption and economic growth for the twenty-first century. This is one of the primary rationales for modeling top-down synthetic biology on the principles of the original Industrial Revolution.

Yet, Ginsberg critiques this mentality that pertained to twentieth-century industrialization and to design: "Faced with the individuality of living things, does the uniform engineering vision, eliminating diversity in favor of a controllable uniformity, seem as desirable?" She describes how the "unique properties of biology are often overlooked in discussions of the industrialization of synthetic biology. Instead," she writes, "we are presented with a vision of 'drop-in' replacements, which use bacteria as a mechanism to produce more of what we already have, rather than doing something more interesting that draws on the particular characteristics of biological systems." Rather than copying techniques of mass production of design through standardization and overproduction, as these "design practices are themselves unsustainable," or becoming obsessed with gene-centrism, she argues that we need to think anew, learning from biology itself rather than from past modes of production.[137] "Life is more than DNA. Fetishizing DNA is limiting, and analogies with the digital world prevent us from seeing biology in full."[138]

A number of issues are at stake in these visions of both design and design education integrating synthetic biology that are not being discussed by many of its proponents. Ginsberg is one of the few synbiodesigners who is thinking critically from within while asking excellent questions about which futures are being envisioned and why. She critiques the limitations of current work in synthetic biology. These include limitations of vision, where the Second Industrial Revolution is imagined to be almost exactly like the first despite the problems created by that original incarnation. They include limitations of practice as well. She critiques the design of "bacteria that pump out non-biodegradable acrylic acid for plastic or isoprene for tires. Once they leave the factory, these plastics and tires may be no less polluting than conventionally made ones."[139]

Similarly, some companies are producing synthetic biofuels that in their use emit greenhouse gases at similar or higher levels than those produced through the burning of fossil fuels.[140] Such uses do not work for "sustainability" but rather shift economic profit from the fossil fuel–based economic sector toward the "glucose economy." "The bioeconomy is sold as a sustainable glucose-powered future, a sweet medicine to remedy our dirty carbon and dangerous nuclear habits," she writes. The "rush to build sugar-powered biofuel infrastructure is often underscored by geopolitical or economic pressures around energy, rather than a desire to maintain biodiversity or seek out good design." Is there even "enough land to feed planes and cars and products as well as people and animals, and can such large-scale monoculture be sustainable?"[141]

This returns us to considerations of spatial and material limits, given that the size of our planet and the material formations it offers are finite. The materials used in the production of microprocessors and computers—not to mention many other products—are being "plundered," to use Steve Pike's word choice, at a rapid rate.[142] Yet, architectural visions of the future—such as Weinstock's "self-aware" cities, artificially living environments such as Beesley's sculptures were they adapted to an architectural scale, and even an abundance of plain old "smart" "green" buildings—rely on microprocessors, sensors, actuators/motors, and distributed communication and control systems.[143] These require both materials and energy, not only in their operation or useful life but throughout their full life cycle. These production processes and the materials and energy used to power them produce by-product pollution and waste. Until architects, designers, manufacturers, consumers, and politicians integrate life cycle analysis into their everyday decision-making, claims of "sustainability" remain unsubstantiated. If molecules can self-assemble simply using energy in chemical bonding, so that then presumably a designer or architect growing something from the bottom up might say no energy is added and the process is "sustainable," then what energy and materials go into getting the molecules isolated in the first place, in order to then combine them, assuming it is a technologically controlled process? Skylar Tibbits's deployable structures to be dropped from helicopters use only gravitational energy for their opening, but this says nothing at all about the energy used to design and manufacture them and the materials from which they are made, transported, and so forth.[144]

By drawing a narrow frame around a product—looking only, say, at its immediate creation and operational use—and then not looking beyond the frame to see the rest of the embedded energy, material extraction, and pollution needed by and produced by the whole life cycle, one can more easily say a product is "sustainable" when it well may not be. Strategies of framing—whether for life cycle analysis or for delineating the boundaries of a complex system—allow us to see or not see the unsustainability or the social and economic inequities that our actions or designs or consumer choices may promote. Framing strategically allows us to imagine and teach that we can engineer something based on a simple but incomplete theory, in the face of contrary knowledge. We can frame something so that it appears to be "bottom-up" even though it may also function "top-down." These strategies of framing work as a process of expulsion, as Saskia Sassen notes in her study of the environmental and social brutalities being enacted under complexity in our current neoliberal global economy.[145] For all these reasons, to ask how something is framed and what that framing reveals are perhaps the most important questions of all. The heavy reliance in discourses of generative architecture on the rhetoric of complexism and current biological theory and practice both naturalizes and distracts from its many modes of instrumentalization: of life and of materiality, through ever bigger data and ever bigger digital infrastructure. These are the strongest but not the only reasons to question the value of the contribution of generative architecture and design, as currently practiced. While some biodesign approaches hold great potential in terms of rethinking materials as grown and biodegradable, lower-tech rather than higher-tech approaches hold more promise for future environmental and generational health and well-being.

APPENDIX

Brief History of Complexity's Intersections with Generative Architecture

The fundamental importance of computer hardware and software for understanding complexity and self-organization is not just definitional, in terms of serving as a major source for the "rules" at play in "self-organization," but also historical. Evelyn Fox Keller's history of self-organization begins with Immanuel Kant's search for a definition of a living organism in 1790 under the new science of biology; he coined the term "self-organization" to distinguish an organism from nonliving things like machines. She describes Kant's definition of an organism: "It is a bounded body capable not only of self-regulation, self-steering, but also, and perhaps most important, of self-formation and self-generation; it is both an organized and a self-organizing being." Furthermore, "an organism is a body which, by virtue of its peculiar and particular organization, is constituted as a 'self'—an entity that, even though not hermetically sealed (or perhaps because it is not hermetically sealed), achieves both autonomy and the capacity for self-generation."[1] By contrast, "inanimate matter lacks both the organization and self-organization of organisms, and machines, though organized, and even designed, are organized and designed from without. The organization and design of organisms is, by contrast, internally generated."[2]

The first part of Keller's history traces how the idea that organisms and machines are different, even if sometimes seeming analogous, was transformed into the idea in cybernetics that animals and machines are actually homologous, as Norbert Wiener famously argued in *Cybernetics; or, Control and Communication in the Animal and the Machine* (1948).[3] The development of the idea of homeostasis, which came out of physiology in the nineteenth and twentieth centuries, played an important role. As homeostasis functions in living organisms, likewise machines can be designed with control mechanisms that use feedback through communication to regulate the machine's functions. Keller writes that if one just includes the designer and the environmental inputs as a part of the "self," then both living organisms and machines can be called self-organizing.[4] Note that including the human designer and environmental inputs along with the machine considerably stretches the idea of a "self," which is usually thought of as a singular living entity. Furthermore, humans have agency, so a significant difference exists between humans' designing and making machines or anything else and that thing on its own self-organizing.

Around the time of World War II with the rise of cybernetics and the creation of the first digital computers, use of the concept and term "self-organization" significantly increased, as many ideas and events coalesced into what began to be known as complexity and general systems theory. Different histories touch on different aspects of these developments, which occurred across the disciplines of cybernetics, computation, biology, embryology, neurophysiology, psychology, psychiatry, meteorology, mathematics, engineering, physics, chemistry, cryptography, artificial intelligence, and computer science.[5] This overview only touches on some of the major developments that intersected with developments in the field of architecture.[6] These interwoven threads of the intersections of complexity theory, evolutionary computation, and architecture generally occurred in three places—London, Cambridge (Massachusetts), and New York—beginning in the late 1950s and early 1960s. This is undoubtedly an oversimplification, since scientific scholars and architects traveled and moved between institutions and read available publications. Furthermore, meetings such as the Macy conferences and the 1959 conference in Chicago on Self-Organizing Systems organized by the U.S. Office of Naval Research served as hubs where thinkers from around the world met to discuss their ideas.

We start in Cambridge after the end of the war, where Wiener was professor of mathematics at the Massachusetts Institute of Technology (MIT) when he published *Cybernetics*. Over the years, a number of his students and colleagues extended facets of cybernetic theory, mathematics, artificial intelligence, and evolutionary computation. Both Oliver Selfidge and John Holland studied with Wiener in the late 1940s, with Selfidge remaining at MIT to work with Marvin Minsky to found the field of artificial intelligence. Holland went on to do graduate study in mathematics and computer science at the University of Michigan, where he was on the faculty during the decades when he developed genetic algorithms and programming for adaptive systems. His research culminated in his pathbreaking *Adaptation in Natural and Artificial Systems* (1975), which influenced architects interested in using computers to generate architectural forms.[7]

Architectural interest in cybernetics and computer programming had a history preceding Holland's publication, though. György Kepes was at MIT starting in 1947, a few years after he published *Language of Vision*.[8] He became interested in Wiener's work, citing him and discussing cybernetics in his book *The New Landscape in Art and Science* (1956).[9] Siegfried Giedion, an architectural historian interested in physics and the author of *Space, Time, and Architecture* (1941), began teaching at MIT and the Harvard Graduate School of Design (GSD) in the 1950s. Their influence extended to the highly interdisciplinary graduate student Christopher Alexander, whose *Notes on the Synthesis of Form* (1964), which used set theory to explain methods of algorithmic design, was influential across fields. This is not surprising, given that he had a bachelor's degree in architecture and a master's of science in mathematics from Cambridge University, and that he received the first doctoral degree in architecture awarded by the GSD and also completed postgraduate study in computer science and transportation theory at MIT and cognitive studies at Harvard. His best seller *A Pattern Language* (1977) is one of the landmark publications applying computer programming to design. Historian Molly Steenson considers him one of the founders of generative architecture, along with Nicholas Negroponte—who studied architecture at MIT in the early 1960s, focusing on computer-aided design—and British architect Cedric Price.[10]

Alexander left Cambridge to teach at the University of California, Berkeley, the year before the Boston Architectural Center hosted the Architecture and the Computer conference in 1964. Three years later, Nicholas Negroponte and Leon Groissier founded the Architecture Machine Group in the Department of Architecture at MIT.[11] British cyberneticist Gordon Pask visited the Architecture Machine Group a number of times between 1968 and 1976; his work on conversation theory and the unusual machines he built contributed to Negroponte's ideas in *The Architecture Machine* (1970). Around the same time, Negroponte and Groissier began teaching a "Computer-Aided Urban Design" studio (1968), and the following year, Pask published "The Architectural Relevance of Cybernetics."[12] Pask also spent time collaborating with architects and teaching at the Architectural Association (AA) in London in the early 1960s, which possibly offered the first computer course for architects in 1963, before Negroponte and Groissier's course in 1968 at what later became the MIT Media Lab in 1985.[13]

South of Boston on the East Coast between the 1940s and 1960s, other significant developments contributed to the formation of complexity theory and its influence on architecture. The branch of the Macy conferences that focused on cybernetics, held in New York City between 1945 and 1953, brought together an interdisciplinary and international group of scholars to consider such themes as Feedback Mechanisms and Circular Causal Systems in Biological and Social Systems, revisited in different guises over the years. Influential American participants were Wiener, John von Neumann, Warren McCullough, Margaret Mead, and Claude Shannon among many others, and British cyberneticists Gregory Bateson and W. Ross Ashby. After 1948, the title of Wiener's book *Cybernetics* became the name of the conference. That same year, mathematician and electrical engineer Claude Shannon, who worked in New York for Bell Labs, published his influential paper "A Mathematical Theory of Communication," which founded the field of information theory. In the mid-1960s, information theory was wedded to complexity theory by Russian mathematician Andrey Kolmogorov and American mathematician and computer scientist Gregory Chaitin, serving as one method by which scientists measure complexity today. Warren Weaver, director of the Division of Natural Sciences of the Rockefeller Foundation in New York City between 1932 and 1955, had met Shannon at Bell Labs and wrote the introduction to his essay.

Weaver's own report to the Rockefeller Foundation, written upon his retirement, summarized many of the developments over the previous quarter century that coalesced in the 1960s and 1970s into complexity theory, which is closely related to general systems theory as explored in Ludwig von Bertalanffy's publication *General Systems Theory* in 1968.

Author Steven Johnson dubs Warren Weaver's summary report to the Rockefeller Foundation as the "founding text of complexity theory."[14] In it, he established three types of scientific problems that were being researched across different disciplines during this time: simple systems having only one or a few variables; systems with thousands or millions of variables analyzable only through the methods of probability and statistics—he called these "disorganized complexity"; and systems somewhere in between, that had many interrelated variables but simple rules that in turn created interesting patterns as part of their processes—he called these "organized complexity." The example of organized complexity that Johnson gives is that of a mechanized billiards table, "where the balls follow specific rules and through their various interactions create a distinct macrobehavior, arranging themselves in a specific shape, or forming a specific pattern over time." To solve problems of organized complexity, Johnson writes, "you needed a machine capable of churning through thousands, if not millions, of calculations per second. . . . Because of his connection to the Bell Labs group, Weaver had seen early on the promise of digital computing, and he knew the mysteries of organized complexity would be much easier to tackle once you could model the behavior in close-to-real time."[15] Systems of organized complexity are apparent everywhere in nature once you learn to see them, and they are what Melanie Mitchell refers to with her definition of nonlinear complex adaptive systems.[16]

A year or two after Weaver's report, when journalist Jane Jacobs was preparing her 1961 attack against New York's "master builder" Robert Moses for the drastic modernist urban planning changes he was implementing in New York City, Jacobs read Weaver's report and developed the idea of organized complexity into her book *The Death and Life of Great American Cities*.[17] In it, she argued that urban zones such as the West Village in New York and similar neighborhoods in other cities thrived because they demonstrated "bottom-up" self-organization that is characteristic of organized complexity. Her argument was powerful and halted much of Moses's planned demolition. It also received significant media and academic coverage and influenced the development of theories that later became identified with postmodernism in architecture. For example, in 1962, architect Robert Venturi began writing one of the founding texts of postmodern architecture, *Complexity and Contradiction in Architecture,* published four years later. Architectural historian Peter Laurence argues that Venturi could not help but be influenced by Jacobs despite the fact that their common fascination with complexity theory originated out of different interests, Jacobs from social complexity and Venturi from an interdisciplinary interest in multiplicities addressed through "literary theories, New Criticism, pop art, and gestalt theory."[18] Venturi's text cites Christopher Alexander's

Notes on the Synthesis of Form and refers to emergence based on social scientist Herbert A. Simon's definition of a complex system as "a large number of parts that interact in a non-simple way," such that the whole is "the result of, and yet more than, the sum of its parts."[19]

Complexity theory as an influence on theories of postmodern architecture is not directly related to the historical development of generative architecture, but it is important to realize the interdisciplinary and multifarious impacts of complexity theory writ large on architecture occurring at these different locations.[20] Charles Jencks, another founder and later historian of postmodern architecture as influenced by complexity theory, had earned his master's in architecture at the Harvard GSD in 1965, and then studied architectural history at University College London, earning his doctorate in 1970. Writings of his from the late 1960s point to his prediction that biology would become a key influence on late twentieth-century architecture, an idea more fully developed in his publications beginning in the mid-1990s.[21] For example, he penned *The Architecture of the Jumping Universe* in 1995, based on complexity theory's tenet that self-organization works nonlinearly, prompting rapid jumps to new levels of organization. And his 2002 revision of his classic *The Language of Post-Modern Architecture* (1977) included new chapters on "Complexity Architecture" and "Fractal Architecture," in which he argued that after the founding of the Santa Fe Institute in the mid-1980s and the spread of the complexity paradigm, postmodernism took a decisive turn toward complexity architecture. Given all these developments, it becomes far less surprising that the history of generative architecture and its intersections with ideas of complexity theory and evolutionary programming occurred in the 1960s, even though it has taken fifty years for it to become well known as a mode of contemporary architectural practice.

This turns our attention to the third location, to London and to the AA, where generative architecture arguably originated at the school, which introduced the use of computers for architectural design. Of course, the AA continued to be and still is a major center teaching generative architecture through the graduate programs at the Design Research Laboratory, founded by Patrik Schumacher and directed by Theodore Spryopoulos, and Emergent Technologies and Design, led now by Michael Weinstock and others. The five-day Course on the Use of Computer Techniques in Building Design and Planning offered in July 1963 actually had to be held at University College Oxford, owing to the fact that that was where the computer was located.[22] Who initiated and who led the course is unclear, but architect Cedric Price was on the faculty at the AA at this time and was collaborating with cyberneticist Gordon Pask on the design of the *Fun Palace* project. This visionary endeavor was intended to be an architectural recreational space that could rearrange its modular internal configuration based on input from computer punch cards specifying users' preferences; parts of the building would be moved around by cranes. Computation was central to its concept, planning, and intended action, and therefore Price and Pask established the Cybernetics Committee, led by Pask, to meet, theorize, and plan the project; these meetings were held in 1964. It is therefore possible that Pask's and Price's presence at the AA influenced the creation of the computer course for architects.

Pask is well known as one of the major British cyberneticists, a group that of course included Alan Turing, W. Ross Ashby, Stafford Beer, and many others. As early as 1949, some of these men—not including Pask—formed the Ratio Club, which met in London to discuss cybernetics after the influence of Wiener's and Shannon's landmark publications.[23] Ashby had created a cybernetic machine known as the homeostat in the late 1940s and was working on his book *Design for a Brain* (1952). His work inspired Beer and Pask, who collaborated in the late 1950s on some electrochemical experiments pertaining to feedback and adaptive systems.[24] Pask began working with Price in the early 1960s, and the introductory document of the Cybernetics Committee for the *Fun Palace* project, which was written by Pask, interestingly describes both the committee and the building as a "self-organising system." It states that the meeting agenda "has been constructed to act as a genetic code. At our first meeting it will be possible for either Cedric Price or myself to indicate, in detail, the chief constraints. . . . The genetic code of the agenda is provided to initiate the evolutionary process and the constraints are not severe enough to inhibit it altogether."[25] Although Pask's description sounds like he is referring to methods of evolutionary computation and something conceptually similar to what Holland in the mid-1970s called genetic algorithms, he is actually talking about the meetings' structure. Still, this sounds incredibly prescient, as only a handful of publications had developed ideas of evolutionary computation before 1964.[26] Pask and Price carried these concepts forward to the modular, computer-controlled *Generator* project of 1976 designed for White Oak Plantation in Florida (but never realized), on which John and Julia Frazer collaborated as computer consultants. John Frazer is undoubtedly one of the chief founders of generative architecture, so his role in this brief history is important.

First a student and then an instructor for many years at the AA, John Frazer published *An Evolutionary Architecture* in 1995 as the culmination of almost thirty years of research. The book describes the "emerging field of architectural genetics" that Frazer pioneered, and marks the beginning of a clearly defined, realizable, and useful computational approach to architectural design. The cover of his book features the "Universal Constructor," built by him and his students in 1990 as a "self-organizing interactive environment," one of a few computational machines assembled by hand at the AA under his direction. His first "self-replicating cellular automata" computer models date to 1979. His use of the terms "self-organizing" and "self-replicating cellular automata" clearly demonstrate his knowledge of and reliance on then-recent biological and computational theories, fitting his goal of investigating "fundamental form-generating processes in architecture, paralleling a wider scientific search for a theory of morphogenesis in the natural world."[27]

Aware of Alan Turing and John von Neumann's work, in the late 1960s

Frazer began using computer resources at the University of Cambridge to develop his "repeating tile = reptile" "seed" system, for which he coded eighteen different spatial orientations. The "seeds" could be combined to form rectangular shapes, and therefore were useful for investigating architectural form genesis for structures that in theory could actually be built.[28] He "evolved" his seed system into pattern formations and structures, plotting his first large-scale 2-D print at Autographics Ltd. in 1968 and sculpting by hand corresponding 3-D models (Figure 3.2). This work is likely the very first architectural design ever prepared on a computer that was then printed out on a plotter. Ironically, in his 1974 *AD* publication, Frazer predicted with regard to his "reptile" analogy that "the associations of a Stegosaurus . . . with an obsolete species is intended to emphasise that such a component approach to architecture, as implied by the system, is probably only of transient significance." Almost fifty years later, the approach is still thriving.[29] To create the "reptile" seed-based designs in the late 1960s and various column designs in the early 1970s, Frazer derived a computational method to "evolve" solutions using a "heuristic algorithm derived from an idea of Donald Michie for MENACE (an educatable OXO machine)." He had reproduced Michie's OXO machine in the early 1960s and then again later that decade with students; owing to the success–reward techniques that allowed the machines to learn how to play against each other, Frazer used the same technique to "educate a column-generating program."[30] In the 1980s or 1990s, he began using genetic algorithms to breed architectural forms, based on the computational system Holland developed for simulating biological evolution published in 1975 as *Adaptation in Natural and Artificial Systems*.[31] Images from 1993, made in collaboration with Peter Graham, demonstrate "the evolution of Tuscan columns by genetic algorithms," in which a "gene" was substituted for James Gibb's "carefully specified proportions" and then bred to create a "population," on which both "natural" and "artificial selection" were applied to determine the "fittest" "perfectly proportioned" designs.[32]

Frazer was by no means working alone at the AA on the development of generative architecture. Beginning in the 1970s, "units" (courses) at the AA were led by architects and others who were interested in cybernetics, computation, biology, and ecology. In short, so many areas overlapped with developments in complex systems theory as well as in the use of computers in architecture that it would have been hard to be a student at the AA during these decades and not be aware of this growing trend of architectural design. Graduates or tutors from the AA who have played leading roles in generative architecture and design thus far besides Frazer include Zaha Hadid, Patrik Schumacher, Michael Hensel, Michael Weinstock, Achim Menges, Neri Oxman, and Andrew Kudless, as well as many others beginning their careers more recently. As is clear from chapters of this book, most of the architectural theorists discussed here are faculty at leading architectural educational institutions: University of Stuttgart Institute of Computational Design; Oslo School of Architecture and Design; AA; International University of Catalunya

School of Architecture; University of Pennsylvania School of Design; Columbia University's Graduate School of Architecture, Planning, and Preservation; Cornell University College of Architecture, Art, and Planning; Bartlett School of Architecture at University College London; University of Greenwich; and University of Waterloo. Yet, of all these institutions thus far in the history of generative architecture, the AA has played the most foundational historical role.

ACKNOWLEDGMENTS

Writing this book over the past ten years has been my most challenging accomplishment. Transforming my research skills from archives and writing history to contemporary criticism entailed more than I ever imagined. While this study has benefited from archival research along with the usual necessary reading, much of the research for this project has been "live" and experiential—by attending classes, doing architectural and scientific projects, presenting talks, and receiving feedback. This intellectual journey would not have been possible without the help of many generous scholars, friends, and humanities organizations that contributed financial support that permitted time away from my work responsibilities at the Department of Design at the University of California at Davis. I therefore want to acknowledge and thank those who helped me the most, as well as everyone who has participated in some way. Although many names follow here in approximately chronological order, many remain unlisted although I am still very grateful to all who encouraged and helped me.

This research began in earnest with funding by the Mellon Foundation to participate in the Penn Humanities Forum (now the Wolf Humanities Center) during the 2008–9 academic year. I am grateful to Wendy Steiner for her leadership of the forum and for the interactions I had with all the fellows in residence, especially Beth Linker and John Tresch. At Penn, I studied the collaboration of Jenny Sabin and Peter Lloyd Jones known as LabStudio, participating in their studio Nonlinear Biological Systems and Design and working with them over the year. My heartfelt thanks to both of them, as well as to Erica Savig, Andrew Lucia, Annette Fierro, and Charles Davis II for their generosity and insights. During my year at Penn, I lectured at the Smithsonian American Art Museum and at Columbia University's GSAPP Inside-Out series on the invitation of Irene Cheng. The comments I received from these talks sharpened my thinking and opened new avenues for research. I am grateful for the opportunity to present this work in progress at the Darwin Celebrations—The Art of Evolution: Charles Darwin and Visual Cultures—at the Courtauld Institute of Art in the summer of 2009. Thanks to Fae Brauer for this invitation and J. D. Talasek at the Cultural Programs of the National Academy of Sciences for his subsequent comments and support.

In the summer of 2009, I spent time in Montreal at the Canadian Centre for Architecture as part of its Visiting Scholars Fellowship program funded by the Andrew Mellon Foundation. Here I delved into the archives of Greg Lynn and Cedric Price and read from their library collections. My thanks especially go to Phyllis Lambert, Mirko Zardini, Alexis Sornin, Howard Shubert,

Volker Welter, Marta Caldeira, and Guido Zuliani. After beginning a new job at UC Davis in 2009, during the 2010–11 academic year I was funded by a Charles Ryskamp Fellowship from the American Council of Learned Societies (ACLS) to continue researching complexity theory and generative architecture. I spent this year in further reading, attending the Association for Computer Aided Design in Architecture conference in New York, and researching for a month in the Archives of the Architectural Association in London. I am very grateful to Pauline Yu and the ACLS for their support, and for the assistance of archivist Edward Bottoms at the Architectural Association.

During the summer of 2011, I began the most amazing part of this journey upon receipt of an Andrew Mellon Foundation New Directions Fellowship. With sixteen months of release from teaching and service to pursue full-time study, I was incredibly fortunate to become a student again in order to receive interdisciplinary training in areas I had not pursued in college: architecture, physics, evolutionary biology, epigenetics, and the history of science. I am so grateful that the Mellon Foundation has this program to encourage and deepen interdisciplinary scholarship, and I appreciate the support of my university through the efforts of Carolyn Thomas at the Davis Humanities Institute and Dean Jessie Ann Owens. My thanks to those who taught me on this journey begins with Benjamin Golder at the University of California at Berkeley summer school, for his friendly chastisement when I was struggling to learn Grasshopper without having learned Rhino. I tried to quit and just audit his class, but Ben would not let me. He told me to "get over it" and start working with others, not by myself. This is something humanities scholars are not trained or encouraged to do. Thanks to him, I jumped that hurdle and took this lesson forward to today, and I hope that I never stop collaborating. I then enrolled in the Emergent Technologies and Design graduate program in Fall 2011 at the Architectural Association, thanks to the generosity of Michael Weinstock and the other tutors—George Jeronimidis, Evan Greenberg, and Mehran Garleghi. While I am grateful for the challenges I faced and friendships begun with all of the 2011 EmTech class, I will name those I worked with most closely: Mara Moral Correa, Vincenzo Reale, Marina Konstantatou, Giancarlo Torpiano, Chun-Feng Liu, Bartek Arendt, Goli Jalali, Yuan Huang, Guy Austern, Mushit Fidelman, Soungmin Yu, Federico Martelli, Mary Polites, and Sebastiaan Leenknegt. My time at EmTech with my peers rekindled my passion for seeking new knowledge, traveling, and meeting friends from around the world.

I returned from London to pursue six months of intensive graduate study at UC Davis in the sciences. The only course offered on self-organization at that time was Jim Crutchfield's Physics 256A and B, Natural Computation and Self-Organization. As Jim is one of the earliest contributors to the Santa Fe Institute, I knew I had to work with him, but in truth I was scared. I had not taken physics since high school and never had studied calculus. Every lecture seemed as if it were being delivered in a foreign language of mathematical symbols. Without the help of the best tutor ever—engineering and physics graduate student Paul Riechers, who is deeply interested in complexity and now has finished his Ph.D.—I could not have completed this endeavor. Instead, by collaborating with Paul on building a van der Pol circuit and studying the nonlinear dynamics of tendril free-coiling (discussed at the end of chapter 2), I gained immensely from my time studying with Jim and the other physicists in his group. During this same period, I also co-led an interdisciplinary faculty and graduate student reading group focused on self-organization and evolutionary biology. My thanks to participants Rick Grosberg (evolution and ecology), Jim Griesemer (philosophy), Brian Johnson (entomology), Jim Crutchfield and Paul Riechers (physics), Xan Chacko and May Ee Wong (cultural studies), and all the others. Since then, I have collaborated as well with biomedical engineer Marc Facciotti, who runs the UC Davis TEAM Molecular Prototyping and BioInnovation Laboratory, headed by Andrew Yao. My thanks extend to both of them and to lighting designer Jonny Hoolko for undertaking his research on bioluminescence with me. Finally, I am grateful to both Evelyn Fox Keller at MIT and Eva Jablonka at the University of Tel Aviv for conducting independent studies with me on the history and theory of self-organization and epigenetics and evolutionary theory, respectively. It is a huge honor to have been able to learn from such amazing female scholars, who are generous and hospitable as well.

After completing study under the New Directions Fellowship, in 2014 at UC Davis I led a cultural studies graduate seminar on Self-Organization in the Humanities, Arts, and Social Sciences. I learned so much from this seminar and particularly want to thank those who shared their insights from their own work in this area, including Meredith Tromble, Robin Hill, Janko Gravner, Jim Griesemer, Sam Nichols, May Ee Wong, Evan Buswell, Colin Johnson, Juan Cajigas Rotundo, Sagit Betser, Erik Porse, and Ksenia Federova. I have also benefited from independent studies with Xan Chacko, Amanda Modell, and Stephanie Maroney, and from all of the life cycle assessments completed by student teams in my Energy, Materials, and Design across Time course, especially the work of Madison Crain, Felix Le, and Riyaz Merchant (discussed near the end of chapter 2). Other colleagues I have learned from include those at the Politics of Parametricism symposium—especially Manuel Shvartzberg, Matthew Poole, Reinhold Martin, Teddy Cruz, and Laura Kurgan; those on the Complexism: Art + Architecture + Biology + Computation, A New Axis in Critical Theory? panels at ISEA in Vancouver 2014, especially Philip Galanter, Meredith Tromble, and Charissa Terranova; and those at the NeoLife SLSA conference in Perth, Australia, including Oron Catts, Ionat Zurr, Jennifer Johung, Elizabeth Stephens, Luis Campos, and many others. My ongoing collaboration with Sacha Laurin, Tania Pozzo, and Irene Flesch has enriched my understanding of biodesign methods and challenges; Sacha's intelligence, energy, and enthusiasm is a constant source of inspiration. The editorial assistance of Kristin Koster in the last few years of this project kept me moving forward, and I am grateful to her and, subsequently, to Pieter Martin at the University of Minnesota Press, for believing in this project.

Finally, close colleagues and friends who have encouraged me in many ways over these ten years deserve mention and thanks. Simon Sadler, James Housefield, and Susan Avila in my home department have spurred me onward, commenting on sections of writing and keeping me focused on finishing. Carolyn Thomas's wise advice and friendship always sets me straight and holds me up when I need it. Likewise, Caren Kaplan's and Spring Warren's struggles to complete their books alongside my own—in London, in coffee shops, at the cottage, over dinners—have helped me feel less alone in the writing portion of this endeavor. My thanks also go to Ken Giles and Sherry Cummings for their support and friendship; Tracy Manuel for talking design with me and being a stellar housemate; and Melissa Chandon for keeping me fit, laughing, and inspiring me to keep up with the example set by her prolific professional output. As always, my father, John Cogdell, edited this manuscript and talked with me about various parts. I continually am thankful for his teaching me how to write and setting an example of lifelong learning applied in the most practical ways. My mother, Ann Cogdell, always listened and loved and blessed my life with her steadiness and support. Lastly, I thank Kieran Kelley for giving me huskies Star and Honey. Along with Goose the cat, their playfulness, affection, and love of life has enriched my own every day, lifting me out of a solely human existence into broader worlds.

NOTES

Introduction

1. Mario Carpo, ed., *The Digital Turn in Architecture, 1992–2012* (London: Wiley, 2013). See also Antoine Picon, *Digital Culture in Architecture* (Basel: Birkhauser, 2010).

2. Google image searches for "generative architecture" and "parametric architecture" offer a number of visual examples that simply demonstrate this resemblance.

3. Philip Galanter, "Complexism and the Role of Evolutionary Art," in *The Art of Artificial Evolution: A Handbook on Evolutionary Art and Music,* ed. Juan Romero and Penousal Machado (New York: Springer Books, 2007), 317.

4. Karl Chu, "Metaphysics of Genetic Architecture and Computation," in *Genetic Architectures II,* ed. Alberto T. Estévez (Santa Fe, N.M.: SITES Books / ESARQ-UIC, 2005), 170.

5. Alberto Estévez, "Appendix for a Definition of Genetic Architecture and Other Related Terms," in *Genetic Architectures II,* ed. Alberto T. Estévez (Santa Fe, N.M.: SITES Books / ESARQ-UIC, 2005), 78.

6. Alberto Estévez, "Genetic Architecture: New Ecologic-Environmental Architectural Design and New Cybernetic-Digital Architectural Design," in *Genetic Architectures,* ed. Alberto T. Estévez (Santa Fe, N.M.: SITES Books / ESARQ-UIC, 2003), 17.

7. Michael Hansmeyer and Benjamin Dillenburger, *Digital Grotesque II,* described at http://digital-grotesque.com/concept/ and http://www.michael-hansmeyer.com/.

8. Michael Weinstock, "Morphogenesis and the Mathematics of Emergence," in "Emergence: Morphogenetic Design Strategies," special issue of *AD,* ed. Michael Hensel, Achim Menges, and Michael Weinstock, 74, no. 3 (May–June 2004): 11–15.

9. Christina Cogdell, *Eugenic Design: Streamlining America in the 1930s* (Philadelphia: University of Pennsylvania Press, 2004).

10. See Wendy Gunn, Ton Otto, and Rachel Charlotte Smith, eds., *Design Anthropology: Theory and Practice* (London: Bloomsbury Press, 2013); Keith Murphy, *Swedish Design: An Ethnography* (Ithaca, N.Y.: Cornell University Press, 2015); as well as two other groups, the Experimental Collaborations project for Ethnography beyond Participant Observation, available at http://xcol.org/, and the New School's Graduate Institute for Design, Ethnography & Social Thought, available at http://www.gidest.org/.

11. Albena Yaneva, *Made by the Office for Metropolitan Architecture: An Ethnography of Design* (Rotterdam: 010 Publishers, 2009).

12. Bruno Latour and Steve Woolgar, *Laboratory Life: The Construction of Scientific Facts* (Beverly Hills, Calif.: Sage Publications, 1979).

13. Stefan Helmreich, "Nature/Culture/Seawater," *American Anthropologist* 113 (2011): 134; in his article, he here cites his book *Alien Ocean: Anthropological Voyages in Microbial Seas* (Berkeley: University of California Press, 2009), 23–25.

14. Helmreich, "Nature/Culture/Seawater," a slightly different version available at http://dspace.mit.edu/openaccess-disseminate/1721.1/61766.

15. Helmreich, "Nature/Culture/Seawater," *American Anthropologist,* 134.

16. Paul Edwards, *A Vast Machine: Computer Models, Climate Data, and the Politics of Global Warming* (Cambridge, Mass.: MIT Press, 2010), 352, 428–30.

17. Harry Collins, "We Cannot Live by Scepticism Alone," *Nature* 458, no. 30 (March 5, 2009): 31.

18. Collins, 31.

19. Edwards, *Vast Machine,* 352, 428–30.

20. See http://architecture2030.org/buildings_problem_why/, which cites data from a 2012 study by the U.S. Energy Information Administration.

21. Michael Hensel and Achim Menges, eds., *Morpho-Ecologies: Towards Heterogeneous Space in Architecture Design* (London: AA Publications, 2007); and Hensel and Menges, eds., "Versatility and Vicissitude: Performance in Morpho-Ecological Design," special issue of *AD,* 78, no. 2 (March–April 2008): 80–87.

22. Steen Rasmussen, Mark Bedau, Liaohai Chen, David Deamer, David Krakauer, Norman Packard, and Peter Stadler, eds., *Protocells: Bridging Nonliving and Living Matter* (Cambridge, Mass.: MIT Press, 2009), xvii; Peter Stadler and Bärbel Stadler, "Replicator Dynamics in Protocells," in *Protocells: Bridging Nonliving and Living Matter,* ed. Steen Rasmussen, Mark Bedau, Liaohai Chen, David Deamer, David Krakauer, Norman Packard, and Peter Stadler (Cambridge, Mass.: MIT Press, 2009), 327.

23. See Rachel Armstrong's TED talk "Architecture that Repairs Itself," July 2009, at http://www.ted.com/talks/rachel_armstrong_architecture_that_repairs_itself.

24. Estévez, "Genetic Architecture," 9, 17.

25. The author was part of the EmTech Emergence seminar led by Weinstock in Fall 2011, where he clearly stated this opinion using these words.

26. Farshid Moussavi and Alejandro Zaera-Polo, "Types, Styles, and Phylogenesis," in "Emergence: Morphogenetic Design Strategies," special issue of *AD,* ed. Michael Hensel, Achim Menges, and Michael Weinstock, 74, no. 3 (May–June 2004): 37.

27. Martin Bressani and Robert Jan van Pelt, "Crystals, Cells, and Networks: Unconfining Territories," in *The Gen(H)ome Project,* ed. Peter Noever and Open Source Architecture (Los Angeles: MAK Center for Art and Architecture, 2006), 66–73.

28. Eric Mennel, "Payments Start for N.C. Eugenics Victims, but Many Won't Qualify," National Public Radio, October 31, 2014, http://www.npr.org/sections/health-shots/2014/10/31/360355784/payments-start-for-n-c-eugenics-victims-but-many-wont-qualify/. See also Genevieve Plaster, "North Carolina Eugenics Victims Still Seeking Justice due to Compensation Technicality," Charlotte Lozier Institute, May 4, 2015, https://lozierinstitute.org/north-carolina-eugenics-victims-still-seeking-justice-due-to-compensation-technicality/.

29. Elizabeth Cohen and John Bonifield, "California's Dark Legacy of Forced Sterilizations," CNN, March 15, 2012, http://www.cnn.com/2012/03/15/health/california-forced-sterilizations/. The recent PBS news story by Lisa Ko, "Unwanted Sterilization and Eugenics Programs in the United States," January 29, 2016, states that in December 2015, "the U.S. Senate voted unanimously to help victims of forced sterilization. North Carolina has paid $35,000 to 220 surviving victims of its eugenics program. Virginia agreed to give surviving victims $25,000 each." Available at http://www.pbs.org/independentlens/blog/unwanted-sterilization-and-eugenics-programs-in-the-united-states/.

30. Corey Johnston, "Female Inmates Sterilized in California Prisons without Approval," Center for Investigative Reporting, July 7, 2013, http://www.geneticsandsociety.org/article/female-inmates-sterilized-california-prisons-without-approval; Bill Chappell, "California's Prison Sterilizations Reportedly Echo Eugenics Era," National Public Radio, July 9, 2013, http://www.npr.org/sections/thetwo-way/2013/07/09/200444613/californias-prison-sterilizations-reportedly-echoes-eugenics-era/.

31. See "California Bans Sterilization of Female Inmates without Consent," NBC News, September 26, 2014, http://www.nbcnews.com/health/womens-health/california-bans-sterilization-female-inmates-without-consent-n212256; and Misty Rojo, "Gov. Jerry Brown signs SB 1135, Prison Anti-Sterilization Bill," *San Francisco Bay View,* September 26, 2014, http://sfbayview.com/2014/09/gov-jerry-brown-signs-sb-1135-prison-anti-sterilization-bill/.

32. Mark Waller, "LaBruzzo Considering Plan to Pay Poor Women $1,000 to Have Their Tubes Tied," *Times-Picayune,* September 23, 2008, http://www.nola.com/news/index.ssf/2008/09/labruzzo_sterilization_plan_fi.html.

33. Aida Edemariam, "A Matter of Life and Death," *The Guardian,* March 27, 2008, https://

www.theguardian.com/science/2008/mar/27/stemcells.medicalresearch/; and Gerard Porter and Malcolm Smith, "Preventing the Selection of 'Deaf Embryos' under the Human Fertilisation and Embryology Act 2008: Problematizing Disability?" *New Genetics and Society* 32, no. 2 (2013): 171–89.

34. Keith Besserud and Joshua Ingram, "Architectural Genomics," in *Silicon + Skin: Biological Processes and Computation,* ed. Andrew Kudless, Neri Oxman, and Marc Swackhamer (Morrisville, N.C.: Lulu Press, 2008), 239–40. Josh Ingram is the same person as Joshua Cotton, the name under which this article was originally published.

35. Besserud and Ingram point to these architectural features as common for optimization: "construction cost, structural efficiency, carbon footprint, daylighting quality, acoustic quality, programmatic compliance, view quality, etc." (240).

36. Amanda Modell, "Mapping the Music Genome: Imaginative Geography in Pandora Internet Radio and the Genographic Project," *Media Fields Journal,* November 14, 2015, http://mediafieldsjournal.squarespace.com/mapping-the-music-genome/.

37. Pengcheng Fu, "Biomolecular Computing: Is It Ready to Take Off?" *Biotechnology Journal* 2 (2007): 91–101.

38. D'Arcy Wentworth Thompson, *On Growth and Form* (Cambridge, U.K.: Cambridge University Press, 1917); Alan Turing, "The Chemical Basis of Morphogenesis," *Philosophical Transactions of the Royal Society of London B* 237, no. 641 (1952): 37–72.

39. Agoston Eiben and Jim Smith, "From Evolutionary Computation to the Evolution of Things," *Nature* 521 (May 28, 2015): 476–82.

40. Sarah Richardson and Hallam Stevens, eds., *Postgenomics: Perspectives on Biology after the Genome* (Durham, N.C.: Duke University Press, 2015).

41. See Anthony Dunne and Fiona Raby, *Speculative Everything: Design, Fiction, and Social Dreaming* (Cambridge, Mass.: MIT Press, 2013); and http://www.dunneandraby.co.uk/content/bydandr/13/0/.

42. Rasmussen et al., *Protocells,* xvii.

43. See http://www.mycoworks.com/; in particular, see the video "Built with the Cleanest Technology on Earth: Nature" on this website.

1. Self-Organizing and Emergent Architecture

1. First studio brief handed out in Boot Camp at the Emergent Technologies and Design program at the Architectural Association (Fall 2011).

2. I applied to EmTech with full disclosure about my professional role at UC Davis, my funding through the Andrew Mellon New Directions Fellowship, and my intent to write a book about generative architecture. I am very grateful that Michael Weinstock graciously accepted me into the program.

3. Melany Mitchell, *Complexity: A Guided Tour* (Oxford, U.K.: Oxford University Press, 2009), 13.

4. Scott Camazine, Jean-Louis Deneubourg, Nigel R. Franks, James Sneyd, Guy Theraula, and Eric Bonabeau, eds., *Self-Organization in Biological Systems* (Princeton, N.J.: Princeton University Press, 2001), 8.

5. See also Stuart Kauffman, *At Home in the Universe* (Oxford, U.K.: Oxford University Press, 1995), 24.

6. Camazine et al., *Self-Organization in Biological Systems,* 8.

7. "Never" is used as an exaggeration here for expressive purposes, but not by much. The only place I have seen the rules specifically addressed is Philip Ball, *Shapes* (Oxford, U.K.: Oxford University Press, 2009), 222–23, where he discussed stigmergy and the creation of termite mounds. He writes, "In this view, it could be said, the future is determined not by relentlessly following a single set of rules, but by responding to what has been done up to that point. The question is, of course: what are the rules?" He is not, however, questioning their existence or origin in complexity theory, but simply asking in this case what they could be.

8. Evelyn Fox Keller, "Organisms, Machines, Thunderstorms . . . Part One," *Historical*

Studies in the Natural Sciences 38, no. 1 (2008), 71, citing W. R. Ashby, "Principles of the Self-Organizing System," in *Principles of Self-Organization,* ed. Heinz von Foerster and George W. Zopf (New York: Pergamon Press, 1962), 267, 269.

9. In the title and argument of J. Scott Turner's book *The Tinkerer's Accomplice: How Design Emerges from Life Itself* (Cambridge, Mass.: Harvard University Press, 2007), design—which is often based on rules or is recognized because of patterns—emerges from life itself, and life itself, he argues, is based on homeostasis (or what he calls Bernard machines, after Claude Bernard).

10. Charissa Terranova, ed., "Complexism: Art + Architecture + Biology + Computation, a New Axis in Critical Theory?" double issue of *Technoetic Arts* 14, nos. 1–2 (June 2016): 3–8; Philip Galanter "Complexism and the Role of Evolutionary Art," in *The Art of Artificial Evolution: A Handbook on Evolutionary Art and Music,* ed. Juan Romero and Penousal Machado (New York: Springer Books, 2007), 311–32; Alan Dorin, "Generative Processes and the Electronic Arts," *Organised Sound* 6, no. 1 (2001): 47–53; Jon McCormack, Alice Eldridge, Alan Dorin, and Peter McIlwain, "Generative Algorithms for Making Music: Emergence, Evolution and Ecosystems," in *The Oxford Handbook of Computer Music,* ed. Roger Dean (Oxford, U.K.: Oxford University Press, 2009), 355–79.

11. See George Katsiaficas, "Comparing Uprisings in Korea and Burma," *Socialism and Democracy* 23, no. 1 (2009): 58–76; Walter C. Clements Jr., "Complexity Theory as a Tool for Understanding and Coping with Ethnic Conflict and Development Issues in Post-Soviet Eurasia," *International Journal of Peace Studies* 7, no. 2 (Autumn–Winter 2002): 1–15; Kai Lehman, "Crisis Foreign Policy as a Process of Self-Organization," *Cambridge Review of International Affairs* 24, no. 1 (March 2011): 27–42; Devan Rosen, Jang Hyun Kim, and Yoonjae Nam, "Birds of a Feather Protest Together: Theorizing Self-Organizing Political Protests with Flock Theory," *Systemic Practice and Action Research* 23 (2010): 419–41; Christian Fuchs and John Collier, "A Dynamic Systems View of Economic and Political Theory," *Theoria: A Journal of Social and Political Theory* (August 2007): 23–52; Christopher G. Hudson, "From Social Darwinism to Self-Organization: Implications for Social Change Theory," *Social Service Review* 74, no. 4 (December 2000): 533–59; R. Keith Sawyer, "Emergence in Sociology: Contemporary Philosophy of Mind and Some Implications for Sociological Theory," *American Journal of Sociology* 107, no. 3 (November 2001): 551–85; Glenn D. Walters, "Developmental Trajectories, Transitions, and Nonlinear Dynamical Systems: A Model of Crime Deceleration and Desistance," *International Journal of Offender Therapy and Comparative Criminology* 46 (2002): 30–44; Glenn D. Walters, "Crime and Chaos: Applying Nonlinear Dynamic Principles to Problems in Criminology," *International Journal of Offender Therapy and Comparative Criminology* 43 (1999): 134–53; Athina Karatzogianni and George Michaelides, "Cyberconflict at the Edge of Chaos: Cryptohierarchies and Self-Organisation in the Open-Source Movement," *Capital and Class* 33 (2009): 143–57.

12. Manuel de Landa, *A Thousand Years of Nonlinear History* (New York: Swerve, 2000); David Hancock, "Organizing Our Thoughts: 'Global Systems' and the Challenge of Writing a More Complex History," *Journal of the Historical Society* 10, no. 3 (September 2010): 319–35; Jia Yi Chow, Keith Davids, Robert Hristovski, Duarte Araújo, and Pedro Passos, "Nonlinear Pedagogy: Learning Design for Self-Organizing Neurobiological Systems," *New Ideas in Psychology* 29 (2011): 189–200; Isabela Granic and Gerald Patterson, "Toward a Comprehensive Model of Antisocial Development: A Dynamic Systems Approach," *Psychological Review* 113, no. 1 (January 2006): 101–31; Edward Selby and Thomas Joiner, "Cascades of Emotion: The Emergence of Borderline Personality Disorder from Emotional and Behavioral Dysregulation," *Review of General Psychology* 13, no. 3 (September 2009): 219–38.

13. Paul Krugman, *The Self Organizing Economy* (Cambridge, Mass.: Wiley-Blackwell, 1996).

14. Karen Ward, *The World in 2050: Quantifying the Shift in the Global Economy* (London: HSBC, 2015), http://www.hsbc.ca/1/PA_ES_Content_Mgmt/content/canada4/pdfs/business/hsbc-bwob-theworldin2050-en.pdf.

15. Venkat Venkatasubramanian, "Fairness Is an Emergent Self-Organized Property of the Free Market for Labor," *Entropy* 12 (2010): 1514–31.

16. Michael Weinstock, "Morphogenesis and the Mathematics of Emergence," in "Emergence: Morphogenetic Design Strategies," special issue of *AD*, ed. Michael Hensel, Achim Menges, and Michael Weinstock, 74, no. 3 (May–June 2004): 11.

17. Weinstock, 15.

18. Weinstock, 17.

19. Michael Weinstock, "Self-Organisation and Material Constructions," in "Techniques and Technologies in Morphogenetic Design," special issue of *AD*, ed. Michael Hensel, Achim Menges, and Michael Weinstock, 76, no. 2 (March–April 2006): 35.

20. Weinstock, 34, 36, 39.

21. Weinstock, "Morphogenesis and the Mathematics of Emergence," 15.

22. Weinstock, 14–15.

23. Weinstock, 15.

24. Weinstock, 17.

25. Weinstock, 13.

26. Weinstock, 14.

27. Biological systems at equilibrium are considered "dead," so to say that organisms maintain equilibrium must mean that balance in and out is achieved, but that equilibrium is in flux constantly, until the point of death.

28. See physicist Philip Ball's three-part book series, *Shapes* (cited above); *Branches* (Oxford, U.K.: Oxford University Press, 2009); *Flow* (Oxford, U.K.: Oxford University Press, 2009). Also, these phrases are basic tenets in the canon of complexity theory.

29. Weinstock, "Morphogenesis and the Mathematics of Emergence," 14.

30. Weinstock, 16–17, citing Francis Heylighen, "Self-Organisation. Emergence and the Architecture of Complexity," *Proceedings of 1st European Conference on System Science* (Paris: AFCET, 1989).

31. Weinstock, 15.

32. Michael Weinstock, *The Architecture of Emergence: The Evolution of Form in Nature and Civilisation* (Chichester, U.K.: Wiley, 2010), 9.

33. Weinstock, 12.

34. Weinstock, 14.

35. Weinstock, 12.

36. Ionat Zurr and Oron Catts, "Are the Semi-Living Semi-Good or Semi-Evil?" *Technoetic Arts* 1, no. 1 (2003): 51, quoting Stephen Jay Gould: "Much of evolution is downward in terms of morphological complexity, rather than upward. We're not marching toward some greater thing." See Gould, "The Pattern of Life's History," *The Third Culture* (New York: Simon & Schuster, 1995), 52.

37. Weinstock, *Architecture of Emergence*, 29.

38. Weinstock, 239–40.

39. Weinstock, 240.

40. Weinstock, 267.

41. This information is gathered from conversations Michael Weinstock and I had during my time at EmTech in the Fall 2011 semester.

42. Weinstock, *Architecture of Emergence*, 245.

43. Weinstock, 269.

44. Michael Weinstock and Mehran Gharleghi, "Intelligent Cities and the Taxonomy of Cognitive Scales," in "System City," special issue of *AD*, ed. Weinstock, profile no. 224 (July–August 2013): 57.

45. Weinstock, "Morphogenesis and the Mathematics of Emergence," 17.

46. Weinstock and Gharleghi, 58.

47. Weinstock and Gharleghi, 57.

48. Weinstock and Gharleghi, 57.

49. Evan Greenberg and George Jeronimidis, "Variation and Distribution: Forest Patterns as a Model for Urban Morphologies," in "System City," special issue of *AD*, ed. Michael

Weinstock, profile no. 224 (July–August 2013): 24–31, also describe cities as homeostatic organisms.

50. Weinstock, *Architecture of Emergence,* 60.

51. Weinstock, 65.

52. Weinstock, 65.

53. Weinstock does state that after collapse and reorganization, some systems return to a simpler organization, but this is not the usual state of affairs.

54. Weinstock's short biography of himself, in print since the early 1990s, reinforces this characterization of Weinstock as an intrepid yet wary adventurer facing the unruly whims of nature. He describes himself as a man of the world since he was a child, born in Germany, having lived in "the Far East and then West Africa, and attended an English public school. He ran away to sea at the age of 17 after reading Conrad. After many years at sea, in traditional wooden sailing ships where he gained shipyard and shipbuilding experience, he studied architecture at the AA and has taught at its School of Architecture since 1989." He also was a member of the "London Fire Brigade (K. 23 Battersea)" and a lifeguard. See "About the Guest Editor Michael Weinstock," in "System City," special issue of *AD,* ed. Michael Weinstock, profile no. 224 (July–August 2013): 7. See also "Intermediate Unit 4," *Architectural Association School of Architecture Prospectus, 1991–92,* 1991, 33.

55. For more information about the Sustainable Environmental Association, see http://www.sustainableenvironmentassociation.net/index.php?option=com_content&view=frontpage&Itemid=1.

56. Michael Hensel and Achim Menges, "Morpho-Ecologies: Towards an Inclusive Discourse on Heterogeneous Architectures," in *Morpho-Ecologies: Towards Heterogeneous Space in Architecture Design,* ed. Hensel and Menges (London: AA Publications, 2007), 53, 58.

57. Achim Menges, "Morpho-Ecologies: Approaching Complex Environments," in "Emergence: Morphogenetic Design Strategies," special issue of *AD,* ed. Michael Hensel, Achim Menges, and Michael Weinstock, 74, no. 3 (May–June 2004): 81, 83.

58. Hensel and Menges, *Morpho-Ecologies,* 43.

59. Hensel and Menges, 51.

60. Michael Hensel and Achim Menges, "Designing Morpho-Ecologies: Versatility and Vicissitude of Heterogeneous Space," in "Versatility and Vicissitude: Performance in Morpho-Ecological Design," special issue of *AD,* ed. Hensel and Menges, 78, no. 2 (March–April 2008): 105.

61. Achim Menges, "Manufacturing Performance," in "Versatility and Vicissitude: Performance in Morpho-Ecological Design," special issue of *AD,* ed. Michael Hensel and Achim Menges, 78, no. 2 (March–April 2008): 43.

62. Menges, 46.

63. See http://www.esf.edu/efb/turner/.

64. J. Scott Turner, "Evolutionary Architecture? Some Perspectives from Biological Design," in "Material Computation: Higher Integration in Morphogenetic Design," special issue of *AD,* ed. Menges, 82, no. 2 (March–April 2012): 32–33.

65. Michael Hensel, "Towards Self-Organisational and Multiple-Performance Capacity in Architecture," in "Techniques and Technologies in Morphogenetic Design," special issue of *AD,* ed. Michael Hensel, Achim Menges, and Michael Weinstock, 76, no. 2 (March–April 2006): 6, 10–11.

66. Michael Hensel, "Computing Self-Organisation: Environmentally Sensitive Growth Modelling," in "Techniques and Technologies in Morphogenetic Design," special issue of *AD,* ed. Michael Hensel, Achim Menges, and Michael Weinstock, 76, no. 2 (March–April 2006): 13.

67. Helen Castle, editor of *AD,* describes how they dislike using the word "green" (she also uses the words "ecological" and "sustainable" but wrongly claims that Hensel and Menges "steer away" from using these latter two terms). See Helen Castle, "Editorial," in "Versatility and Vicissitude: Performance in Morpho-Ecological Design," special issue of *AD,* ed. Michael Hensel and Achim Menges, 78, no. 2 (March–April 2008): 5.

68. Michael Hensel and Achim Menges, "Versatility and Vicissitude: An Introduction to Performance in Morpho-Ecological Design," in "Versatility and Vicissitude: Performance in Morpho-Ecological Design," special issue of *AD*, ed. Michael Hensel and Achim Menges, 78, no. 2 (March–April 2008): 7.

69. Michael Hensel, "(Synthetic) Life Architectures: Ramifications and Potentials of a Literal Biological Paradigm for Architectural Design," in "Techniques and Technologies in Morphogenetic Design," special issue of *AD*, ed. Michael Hensel, Achim Menges, and Michael Weinstock, 76, no. 2 (March–April 2006): 23.

70. Achim Menges and Steffen Reichert, "Material Capacity: Embedded Responsiveness," in "Material Computation: Higher Integration in Morphogenetic Design," special issue of *AD*, ed. Menges, 82, no. 2 (March–April 2012): 52–59.

71. Castle, "Editorial," 5.

72. Achim Menges, "Material Resourcefulness: Activating Material Information in Computational Design," in "Material Computation: Higher Integration in Morphogenetic Design," special issue of *AD*, ed. Menges, 82, no. 2 (March–April 2012): 42.

73. Michael Hensel, Defne Sunguroğlu Hensel, Mehran Gharleghi, and Salmaan Craig, "Towards an Architectural History of Performance: Auxiliarity, Performance, and Provision in Historical Persian Architectures," in "Iran: Past, Present and Future," special issue of *AD*, ed. Michael Hensel and Mehran Gharleghi, 82, no. 3 (2012): 26–37.

74. Michael Hensel, "Performance-Oriented Design Precursors and Potentials," in "Versatility and Vicissitude: Performance in Morpho-Ecological Design," special issue of *AD*, ed. Michael Hensel and Achim Menges, 78, no. 2 (March–April 2008): 50; see also Menges, "Material Resourcefulness," 50.

75. See http://www.sustainableenvironmentassociation.net/index.php?option=com_content&view=article&id=53&Itemid=61. These projects were published in Hensel et al., "Towards an Architectural History of Performance," 26–37.

76. Hensel, "Performance-Oriented Design Precursors and Potentials," 49, italics added.

77. Hensel, 49, 53.

78. Hensel, "(Synthetic) Life Architectures," 18.

79. Hensel, 19.

80. See also Hensel and Menges's essay "Morpho-Ecologies," 24–28.

81. Hensel and Menges, 24, 26.

82. At the AA, Menges and Hensel worked with Eiichi Matsuda, in 2003–4, on an aggregated structure project; in 2004, they worked with Anne Hawkins and Catie Newell on another at Rice University. See Achim Menges, "Aggregates," in "Versatility and Vicissitude: Performance in Morpho-Ecological Design," special issue of *AD*, ed. Michael Hensel and Achim Menges, 78, no. 2 (March–April 2008): 86–87. See also Karola Dierichs and Achim Menges, "Aggregate Structures: Material and Machine Computation of Designed Granular Substances," in "Material Computation: Higher Integration in Morphogenetic Design," special issue of *AD*, ed. Menges, 82, no. 2 (March–April 2012): 74–81 (esp. image of robotic construction, p. 80); as well as Karola Dierichs and Achim Menges, "Granular Morphologies: Programming Material Behaviour with Designed Aggregates," in "Fusing the Physical and Computational," special issue of *AD*, ed. Menges, 85, no. 5 (September–October 2015): 86–91 (esp. image of granular arch, p. 90).

83. Philip Ball, "Pattern Formation in Nature: Physical Constraints and Self-Organising Characteristics," in "Material Computation: Higher Integration in Morphogenetic Design," special issue of *AD*, ed. Achim Menges, 82, no. 2 (March–April 2012): 22–27.

84. See http://architecture2030.org/buildings_problem_why/.

85. Michael Hensel and Christian Hermansen Cordua, "Relating Perceptions of Constructions, Experimental and Local," and Hensel, "Rural Studio: Incarnations of a Design-and-Build Programme," both in "Constructions: An Experimental Approach to Intensely Local Architectures," special issue of *AD*, ed. Hensel and Hermansen Cordua, 85, no. 2 (March–April 2015): 8–15, 40–47.

86. Or, is it the other way around, that computers have made complexity theory possible?

87. Thanks to my colleague James Housefield for suggesting the need to reference Marc-Antoine Laugier's primitive hut.

88. For a very interesting study of the fractal patterns in the architecture of different cultures in Africa, see the work of Ron Egash, namely, his TED talk "The Fractals at the Heart of African Design," 2007, available at http://www.ted.com/talks/ron_eglash_on_african_fractals; and his book *African Fractals: Modern Computing and Indigenous Design* (New Brunswick, N.J.: Rutgers University Press, 1999). Egash is very clear that Africans creating these designs are very self-conscious and self-aware of their mathematical strategy.

89. Skylar Tibbits, "Design to Self-Assembly," in "Material Computation: Higher Integration in Morphogenetic Design," special issue of *AD,* ed. Achim Menges, 82, no. 2 (March–April 2012): 72.

90. Saskia Sassen, *Expulsions: Brutality and Complexity in the Global Economy* (Cambridge, Mass.: Harvard University Press, 2014).

91. Weinstock, "Morphogenesis and the Mathematics of Emergence," 15.

92. Hensel and Menges, "Morpho-Ecologies," 59.

93. Hensel and Menges, 51.

94. Patrik Schumacher, "Hegemonic Parametricism Delivers a Market-Based Urban Order," in "Architectural Design Parametricism 2.0," special issue of *AD,* ed. Schumacher, 86, no. 2 (March–April 2016): 115.

95. Schumacher, 118.

96. Schumacher, 118, 120.

97. Schumacher, 119.

98. Schumacher, 120.

99. Schumacher, 120, 123.

100. Schumacher, 123.

101. Christina Cogdell, "Breeding Ideology: Parametricism and Biological Architecture," in *The Politics of Parametricism: Digital Technologies in Architecture,* ed. Matthew Poole and Manuel Shvartzberg (London: Bloomsbury, 2015), 123–37.

102. On Teague, see Jeffrey Meikle, *Twentieth-Century Limited: Industrial Design in America, 1925–1939* (1979; repr., Philadelphia: Temple University Press, 2001), esp. chap. 6, "Everything from a Match to a City."

103. See Christina Cogdell, *Eugenic Design: Streamlining America in the 1930s* (Philadelphia: University of Pennsylvania Press, 2004), esp. chap. 4, "Flow Is the Word: Biological Efficiency and Streamline Design."

104. Email to the author supposedly from Barack Obama, July 2, 2016, "paid for by Organizing for Action."

105. Cogdell, *Eugenic Design,* xi.

106. Thanks to Kristin Koster for texting me the photo of a bottle of Emergent White IPA in June 2016. See http://boulderbeer.com/emergent-white-ipa/.

2. Material Computation

1. I am not referring to something like a creator (much less Creator) in what is referred to in Christian circles as "intelligent design," at least not for "nature." But since I am writing about design and architecture, I think making agency clear is important, since programmers script and architects and designers both design and script. On this, see J. Scott Turner, *The Tinkerer's Accomplice: How Design Arises from Life Itself* (Cambridge, Mass.: Harvard University Press, 2007).

2. For a description of the journal *Natural Computing,* see http://link.springer.com/journal/11047. The journal website states, "Natural computing includes evolutionary algorithms, neural networks, molecular computing, and quantum computing." Topics that the journal focuses on include theory of computation, evolutionary biology, processor architectures, artificial intel-

ligence including robotics, statistical physics, dynamical systems complexity, and related subjects (one of which is evolutionary and developmental biology).

3. Achim Menges, "Polymorphism," in "Techniques and Technologies in Morphogenetic Design," special issue of *AD,* ed. Michael Hensel, Achim Menges, and Michael Weinstock, 76, no. 2 (March–April 2006): 79; Achim Menges, "Material Computation: Higher Integration in Morphogenetic Design," in "Material Computation: Higher Integration in Morphogenetic Design," special issue of *AD,* ed. Achim Menges, 82, no. 2 (March–April 2012): 17; Achim Menges, "Material Resourcefulness: Activating Material Information in Computational Design," in "Material Computation: Higher Integration in Morphogenetic Design," special issue of *AD,* ed. Achim Menges, 82, no. 2 (March–April 2012): 35–36.

4. On LIPHE, see http://www.mcgill.ca/architecture/facilities/liphe.

5. Menges, "Material Resourcefulness," 42.

6. Achim Menges and Steffen Reichert, "Material Capacity: Embedded Responsiveness," in "Material Computation: Higher Integration in Morphogenetic Design," special issue of *AD,* ed. Achim Menges, 82, no. 2 (March–April 2012): 53.

7. Menges, "Material Resourcefulness," 40–42.

8. Menges, 37.

9. Menges's analysis of the use of wood compared to steel does not take into account the embedded energy of the digital tools used to design and manufacture wood versus steel structures, perhaps because they are likely very similar. Adding this into the overall analysis of a structure made from either material significantly increases its overall embedded energy.

10. Menges and Reichert, "Material Capacity," 54, 58.

11. Menges, "Material Resourcefulness," 36–37.

12. Menges, "Material Computation," 21, citing Sanford Kwinter, "The Computational Fallacy," in *Computational Design Thinking,* ed. Achim Menges and Sean Ahlquist (London: John Wiley & Sons, 2011), 211.

13. Menges, "Material Computation," 16.

14. Menges, 16–17.

15. Toni Kotnik and Michael Weinstock, "Material, Form, and Force," in "Material Computation: Higher Integration in Morphogenetic Design," special issue of *AD,* ed. Achim Menges, 82, no. 2 (March–April 2012): 111; Achim Menges, "Introduction: Fusing the Computational and the Physical—Towards a Novel Material Culture," in "Fusing the Physical and Computational," special issue of *AD,* ed. Menges, 85, no. 5 (September–October 2015): 15.

16. Santiago Huerta, "Structural Design in the Work of Gaudi," *Architectural Science Review* 49, no. 4 (2006): 324–39, available at http://oa.upm.es/703/1/Huerta_Art_002.pdf.

17. Michael Hensel and Achim Menges, "Membrane Spaces," in "Versatility and Vicissitude: Performance in Morpho-Ecological Design," special issue of *AD,* ed. Hensel and Menges, 78, no. 2 (March–April 2008): 75.

18. Hensel and Menges.

19. Karola Dierichs and Achim Menges, "Aggregate Structures: Material and Machine Computation of Designed Granular Substances," in "Material Computation: Higher Integration in Morphogenetic Design," special issue of *AD,* ed. Achim Menges, 82, no. 2 (March–April 2012): 76.

20. Geo-engineering software can mathematically model granulate behavior using different methods: "molecular dynamics," "discrete element method," and "event-driven molecular dynamics," as well as "rigid body dynamic" from animation software. See Dierichs and Menges, 79–80.

21. Dierichs and Menges, 79.

22. P. Bak, C. Tang, and K. Wiesenfeld, "Self-Organized Criticality: An Explanation of 1/f Noise," *Physical Review Letters* 59, no. 4 (1987): 381–84.

23. Dierichs and Menges, "Aggregate Structures," 80–81.

24. Dierichs and Menges, 79–80.

25. Neri Oxman, "Programming Matter," in "Material Computation: Higher Integration in Morphogenetic Design," special issue of *AD,* ed. Achim Menges, 82, no. 2 (March–April 2012): 92.

26. Oxman, 95.

27. Oxman, 92.

28. Skylar Tibbits, "Design to Self-Assembly," in "Material Computation: Higher Integration in Morphogenetic Design," special issue of *AD,* ed. Achim Menges, 82, no. 2 (March–April 2012): 69.

29. Tibbits, 69.

30. Tibbits, 69.

31. Tibbits, 69–70.

32. Tibbits, 70.

33. Tibbits, 70.

34. Images of Logic Matter are available at http://selfassemblylab.mit.edu/logic-matter/, including the ones with hands that show the components being manipulated.

35. Tibbits, 70, italics added.

36. Images of *Biased Chains* are available at http://www.selfassemblylab.net/BiasedChains.php.

37. Tibbits, "Design to Self-Assembly," 71.

38. Tibbits, 71.

39. Tibbits, 72.

40. Benjamin and I met when I spoke at Columbia University's Graduate School of Architecture, Planning, and Preservation in 2009 about the current work of LabStudio at the University of Pennsylvania. LabStudio is a team comprising architect Jenny Sabin (now at Cornell University) and molecular biologist Peter Lloyd Jones (now at the Medical College of Thomas Jefferson University). I mention this because the project Benjamin and Federici tackled in 2011 is very similar to the work of Sabin and Jones of two years before, which is discussed in chapter 5.

41. David Benjamin and Fernan Federici, "Bio Logic," in *Synthetic Aesthetics: Investigating Synthetic Biology's Designs on Nature,* ed. Alexandra Daisy Ginsberg, Jane Calvert, Pablo Schyfter, Alistair Elfick, and Drew Endy (Cambridge, Mass.: MIT Press, 2014), 143–54; Pablo Schyfter, "Scale and Metaphor," in *Synthetic Aesthetics: Investigating Synthetic Biology's Designs on Nature,* ed. Alexandra Daisy Ginsberg, Jane Calvert, Pablo Schyfter, Alistair Elfick, and Drew Endy (Cambridge, Mass.: MIT Press, 2014), 155–64.

42. Tom Knight's "biobricks" are not the same thing as designer Ginger Krieg Dosier's BioBrick, a brick made from bacteria, urea, calcium ions, and sand, featured in William Myers, *BioDesign: Art, Science, Creativity* (New York: Museum of Modern Art, 2012), 78–79, 258–59.

43. "Biobricks" is the name given to the "parts" available for purchase from the Registry of Standard Biological Parts; see http://parts.igem.org/Catalog.

44. Benjamin and Federici, "Bio Logic," 144.

45. Benjamin and Federici, 144–47.

46. In the same chapter, Federici and Benjamin conducted other experiments as well, which I am not covering here.

47. Pengcheng Fu, "Biomolecular Computing: Is It Ready to Take Off?" *Biotechnology Journal* 2 (2007): 91.

48. Fu, 91–92.

49. Fu, 92, referring to Leonard Adleman's work of 1994.

50. Leonard Adleman, "Molecular Computation of Solutions to Combinatorial Problem," *Science* 266 (1994): 1021–24.

51. Fu, "Biomolecular Computing," 92–93.

52. Fu, 94–95.

53. See also Ted Sargent, "Nanotechnology: Design in the Quantum Vernacular," in *Design and the Elastic Mind,* ed. Paola Antonelli (New York: Museum of Modern Art, 2008), 82–83.

54. David Depew, "From Heat Engines to Digital Printouts: A Tropology of the Organism from the Victorian Era to the Human Genome Project," in *Memory Bytes: History, Technology, and Digital Culture,* ed. Lauren Rabinowitz and Abraham Geil (Durham, N.C.: Duke University Press, 2003), 47–75. Depew traces the history of the idea that DNA is a "code of life"—meaning, like a computational programming code.

55. Fu, "Biomolecular Computing," 98.

56. Alexis Courbet, Franck Molina, and Patrick Amar, "Computing with Synthetic Protocells," *Acta Biotheoretica* 63 (2015): 309–23.

57. Myers, *BioDesign,* 124–25, 186–87.

58. Aspects of Benjamin and Federici's methods are vaguely similar to aspects of computational mechanics, which uses information recorded through observation of a system over time to deduce its structure in the form of an epsilon-machine. Benjamin and Federici do not observe the same system through time but rather compare one set of data from one system to that of another system to ascertain a correlating mathematical expression of pattern.

59. J. P. Crutchfield and D. P. Feldman, "Regularities Unseen, Randomness Observed: Levels of Entropy Convergence," *Chaos* 13, no. 1 (2003): 25–54, written in 2001 as Santa Fe Institute Working Paper 01-02-012.

60. James P. Crutchfield, PowerPoint slides for Lectures 1 and 21, PHY 256A and B, Natural Computation and Self-Organization, UC Davis, Winter and Spring semesters, 2012. The ongoing class website can be found at http://csc.ucdavis.edu/~chaos/courses/ncaso/.

61. James P. Crutchfield, "Between Order and Chaos," *Nature Physics* 8 (2012): 22, available at http://www.semanticscholar.org/paper/Between-Order-and-Chaos-Odell/2574b6d180271 6f5b95dfbf39d438e4ef953b189/pdf.

62. Crutchfield, 22–23.

63. James T. Crutchfield, J. Doyne Famer, Norman H. Packard, and Robert S. Shaw, "Chaos," *Scientific American* 254, no. 12 (December 1986): 49.

64. Steven Strogatz, *Nonlinear Dynamics and Chaos: With Applications to Physics, Biology, Chemistry, and Engineering* (Boulder, Colo.: Westview Press, 2001).

65. Crutchfield et al., "Chaos," 51.

66. Crutchfield et al., 51.

67. Crutchfield, "Between Order and Chaos," 17.

68. Crutchfield, 17.

69. Crutchfield, 17.

70. Crutchfield, 18.

71. Crutchfield, 18.

72. Crutchfield, 18.

73. Cosma Shalizi and James Crutchfield, "Computational Mechanics: Pattern and Prediction, Structure and Simplicity," Santa Fe Institute Working Paper 99-07-044 (January 4, 2011), 2, available at http://arxiv.org/abs/cond-mat/9907176, published as "Computational Mechanics: Pattern and Prediction, Structure and Simplicity," *Journal of Statistical Physics* 104 (2001): 819–81.

74. Robert Payne and Claire Grierson, "A Theoretical Model for ROP Localisation by Auxin in Arabidopsis Root Hair Cells," *PLoS ONE* 4, no. 12 (2009): e8337; Hironori Fujita, Koichi Toyokura, Kiyotaka Okada, and Masayoshi Kawaguchi, "Reaction-Diffusion Pattern in Shoot Apical Meristem of Plants," *PLoS ONE* 6, no. 3 (2011): e18243.

75. Crutchfield and Feldman, "Regularities Unseen, Randomness Observed"; Shalizi and Crutchfield, "Computational Mechanics"; C. C. Strelioff, J. P. Crutchfield, and A. Hubler, "Inferring Markov Chains: Bayesian Estimation, Model Comparison, Entropy Rate, and Out-of-Class Modeling," Santa Fe Institute Working Paper (March 2007), available at http://arxiv.org/abs/math.ST/0703715.

76. Susanne Still, James Crutchfield, and Christopher Ellison, "Optimal Causal Inference" (August 2007), available at http://arxiv.org/abs/0708.1580v1.

77. On the need to reduce dimensions, see Pengcheng Fu and Cliff Hooker, "Outstanding

Issues in Systems and Synthetic Biology," in *Systems Biology and Synthetic Biology*, ed. Pengcheng Fu and Sven Panke (London: John Wiley & Sons, 2009), 611–42.

78. Byung-Chul Choi, Hang-Sik Shin, Su-Yol Lee, and Tak Hur, "Life Cycle Assessment of a Personal Computer and Its Effective Recycling Rate," *International Journal of Life Cycle Assessment* 11, no. 2 (March 2006, online 2004): 122–28.

79. On CRT and LCD screens, see Vikrant Bhakar, Aashray Agur, A. K. Digalwar, and Kuldip Singh Sangwan, "Life Cycle Assessment of CRT, LCD, and LED Monitors," *Procedia CIRP* 29 (2015): 432–37, available at http://www.sciencedirect.com/science/article/pii/S2212827115000414. CIRP is the International Academy for Production Engineering. See also Paul Teehan and Milind Kandlikar, "Sources of Variation in Life Cycle Assessments of Desktop Computers," *Journal of Industrial Ecology* 16, no. S1 (2012): S182–94, available at https://onlinelibrary.wiley.com/doi/pdf/10.1111/j.1530-9290.2011.00431.x; and Madison Crain, Riyaz Merchant, and Felix Le, three individual papers covering the "General Life Cycle of a Silicon Wafer MOSFET Transistor," March 2016, available at http://www.designlife-cycle.com/mosfet/.

80. One meaning of the word "sand" refers to particle sizes (between 0.6 and 2 millimeters), so technically, the text in the marketing brochure referring to "sand" is accurate, as the chips do begin with crushed quartz particles. See Intel, "From Sand to Circuits: How Intel Makes Integrated Circuit Chips," 2008, available at http://web.archive.org/web/20170110155945/http://www.intel.com/Assets/PDF/General/308301003.pdf.

81. Felix Le, "Waste Products of MOSFETs: There's a Lot," March 2016, 3, available at http://www.designlife-cycle.com/mosfet/.

82. Madison Crain, "MOSFET Transistors: Materials," March 2016, 4, available at http://www.designlife-cycle.com/mosfet/; see also "How Do They Make Silicon Wafers and Computer Chips?" March 5, 2018, 8:42 video, available at http://www.youtube.com/watch?v=aWVywhzuHnQ.

83. Crain, 2; Michael Welland, "Sand to Chips: What's the Real Story?" August 7, 2009, available at http://throughthesandglass.typepad.com/through_the_sandglass/2009/08/sand-to-chips—-whats-the-real-story.html.

84. Welland.

85. Eric Williams, Robert Ayres, and Miriam Heller, "Energy and Chemical Use in the Production for Microchips," *IEEE,* February 2002, 186.

86. Riyaz Merchant, poster diagram and his text "The Energy Story," March 2016, available at http://www.designlife-cycle.com/mosfet/.

87. Le, "Waste Products of MOSFETs," 4.

88. Le, 4.

89. Crain, "MOSFET Transistors," 6; Le, "Waste Products of MOSFETs," 4.

90. "How Do They Make Silicon Wafers and Computer Chips?"; and Wikipedia, s.v. "Transistor Count," last modified March 29, 2018, available at http://en.wikipedia.org/wiki/transistor_count.

91. See Eric Williams, "Environmental Impacts of Microchip Manufacture," *Thin Solid Films* 461 (2004): 5. Riyaz Merchant writes, "When all stages of the lifecycle of these wafer based transistors are accounted for, the iceberg of energy weighs in at 1890 billion kWh per year, enough power to keep 173 million US residential households running. This enormous amount of energy comes mainly from electricity, which is a secondary source derived from the burning of fossil fuels. With the amount of semiconductor devices predicted to double by the year 2030, society is faced with a daunting task of being able to continue to supply the massive energy required to produce one of the physically smallest innovations in human history" ("Energy Story," 8–9). His calculation is based on the number of transistors made in 2013.

92. Williams, 2.

93. Williams, Ayres, and Heller, "Energy and Chemical Use," 188.

94. Eric Williams, "Energy Intensity of Computer Manufacturing: Hybrid Assessment Combining Process and Economic Input–Output Methods," *Environmental Science and Technology* 38, no. 22 (2004): 6166. See also Philip Ball, "Heavy Computing," *Nature Materials* 3 (May 2004): 287.

95. Alastair Iles, "Mapping Environmental Justice in Technology Flows: Computer Waste Impacts in Asia," *Global Environmental Politics* 4, no. 4 (November 2004): 76, 78.

96. Iles, 86.

97. Iles, 84–87.

98. Iles, 88.

99. For example, see Giulio Boccaletti, Markus Loffler, and Jeremy Oppenheim, "How IT Can Cut Carbon Emissions," *McKinsey Quarterly,* October 2008; and Kris de Decker, "The Monster Footprint of Digital Technology," *Energy Bulletin,* June 16, 2009, available at http://www.lowtechmagazine.com/2009/06/embodied-energy-of-digital-technology.html.

100. Andreas Manhart, Matthias Buchert, Daniel Bleher, and Detlef Pingel, "Recycling of Critical Metals from End-of-Life Electronics," in *Electronics Goes Green, 2012* (Piscataway, N.J.: IEEE, 2012), 2.

101. Eelco Smit, Jan Scheijgrond, and Jan Severin, "Resource Scarcity: An OEM Perspective," in *Electronics Goes Green, 2012* (Piscataway, N.J.: IEEE, 2012), 1–5; Mario Schmidt, "Resource Efficiency: What Are Critical Metals and How Scarce Are They?" (paper presented at the Electronic Displays Conference, February 29–March 1, 2012, Nuremberg, Germany), available at http://www.hs-pforzheim.de/fileadmin/user_upload/uploads_redakteur/Forschung/INEC/Dokumente/Team__Publikationen_/Electronic_Displays_2012_Schmidt.pdf. Other critical metals used in personal computers, in addition to those listed above, include antimony and magnesium.

102. See http://www.statista.com/statistics/269049/global-pc-shipment-forecast-since-2009/; and http://www.worldometers.info/computers/, which as of May 2018 when the study was done, estimated the number of personal computers sold this year at about eighty-six million. It forecasts 256.3 million for 2018 and 248.4 million for 2022.

103. Smit, Scheijgrond, and Severin, "Resource Scarcity," 2–3.

104. Smit, Scheijgrond, and Severin, 3.

105. Schmidt, "Resource Efficiency," Table 1, 2.

106. Schmidt, 3–4.

107. Manhart et al., "Recycling of Critical Metals," 3.

108. de Decker, "Monster Footprint of Digital Technology."

109. Stefan Helmreich, "Nature/Culture/Seawater," *American Anthropologist* 113 (2011): 132–44.

3. Morphogenesis and Evolutionary Computation

1. Achim Menges and Sean Ahlquist, eds., introduction to D'Arcy Thompson, "On the Theory of Transformations, or the Comparison of Related Forms," in *Computational Design Thinking* (West Sussex, U.K.: Wiley, 2011), 32.

2. Sanjeev Kumar and Peter Bentley, "Biologically Inspired Evolutionary Development," in *Evolvable Systems: From Biology to Hardware,* ed. Andy Tyrrell, Pauline Haddow, and Jim Torresen (New York: Springer, 2003), 57.

3. On Evo DeVO at LIPHE, see http://www.mcgill.ca/architecture/resources/liphe; and Aaron Sprecher and Chandler Ahrens, "Adaptive Knowledge in Architecture," in "Digital Property: Open-Source Architecture," special issue *AD,* ed. Wendy W. Fok and Antoine Picon, 86, no. 5 (September–October 2016): 25–35.

4. Helene Furjàn and Peter Lloyd Jones, "Epigenesis: Bio-Architectures," in *The Gen(H)ome Project,* ed. Peter Noever and Open Source Architecture (Los Angeles: MAK Center for Art and Architecture, 2006), 82–89.

5. Aspects of Haeckel's theory of recapitulation bear some resemblance to what we now know from evo-devo in that very distantly related organisms share a common set of homeotic genes that affect organismal development. Differences in gene activation, rather than differences in gene sequences or numbers, account for many of the major morphological differences between species.

6. Snait Gissis and Eva Jablonka, eds., *Transformation of Lamarckism: From Subtle Fluids to Molecular Biology* (Cambridge, Mass.: MIT Press, 2011).

7. In Germany in the 1930s and 1940s, Hollerith punch cards and tabulating machines designed, leased, and maintained by IBM Germany (Dehomag) were used keep track of large amounts of census data, including location of Jews, ethnicity, economic status, as well as scientific trait survey data, food and labor supplies, human transportation, and death records throughout the Holocaust. See Edwin Black, *IBM and the Holocaust* (Rockville, Md.: Dialog Press, 2012). This is the earliest historical overlap between the uses of computation and biological theories of evolution for highly unethical statistical and political purposes.

8. This is the focus of Lily Kay's *Who Wrote the Book of Life? A History of the Genetic Code* (Cambridge, Mass.: MIT Press, 2000). Her argument is summarized and added on to by David Depew in "From Heat Engines to Digital Printouts: A Tropology of the Organism from the Victorian Era to the Human Genome Project," in *Memory Bytes: History, Technology, and Digital Culture,* ed. Lauren Rabinowitz and Abraham Geil (Durham, N.C.: Duke University Press, 2003), 47–75. Kay cites Watson and Crick's second *Nature* article as the publication where they use the word "code": "It therefore seems likely that the precise sequence of the bases is the code which carries the genetical information" (59). She also recounts earlier ideas of Erwin Schrödinger on the likely existence of a "code-script" at the root of life (60–62).

9. Agoston Eiben and Jim Smith, "From Evolutionary Computation to the Evolution of Things," *Nature* 521 (May 28, 2015): 476, citing A. M. Turing, *Machine Intelligence 5,* ed. B. Meltzer and D. Michie (Edinburgh, U.K.: Edinburgh University Press, 1969). See also Thomas Back, Ulrich Hammel, and Paul Schwefel, "Evolutionary Computation: Comments on the History and Current State," *IEEE Transactions on Evolutionary Computation* 1, no. 1 (April 1997): 3–17.

10. Alan Turing, "The Chemical Basis of Morphogenesis," *Philosophical Transactions of the Royal Society of London B* 237, no. 641 (1952): 37–72; Philip Ball, *Shapes* (Oxford, U.K.: Oxford University Press, 2009), 154.

11. Turing, 41, also quoted in Ball, 155.

12. Ball, 155.

13. Turing, in "Chemical Basis of Morphogenesis," 38, suggests that morphogens are similar to Conrad Waddington's "evocators" or that they may be hormones or even genes as a specific subset.

14. Ball, *Shapes,* 156.

15. See Ball's footnote on page 156 regarding Turing's wish for a computer to compute the reaction-diffusion equations.

16. Ball, 157. See also Florian Maderspacher, "Colour Patterns: Channeling Turing," *Current Biology* 22, no. 8 (April 2012): R266–68; Jonathon Howard, Stephan Grill, and Justin Bois, "Turing's Next Steps: The Mechanochemical Basis of Morphogenesis," *Nature Reviews in Molecular and Cell Biology* 12 (June 2011): 392–98; Siegfried Roth, "Mathematics and Biology: A Kantian View on the History of Pattern Formation Theory," *Development, Genes, and Evolution* 221, no. 5 (December 2011): 255–79; Shigeru Kondo and Takashi Miura, "Reaction-Diffusion Model as a Framework for Understanding Biological Pattern Formation," *Science* 329 (24 September 2010): 1616–20; Philip Maini, "The Impact of Turing's Work on Pattern Formation in Biology," *Mathematics Today,* August 2004, 140–41.

17. Eiben and Smith, "From Evolutionary Computation to the Evolution of Things," 477, 479; see also Melanie Mitchell, *An Introduction to Genetic Algorithms* (Cambridge, Mass.: MIT Press, 1996), 2.

18. Eiben and Smith, 480.

19. Mitchell, *Introduction to Genetic Algorithms,* 181–82.

20. Eiben and Smith, "From Evolutionary Computation to the Evolution of Things," 478–79.

21. Mitchell, *Introduction to Genetic Algorithms,* 4–5, 181.

22. Mitchell, 181–82.

23. Kay, *Who Wrote the Book of Life?*; Depew, "From Heat Engines to Digital Printouts."

24. Depew, 58–61.

25. Francis Crick, "Central Dogma of Molecular Biology," *Nature* 227 (August 8, 1970): 561–63. In this article he qualifies and revises some of his earlier claims about the unidirectionality of flow from DNA to RNA to proteins, owing to discoveries by other scientists that showed this was not always the case; see also Francis Crick, "On Protein Synthesis," *Symposia of the Society for Experimental Biology* 12 (1958): 138–63.

26. Depew, "From Heat Engines to Digital Printouts," 61.

27. Depew, 61.

28. Depew, 67–69.

29. Depew, 68.

30. Depew, 70.

31. Depew, 69, italics added. Depew is also coauthor, along with Bruce Weber, of *Darwinism Evolving: Systems Dynamics and the Genealogy of Natural Selection* (Cambridge, Mass.: MIT Press, 1995).

32. Hallam Stevens, "Networks: Representations and Tools in Postgenomics," in *Postgenomics: Perspectives on Biology after the Genome,* ed. Sarah Richardson and Hallam Stevens (Durham, N.C.: Duke University Press, 2015), 103.

33. Stevens, 104.

34. Depew, "From Heat Engines to Digital Printouts," 68.

35. Sarah Richardson and Hallam Stevens, "Approaching Postgenomics," in *Postgenomics: Perspectives on Biology after the Genome,* ed. Sarah Richardson and Hallam Stevens (Durham, N.C.: Duke University Press, 2015), 237.

36. John Frazer, *An Evolutionary Architecture* (London: Architectural Association, 1995), 10–11.

37. Alberto Estévez, "Biomorphic Architecture," in *Genetic Architectures II: Digital Tools and Organic Forms,* ed. Estévez (Santa Fe, N.M.: SITES Books / ESARQ-UIC, 2005), 78.

38. See Michael Weinstock, "Evolution and Computation," in Michael Hensel, Achim Menges, and Michael Weinstock, *Emergent Technologies and Design: Towards a Biological Paradigm for Architecture* (New York: Routledge, 2010), 25–41.

39. Achim Menges, "Biomimetic Design Processes in Architecture: Morphogenetic and Evolutionary Computational Design," *Bioinspiration and Biomimicry* 7, no. 1 (2012): 015003. The most recent works on evolutionary theory included in his sources are Stephen Jay Gould, *The Structure of Evolutionary Theory* (Cambridge, Mass.: Harvard University Press, 2002); and Gerd Müller and Stuart Newman, *Origination of Organismal Form* (Cambridge, Mass.: MIT Press, 2003). Otherwise, his references point to Julian Huxley, *Evolution: The Modern Synthesis* (Cambridge, Mass.: MIT Press, 1942); Ernst Mayr, "Typological Versus Population Thinking," *Darwin and the Evolutionary Theory in Biology* (Washington, D.C.: Anthropological Society of Washington, 1959), 409–12; Walter J. Bock, "Preadaptation and Multiple Evolutionary Pathways," *Evolution* 13 (1959): 194–211; and Mary C. McKitrick, "Phylogenetic Constraints in Evolutionary Theory," *Annual Reviews in Ecological Systems* 24 (1993): 307–30.

40. The entry for neo-Darwinism in Wikipedia claims that the modern synthesis and neo-Darwinism are still the "current evolutionary theory" without note of all the changes since the turn of the twentieth century. This points to the power of this theory overall. See Wikipedia, s.v. "Neo-Darwinism," last modified April 14, 2018, available at http://en.wikipedia.org/wiki/Neo-Darwinism.

41. Depew and Weber, *Darwinism Evolving,* 299–301.

42. Depew asserts this in "From Heat Engines to Digital Printouts," 64.

43. Depew and Weber, *Darwinism Evolving,* 346.

44. Depew and Weber, 342; see also Wikipedia, s.v. "One Gene–One Enzyme Hypothesis," last modified September 29, 2017, available at http://en.wikipedia.org/wiki/One_gene-one-_enzyme_hypothesis. See also Mark Hickman and John Cairns, "The Centenary of the One-Gene One-Enzyme Hypothesis," *Genetics* 163, no. 3 (April 2003): 839–41, which cites predecessors to Beadle and Tatum.

45. Alexander Palazzo and T. Ryan Gregory, "The Case for Junk DNA," *PLoS Genetics* 10, no. 5 (May 2014): e1004351, available at http://www.ncbi.nlm.nih.gov/pmc/articles/PMC4014423/.

46. Richard Dawkins, *The Selfish Gene* (Oxford, U.K.: Oxford University Press, 1976).

47. Mitchell, *Introduction to Genetic Algorithms,* 2.

48. Mitchell, 5.

49. Mitchell, 5.

50. Mitchell, 5.

51. Mitchell, 6.

52. Mitchell, 6.

53. Mitchell, 6.

54. Mitchell, 6.

55. Depew, "From Heat Engines to Digital Printouts," 67–69.

56. The roof was for Coventry Preparatory School and published first in John Frazer, "Reptiles," *AD* 4 (1974): 231–39; and later in Frazer, *Evolutionary Architecture,* 23.

57. Email from John Frazer to the author, June 20, 2016.

58. Frazer, *Evolutionary Architecture,* 11, 58.

59. See one listing of their holdings from the Yokohama Terminal project at http://www.moma.org/collection/works/95093, which refers to a C-print of the geometry of the girders. When I visited MoMA in 2008, I saw some of the Yokohama design prints on display in the design section of the museum's permanent collection. I remember a plaque on the wall that described how the girders were designed using genetic algorithms, but I cannot find pictures of the text and am not sure my memory is accurate on this point. See also David Langdon, "Yokohama International Passenger Terminal, Foreign Office Architects (FOA)," *AD Classics,* October 7, 2014, available at http://www.archdaily.com/554132/ad-classics-yokohama-international-passenger-terminal-foreign-office-architects-foa, for a description of the difficulty and uniqueness of the girder design.

60. FOA, "Phylogenesis: FOA's Ark," in *Phylogenesis: FOA's Ark,* ed. Michael Kubo, Albert Ferre, Farshid Moussavi, and Alejandro Zaera-Polo (Barcelona: Actar, 2003), 8–9.

61. FOA, 11.

62. Michael Weinstock, "Morphogenesis and the Mathematics of Emergence," in "Emergence: Morphogenetic Design Strategies," special issue of *AD,* ed. Michael Hensel, Achim Menges, and Michael Weinstock, 74, no. 3 (May–June 2004): 16.

63. Weinstock, "Evolution and Computation," 29.

64. Weinstock, 34, 38.

65. Benjamin recommended this website on his course brief and I participated in a critique in the Spring 2009 semester for this studio.

66. See Marek Obitko's website about genetic algorithms, available at http://www.obitko.com/tutorials/genetic-algorithms/biological-background.php.

67. Keith Besserud and Joshua Ingram, "Architectural Genomics," in *Silicon + Skin: Biological Processes and Computation,* ed. Andrew Kudless, Neri Oxman, and Marc Swackhamer (Morrisville, N.C.: Lulu Press, 2008), 239–40.

68. Besserud and Ingram, 243.

69. Besserud and Ingram, 240.

70. Besserud and Ingram, 240–41. Eiben and Smith write, "Nevertheless, it is important to understand that evolutionary algorithms are not optimizers, but approximators, and they are not optimal since we might not know whether the fitness of the best evolved solution is in fact the highest value possible" ("From Evolutionary Computation to the Evolution of Things," 478).

71. Other examples of fitness criteria for architectural GAs are mentioned in Menges, "Biomimetic Design Processes in Architecture," 4.

72. Weinstock, "Morphogenesis and the Mathematics of Emergence," 12.

73. Eiben and Smith, "From Evolutionary Computation to the Evolution of Things," 477.

74. Depew, "From Heat Engines to Digital Printouts," 68.

75. Christina Cogdell, *Eugenic Design: Streamlining America in the 1930s* (2004; repr., Philadelphia: University of Pennsylvania Press, 2010), 46.

76. See Sean Carroll's summary of this history in *Endless Forms Most Beautiful: The New Science of Evo Devo* (New York: Norton, 2005), 6–7.

77. Evelyn Fox Keller, "The Postgenomic Genome," in *Postgenomics: Perspectives on Biology after the Genome,* ed. Sarah Richardson and Hallam Stevens (Durham, N.C.: Duke University Press, 2015), 14.

78. Depew and Weber, *Darwinism Evolving,* 351.

79. Depew and Weber, 351.

80. Jyoti Madhusoodanan, "Human Gene Set Shrinks Again," *The Scientist,* July 8, 2014, available at http://www.the-scientist.com/?articles.view/articleNo/40441/title/Human-Gene-Set-Shrinks-Again/.

81. Although publications proposing the realignment of evolutionary and developmental biology based on evidence that led to evo-devo began before 2000, that was the year that the *Proceedings of the National Academy of Sciences* was devoted to pursuing the theory of evo-devo, with its resulting publication (97, no. 9 [2000]).

82. Frazer, *Evolutionary Architecture,* 20.

83. Carroll, *Endless Forms Most Beautiful,* 15, 64.

84. Some of these scientists worked with Carroll in the same lab—he mentions Allen Laughon in addition to himself, as well as scientists in Basel, Switzerland, Bill McGinnis and Mike Levine working in Walter Gehring's lab. See Carroll, 63–64.

85. Carroll, 62–63.

86. Carroll, 9.

87. Carroll, 29.

88. Carroll, 19–28.

89. On broken symmetries, see Ian Stewart, "Broken Symmetries and Biological Patterns," in *On Growth, Form, and Computers,* ed. Sanjeev Kumar and Peter Bentley (San Diego: Elsevier Press, 2003), 181–202; see also Ball, *Shapes,* 23–25 and throughout.

90. Carroll, *Endless Forms Most Beautiful,* 33–34.

91. Carroll, 64, 71.

92. Carroll, 88.

93. Carroll, 65.

94. Ball, *Shapes,* 275.

95. Carroll, *Endless Forms Most Beautiful,* 89–98.

96. Carroll, 44–45.

97. Email from Sean Carroll to the author, August 18, 2016.

98. Ball, *Shapes,* 163, 176, 189, 242–45, 266–71, esp. 277–80.

99. Carroll, *Endless Forms Most Beautiful,* 11.

100. Carroll, 11.

101. Carroll, 106.

102. Kumar and Bentley, "Biologically Inspired Evolutionary Development," 58.

103. Kumar and Bentley, 61.

104. Kumar and Bentley, 60; see also Eva Jablonka and Marion Lamb, *Evolution in Four Dimensions: Genetic, Epigenetic, Behavioral, and Symbolic Variation in the History of Life* (Cambridge, Mass.: MIT Press, 2005), 33. They write, "The discoveries in molecular biology inevitably led to a partial revision of the Modern Synthesis version of Darwinian evolution: The gene, the unit of heredity in the Modern Synthesis, became a DNA sequence, which codes for a protein product or an RNA molecule." On page 67, they recount how the definition of a "gene" is in question, a fact echoed by Carl Zimmer in "Now: The Rest of the Genome," *New York Times,* November 10, 2008, available at http://www.nytimes.com/2008/11/11/science/11gene.html.

105. For example, see Paul Myers, "*Hox* Genes in Development: The *Hox* Code," *Nature Education* 1(1), no. 2 (2008), available at http://www.nature.com/scitable/topicpage/hox-genes-in-development-the-hox-code-41402.

106. Zimmer.

107. Kumar and Bentley, "Biologically Inspired Evolutionary Development," 61.

108. Kumar and Bentley, 62.

109. Kumar and Bentley, 63.

110. Weinstock, "Evolution and Computation," 40.

111. Weinstock, 40. Although Carroll's book *Endless Forms Most Beautiful* was on the reading list for the 2011 EmTech class, in Weinstock's 2010 essay "Evolution and Computation" he does not cite Carroll anywhere, despite drawing heavily on Carroll's book for his description of the history and ideas of evo-devo.

112. Weinstock, "Evolution and Computation," 40; see also Carroll's explanation that "differences in form arise from evolutionary changes in where and when genes are used, especially those genes that affect the number, shape, or size of a structure" (*Endless Forms Most Beautiful,* 11).

113. Weinstock, "Evolution and Computation," 40.

114. Weinstock, 40.

115. See Sprecher and Ahrens, "Adaptive Knowledge in Architecture"; and http://www.mcgill.ca/architecture/resources/liphe. From these sources, it is not possible to discern how the Evo DeVO Project uses the theory of evo-devo as a model; most of Sprecher's references are to information technology rather than biology.

116. Menges, "Biomimetic Design Processes in Architecture," 2.

117. Menges, 4, 6, 9.

118. Menges, 4–7.

119. For example, see James Shapiro, "Revisiting the Central Dogma in the 21st Century," paper presented at a symposium on Natural Genetic Engineering—Natural Genome Editing, July 2–6, 2008, available at http://shapiro.bsd.uchicago.edu/Shapiro2009.AnnNYAcadSciMS.RevisitingCentral%20Dogma.pdf.

120. Yan Boucher, Christophe Douady, Thane Papke, David Walsh, Mary Ellen Boudreau, Camilla Nesbo, Rebecca Case, and Ford Doolittle, "Lateral Gene Transfer and the Origins of Prokaryotic Groups," *Annual Review of Genetics* 37 (2003): 283–328; and Victor Kunin, Leon Goldovsky, Nikos Darzentas, and Christos Ouzounis, "The Net of Life: Reconstructing the Microbial Phylogenetic Network," *Genome Research* 15 (2005): 954–59, available at http://genome.cshlp.org/content/15/7/954.full.

121. See John Dupre, "The Polygenomic Organism," in *Postgenomics: Perspectives on Biology after the Genome,* ed. Sarah Richardson and Hallam Stevens (Durham, N.C.: Duke University Press, 2015), 56–72. See also Sarah Williams, "Humans May Harbor More Than 100 Genes from Other Organisms," *Science,* March 12, 2015, available at http://www.sciencemag.org/news/2015/03/humans-may-harbor-more-100-genes-other-organisms. The Wikipedia entry for "Horizontal Gene Transfer," in the section on "Eukaryotes," lists a number of instances of HGT between bacteria and eukaryotic organisms, including source citations; see http://en.wikipedia.org/wiki/horizontal_gene_transfer, last modified May 1, 2018.

122. Lynn Margulis and Dorion Sagan, *Acquiring Genomes: A Theory of the Origin of Species* (New York: Basic Books, 2003).

123. Dupre, "Polygenomic Organism," 57–58; and David Riley, Karsten Sieber, Kelly Robinson, James White, Ashwinkumar Ganesan, Syrus Nourbakhsh, and Julie Dunning Hotopp, "Bacteria–Human Somatic Cell Lateral Gene Transfer in Cancer Samples," *PLoS Computational Biology* 9, no. 6 (2013): e1003107, available at http://journals.plos.org/ploscompbiol/article/asset?id=10.1371%2Fjournal.pcbi.1003107.pdf.

124. "Darwin Was Wrong: Cutting Down the Tree of Life," cover of *New Scientist,* January 24–30, 2009; Ian Sample, "Evolution: Charles Darwin Was Wrong about the Tree of Life," *The Guardian,* January 21, 2009, available at http://www.theguardian.com/science/2009/jan/21/charles-darwin-evolution-species-tree-life.

125. Michel Morange, "The Relations between Genetics and Epigenetics: A Historical Point of View," in "From Epigenesis to Epigenetics: The Genome in Context," special issue of *Annals of the*

New York Academy of Sciences, ed. Linda van Speybroeck, Gertrudis Van de Vijver, and Dani De Waele, 981 (December 2002): 51; and Eva Jablonka and Marion Lamb, "The Changing Concept of Epigenetics," in "From Epigenesis to Epigenetics: The Genome in Context," special issue of *Annals of the New York Academy of Sciences,* ed. Linda van Speybroeck, Gertrudis Van de Vijver, and Dani De Waele, 981 (December 2002): 82.

126. Keller, "Postgenomic Genome," 14; Morange, "Relations between Genetics and Epigenetics," 55, italics added.

127. Morange, 52–53.

128. Morange, 52–53.

129. Morange, 51.

130. Jablonka and Lamb, "Changing Concepts of Epigenetics," 88, citing C. Wu and J. R. Morris, "Genes, Genetics, and Epigenetics: A Correspondence," *Science* 293 (2001): 1103–5, who cite V. Russo, R. Martienssen, and A. Riggs, eds., *Epigenetic Mechanisms of Gene Regulation* (Woodbury, N.Y.: Cold Spring Harbor Laboratory Press, 1996). See also Sarah Richardson, "Maternal Bodies in the Postgenomic Order: Gender and the Explanatory Landscape of Epigenetics," in *Postgenomics: Perspectives on Biology after the Genome,* ed. Sarah Richardson and Hallam Stevens (Durham, N.C.: Duke University Press, 2015), 212. Another definition is proposed by Adrian Bird in "Perceptions of Epigenetics," *Nature* 447 (May 24, 2007): 396–98, available at http://www.nature.com/nature/journal/v447/n7143/full/nature05913.html.

131. Pilar Cubas, Coral Vincent, and Enrico Coen, "An Epigenetic Mutation Responsible for Natural Variation in Floral Symmetry," *Nature* 401 (September 9, 1999): 157–61; Michael Ronemus, "Flower Power," *Nature Genetics* 23, no. 2 (1999): 132.

132. Morange, "Relations between Genetics and Epigenetics," 56.

133. Jablonka and Lamb, *Evolution in Four Dimensions,* 127–28.

134. For different interpretations and definitions of the word "genome," see Keller, "Postgenomic Genome," 26–27.

135. Jablonka and Lamb, *Evolution in Four Dimensions,* 142.

136. Richardson, "Maternal Bodies in the Postgenomic Order," throughout; Jablonka and Lamb, *Evolution in Four Dimensions,* 137–46.

137. Hugh Morgan, Heidi Sutherland, David Martin, and Emma Whitelaw, "Epigenetic Inheritance at the Agouti Locus in the Mouse," *Nature Genetics* 23, no. 3 (1999): 314; Emma Whitelaw and David Martin, "Retrotransposons as Epigenetic Mediators of Phenotypic Variation in Mammals," *Nature Genetics* 27 (April 2001): 361–65.

138. Jablonka and Lamb, *Evolution in Four Dimensions,* 144; Richardson, "Maternal Bodies in the Postgenomic Order," 212, citing Moshe Szyf, Ian Weaver, Francis Champagne, Josie Diorio, and Michael Meaney, "Maternal Programming of Steroid Receptor Expression and Phenotype through DNA Methylation in the Rat," *Frontiers in Neuroendocrinology* 26, nos. 3–4 (2005): 139–62.

139. Jablonka and Lamb, "Changing Concepts of Epigenetics," 94–95; Gissis and Jablonka, *Transformations of Lamarckism.*

140. Jablonka and Lamb, *Evolution in Four Dimensions,* 128.

141. Bird, "Perceptions of Epigenetics," 396.

142. See the ENCODE Project website at http://www.encodeproject.org/. The idea that there is one human genome—*the* human genome—when, in fact, variations occur between the genomes of individual people, should be recognized as a statistical concept based on the idea of a norm. The Human Genome Project only decoded the genomes of a few individuals pieced together by parts, and since then, the 1000 Genomes Project and 23andMe are adding a huge amount of data to the statistical averages.

143. Zimmer.

144. Keller, "Postgenomic Genome," 17–18, 20.

145. Bradley E. Bernstein, John A. Stamatoyannopoulos, Joseph F. Costello, Bing Ren, Aleksandar Milosavljevic, Alexander Meissner, Manolis Kellis, Marco A. Marra, Arthur L. Beaudet, Joseph R. Ecker, Peggy J. Farnham, Martin Hirst, Eric S. Lander, Tarjei S. Mikkelsen,

and James A. Thomson, "The NIH Roadmap Epigenomics Mapping Consortium," *Nature Biotechnology* 28, no. 10 (October 2010): 1045–48. See also Jae-Bum Bae, "Perspectives of International Human Epigenome Consortium," *Genomics Information* 11, no. 1 (March 2013): 7–14. The abstract collapses epigenetics into genetics, describing the work of the consortium as a "giant step toward the conquest of unexplored regions of the human genome." A similar reabsorption of epigenetics into genetics is hashed out in Mark Ptashne, Oliver Hobert, and Eric Davidson in "Questions over the Scientific Basis of the Epigenome Project," *Nature* 464, no. 487 (March 25, 2010), available at http://www.nature.com/nature/journal/v464/n7288/full/464487c.html. For a general website of these projects, see http://www.roadmapepigenomics.org/.

146. "Time for the Epigenome," *Nature* 463, no. 587 (February 4, 2010), available at http://www.nature.com/nature/journal/v463/n7281/full/463587a.html.

147. "Time for the Epigenome."

148. Jablonka and Lamb, "Changing Concepts of Epigenetics," 89; Jablonka and Lamb, *Evolution in Four Dimensions,* 123.

149. Jablonka and Lamb, "Changing Concepts of Epigenetics," 91–92.

150. Sathish Periyasamy, William Alexander Gray, and Peter Kille, "The Epigenetic Algorithm," *IEEE Congress on Evolutionary Computation,* 2008, 3228–30.

151. Periyasamy, Gray, and Kille, 3232. See also Steen Rasmussen, Mark Bedau, Liaohai Chen, David Deamer, David Krakauer, Norman Packard, and Peter Stadler, eds., *Protocells: Bridging Nonliving and Living Matter* (Cambridge, Mass.: MIT Press, 2009), xx.

152. Periyasamy, Gray, and Kille, "Epigenetic Algorithm," 3228.

153. Periyasamy, Gray, and Kille, 3228.

154. Periyasamy, Gray, and Kille, 3228.

155. Periyasamy, Gray, and Kille, 3230.

156. James Shapiro, "Genome Organization and Reorganization in Evolution: Formatting for Computation and Function," in "From Epigenesis to Epigenetics: The Genome in Context," special issue of *Annals of the New York Academy of Sciences,* ed. Linda van Speybroeck, Gertrudis Van de Vijver, and Dani De Waele, 981 (December 2002): 113.

157. J. Scott Turner, "Evolutionary Architecture? Some Perspectives from Biological Design," in "Material Computation: Higher Integration in Morphogenetic Design," special issue of *AD,* ed. Menges, 82, no. 2 (March–April 2012): 31, 33.

158. Frazer, *Evolutionary Architecture,* 83, 99.

159. Furjàn and Jones, "Epigenesis," 87.

160. Frazer, *Evolutionary Architecture,* 102, citing Richard Dawkins, *The Extended Phenotype* (Oxford, U.K.: Oxford University Press, 1982); W. Katavolos, "Organics," in *Programmes and Manifestoes on 20th-Century Architecture,* ed. Ulrich Conrads (London: Lund Humphries, 1970); Charles Jencks, *Architecture 2000: Predictions and Methods* (London: Studio Vista, 1971); Peter Cook, ed., *Archigram* 9 (1970); A. Graham Cairns-Smith, *Genetic Takeover and the Mineral Origins of Life* (Cambridge, U.K.: Cambridge University Press, 1982).

161. Eiben and Smith, "From Evolutionary Computation to the Evolution of Things," 480.

162. Sara Shostak and Margot Moinester, "The Missing Piece of the Puzzle? Measuring the Environment in the Postgenomic Moment," in *Postgenomics: Perspectives on Biology after the Genome,* ed. Sarah Richardson and Hallam Stevens (Durham, N.C.: Duke University Press, 2015), 195.

163. Shostak and Moinester, 197.

164. Michelle Murphy, *Sick Building Syndrome and the Problem of Uncertainty: Environmental Politics, Technoscience, and Women Workers* (Durham, N.C.: Duke University Press, 2006).

165. Besserud and Ingram, "Architectural Genomics," 140.

4. Context Matters

1. The only other publication-documented generative architect–biological scientist duo, that of David Benjamin and synthetic biologist Fernan Federici, to work in a similar manner

to Sabin and Jones possibly based their own approach on that of LabStudio. See the section on biocomputation addressing Benjamin and Federici's work in chapter 2 for comparison.

2. See related images and study at Rene Chapados, Khotaro Abe, Kaori Ihida-Stansbury, David McKean, Adam Gates, Michael Kern, Sandra Merklinger, John Elliott, Anne Plant, Hiroaki Shimokawa, and Peter Lloyd Jones, "ROCK Controls Matrix Synthesis in Vascular Smooth Muscle Cells: Coupling Vasoconstriction to Vascular Remodeling," *Circulation Research* 99 (September 21, 2006): 837–44. "TN1/green fluorescent protein (TN1-GFP)" revealed the extracellular matrix (ECM); "fluorescein isothiocyanate (FITC)-conjugated goat anti-rabbit IgG" revealed the nucleus; and "For F-actin, cells were stained with AlexaFluor 594 phalloidin" (838).

3. Rosalind Franklin, Photograph 51, X-ray diffraction image of sodium deoxyribose nucleate (1952), in Franklin and Ray Gosling, "Molecular Configuration in Sodium Thymonucleate," *Nature* 171, no. 4356 (April 1953): 740.

4. Celeste Nelson and Mina Bissell define the "microenvironment" as "local and systemic constituents surrounding a cell, including ECM, other cells, and soluble factors released locally or transmitted from other organs, such as hormones." See Nelson and Bissell, "Of Extracellular Matrix, Scaffolds, and Signaling: Tissue Architecture Regulates Development, Homeostasis, and Cancer," *Annual Review of Cell and Developmental Biology* 22 (2006): 288.

5. On cells as tensegrity structures, see Donald Ingber, "The Architecture of Life," *Scientific American*, January 1998, 48–57; and more recently, Donald Ingber, Ning Wang, and Dimitrije Stamenovic, "Tensegrity, Cellular Biophysics, and the Mechanics of Living Systems," *Reports on Progress in Physics* 77, no. 4 (2014): 046603, https://www.ncbi.nlm.nih.gov/pmc/articles/PMC4112545/.

6. See http://smartgeometry.org/.

7. Jenny Sabin and Peter Lloyd Jones, "LabStudio: Nonlinear Design Diagnostics and Tooling," short fund-raising proposal shared with the author in 2009.

8. Donald Ingber and James Jamieson, "Cells as Tensegrity Structures: Architectural Regulation of Histodifferentiation by Physical Forces Transduced over Basement Membrane," in *Gene Expression during Normal and Malignant Differentiation*, ed. Leif C. Andersson, Carl G. Gahmberg, and P. Ekblom (Orlando: Academic Press, 1985), 13–32.

9. Ingber, Wang, and Stamenovic, "Tensegrity, Cellular Biophysics, and the Mechanics of Living Systems," 5.

10. Nelson and Bissell, "Extracellular Matrix, Scaffolds, and Signaling," 297–98. They describe how cell rounding "leads to histone modifications," which affect gene accessibility and regulation.

11. Ingber, Wang and Stamenovic, "Tensegrity, Cellular Biophysics, and the Mechanics of Living Systems," 1.

12. Nelson and Bissell, "Extracellular Matrix, Scaffolds, and Signaling," 288; Christy Hebner, Valerie Weaver, and Jayanta Debnath, "Modeling Morphogenesis and Oncogenesis in Three-Dimensional Breast Epithelial Cultures," *Annual Review of Pathology: Mechanisms of Disease* 3 (2008): 313–39.

13. J. Scott Turner, "Evolutionary Architecture? Some Perspectives from Biological Design," in "Material Computation: Higher Integration in Morphogenetic Design," special issue of *AD*, ed. Menges, 82, no. 2 (March–April 2012): 31, 33.

14. Valerie Weaver, Ole Petersen, Fei Yuan Wang, Carolyn Larabell, Per Briand, Caroline Damsky, and Mina Bissell, "Reversion of the Malignant Phenotype of Human Breast Cells in Three-Dimensional Culture and In Vivo by Integrin Blocking Antibodies," *Journal of Cell Biology* 137, no. 1 (April 7, 1997): 231–45. See also Mina Bissell's talk "Genes and the Microenvironment: Two Faces of Breast Cancer," available about thirty minutes into this video at http://www.youtube.com/watch?v=g5H9NLjO-0E.

15. Bissell, "Genes and the Microenvironment." Elsewhere, she rephrases this as follows: "Tissue architecture is both a consequence and a cause (the end and the beginning)." See Nelson and Bissell, "Extracellular Matrix, Scaffolds, and Signaling," 289.

16. Two articles explaining the importance of three-dimensional cultures are Genee Lee,

Paraic Kenny, Eva Lee, and Mina Bissell, "Three-Dimensional Culture Models of Normal and Malignant Breast Epithelial Cells," *Nature Methods* 4, no. 4 (April 2007): 359–65; and Hebner, Weaver, and Debnath, "Modeling Morphogenesis and Oncogenesis in Three-Dimensional Breast Epithelial Cultures."

17. David McKean, Lila Sisbarro, Dusko Ilic, Nihal Kaplan-Alburquerque, Raphael Nemenoff, Mary Weiser-Evans, Michael Kern, and Peter Lloyd Jones, "FAK Induces Expression of Prx1 to Promote Tenascin-C-Dependent Fibroblast Migration," *Journal of Cell Biology* 161, no. 2 (April 28, 2003): 393–402.

18. Kaori Ihida-Stansbury, David McKean, Sarah Gebb, James Martin, Troy Stevens, Raphael Nemenoff, Ann Akeson, Jessica Vaughn, and Peter Lloyd Jones, "Paired-Related Homeobox Gene *Prx1* Is Required for Pulmonary Vascular Development," *Circulation Research* 94 (June 11, 2004): 1507–14. See also Peter Lloyd Jones, "Pulmonary Vascular Development," in *Endothelial Biomedicine,* ed. William Aird (Cambridge, U.K.: Cambridge University Press, 2007), 176–90.

19. Chapados et al., "ROCK Controls Matrix Synthesis in Vascular Smooth Muscle Cells." See also Peter Lloyd Jones, "Move On! Smooth Muscle Cell Behavior Paired Down," *Circulation Research* 100, no. 6 (March 30, 2007): 757–60; Agne Taraseviciute, Benjamin Vincent, Pepper Schedin, and Peter Lloyd Jones, "Quantitative Analysis of 3-D Human Mammary Epithelial Tissue Architecture Reveals a Role for Tenascin-C in Regulating C-Met Function," *American Journal of Pathology* 176, no. 2 (February 2010): 827–38.

20. Sabin and Jones cite Marvin Cassman as the source of the epigraph on their course description; see Cassman, Adam Arkin, Frank Doyle, Fumiaki Katagiri, Douglas Lauffenburger, and Cynthia Stokes, *WTEC Panel Report on International Research and Development in Systems Biology* (Baltimore: World Technology Evaluation Center, 2005), 2, available at https://www.researchgate.net/profile/Adam_Arkin/publication/226941915_Data_and_Databases/links/09e415107356f39e6f000000/Data-and-Databases.pdf.

21. Jenny Sabin and Peter Lloyd Jones, "Nonlinear Systems Biology and Design: Surface Design," in *Silicon + Skin: Biological Processes and Computation,* ed. Andrew Kudless, Neri Oxman, and Marc Swackhamer (Morrisville, N.C.: Lulu Press, ACADIA, 2008), 55; Eva Jablonka and Marion Lamb, *Evolution in Four Dimensions: Genetics, Epigenetics, Behavioral, and Symbolic Variation in the History of Life* (Cambridge, Mass.: MIT Press, 2006), 113.

22. Sabin and Jones, 64.

23. Katharine Miller, "Seeing Science," *Biomedical Computation Review,* Summer 2010, 26; Martin Krzywinski and Erica Savig, "Multidimensional Data," *Nature Methods* 10, no. 7 (2013): 595.

24. See http://www.jennysabin.com/branching-morphogenesis/.

25. Another sculptural piece by Sabin, Jones, Andrew Lucia, and Annette Fierro, *Ground Substance,* was featured on the cover of the *American Journal of Pathology,* February 2010.

26. Sabin's piece was featured as the opening photograph, by Byron Smith, in Ken Johnson, "Cooper Hewitt Triennial Offers a Bold Look at 'Beauty,'" *New York Times,* February 11, 2016, available at http://www.nytimes.com/2016/02/12/arts/design/cooper-hewitt-triennial-offers-a-bold-look-at-beauty.html.

27. See Beesley's writings on the *Hylozoic* series, available at http://philipbeesleyarchitect.com/publications/digital-publications.php.

28. Sabin used a photo-luminescent yarn for this piece, per an email from her to the author, August 26, 2016.

29. Sabin and Jones, "Nonlinear Systems Biology and Design," 56.

30. Jenny Sabin, Andrew Lucia, Giffen Ott, and Simin Wang, "Prototyping Interactive Nonlinear Nano-to-Micro Scaled Material Properties and Effects at the Human Scale," in *Proceedings of the Society and Modeling International (SimAud)* (San Diego: Society for Computer Simulation International, 2014), 2.

31. Simin Wang, Andrew Lucia, and Jenny Sabin, "Simulating Nonlinear Nano-to-Micro Scaled Material Properties and Effects at the Architectural Scale," in *Proceedings of the Society*

and Modeling International (SimAud) (San Diego: Society for Computer Simulation International, 2014), 3.

32. See Michael Hansmeyer and Benjamin Dillenburger, "Dataflow," n.d., at http://digital-grotesque.com/design/. "The geometry of the grottos consist of 260 million and 1.35 billion individual faces respectively. This large amount of data cannot be adequately processed by existing CAD software. Customized algorithms were therefore developed to calculate the construction details and to convert the form into printable data." Given that they had thirty billion spatial data points, "such an enormous amount of information cannot be processed as a single entity in the computer; the geometry is loaded only where needed, streamed layer per layer."

33. Wang, Lucia, and Sabin, "Simulating Nonlinear Nano-to-Micro Scaled Material Properties and Effects," 7.

34. Wang, Lucia, and Sabin, 1.

35. Jenny Sabin, "Transformative Research Practice: Architectural Affordances and Crisis," *Journal of Architectural Education* 69, no. 1 (March 2015): 66.

36. Hyung Chul Kim and Vasilis Fthenakis, "Life Cycle Energy and Climate Change Implication of Nanotechnologies; A Critical Review," n.d., 1, posted on Center for Life Cycle Analysis at Columbia University website, available at http://www.clca.columbia.edu/244_Kim-Fthenakis-LCA-of-nanotech-revised-07-17.pdf. See also Kris de Decker, "The Monster Footprint of Digital Technology," *Low Tech Magazine,* June 2009, available at http://www.lowtechmagazine.com/2009/06/embodied-energy-of-digital-technology.html.

37. Kim and Fthenakis, 1.

38. Sabin, "Transformative Research Practice," 67.

39. Sabin, 63, 71.

5. Growing Living Buildings

1. William Myers, *BioDesign: Nature, Science, Creativity* (New York: Museum of Modern Art, 2012), 58–61.

2. For examples, see Myers, 22–61, which includes the projects Harmonia 57, Gutman Visitor Center, Root Bridges of Meghalaya, Cattedrale Vegetale, Baubotanik Tower, Lake Constance Footbridge, Bio Milano, Editt Tower, and Fab Tree Hab, among others; Bill Watts and Sean Affleck, "Living Buildings," in "Neoplasmatic Design," special issue of *AD,* ed. Marcos Cruz and Steve Pike, 78, no. 6 (November–December 2008): 78–79; and Ton Venhoeven, "Wonderwall," in "Neoplasmatic Design," special issue of *AD,* ed. Marcos Cruz and Steve Pike, 78, no. 6 (November–December 2008): 80–81.

3. Stewart Brand, "Review of *Evolution and Design of the Plant Kingdom,*" in *The Last Updated Whole Earth Catalog,* ed. Stewart Brand, 1974, 84.

4. Myers, *BioDesign,* 132–33.

5. John Schwartz, "Museum Kills Live Exhibit," *New York Times,* May 13, 2008, available at http://www.nytimes.com/2008/05/13/science/13coat.html.

6. Helen Castle, "Editorial," in "Neoplasmatic Design," special issue of *AD,* ed. Marcos Cruz and Steve Pike, 78, no. 6 (November–December 2008): 4.

7. Marcos Cruz and Steve Pike, "Neoplasmatic Design: Design Experimentation with Bio-Architectural Composites," in "Neoplasmatic Design," special issue of *AD,* ed. Marcos Cruz and Steve Pike, 78, no. 6 (November–December 2008): 8, 12.

8. Marcos Cruz, "Synthetic Neoplasms," in "Neoplasmatic Design," special issue of *AD,* ed. Marcos Cruz and Steve Pike, 78, no. 6 (November–December 2008): 42.

9. See Dennis Dollens, *Digital–Botanic Architecture* (Santa Fe, N.M.: SITES Books / ESARQ-UIC, 2005), 57–67; Castle, "Editorial," 4; Cruz and Pike, "Neoplasmatic Design," 6, 12, 15; Oron Catts and Ionat Zurr, "Growing Semi-Living Structures: Concepts and Practices for the Use of Tissue Technologies for Non-Medical Purposes," in "Neoplasmatic Design," special issue of *AD,* ed. Marcos Cruz and Steve Pike, 78, no. 6 (November–December 2008): 30–35; Oron Catts and Ionat Zurr, "The Vitality of Matter and the Instrumentalisation of Life," in "The Innovation

Imperative: Architectures of Vitality," special issue of *AD,* ed. Pia Ednie-Brown, Mark Burry, and Andrew Burrow, 83, no. 1 (January–February 2013): 70–75.

10. Conversation between Oron Catts and the author, February 2011, Dublin.

11. Dollens, *Digital–Botanic Architecture,* 58.

12. If one synthesizes the DNA sequence from scratch using DNA synthesis, then usually the process is considered to fall under synthetic biology rather than genetic engineering. However, the new technique of CRISPR/Cas9 is used in both approaches.

13. Gretchen Reynolds, "Artificial Wombs: Will We Grow Babies outside Their Mother's Bodies?" *Popular Science,* August 1, 2005, available at http://www.popsci.com/scitech/article/2005-08/artificial-wombs.

14. See their firm's website, http://hwkn.com/. For Matthias Hollwich's and Marc Kushner's video *Econic Design,* see http://www.youtube.com/watch?v=_AEx9U7x860.

15. Rachel Armstrong, "Artificial Evolution: A Hands-Off Approach for Architects," in "Neoplasmatic Design," special issue of *AD,* ed. Marcos Cruz and Steve Pike, 78, no. 6 (November–December 2008): 83.

16. On sustainability as a goal, or partial goal, see Cruz and Pike, "Neoplasmatic Design," 12–13.

17. Jennifer Doudna and Emanuelle Charpentier, "The New Frontier of Genome Engineering with CRISPR/Cas9," *Science* 346, no. 6213 (November 28, 2014): 1077, available at http://science.sciencemag.org/content/346/6213/1258096; Henriette O'Geen, Abigail Yu, and David Segal, "How Specific Is CRISPR/Cas9 Really?" *Current Opinion in Chemical Biology* 29 (2015): 72–78; and Haifeng Wang, Marie La Russa, and Lei Qi, "CRISPR/Cas9 in Genome Editing and Beyond," *Annual Review of Biochemistry* 85 (2016): 227–64.

18. Cruz and Pike, "Neoplasmatic Design," 8–9.

19. Marcos Cruz, "Designer Surgeons," in "Neoplasmatic Design," special issue of *AD,* ed. Marcos Cruz and Steve Pike, 78, no. 6 (November–December 2008): 46–51.

20. Oron Catts and Ionat Zurr, "Semi-Living Art," in *Signs of Life: Bio Art and Beyond,* ed. Eduardo Kac (Cambridge, Mass: MIT Press, 2007), 231–48. See also Catts and Zurr, "Growing Semi-Living Structures," 32.

21. Catts and Zurr, "Semi-Living Art," 233–34.

22. Catts and Zurr.

23. They critique capitalism and extreme profit-taking in Ionat Zurr and Oron Catts, "Are the Semi-Living Semi-Good or Semi-Evil?" *Technoetic Arts* 1, no. 1 (2003): 60, and discuss Margulis's theory of endosymbiogenesis and cooperative evolution, in contrast to Darwinian competitive "survival of the fittest" (51). Catts, in an email to the author (August 26, 2016), stated that the original logo he designed for SymbioticA in 1999 was a direct reference to endosymbiogenesis, where one cell swallows another to create a new cooperative function, which is how Margulis describes the origin of eukaryotic cells from the fusion of two prokaryotic cells.

24. For example, Catts has just been appointed as professor of contestable design at the Royal College of Art in 2016. Zurr and he describe their uneasiness in "Are the Semi-Living Semi-Good or Semi-Evil?" 58–60.

25. Catts and Zurr, "Semi-Living Art," 237–43. They also discuss the in vitro meat piece in Zurr and Catts, "Are the Semi-Living Semi-Good or Semi-Evil?" 48.

26. Catts and Zurr, "Growing Semi-Living Structures," 34.

27. Dollens, *Digital–Botanic Architecture,* 62.

28. Dollens, 62–63.

29. Dollens, 66.

30. Catts and Zurr, "Semi-Living Art," 237–43.

31. On thickness of tissue and diffusability of oxygen and nutrients, see Hyun-Wook Kang, Sang Jin Lee, In Kap Ko, Carlos Kengla, James Yoo, and Anthony Atala, "A 3D Bioprinting System to Produce Human-Scale Tissue Constructs with Structural Integrity," *Nature Biotechnology* 34, no. 3 (March 2016): 312.

32. On the sugar or carbohydrate glass method, see Jordan Miller, Kelly Stevens, Michael

Yang, Brendon Baker, Duc-Huy Nguyen, Daniel Cohen, Estevan Toro, Alice Chen, Peter Galie, Xiang Yu, Ritika Chaturvedi, Sangeeta Bhatia, and Christopher Chen, "Rapid Casting of Patterned Vascular Networks for Perfusable Engineered Three-Dimensional Tissues," *Nature Materials* 11, no. 9 (2012): 768–74. The other method uses "sacrificial Pluronic F-127 hydrogel"; see Kang et al., "3D Bioprinting System," 312–19.

33. David Kolesky, Kimberly Homan, Mark Skylar-Scott, and Jennifer Lewis, "Three-Dimensional Bioprinting of Thick Vascularized Tissues," *Proceedings of the National Academy of Sciences* 113, no. 12 (2016): 3179–84.

34. See William Harris, "How 3-D Bioprinting Works," n.d., available at http://health.howstuffworks.com/medicine/modern-technology/3-d-bioprinting1.htm. Wei Sun of the Drexel University Computer-Aided Tissue Engineering (CATE) laboratory was an innovator in "direct cell writing"; conversation of Wei Sun with the author in early 2009.

35. Other methods exist as well; see Christian Mandrycky, Zongjie Wang, Keekyoung Kim, and Deok-Ho Kim, "3D Bioprinting for Engineering Complex Tissues," *Biotechnology Advances* 34 (2016): 423. This article offers good overview of the state of current bioprinting technologies. See also Ibrahim Ozbolat and Monika Hospodiuk, "Current Advances and Future Perspectives in Extrusion-Based Bioprinting," *Biomaterials* 76 (2016): 321–43; Kang et al., "3D Bioprinting System," for their "integrated tissue-organ printer" approach; and Yin Yu, Kazim Moncal, Jianqiang Li, Weijie Peng, Iris Rivero, James Martin, and Ibrahim Ozbolat, "Three-Dimensional Bioprinting Using Self-Assembling Scalable Scaffold-Free 'Tissue Strands' as a New Bioink," *Scientific Reports* 6, article no. 28714 (June 27, 2016), available at http://www.nature.com/articles/srep28714. Also, it is also common to use different types of stem cells and then cause them to differentiate post-printing via chemical cues into the desired cells rather than printing different types at the outset.

36. See Kang et al., "3D Bioprinting System," 315.

37. Mandrycky et al., "3D Bioprinting for Engineering Complex Tissues," 423.

38. Cor van der Weele and Johannes Tramper, "Cultured Meat: Every Village Its Own Factory?" *Trends in Biotechnology* 32, no. 6 (June 2014): 294–96.

39. On modular 3-D printing, see the work of Virginia San Fratello and Ronald Rael through their practice Rael San Fratello, available at http://www.rael-sanfratello.com/; and also Emerging Objects, available at http://www.emergingobjects.com/.

40. See "Creating a Beating Heart in a Lab," December 22, 2009, available at http://www.youtube.com/watch?v=j9XzN0-TQZc; also "New Heart Built with Stem Cells," April 27, 2008, available at http://www.youtube.com/watch?v=j9hEFUpTVPA.

41. Searches in the online academic database Biosis on August 27, 2016, for "tissue engineering" and "epigenetics" returned only seventy-four articles; searching for "genetic engineering" and "epigenetics" returned only seventy-one; and searches for "synthetic biology" and "epigenetics" returned only twenty-three. The deep significance of epigenetic factors as gene regulators and their important role in maintaining cellular architecture during the use of biotechnologies establishes a significant hurdle to be overcome, once it is acknowledged. It seems the process is only yet beginning. In tissue engineering, the use of stem cells with the goal of later differentiation requires knowledge of the epigenetic signals that lead to particular paths of differentiation. Also, when cells are being cultured in vitro, their epigenetic signals can destabilize over time, so the longer a tissue is being cultured, the greater the chance for epigenetic changes to cell identity and function prior to implantation. See Serena Redaelli, Angela Bentivegna, Dana Foudah, Mariorosaria Miloso, Juliana Redondo, Gabriele Riva, Simona Baronchelli, Leda Dalpra, and Giovanni Tredici, "From Cytogenomic to Epigenomic Profiles: Monitoring the Biologic Behavior of In Vitro Cultured Human Bone Marrow Mesenchymal Stem Cells," *Stem Cell Research and Therapy* 3, no. 47 (2012): 17 pp.; Zhilong Li, Chenxiong Liu, Zhenhua Xie, Pengyue Song, Robert Zhao, Ling Guo, Zhigang Liu, and Yaojiong Wu, "Epigenetic Dysregulation in Mesenchymal Stem Cell Aging and Spontaneous Differentiation," *PLoS ONE* 6, no. 6 (June 2011): e20526; Biao Huang, Gang Li, and Xiao Hua Jiang, "Fate Determination in Mesenchymal Stem Cells: A Perspective from Histone-Modifying Enzymes," *Stem Cell Research and*

Therapy 6, no. 35 (2015): 9 pp.; and Maggie Zi Chow, Kenneth Boheler, and Ronald Li, "Human Pluripotent Stem Cell-Derived Cardiomyocytes for Heart Regeneration, Drug Discovery, and Disease Modeling: From the Genetic, Epigenetic, and Tissue Modeling Perspectives," *Stem Cell Research and Therapy* 4, no. 97 (2013): 13 pp.

42. Matias del Campo and Sandra Manninger, "Speculations on Tissue Engineering and Architecture," in *Silicon + Skin: Biological Processes and Computation,* ed. Andrew Kudless, Neri Oxman, and Marc Swackhamer (Morrisville, N.C.: Lulu Press, 2008), 84.

43. del Campo and Manninger, 86.

44. To learn the techniques of engineering synthetic biology, design student Jonny Hoolko and I worked for six months in Marc Facciotti's TEAM Molecular Prototyping and BioInnovation Laboratory at the University of California at Davis in 2015. Jonny is a lighting designer who studied LED color tuning for his undergraduate honors thesis; he wanted to understand bioluminescence better as a lighting option because organisms emit almost zero heat with it. We inserted the genes of fireflies and *Vibrio fischerii* into *Escherichia coli* in order to learn the techniques of synthetic biology as a potential tool for bio-based lighting design. While we succeeded at producing colored light in many combinations, the light was so dim and short-lived that it was difficult to photograph. This does not bode well for simple translation into the lighting industry.

45. For more on the interrelation of tissue form and function, see the discussion in this book in chapters 3 and 4, particularly the work of Mina Bissell and Peter Lloyd Jones.

46. Developments in epigenomics are discussed in the latter part of chapter 3 of this book. On the NIH Roadmap Epigenomics Mapping Consortium, see http://www.roadmapepigenomics.org/.

47. Catts and Zurr, "Vitality of Matter and the Instrumentalisation of Life," 72.

48. Catts and Zurr, "The Ethics of the Experiential Engagement with the Manipulation of Life," in *Tactical Biopolitics: Art, Activism, and Technoscience,* ed. Beatriz da Costa and Kavita Philip (Cambridge, Mass.: MIT Press, 2008), 141n19. See also Zhanqiu Yang and Hai-Rong Xiong, "Culture Conditions and Types of Growth Media for Mammalian Cells," in *Biomedical Tissue Culture* (London: Intech, 2012), 4–5, available at http://cdn.intechopen.com/pdfs/40247/InTech-Culture_conditions_and_types_of_growth_media_for_mammalian_cells.pdf. They write under the section "Natural Medium," in the list of requirements for nutrient media, that "today, serum is still the widely used natural medium. . . . Serum can derive from different animals. Current serum used in tissue culture is cattle serum. Human serum, horse serum is used for some specific cells. Cattle serum has several advantages as used in cell culture: adequate resource, mature preparation technique, long application time. Cattle serum includes bovine calf serum, newborn calf serum, and fetal bovine serum. Take sample for cattle serum from Gibco Life Technologies Company, fetal bovine serum derives from caesarean section fetal bovine; newborn calf serum comes from newborn calf born within 24h; bovine calf serum comes from calf with 10 to 30 days. Fetal bovine serum has highest quality because the fetal bovine doesn't expose to outside environment and has lowest antibodies and complement."

49. Alok Jha, "Synthetic Meat: How the World's Costliest Burger Made It to the Plate," *The Guardian,* August 5, 2013, http://www.theguardian.com/science/2013/aug/05/synthetic-meat-burger-stem-cells, quoting "Julian Savulescu, professor of practical ethics at the University of Oxford." The scientist creating the synthetic meat featured in this article is Dr. Mark Post at Maastricht University in the Netherlands.

50. Daniel Grushkin, "Meet the Woman Who Wants to Grow Clothing in a Lab," *Popular Science,* February 17, 2015, available at http://www.popsci.com/meet-woman-who-wants-growing-clothing-lab; on Zoa and their process of engineering yeast cells to produce collagen, see Astrid Wendlandt, "Fashion's Interest in Alternative Fabrics Keeps Growing," *New York Times,* November 12, 2017, available at http://www.nytimes.com/2017/11/12/style/alternative-fabrics-sustainability-recycling.html; and Mary Page Bailey, "Protein Engineering Yields Animal-Free Leather," *Chemical Engineering,* May 1, 2018, available at http://www.chemengonline.com/protein-engineering-yields-animal-free-leather/.

51. Catts and Zurr, "Ethics of the Experiential Engagement with the Manipulation of Life," 135.

52. See "First Self-Replicating Synthetic Bacterial Cell," J. Craig Venter Institute, May 20, 2010, at https://www.jcvi.org/first-self-replicating-synthetic-bacterial-cell-constructed-j%C2%A0craig-venter-institute-researchers; Ewen Calloway, "'Minimal' Cell Raises Stakes in Race to Harness Synthetic Life," *Nature* 531, no. 7596 (March 24, 2016), available at http://www.nature.com/news/minimal-cell-raises-stakes-in-race-to-harness-synthetic-life-1.19633; Catts and Zurr, "Vitality of Matter and the Instrumentalisation of Life," 72–73.

53. Paul Rothemund, "Casting Spells with DNA," October 18, 2007, available at http://www.youtube.com/watch?v=Yn1snjEtk54.

54. Paola Antonelli, *Design and the Elastic Mind* (New York: Museum of Modern Art, 2008), 115.

55. Zurr and Catts, "Are the Semi-Living Semi-Good or Semi-Evil?" 47–49.

56. Zurr and Catts, 51.

57. Zurr and Catts, 51.

58. Email from Catts to the author, August 26, 2016.

59. Zurr and Catts, "Are the Semi-Living Semi-Good or Semi-Evil?" 51.

60. Giorgio Bernardi, "Chromosome Architecture and Genome Organization," *PLoS ONE* 10, no. 11 (November 30, 2015): e0143739; Diego Cattoni, Alessandro Valeri, Antoine Le Gall, and Marcelo Nollmann, "A Matter of Scale: How Emerging Technologies Are Redefining Our View of Chromosome Architecture," *Trends in Genetics* 31, no. 8 (August 2015): 454–64; Jerod Ptacin and Lucy Shapiro, "Chromosome Architecture Is a Key Element of Bacterial Cellular Organization," *Cellular Microbiology* 15, no. 1 (January 2013): 45–52.

61. For more information about ENCODE and epigenetics, see chapter 3 of this book. The review is that of O'Geen, Yu, and Segal, "How Specific Is CRISPR/Cas9 Really?" 76.

62. See the discussion of this in chapter 4 of this book; and Evelyn Fox Keller, "The Post genomic Genome," in *Postgenomics: Perspectives on Biology after the Genome,* ed. Sarah Richardson and Hallam Stevens (Durham, N.C.: Duke University Press, 2015), 18–20.

63. Conversation between Matthias Hollwich and the author, February 2009, Philadelphia.

64. Hollwich and Kushner, *Econic Design.*

65. See http://architecture2030.org/buildings_problem_why/, which cites data from a 2012 study by the U.S. Energy Information Administration.

66. Hollwich and Kushner, *Econic Design.*

67. Regarding the name MEtreePOLIS, take note of the emphases, lest you think Hollwich and Kushner are playing it straight. They could have spelled it "meTREEpolis," but that would conform to the text and image of most "sustainability" marketing campaigns, suggesting a specious reformed humility in light of newfound recognition of the dominance of nature over the self and the fabric of the city. Rather, they hold firmly to their initial claim that since humans won't change their habits to be in touch with the environment, architects and other designers of the future "will use technology to change nature to be in tune with us." They therefore accentuate the "ME" and the "POLIS," since all trees are actually gone, and nature has been replaced with "enhanced" nature, seemingly dictated and controlled by the economic and environmental needs of a self-centered city-state.

68. See http://www.uic.es/en/esarq/studies.

69. Alberto Estévez, "Genetic Architecture: New Ecologic-Environmental Architectural Design and New Cybernetic-Digital Architectural Design," in *Genetic Architectures,* ed. Alberto T. Estévez (Santa Fe, N.M.: SITES Books / ESARQ-UIC, 2003), 17.

70. Estévez, 11.

71. Alberto Estévez, "Biomorphic Architecture: First History of Genetic Architecture or, Is Genetic Architecture Biomorphic?" in *Genetic Architectures II,* ed. Alberto T. Estévez (Santa Fe, N.M.: SITES Books / ESARQ-UIC, 2005), 74.

72. Estévez, "Genetic Architecture," 17, 7.

73. Estévez, "Biomorphic Architecture," 74.

74. Estévez, "Genetic Architecture," 9, 17.

75. Alberto Estévez, "Genetic Architectures: New Bio and Digital Techniques," in *Genetic Architectures III: New Bio and Digital Techniques,* ed. Alberto Estévez (Santa Fe, N.M.: SITES Books / ESARQ-UIC, 2009), 26.

76. On digital topology, see chapter 4; as well as David Depew, "From Heat Engines to Digital Printouts: A Tropology of the Organism from the Victorian Era to the Human Genome Project," in *Memory Bytes: History, Technology, and Digital Culture,* ed. Lauren Rabinowitz and Abraham Geil (Durham, N.C.: Duke University Press, 2003), 47–75.

77. See http://www.uic.es/en/research-groups/genetic-architecture.

78. See http://www.uic.es/en/research-groups/genetic-architecture.

79. Agustí Fontarnau, "Genetics Fundamentals," in *Genetic Architectures III: New Bio and Digital Techniques,* ed. Alberto Estévez (Santa Fe, N.M.: SITES Books / ESARQ-UIC, 2009), 121.

80. See the brochure at http://www.uic.es/sites/default/files/Folletos/university_masters_degree_in_biodigital_architecture.pdf; and the website, under the section "More" where the section "Labs" only contains information about the "Equipment and Digital Manufacturing Lab," at http://www.biodigitalarchitecture.com/labs.html.

81. Estévez, "Genetic Architecture," 15, 17.

82. Estévez, 17.

83. Estévez, 5.

84. Estévez, "Biomorphic Architecture," 56.

85. del Campo and Manninger, "Speculations on Tissue Engineering and Architecture," 86.

86. Alberto Estévez with Maria Serer, *Genetic Barcelona Pavilion* (2007), in *Genetic Architectures III: New Bio and Digital Techniques,* ed. Alberto Estévez (Santa Fe, N.M.: SITES Books / ESARQ-UIC, 2009), 20.

87. Estévez, "Genetic Architecture," 15, 17.

88. Estévez, "Biomorphic Architecture," 71–72.

89. Estévez, 56–57. He also wrote, in 2003, "Who will be the new Christopher Columbus? Who will be the first to achieve manmade software identical to natural software, to DNA, cloning software that architects can use to simulate, graphically, the design of genetic houses with the same strings of information, the same ones and zeros, that nature uses?" See Estévez, "Genetic Architecture," 17.

90. Estévez, "Genetic Architecture," 11, 17; Estévez, "Biomorphic Architecture," 74.

91. Steve Pike, "Manipulation and Control of Micro-Organic Matter in Architecture," in "Neoplasmatic Design," special issue of *AD,* ed. Marcos Cruz and Steve Pike, 78, no. 6 (November–December 2008): 18.

92. On the involuntary sterilization of Native American women in the 1960s and 1970s, see Jane Lawrence, "The Indian Health Service and the Sterilization of Native American Women," *American Indian Quarterly* 24, no. 3 (Summer 2000): 400–419; Gregory Rutecki, "Forced Sterilization of Native Americans: Later Twentieth Century Physician Cooperation with National Eugenic Policies?" *Ethics and Medicine* 27, no. 1 (Spring 2011): 32–43.

93. For a lengthier analysis of *Econic Design,* see Christina Cogdell, "Tearing Down the Grid," *Design and Culture* 3, no. 1 (2011): 75–84.

94. Joseph Strauss, "Patents on Biomaterial: A New Colonialism or a Means for Technology Transfer and Benefit-Sharing?" in *Bioethics for a Small World,* ed. Felix Thiele and Richard Ashcroft (Berlin: Springer, 2005), 45–72; John Merson, "Bio-Prospecting or Bio-Piracy: Intellectual Property Rights and Biodiversity in a Colonial and Postcolonial Context," *Osiris—Nature and Empire: Science and the Colonial Enterprise,* 2nd ser., 15 (2000): 282–96; Stuart Newman, "The Role of Genetic Reductionism in Biocolonialism," *Peace Review* 12, no. 4 (2000): 517–24; and Katy Moran, Steven King, and Thomas Carlson, "Biodiversity Prospecting: Lessons and Prospects," *Annual Review of Anthropology* 30 (2001): 505–26.

95. Statistics and quote from Wikipedia, s.v. "Kudzu," http://en.wikipedia.org/wiki/kudzu, last modified April 26, 2018.

96. All quotes come from the narrative in the video; see Hollwich and Kushner, *Econic Design*.

97. Zurr and Catts, "Are the Semi-Living Semi-Good or Semi-Evil?" 51.

98. Zurr and Catts, 59. They continue: "There are many issues that have to be resolved by humanity as a whole before we can proceed with large-scale exploitation of modified/designed living biological systems. This is of grave concern as decisions which are being made now will determine the directions in which exploitation of living systems take. It is of particular concern as we are entering an era of conflict and intolerance to the other, coupled with an extreme form of capitalism and profit taking" (60). On this theme, see also James Shapiro, "Bacteria Are Small but Not Stupid: Cognition, Natural Genetic Engineering, and Socio-Bacteriology," *Studies in the History and Philosophy of Biological and Biomedical Science* 38 (2007): 807–19.

99. Cruz and Pike, "Neoplasmatic Design," 13.

100. Cruz and Pike, 14.

101. Catts and Zurr, "Growing Semi-Living Structures," 32–33, italics added.

102. Catts and Zurr, "Vitality of Matter and the Instrumentalisation of Life," 75, italics added.

103. Zurr and Catts, "Are the Semi-Living Semi-Good or Semi-Evil?" 59.

104. On the love of dinosaurs in the synthetic biology community and company known as Ginkgo Bioworks, see Luis Campos, "Jurassic Ark: Or, A Menagerie of Methods for Thinking Historically about De-Extinction," paper presented at the NeoLife 2015 Conference of the Society for Literature, Science, and Art, Perth, Australia, October 2, 2015.

105. E. M. Meyerowitz, "Plants Compared to Animals: The Broadest Comparative Study of Development," *Science* 295, no. 5559 (2002): 1482–85. Scientists even hotly debate whether naturally occurring chimeras are the fusion of two animal species. See Donald Williamson, "The Origins of Larvae," *American Scientist* 95, no. 6 (November–December 2007): 509; and rebuttals by Michael Hart, Richard Strathmann, and Jonathan Allen, "Whence Larvae," *American Scientist* 96, no. 2 (March–April 2008): 91.

106. Sean Carroll, *Endless Forms Most Beautiful: The New Science of Evo Devo* (New York: Norton, 2005).

107. T. J. Clark, *Picasso and Truth: From Cubism to Guernica* (Princeton, N.J.; Princeton University Press, 2013), 116–17.

108. Castle, "Editorial," 4. This was also a problem with the Museum of Modern Art exhibition *Design and the Elastic Mind* (2008) in my opinion. See my review, Christina Cogdell, "Design and the Elastic Mind, Museum of Modern Art (Spring 2008)," *Design Issues* 25, no. 3 (Summer 2009): 92–101.

6. "Protocell" Architecture and SynBioDesign

1. On the pursuit of protocells characterized as the creation of "wet artificial life," see Steen Rasmussen, Mark Bedau, Liaohai Chen, David Deamer, David Krakauer, Norman Packard, and Peter Stadler, eds., *Protocells: Bridging Nonliving and Living Matter* (Cambridge, Mass.: MIT Press, 2009), xvii. Here also the authors claim, "The holy grail of wet artificial life is the construction of protocells."

2. Peter Stadler and Bärbel Stadler, "Replicator Dynamics in Protocells," in *Protocells: Bridging Nonliving and Living Matter,* ed. Steen Rasmussen, Mark Bedau, Liaohai Chen, David Deamer, David Krakauer, Norman Packard, and Peter Stadler (Cambridge, Mass.: MIT Press, 2009), 317, 327; Rasmussen et al., *Protocells,* xvii.

3. Ewen Calloway, "'Minimal' Cell Raises Stakes in Race to Harness Synthetic Life," *Nature* 531, no. 7596 (March 24, 2016), available at http://www.nature.com/news/minimal-cell-raises-stakes-in-race-to-harness-synthetic-life-1.19633.

4. Clyde Hutchison III, Ray-Yuan Chuang, Vladimir Noskov, Nacyra Assad-Garcia, Thomas Deerinck, Mark Ellisman, John Gill, Krishna Kannan, Bogumil Karas, Li Ma, James Pelletier, Zhi-Qing Qi, R. Alexander Richter, Elizabeth Strychalski, Lijie Sun, Yo Suzuki, Billyana Tsvetanova, Kim Wise, Hamilton Smith, John Glass, Chuck Merryman, Daniel Gibson,

and J. Craig Venter, "Design and Synthesis of a Minimal Bacterial Genome," *Science* 351, no. 6280 (March 25, 2016): 1414.

5. Rasmussen et al., *Protocells,* xvii.

6. Rasmussen et al., xv.

7. Rachel Armstrong, "Self-Repairing Architecture," June 24, 2010, *Next Nature Network,* available at https://www.nextnature.net/2010/06/self–repairing-architecture/.

8. See Rachel Armstrong's TED talk "Architecture that Repairs Itself," July 2009, at http://www.ted.com/talks/rachel_armstrong_architecture_that_repairs_itself.

9. Philip Beesley and Rachel Armstrong, "Soil and Protoplasm: The Hylozoic Ground Project," in "Protocell Architecture," special issue of *AD,* ed. Neil Spiller and Rachel Armstrong, 81, no. 2 (March–April 2011): 86.

10. Armstrong, "Self-Repairing Architecture."

11. Armstrong.

12. Armstrong.

13. David Benjamin and Fernan Federici, "Bio Logic," in *Synthetic Aesthetics: Investigating Synthetic Biology's Designs on Nature,* ed. Alexandra Daisy Ginsberg, Jane Calvert, Pablo Schyfter, Alistair Elfick, and Drew Endy (Cambridge, Mass.: MIT Press, 2014), 143–54.

14. Williams Myers's interview with David Benjamin in Myers, *BioDesign: Nature, Science, Creativity* (New York: Museum of Modern Art, 2012), 257.

15. On Benjamin's *Hy-Fi,* see http://momaps1.org/yap/view/17. See also Blaine Brownell, "David Benjamin's Building Blocks," *Architect* 103, no. 3 (2014): 22; and "Organic BioBrick Made from Mushrooms Make for Cool Construction," *American Ceramic Society Bulletin* 93, no. 8 (August 28, 2014): 6–7.

16. See Phil Ross's website, http://www.mycoworks.com.

17. Rasmussen et al., *Protocells,* xv.

18. Timothy Gardner, Charles Cantor, and James Collins, "Construction of a Genetic Toggle Switch in *Escherichia coli,*" *Nature* 403 (January 20, 2000): 339–42. In the same issue, see Michael Elowitz and Stanislas Leibler, "A Synthetic Oscillatory Network of Transcriptional Regulators," 335–38.

19. Alexandrine Froger and James Hall, "Transformation of Plasmid DNA into *E. coli* Using the Heat Shock Method," *Journal of Visualized Experiments* 6 (2007): 253, available at http://www.ncbi.nlm.nih.gov/pmc/articles/PMC2557105/. This was also the process that Jonny Hoolko and I used in a lab at UC Davis when I learned basic techniques of engineering synthetic biology by inserting the genes for bioluminescence from fireflies and *Vibrio fischerii* into *E. coli* (Spring 2015).

20. Luis Campos, "The BioBrick Road," *BioSocieties* 7, no. 2 (2012): 115–39. Campos critiques the imprecision of the definition, methodology, and actuality of BioBricks, the fundamental gene sequences available through the Registry of Standard Biological Parts. He shows that, at least as of 2012, they are anything but "standard" (standardized), as the precursor and following sequences before and after the desired gene sequence are not standardized, and therefore actually function differently in different organisms to which they are inserted.

21. A "part" has a promoter, ribosome binding site, start codon, DNA protein coding sequence, stop codon, and terminator. These are the six major parts of a "transcriptional unit." For websites on the parts registry, see http://parts.igem.org/Help:An_Introduction_to_BioBricks and http://parts.igem.org/Catalog. There is also now a BioBricks Foundation, whose history is outlined at http://biobricks.org/biobricks-history/.

22. Alistair Elfick and Drew Endy, "Synthetic Biology: What It Is and Why It Matters," in *Synthetic Aesthetics: Investigating Synthetic Biology's Designs on Nature,* ed. Alexandra Daisy Ginsbert, Jane Calvert, Pablo Schyfter, Alistair Elfick, and Drew Endy (Cambridge, Mass.: MIT Press, 2014), 19.

23. Elfick and Endy, 19.

24. Elfick and Endy, 19–20.

25. Alexandra Daisy Ginsberg, "Design as the Machines Come to Life," in *Synthetic Aesthetics:*

Investigating Synthetic Biology's Designs on Nature, ed. Alexandra Daisy Ginsberg, Jane Calvert, Pablo Schyfter, Alistair Elfick, and Drew Endy (Cambridge, Mass.: MIT Press, 2014), 41, 52.

26. On the growing national and international bioeconomy, see the White House, *National Bioeconomy Blueprint* (Washington, D.C.: Government Printing Office, 2012), available at http://obamawhitehouse.archives.gov/sites/default/files/microsites/ostp/national_bioeconomy_blueprint_april_2012.pdf; Manfred Kircher, "The Emerging Bioeconomy: Industrial Drivers, Global Impact, and International Strategies," *Industrial Biotechnology* 10, no. 1 (February 2014): 11–18.

27. These are critiqued in Campos, "BioBrick Road."

28. Two notable exhibitions including these works, cited throughout this book, are Paola Antonelli's *Design and the Elastic Mind* (New York: Museum of Modern Art, 2008); and Myers's *BioDesign.* More recently, the Synthetic Aesthetics research project (2009–12) funded by the National Science Foundation (United States) and the Engineering and Physical Science Research Council (United Kingdom), and its resultant book—Alexandra Daisy Ginsberg, Jane Calvert, Pablo Schyfter, Alistair Elfick, and Drew Endy, eds., *Synthetic Aesthetics: Investigating Synthetic Biology's Designs on Nature* (Cambridge, Mass.: MIT Press, 2014)—features collaborative projects between designers and scientists exploring the potentials of synbiodesign.

29. Alexandra Daisy Ginsberg, "Transgressing Biological Boundaries," in *Synthetic Aesthetics: Investigating Synthetic Biology's Designs on Nature,* ed. Alexandra Daisy Ginsberg, Jane Calvert, Pablo Schyfter, Alistair Elfick, and Drew Endy (Cambridge, Mass.: MIT Press, 2014), 299.

30. See http://design-interactions.rca.ac.uk/studio/explore/synthetic-biology.

31. Michael Burton, *Nanotopia* and *Future Farm,* 2006–7, available at http://www.michael-burton.co.uk/HTML/nanotopia.htm and http://www.michael-burton.co.uk/HTML/future_farm.htm. See also Antonelli, *Design and the Elastic Mind,* 107–8. Burton's work is also discussed in Anthony Dunne, "Design for Debate," in "Neoplasmatic Design," special issue of *AD,* ed. Marcos Cruz and Steve Pike, 78, no. 6 (November–December 2008): 90–93.

32. See http://design-interactions.rca.ac.uk/studio/alexandra-daisy-ginsberg/designing-for-the-sixth-extinction-2013-15.

33. Alexandra Daisy Ginsberg, "Design Evolution," in *Synthetic Aesthetics: Investigating Synthetic Biology's Designs on Nature,* eds. Alexandra Daisy Ginsberg, Jane Calvert, Pablo Schyfter, Alistair Elfick, and Drew Endy (Cambridge, Mass.: MIT Press, 2014), 130.

34. See "Design Fictions," 2011, available at http://natsaiaudrey.co.uk/DESIGN-FICTIONS-Posthumanity-in-the-Age-of-Synthetics; Myers, *BioDesign,* 176.

35. Myers, 172.

36. See Amy Congdon, *Biological Atelier,* n.d., at http://postextiles.com/?p=372.

37. Myers, *BioDesign,* 267. See Sawa's own website at http://algaeprinting.com/.

38. Although Sawa employs the term "artificial cell," which could perhaps be something other than a protocell, her use of the past tense likely is based on confusion raised by Armstrong's use of "protocell" to describe pre-protocells in her work.

39. On kill switches for use by design, see Ginsberg, "Design Evolution," 113–14.

40. Myers, *BioDesign,* 267.

41. Myers, 68, 123.

42. Myers, 186.

43. Myers, 126.

44. Olga Zhaxybayeva and W. Ford Doolittle, "Lateral Gene Transfer," *Current Biology* 21, no. 7 (April 12, 2011): R242–46, available at http://www.cell.com/current-biology/abstract/S0960-9822(11)00101-1.

45. Ginsberg, "Design as the Machines Come to Life," 54; Ginsberg, "Transgressing Biological Boundaries," 288.

46. Rasmussen et al., *Protocells,* xiv, caption for figure I.1.

47. Pablo Razeto-Barry, "Autopoiesis 40 Years Later: A Review and a Reformulation," *Origins of Life and Evolution of Biospheres* 42 (2012): 543–67; Pier Luigi Luisi, "Autopoiesis: A Review and a Reappraisal," *Naturwissenschaften* 90 (2003): 49–59.

48. Luisi states, "An autopoietic unit is a system that is capable of self-sustaining owing to an inner network of reactions that re-generate all the system's components" (51).

49. Luisi, 52.

50. Tibor Gánti first proposed the chemoton concept in "Organization of Chemical Reactions into Dividing and Metabolizing Units: The Chemotons," *BioSystems* 7 (1975): 15–21. Quote here from Eors Szathmary, Mauro Santos, and Chrisantha Fernando, "Evolutionary Potential and Requirements for Minimal Protocells," *Top Currents in Chemistry* 259 (2005): 170. The editors of Rasmussen et al., *Protocells,* xiv, use Gánti's chemoton concept as their basic definition of a protocell.

51. Frank Harold, "Molecules into Cells: Specifying Spatial Architecture," *Microbiology and Molecular Biology Reviews* 69, no. 4 (2005): 544.

52. Alicja Dzieciol and Stephen Mann, "Designs for Life: Protocells Models in the Laboratory," *Chemical Society Reviews* 42 (2012): 80.

53. Dzieciol and Mann, 80. The authors specify the characteristics of living cells as sharing a "semi-permeable membrane . . . genetic information . . . template polymerization to copy hereditary information . . . transcription of the genetic information stored in DNA into RNA, and translation of RNA into proteins (the 'central dogma') . . . metabolism . . . [and] homeostasis."

54. Ricard Sole, Andrea Munteanu, Carlos Rodriguez-Caso, and Javier Macia, "Synthetic Protocell Biology: From Reproduction to Computation," *Philosophical Transactions of the Royal Society B* 362 (2007): 1727–39. See also Daniel Hammer and Neha Kamat, "Towards and Artificial Cell," *Federation of European Biochemical Societies Letters* 586 (2012): 2882–90.

55. Ian Sample, "DNA Alternative Created by Scientists," *The Guardian,* April 19, 2012, available at http://www.theguardian.com/science/2012/apr/19/dna-alternative-xnas-science-genetics; Ginsberg, "Design as the Machines Come to Life," 54.

56. John Maynard Smith and Eors Szathmary, *The Major Transitions in Evolution* (Oxford, U.K.: Oxford University Press, 1995), 100–101.

57. A founding text on "The Origin of Protocells" is chapter 7 in Smith and Szathmary, 98–118. See also See Irene Chen and Peter Walde, "From Self-Assembled Vesicles to Protocells," *Cold Spring Harbor Perspectives in Biology* 2, no. 7 (July 2010): a002170, available at http://cshperspectives.cshlp.org/content/2/7/a002170.full.

58. Rasmussen et al., *Protocells*; Mark Bedau, John McCaskill, Norman Packard, and Steen Rasmussen, "Living Technology: Exploiting Life's Principles in Technology," *Artificial Life* 16 (2010): 89–97.

59. Martin Hanczyc, "Structure and the Synthesis of Life," in "Protocell Architecture," special issue of *AD,* ed. Neil Spiller and Rachel Armstrong, 81, no. 2 (March–April 2011): 31.

60. Bedau et al., "Living Technology," 91.

61. Bedau et al., 91.

62. Bedau et al., 91.

63. Bedau et al., 91.

64. Bedau et al., 91.

65. Philip Beesley, ed., *Near-Living Architecture: Works in Progress from the Hylozoic Ground Collaboration, 2011–2013* (Toronto: Riverside Architectural Press, 2014).

66. Rasmussen et al., *Protocells,* xvii.

67. Beesley, *Near-Living Architecture,* 113.

68. Hanczyc, "Structure and the Synthesis of Life," 31.

69. Rachel Armstrong, "How Protocells Can Make 'Stuff' Much More Interesting," in "Protocell Architecture," special issue of *AD,* ed. Neil Spiller and Rachel Armstrong, 81, no. 2 (March–April 2011): 77.

70. The waste barge in the waterways could remove the excess oil by dragging something absorbent through the area afterward; see Jessica Griggs, "Creating Buildings That Repair Themselves," *Enniodufour* (blog), February 23, 2012, available at http://enniodufour.typepad.com/blog/2012/02/creating-buildings-that-repair-themselves.html. This is a classic example of technofix thinking.

71. Rachel Armstrong, "Future Venice: Growing and Artificial Reef under the City," *En Vie / Alive,* 2013, available at http://thisisalive.com/future-venice-growing-an-artificial-reef-under-the-city/; Ben Hobson, "Growing a 'Giant Artificial Reef' Could Stop Venice Sinking," *Dezeen,* May 30, 2014, available at http://www.dezeen.com/2014/05/30/movie-rachel-armstrong-future-venice-growing-giant-artificial-reef/; Steve Tooze, "Rachel Armstrong: Grow Your Own City," *Future Laboratory,* March 15, 2010, available at http://www.lsnglobal.com/opinion/article/1626/rachel-armstrong-grow-your-own-city; Rachel Armstrong, "How Protocells Will Create the Next Wonders of the World," in *The Technology of Us,* e-book available at http://technologyofus.com/armstrong-protocells/.

72. Paul Preissner, "Back to the Future," in "Protocell Architecture," special issue of *AD,* ed. Neil Spiller and Rachel Armstrong, 81, no. 2 (March–April 2011): 108.

73. Rachel Armstrong, "Living Buildings: Plectic Systems Architecture," *Technoetic Arts* 7, no. 2 (2009): 92.

74. Bruce Sterling, "Architecture Fiction: Rachel Armstrong" *Wired,* December 21, 2011, available at http://www.wired.com/2011/12/architecture-fiction-rachel-armstrong/.

75. Rachel Armstrong and Neil Spiller, "A Manifesto for Protocell Architecture: Against Biological Formalism," in "Protocell Architecture," special issue of *AD,* ed. Spiller and Armstrong, 81, no. 2 (March–April 2011): 25.

76. Simon Sellars interview with Rachel Armstrong, "Living Architecture," *Australian Design Review,* December 2011, available at http://www.australiandesignreview.com/features/15151-interview-rachel-armstrong. I am also reminded of Parul Sehgar's editorial "The Profound Emptiness of Resilience," *New York Times Magazine,* December 1, 2015, available at http://www.nytimes.com/2015/12/06/magazine/the-profound-emptiness-of-resilience.html.

77. Armstrong, "Living Buildings," 82.

78. Armstrong, "Self-Repairing Architecture." This is like her self-repairing shoe—see Bruce Sterling, "Architectural Fiction: Rachel Armstrong, Protocell Shoe," *Wired,* January 2, 2012, available at http://www.wired.com/2012/01/architecture-fiction-rachel-amstrong-protocell-shoe/.

79. Lisa Iwamoto, "Line Array: Protocells as Dynamic Structure," in "Protocell Architecture," special issue of *AD,* ed. Neil Spiller and Rachel Armstrong, 81, no. 2 (March–April 2011): 112–21.

80. Iwamoto, 113, 121, italics added.

81. Griggs, "Creating Buildings That Repair Themselves"; Petra Bogias, "Living Agents in Construction: Protocells and Natural Computing with Rachel Armstrong," *Bridge,* January 10, 2014, available at http://waterlooarchitecture.com/bridge/blog/2014/01/10/living-agents-in-construction-protocells-and-natural-computing-with-rachel-armstrong/.

82. Armstrong and Spiller, "Manifesto for Protocell Architecture," 25, italics added.

83. Armstrong, "Living Buildings," 80.

84. Armstrong, "How Protocells Can Make 'Stuff' Much More Interesting," 72.

85. Armstrong, 77.

86. Armstrong, 72.

87. Hanczyc, "Structure and the Synthesis of Life."

88. See Leroy Cronin, "Defining New Architectural Design Principles with 'Living' Inorganic Materials," in "Protocell Architecture," special issue of *AD,* ed. Neil Spiller and Rachel Armstrong, 81, no. 2 (March–April 2011): 36–37.

89. Cronin, 41.

90. M. Boden, "Autopoiesis and Life," *Cognitive Science Questions* 1 (2000): 115–43, available at http://www.univie.ac.at/constructivism/archive/fulltexts/2469.html. See Eric Smith, Harold J. Morowitz, and Shelley D. Copley, "Core Metabolism as a Self-Organizing System," in *Protocells: Bridging Nonliving and Living Matter,* ed. Steen Rasmussen, Mark Bedau, Liaohai Chen, David Deamer, David Krakauer, Norman Packard, and Peter Stadler (Cambridge, Mass., MIT Press, 2009), 433–60; Mark Bedau, "Weak Emergence," in "Mind, Causation, and World," special issue of *Philosophical Perspectives,* ed. James E. Tomberlin, 11 (1997): 375–99. Thanks to

James Griesemer for introducing this literature to me in his Philosophy of Science seminar on Emergence, UC Davis, Spring 2012.

91. Evelyn Fox Keller, "Organisms, Machines, and Thunderstorms: A History of Self-Organization, Part One," *Historical Studies in the Natural Sciences* 38, no. 1 (2008): 47–48. Kant defines self-organization in *Critique of Judgment* (1790).

92. On prioritization of the central dogma by synthetic biologists, see Elfick and Endy, "Synthetic Biology," 9–10.

93. Experience of and conversation held with a scientist by the author, Spring 2015, Davis, California.

94. Campos, "BioBrick Road."

95. Patrik Schumacher, "Hegemonic Parametricism Delivers a Market-Based Urban Order," in "Architectural Design Parametricism 2.0," special issue of *AD,* ed. Schumacher, 86, no. 2 (March–April 2016): 114–23.

96. One recent publication addressing synthetic biology from a systems biology perspective is Joana Xavier, Kiran Raosaheb Patil, and Isabel Rocha, "Systems Biology Perspectives on Minimal and Simpler Cells," *Microbiology and Molecular Biology Reviews* 78, no. 3 (September 2014): 487–509.

97. Natalja Strelkowa, "Stochastic Complexity Analysis in Synthetic Biology," in *How Nature Works: Complexity in Interdisciplinary Research and Applications,* ed. Ivan Zelinka, Ali Sanayei, Hector Zenil, and Otto E. Rössler (New York: Springer, 2013), 162.

98. Jeffrey Tabor, Travis Bayer, Zachary Simpson, Matthew Levy, and Andrew Ellington, "Engineering Stochasticity in Gene Expression," *Molecular Biosystems* 4, no. 7 (July 2008): 754.

99. Sara Hooshangi, Stephan Thiberge, and Ron Weiss, "Ultrasensitivity and Noise Propagation in a Synthetic Transcriptional Cascade," *Proceedings of the National Academy of Sciences* 102, no. 10 (8 March 2005): 3581.

100. Pengcheng Fu and Cliff Hooker, "Outstanding Issues in Systems and Synthetic Biology," in *Systems Biology and Synthetic Biology,* ed. Pengcheng Fu and Sven Panke (London: John Wiley & Sons, 2009), 611–42.

101. Fu and Hooker, 613.

102. Michael Bolker, "Complexity in Synthetic Biology: Unnecessary or Essential," in *Synthetic Biology: Character and Impact,* ed. Bernd Giese, Christian Pade, Henning Wigger, and Arnim von Gleich (New York: Springer, 2015), 59.

103. Hanczyc, "Structure and the Synthesis of Life," 26.

104. Hanczyc, 27–28.

105. Hanczyc, 26; Stadler and Stadler, "Replicator Dynamics in Protocells," 317, 327.

106. Anthony Dunne, "Design for Debate," in "Neoplasmatic Design," special issue of *AD,* ed. Marcos Cruz and Steve Pike, 78, no. 6 (November–December 2008): 92n3.

107. Michael Weinstock, "Morphogenesis and the Mathematics of Emergence," in "Emergence: Morphogenetic Design Strategies," special issue of *AD,* ed. Michael Hensel, Achim Menges, and Michael Weinstock, 74, no. 3 (May–June 2004): 12.

108. Sathish Periyasamy, William Alexander Gray, and Peter Kille, "The Epigenetic Algorithm," *IEEE Congress on Evolutionary Computation,* 2008, 3228.

109. CRISPR/Cas9 has spurred the convening of interdisciplinary panels at different universities that are meeting to consider the ethical implications of what they see as an imminent future use of this technology in medicine. See, for example, the event CRISPR Technology: Responsible Discourse about Science and Bioethics, held on May 26, 2016, at UC Davis (http://innovation.ucdavis.edu/events/crispr-technology-responsible-discourse-about-science-and-bioethics). A similar international summit was held in Washington, D.C., early in December 2015 (http://news.berkeley.edu/2015/12/01/crispr-inventor-calls-for-pause-in-editing-heritable-genes/).

110. Juan Enriquez and Steve Gullans, *Evolving Ourselves: How Unnatural Selection and Nonrandom Mutation Are Changing Life on Earth* (New York: Penguin, 2015), 133.

111. Enriquez and Gullans, 135.

112. In 2015, *Nature Biotechnology* solicited input from fifty scientists to discuss the ethics

of using CRISPR for human genetic engineering; see "CRISPR Germline Engineering: The Community Speaks," *Nature Biotechnology* 33 (May 12, 2015): 478–86.

113. Enriquez and Gullans, *Evolving Ourselves*, 136–37.

114. See "3-Person IVF: A Resource Page," Center for Genetics and Society, available at http://www.geneticsandsociety.org/internal-content/3-person-ivf-resource-page.

115. Enriquez and Gullans, *Evolving Ourselves*, 142, 157.

116. Christina Cogdell, *Eugenic Design: Streamlining America in the 1930s* (2004; repr., Philadelphia: University of Pennsylvania Press, 2010), 22–23, 110, 236.

117. Neil Spiller and Rachel Armstrong, "It's a Brand New Morning," in "Protocell Architecture," special issue of *AD*, ed. Neil Spiller and Rachel Armstrong, 81, no. 2 (March–April 2011): 20, 25.

118. See Roberto Bottazzi, "A Fuller Understanding," *Architectural Review* 233, no. 1392 (February 2013): 4 pp.; and "Architecture & Ecology: Tuesday 4 December," *Architectural Review*, n.d., available at http://www.architectural-review.com/rethink/architecture-and-ecology-tuesday-4-december/8637625.fullarticle.

119. Botazzi, "Fuller Understanding."

120. Richard Simon, "The Futures of Humanity: Anarchism, Technoscience, and the Sociology of God," *Contemporary Sociology: A Journal of Reviews* 42, no. 726 (2013): 726.

121. Wikipedia, s.v. "Transhumanism," available at http://en.wikipedia.org/wiki/transhumanism, last modified May 7, 2018.

122. Rasmussen et al., *Protocells*, xx.

123. Susanna Soares, *New Organs of Perception*, 2007, and *Genetic Trace*, 2007, available at http://www.susanasoares.com/index.php?id=73 and http://www.susanasoares.com/?id=77. See also Antonelli, *Design and the Elastic Mind*, 110.

124. Here she is citing Kate Douglas, "Are We Still Evolving?" *New Scientist*, March 11, 2006, available at http://www.evcforum.net/DataDropsite/NewScientistAreWeEvolving.html.

125. See Aida Edemariam, "A Matter of Life and Death," *The Guardian*, March 27, 2008, available at http://www.theguardian.com/science/2008/mar/27/stemcells.medicalresearch. See also Ailsa Stevens, "Debating Deafness and Embryo Selection: Are We Undermining Reproductive Confidence in the Deaf Community?" *BioNews*, April 21, 2008, available at http://www.bionews.org.uk/page_37988.asp.

126. On state sterilization laws in the United States, see Cogdell, *Eugenic Design*, 3, 40, 98, 104, 106, 196, 220; Daniel Kevles, *In the Name of Eugenics: Genetics and the Uses of Human Heredity* (Cambridge, Mass.: Harvard University Press, 1998); and Phillip Reilly, *The Surgical Solution: A History of Involuntary Sterilization in the United States* (Baltimore: Johns Hopkins University Press, 1991).

127. Armstrong, "How Protocells Can Make 'Stuff' Much More Interesting."

128. Mark Waller, "LaBruzzo Considering Plan to Pay Poor Women $1,000 to Have Tubes Tied," *Times-Picayune*, September 23, 2008, available at http://www.nola.com/news/index.ssf/2008/09/labruzzo_sterilization_plan_fi.html. See Oron Catts and Ionat Zurr's critique of the "engineering mindset" in "Countering the Engineering Mindset: The Conflict of Art and Synthetic Biology," in *Synthetic Aesthetics: Investigating Synthetic Biology's Designs on Nature*, ed. Alexandra Daisy Ginsbert, Jane Calvert, Pablo Schyfter, Alistair Elfick, and Drew Endy (Cambridge, Mass.: MIT Press, 2014), 27–38.

129. Sheila Weiss, "The Race Hygiene Movement in Germany, 1904–1945," in *The Wellborn Science: Eugenics in Germany, France, Brazil, and Russia*, ed. Mark Adams (Oxford, U.K.: Oxford University Press, 1990), 26, 49; Cogdell, *Eugenic Design*, 230–32.

130. Enriquez and Gullans, *Evolving Ourselves*.

131. Lesia Bilitchenko, Adam Liu, and Douglas Densmore, "The Eugene Language for Synthetic Biology," *Methods in Enzymology* 498, no. 2 (2011): 153–72.

132. Eric Mennel, "Payments Start for N.C. Eugenics Victims, but Many Won't Qualify," *All Things Considered*, October 31, 2014, available at http://www.npr.org/sections/health-shots/2014/10/31/360355784/payments-start-for-n-c-eugenics-victims-but-many-wont-qualify.

133. Hunter Schwarz, "Following Reports of Forced Sterilization of Female Prison Inmates, California Passes Ban," *Washington Post*, September 26, 2014, available at https://www.washingtonpost.com/blogs/govbeat/wp/2014/09/26/following-reports-of-forced-sterilization-of-female-prison-inmates-california-passes-ban/.

134. Ginsberg, "Design Evolution," 110.

135. Ginsberg, 114, italics added.

136. Dana Kulic, Rob Gorbet, and Ali-Akbar Samadani, "Using Affect to Increase Empathy in Near-Living Architecture," in *Near-Living Architecture: Works in Progress from the Hylozoic Ground Collaboration, 2011–2013*, ed. Philip Beesley (Toronto: Riverside Architectural Press, 2014), 64–72.

137. Ginsberg," Transgressing Biological Boundaries," 293, 297–98.

138. Ginsberg, "Design Evolution," 134.

139. Ginsberg, 115.

140. Ginsberg, 115, 120; Ethan Huff, "Biofuels Emit 400 Percent More CO2 Than Regular Fuels," *Natural News*, August 10, 2010, available at http://www.naturalnews.com/029421_biofuels_CO2.html. The article is about corn and soy biofuel, not algal biofuel, as is envisioned by some of the synbiodesign projects included in Myers, *BioDesign*.

141. Ginsberg, 120–22. See also Vaclav Smil, *Energy in World History* (Boulder, Colo.: Westview Press, 1994), 91, 246, on the shortage of land to grow feed for horses if we hypothetically returned to animal power for farming.

142. Steve Pike, "Manipulation and Control of Micro-Organic Matter in Architecture," in "Neoplasmatic Design," special issue of *AD*, ed. Marcos Cruz and Steve Pike, 78, no. 6 (November–December 2008): 18.

143. Michael Weinstock and Mehran Gharleghi, "Intelligent Cities and the Taxonomy of Cognitive Scales," in "System City: Infrastructure and the Space of Flows," special issue of *AD*, ed. Weinstock, 83, no. 3 (July–August 2013): 65.

144. Skylar Tibbits, "Design to Self-Assembly," in "Material Computation: Higher Integration in Morphogenetic Design," special issue of *AD*, ed. Achim Menges, 82, no. 2 (March–April 2012): 72.

145. Saskia Sassen, *Expulsions: Brutality and Complexity in the Global Economy* (Cambridge, Mass.: Harvard University Press, 2014).

Appendix

1. Evelyn Fox Keller, "Organisms, Machines, Thunderstorms: A History of Self-Organization, Part One," *Historical Studies in the Natural Sciences* 38, no. 1 (2008): 49.

2. Keller, 50.

3. Keller, 47.

4. Keller, 69. She writes, "More precisely, only if the 'self' is enlarged to include the system to which the machine is coupled can one speak of self-organization."

5. Keller, "Organisms, Machines, Thunderstorms: A History of Self-Organization, Part One"; Keller, "Organisms, Machines, Thunderstorms: A History of Self Organization, Part Two," *Historical Studies in the Natural Sciences* 39, no. 1 (2009): 1–31; Steven Johnson, *Emergence: The Connected Lives of Ants, Brains, Cities, and Software* (New York: Scribner, 2001); Melanie Mitchell, *Complexity: A Guided Tour* (Oxford, U.K.: Oxford University Press, 2011); Andrew Pickering, *The Cybernetic Brain: Sketches of Another Future* (Chicago: University of Chicago Press, 2011); Ralph Abraham, "The Genesis of Complexity," in *Advances in Systems Theory, Complexity, and the Human Sciences*, ed. Edgar Morin and Alfonso Montuori (Cresskill, N.J.: Hampton Press, 2008); Minka Woermann, "What Is Complexity Theory?" n.d., available at http://www.academia.edu/823563/What_is_complexity_theory; Steve J. Heims, *The Cybernetics Group* (Cambridge, Mass.: MIT Press, 1991).

6. On these intersections, see Charles Jencks, *The New Paradigm in Architecture* (New Haven, Conn.: Yale University Press, 2002); "Charles Jencks on Architecture and Theory," April 1, 2012, interview with ArchiTeam Point of View, available at http://www.architravel.com/pointofview/interview/charles-jencks-on-architecture-and-theory/; Reinhold Martin, "Complexities," *Jour-*

nal of Architecture 3, no. 3 (2001): 187–209; Reinhold Martin, *The Organizational Complex: Architecture, Media, and Corporate Space* (Cambridge, Mass.: MIT Press, 2003); Mark Wigley, "Network Fever," *Grey Room* 4 (Summer 2001): 82–122; Simon Sadler, *Archigram: Architecture without Architecture* (Cambridge, Mass.: MIT Press, 2005); Simon Sadler, "An Architecture of the Whole," *Journal of Architectural Education* 61, no. 4 (May 2008): 108–29; Greg Lynn, curator, *Archaeology of the Digital* (Montreal: Canadian Centre for Architecture, 2013); Lynn, curator, *Archaeology of the Digital: Media and Machines* (Montreal: Canadian Centre for Architecture, 2014); Lynn, curator, *Archaeology of the Digital: Complexity and Convention* (Montreal: Canadian Centre for Architecture, 2016); Molly Wright Steenson, "Architectures of Information: Christopher Alexander, Cedric Price, and Nicholas Negroponte and MIT's Architecture Machine Group" (Ph.D. diss., Princeton University, 2014), available at http://dataspace.princeton.edu/jspui/handle/88435/dsp01pn89d6733; Christopher Hight, *Architectural Principles in the Age of Cybernetics* (New York: Routledge, 2007); Hight, "The Transgenic Territories of Oikonomia," in *The Gen(H)ome Project,* ed. Peter Noever and Open Source Architecture (Los Angeles: MAK Center for Art and Architecture, 2006), 38–45; Mario Carpo, *The Digital Turn in Architecture, 1992–2012* (London: Wiley, 2013); and Antoine Picon, *Digital Culture in Architecture* (Basel: Birkhauser, 2010).

7. See Johnson, *Emergence,* 59; and Thomas Back, Ulrich Hammel, and Paul Schwefel, "Evolutionary Computation: Comments on the History and Current State," *IEEE Transactions on Evolutionary Computation* 1, no. 1 (April 1997): 3–17. They write, "But somewhat surprisingly, the researchers in the various disciplines of evolutionary computation remained isolated from each other until the meetings in the early 1990s" (4). Other important publications by John Holland are *Hidden Order: How Adaptation Builds Complexity* (New York: Basic Books, 1995); *Emergence: From Chaos to Order* (New York: Basic Books, 1998); *Signals and Boundaries: Building Blocks for Complex Adaptive Systems* (Cambridge, Mass.: MIT Press, 2012); and *Complexity: A Very Short Introduction* (Oxford, U.K.: Oxford University Press, 2014).

8. György Kepes, *Language of Vision* (Chicago: Paul Theobald, 1944).

9. Martin, "Complexities," 196.

10. See http://www.aboutus.com/Christopher_Alexander and http://pcad.lib.washington.edu/person/3534/; Steenson, "Architectures of Information," 31–97.

11. Steenson, 11.

12. Gordon Pask, "The Architectural Relevance of Cybernetics," *AD,* September 1969, 494–96.

13. Usman Haque, "The Architectural Relevance of Gordon Pask," *AD* 77, no. 4 (July–August 2007): 54–61. See also Nicholas Negroponte, *Soft Architecture Machines* (Cambridge, Mass.: MIT Press 1976); Steenson, "Architectures of Information," 9; Molly Wright Steenson, "Nicholas Negroponte, Leon Groisser, Jerome Wiesner, The Architecture Machine Group and the Media Lab at Massachusetts Institute of Technology MIT *Cambridge MA, USA,* 1967–1985," n.d., available at http://radical-pedagogies.com/search-cases/a13-architecture-machine-group-media-lab-massachusetts-institute-technology-mit/.

14. Johnson, *Emergence,* 46. Ludwig von Bertalanffy is also often credited with this for his *General System Theory: Foundations, Development, Applications* (New York: George Braziller, 1968).

15. Johnson, 48–49.

16. See summary of Weaver's report in Johnson, 50; and Mitchell, *Complexity,* 13.

17. Johnson, *Emergence,* 50. Although Johnson states that Weaver's report to the Rockefeller Foundation in the late 1950s is where Jacobs saw his theory of organized and disorganized complexity, Weaver had published this theory much earlier; see Warren Weaver, "Science and Complexity," *American Scientist* 36 (1948): 536–44.

18. Peter Laurence, "Contradictions and Complexities: Jane Jacobs's and Robert Venturi's Complexity Theories," *Journal of Architectural Education* 59, no. 3 (February 2006): 49.

19. Robert Venturi, *Complexity and Contradiction in Architecture* (New York: Museum of Modern Art in association with the Graham Foundation, 1966), 88.

20. These influences were also occurring at other locations, for example Northern California, where Alexander was working and counterculture theorist Stewart Brand and the *Whole Earth Catalog* began popularizing whole systems architecture. See Sadler, "Architecture of the Whole."

21. John Frazer, *An Evolutionary Architecture* (London: Architectural Association Publications, 1995), 10, citing Charles Jencks, *Architecture 2000: Predictions and Methods* (London: Studio Vista, 1971). Frazer's *Evolutionary Architecture* is available at http://issuu.com/aaschool/docs/an-evolutionary-architecture-webocr.

22. See "AA Computer Course" leaflet from 1963, in Box 2007: 55 Ag No 2342, Archives at the Architectural Association, London.

23. Phil Husbands and Owen Holland, "The Ratio Club: A Hub of British Cybernetics," in *The Mechanical Mind in History,* ed. Phil Husbands, Owen Holland, and Michael Wheeler (Cambridge, Mass.: MIT Press, 2008), 91–148.

24. Andrew Pickering, "Cybernetics and the Mangle: Ashby, Beer, Pask," *Social Studies of Science* 32, no. 3 (June 2002): 7, available at http://citeseerx.ist.psu.edu/viewdoc/download?doi=10.1.1.15.882&rep=rep1&type=pdf. The article appeared in French translation in A. Dahan and D. Pestre, eds., *La reconfiguration des sciences pour l'action dans les années 1950* (Paris: Presses de l'EHESS, 2002). In 1961, Pask also published with Heinz von Foerster, "A Predictive Model for Self-Organizing Systems, Part I," *Cybernetica* 3 (1961): 258–300; and "A Predictive Model for Self-Organizing Systems, Part II," *Cybernetica* 4 (1961): 20–55.

25. "Fun Palace Project. Cybernetics Committee. Introductory Document, Circulation List and Basic Plans," 10–11, DR1995:0188:525:004:009, Cedric Price Archive, Canadian Centre for Architecture, Montreal.

26. Regarding whether Pask was referring to evolutionary computation, John Frazer in an email to the author on June 20, 2016, stated, "I only heard Gordon talk of genetic code in the sense we used it until 1990+ when he was invited to join our project. I do not think Gordon was thinking of evolutionary computation or genetic algorithms or parameters." For articles on the history of evolutionary computation, see Back, Hammel, and Schwefel, "Evolutionary Computation," 3, 12nn1–4, citing Hans-Joachim Bremermann, "Optimization through Evolution and Recombination," in *Self-Organizing Systems,* ed. Marshall C. Yovits, George T. Jacobi, and G. D. Goldstein (Washington, D.C.: Spartan, 1962); Richard M. Friedberg, "A Learning Machine: Part I," *IBM Journal* 2, no. 1 (January 1958): 2–13; Richard M. Friedberg, Bradford Dunham, and James H. North, "A Learning Machine: Part II," *IBM Journal* 3, no. 7 (July 1959): 282–87; and George E. P. Box, "Evolutionary Operation: A Method for Increasing Industrial Productivity," *Applied Statistics* 6, no. 2 (1957): 81–101.

27. Frazer, *Evolutionary Architecture,* 9.

28. See John Frazer, "Reptiles," *AD* 4 (1974): 231–39.

29. Frazer, 235.

30. Email from John Frazer to the author, June 20, 2016.

31. See Frazer's citation of Holland in *An Evolutionary Architecture,* 13.

32. See Frazer, 63; and http://www.obitko.com/tutorials/genetic-algorithms/.

INDEX

CHRISTINA COGDELL is professor in the Department of Design at the University of California at Davis. She is the author of *Eugenic Design: Streamlining America in the 1930s* and coeditor of *Popular Eugenics: National Efficiency and American Mass Culture in the 1930s.*